Experimental Hypnosis

Experimental Hypnosis

Experimental Hypnosis

A SYMPOSIUM OF ARTICLES ON RESEARCH BY
MANY OF THE WORLD'S LEADING AUTHORITIES

Edited by LESLIE M. LeCRON

THE CITADEL PRESS   •   NEW YORK

Chapter 9, part 1, "Time Distortion in Hypnosis," *Bulletin*, Georgetown University Medical
Center, April–May, 1948.

Chapter 9, part 2, "Time Distortion in Hypnosis II" (Digest), *Bulletin*, Georgetown University Medical Center, October–November, 1950.

Chapter 13, "Hypnodontics," from *Hypnodontics—Hypnosis in Dentistry*, Copyright by Dental Items of Interest Publishing Company, Inc.,
Brooklyn, 1952.

Acknowledgments*

For permission to quote the editor expresses his gratitude to the following publishers and authors:

From

Alexander, F., and French, T. M.: *Psychoanalytic Therapy*, The Ronald Press Company, New York, 1946 [p. 178].

Barkhuus, A.: "Native medicine in Ethiopia," *Ciba Symposia*, **9**, 1947 [p. 17].

Bateson, G., and Mead, M.: *Balinese Character*, New York Academy of Sciences, New York, 1942 [p. 18].

E. A.: "Arctic medicine in South America," *Ciba Symposia*, **10**, 1948 [p. 16].

Erickson, M. H.: "An experimental investigation of the possible antisocial use of hypnosis," *Psychiatry*, **2**:391, 1939 [pp. 382, 383, 384, 385, 386, 387].

Erickson, M. H.: "Experimental demonstrations of the psychopathology of everyday life," *Psychoanalyt. Quart.*, **8**:338, 1939 [pp. 391, 394–395].

Erickson, M. H.: "Hypnosis in medicine," *M. Clin. North America*, **28**:639, 1944 [pp. 389–390].

Estabrooks, G. H.: "Hypnosis: its tremendous potential as a war weapon," *Argosy*, **330**:26, February, 1950 [pp. 385, 400].

Freuchen, Peter: *Arctic Adventure*, Halcyon House, New York, 1938 [p. 15].

Hastings, J.: *Encyclopedia of Religion and Ethics*, Charles Scribner's Sons, New York, 1908 [p. 7].

Hyde, W.: "Case reports," *North-West Dentistry*, **28**:154, July, 1949 [pp. 346–347].

Pattie, F. A.: "Some American contributions to the science of hypnosis," reprinted from *The American Scholar*, Vol. 12, no. 4, Autumn, 1943, by permission of the publishers [p. 388].

Rowland, L. W.: "Will hypnotized persons try to harm themselves or others?" *J. Abnorm. & Social Psychol.*, **34**:114, 1939. Courtesy of the American Psychological Association [pp. 400–401].

* Numbers in brackets refer to pages in this text.

Alfred Lord Tennyson: *A Memoir by His Son,* Vol. 1, The Macmillan Company, New York, 1897 [p. 7].

Watkins, J. G.: "Anti-social compulsions induced under hypnotic trance," *J. Abnorm. & Social Psychol.,* **42**:256, 1947. Courtesy of the American Psychological Association [pp. 402–403].

Weitzenhoffer, A. M.: "The production of anti-social acts under hypnosis," *J. Abnorm. & Social Psychol.,* **44**:420, 1949. Courtesy of the American Psychological Association [p. 379].

White, R. W.: "A preface to the theory of hypnotism," *J. Abnorm. & Social Psychol.,* **36**:477, 1941. Courtesy of the American Psychological Association [pp. 390–391].

Wolberg, L. R.: "Hypnotic experiments in psychosomatic medicine," *Psychosom. Med.,* **9**:337, 1947. Courtesy of Paul B. Hoeber, Inc. [p. 390].

Introduction

It was in 1779 that Mesmer first published his theories and discoveries regarding "animal magnetism." Since that time the popular and scientific literature on hypnotism has added up to thousands of books and articles. It would seem that more than one hundred and seventy years of the modern history of hypnotism should have afforded us a good understanding and knowledge of the subject. Actually, the contrary is the case, for as yet we know almost nothing about hypnosis, and no entirely adequate theory has even been advanced to explain it. The question "What is a trance?" remains unanswered, nor do we know very much as to what actually can be accomplished in a practical way with hypnosis.

By 1825 most hypnotic phenomena had been recognized, even if not understood. Hypnotic anesthesias and analgesias, positive and negative hallucinations, catalepsy, memory recall, posthypnotic suggestions, etc., all had been reported by then, along with claims as to many other results which supposedly could be brought about through hypnotic suggestion. It was stated that strange telepathic and clairvoyant powers could be evoked under hypnosis, and that many physiological changes in the body could be produced. Yet, with seventeen decades of experience and experiment, many of these matters are still scientifically unproved. Controversies still rage over some points such as whether or not a skin blister can be produced by hypnotic suggestion; whether or not a hypnotized person can be induced to commit a crime or an antisocial act; whether rapport is an actual phenomenon of hypnosis; and we still know very little as to the physical effects which can be produced. American researchers have devoted their attention primarily to the psychological and theoretical aspects of hypnosis. The physiological phases have been almost completely neglected here, though in Europe they have had some attention.

There are various reasons for our continued ignorance concerning hypnosis. Like medicine, hypnotism sprang from magic. While medicine has lost this stigma and has become respectable, hypnotism, unfortunately, is still regarded, in the eyes of the public and of scientists alike, as akin to witchcraft—to the shame of the scientists. Popular misconceptions remain prevalent, and hypnosis is considered to be awesome and mysterious, something of which the average person is curious but fearful. Most persons believe that damage to the mind may result from hypnotization; that the hypnotist can detrimentally control the will of the subject; that under hypnosis one loses consciousness; that a person will talk and perhaps betray "state secrets" if he submits to hypnosis; and still other ideas are held which are completely contrary to fact.

Because of its bad odor with the public, until recently the medical profession has been reluctant to use hypnosis, despite its definite advantages in psychotherapy. Most psychologists have also ignored and avoided its investigation, though hypnotism is to be classified as a branch of the science of psychology.

Modern investigation of hypnosis has been carried on by a relatively small number of psychologists and psychiatrists who have found themselves fascinated by its phenomena and possibilities. Much of the research has been individual, though there are some universities and colleges whose authorities are sufficiently liberal to permit experimentation. Many schools forbid such investigation, refusing use of facilities for its study. For instance, the University of California at Berkeley, where much of the early atomic research was conducted, will not permit a demonstration of hypnosis in a psychology class nor an experiment to be made in the laboratory. Atomic contamination may be risked; the contamination from hypnosis is too dangerous! Oddly, the same university has no such ban at its Los Angeles campus.

During World War II many psychotherapists turned to hypnosis in a desperate attempt to find a brief method of dealing with "battle fatigue." Owing to this fact, hypnotism has begun to find acceptance with the medical profession, with psychologists, and also with the public. Gradually, it is losing its bad reputation and is becoming an acceptable psychotherapeutic tool and also an acceptable implementation in dentistry.

Recently, no less than five different groups of scientists interested in hypnosis have been organized into technical societies. Three of these are dental societies, and they will be discussed in the chapters on hypnodontics. The Society for Clinical and Experimental Hypnosis was formed in 1949 for the purpose of bringing together into one scientific group those professional workers utilizing hypnosis in experimental and clinical areas. It is made up mostly of psychiatrists and psychologists and aims to act as a center for information, for the development of standards for qualified therapists, to sponsor conferences on problems in hypnosis, and to stimulate research. Monthly meetings, which include the reading of scientific papers, are held in New York. Membership is by invitation, with the highest standards as a requisite. Most of the leading scientific authorities on hypnosis now are members of this group. In England a somewhat similar organization was set up at about the same time. It is designated as The British Society of Medical Hypnotists and issues a quarterly journal devoted to articles on hypnosis. These groups indicate the extent of the rising professional and scientific interest in the subject.

Practitioners who adopt hypnosis inevitably will demand more scientific knowledge of hypnosis and the ways in which it may be used. But experimentation involves expense, and money is needed for any intensive investigation. Within the past few years funds have been granted to the Menninger Clinic by the Rockefeller and Macy Foundations for investigation of hypnoanalysis, but, as far as is known to the editor, no grant has ever been made for the study of hypnosis itself. Such foundations and the U.S. Department of Public Health might well make such grants, for increased knowledge of hypnotism and its practical uses undoubtedly would prove valuable.

In 1933 Dr. Clark Hull of Yale published his book *Hypnosis and Suggestibility* [1] * which is a report on a series of experiments conducted under his guidance. This research was carried out by a num-

---

* Superior numbers refer to the lists of books and articles following the sections in which the numbers appear.

ber of his assistants and associates and by graduate students studying for advanced degrees in psychology. Their work cleared up some aspects of hypnosis, failed to shed light on others, and made the situation even more confused as to still others. This was the first (and only) intensive investigation of hypnosis and suggestion conducted according to modern scientific investigative methods. Hull can be regarded as having shown the way toward obtaining a proper understanding and knowledge of hypnotism. Undoubtedly, this is his main contribution, and one which is as important as that of Bernheim when he showed that hypnotism is largely based on suggestion and that no mysterious force or "animal magnetism" is involved in producing the hypnotic state or its phenomena.

Hull saw that the controlled experiment is essential for the proper evaluation of hypnosis. He was the first to use controlled experiments to any extent in the study of hypnotic phenomena, though P. C. Young is to be credited with the first adequately controlled experiment, the results of which were published in 1925.[2]

For the reader to understand and intelligently assess some of the articles which follow, he should know the principle of the controlled experiment. Basically, this is the "method of difference" which, through comparison, arrives definitely at the causes of a phenomenon. Hull quotes J. S. Mill[3] on the principle upon which the method is based. Mill says that in investigating a phenomenon if a circumstance occurs in one instance and not in another, and they are alike otherwise in circumstances, then that circumstance "is the effect or cause or an indispensable part of the cause of the phenomenon."

Following publication of Hull's book, most hypnotic experimenters have used this procedure. These investigators have published their findings in scientific journals, and new information is constantly being made available. Thus, our knowledge is slowly increasing, though we still have far to go.

Unfortunately, there is no standardization in methods of investigation or of reporting on hypnotic research. Often, it is difficult to assay the work from the reports, and many experiments must be considered inconclusive, or possibly even in error because the investigator has not obtained in his subjects a trance of sufficient depth.

The need for a deep trance in experimental work has been emphasized by Erickson,[4] and, in speaking of a deep trance, he refers to a state deeper than that usually designated as the "somnambulistic" stage. Few experimenters take the time and trouble necessary to evoke such a deep state of hypnosis, many not even being aware that deeper stages can be produced. Even with the best of subjects, induction of such a deep trance may at first require 2 hours or more of effort, though with practice and by suggestion this can be reduced to only a few minutes. In any given experiment with a particular subject, it may be impossible to obtain positive results during the ordinary somnambulistic trance, when such results might be attained in this deeper state. A discussion by Erickson of deep trances and their induction is one of the most signficant of the articles presented in the following pages.

For the proper evaluation of any experiment, it frequently is of great importance to know the exact wording of the suggestions which are given the subject and also the attitude toward the test of both the subject and the operator. These things may greatly influence the end results. Of course, even if the words are reported, it is impossible to describe all the nuances of inflection and tone of voice, and the many intangible, indirect suggestions which might be conveyed to the subject and which might influence results. Operator attitude is highly important, for the subject, through minimal cues, quickly learns the expectations of the hypnotist, and, if the operator anticipates a negative result, in all probability the subject will provide one.

In experimentation, much better results will usually be obtained if the hypnotized subject is treated as a normal human being rather than a robot, and if he is brought from a lethargic condition into a state of alertness. This permits him to take a more active participating role, and usually he is greatly interested in the experiment or he would not have lent himself to the project.

Still another important matter in reporting hypnotic studies is, at the conclusion, to learn the subject's observations as to his behavior during an experiment. This may aid considerably in explaining and interpreting the results.

During some kinds of hypnotic research, if the subject is kept in a passive state, he may fall into a normal sleep. The possible results of the test could be changed by this. In such studies it is important, sometimes, to know whether or not the subject remained in the hypnotic state, and the knee-jerk test described by Bass [5] should then be used as a control.

All of these points, if adopted by researchers, would facilitate interpretation and would make almost any experiment of greater value. Frequently, explanations could then be made for the failure of one experimenter to secure a positive result when the same test has been successfully performed by someone else; for instance, in the production of hallucinations, blistering, and other phenomena.

Because intangibles are being dealt with, it has never been easy to experiment in any field of psychology, and it is particularly difficult with hypnosis. So far, we know very little about the human mind, especially as to its subconscious phases or the factors governing behavior. And in hypnosis we must take into consideration conscious and subconscious, normal and abnormal behavior and conditions.

In the chapters which follow, the terms "subconscious" or "unconscious" will frequently be encountered, and they are synonymous. Psychologists have used various other terms for describing that stratum of mental activity below the conscious level, such as "subjective," "subliminal," and "superconscious." The editor favors the word *subconscious* because *unconscious* is also used to describe the state of being not conscious or "out," as when asleep, drugged, in a faint, or knocked out by a blow. Probably the term "unconscious" is preferred by most psychologists, Freud having adopted it.

It has been the intention of the editors and of the contributors to this book to add something to our knowledge of hypnotism. The leading authorities throughout the world were requested to undertake experiments or to write about some particular phase of hypnosis which needs clarification. Ideally, it would have been best to have outlined a comprehensive, synthesized list of topics for investigation, but, practically, this was impossible because it was necessary to consider the interests and desires of the individual contributions as to the themes with which they wished to deal. Hence, topics could not be assigned arbitrarily, and many important subjects have been omitted. Of course, it would be impossible to treat in a single volume all the various phases of hypnosis which might well have been the object of investigation. It is hoped that the present work will stimulate further study, particularly coordinated experimentation in university laboratories.

This volume has been primarily intended to report on research in hypnosis itself rather than on practical applications. However, hypnotic phenomena are utilized in psychotherapy, and, in dealing with the phenomena, psychotherapy therefore enters into the picture and becomes important. Some of the chapters venture into that field.

Most of the articles are published here for the first time. Because they supplement another chapter or are of unusual interest, two are reprinted from scientific journals.

Each contribution presents the opinions and findings of its author. Other contributors may not agree with the conclusions arrived at by the author, for many phases of hypnosis are highly controversial. The introduction, the connecting material between chapters, and one of the articles have been written by the editor, and these sections represent only his opinions, not necessarily those of the contributors, or any one of them.

When writing scientific articles, and particularly if they report on research, the author expects others to be critical, and criticism may be unfavorable to his own findings and opinions. This is a healthy state of affairs, for it keeps the scientist from dogmatism and from jumping to conclusions too readily. Such criticism will be found in some of these papers, and the lay reader should realize that it is entirely impersonal.

In editing the foreign contributions, it should be mentioned that English and American spelling is sometimes at variance. As the book is published in the United States, wherever there is a difference it was thought best, for uniformity, to adopt the American form of spelling, and apologies are tendered to the British collaborators.

The references which follow each article *in toto* make up a very comprehensive bibliography of modern hypnotic literature and include some of the more important work of earlier times.

It has been the intention to promote by means of this volume an interest in hypnosis among the general public as well as among scientists. If hypnosis is ever to become of real value it must meet with public approval, and such approval can only come through a proper understanding of hypnotism. Therefore, the text has been written in the usual form for scientific articles, but the contributors were asked in most cases to modify the usual technical language to some extent in order to make the book more readily understandable by lay readers.

The editor would like to express here his appreciation for the splendid cooperation and the many suggestions given him by the contributors who have made possible this collaborative work.

LESLIE M. LeCRON

8217 Beverly Blvd.
Los Angeles, Calif.
January, 1952

REFERENCES

1. Hull, C.: *Hypnosis and Suggestibility*, Appleton-Century-Crofts, Inc., New York, 1933.

2. Young, P. C.: "An experimental study of mental and physical functions in the normal and hypnotic states," *Am. J. Psychol.*, **36**:214, 1925.

3. Mill, J. S.: *A System of Logic*, Longmans, Green & Co., Inc., New York, 1919.

4. Erickson, M. H.: "A study of clinical and experimental findings on hypnotic deafness," *J. Gen. Psychol.*, **19**:127, 1938.

5. Bass, M. J.: "Differences of the hypnotic trance from normal sleep," *J. Exper. Psychol.*, **14**:382, 1931.

Table of Contents

List of Contributors

MILTON ABRAMSON, M.D., PH.D., Clinical Instructor, Department of Obstetrics and Gynecology, University of Minnesota, Minneapolis, Minnesota; Associate, Department of Obstetrics and Gynecology, Minneapolis General Hospital

THOMAS O. BURGESS, PH.D., Department of Psychology, Concordia College, Moorhead, Minnesota

JAMES A. CHRISTENSON, JR., PH.D., Chief Clinical Psychologist, Veterans Administration Mental Hygiene Clinic, Tampa, Florida; Clinical Psychologist Pinellas County Child Guidance Clinic, St. Petersburg, Florida

LINN F. COOPER, M.D., 2222 Q Street, N. W., Washington, D.C.

MILTON H. ERICKSON, M.D., 32 West Cypress Street, Phoenix, Arizona

W. D. FURNEAUX, A.I.P., B.Sc., Institute of Psychiatry, University of London, England.

WILLIAM T. HERON, PH.D., Professor of Psychology, University of Minnesota, Minneapolis, Minnesota

J. STEPHEN HORSLEY, M.D., St. Margarets, Wimborne, Dorset, England

LESLIE M. LECRON, B.A., 8217 Beverly Boulevard, Los Angeles 48, California

AARON A. MOSS, D.D.S., 20 Morristown Road, Bernardsville, New Jersey

ANITA M. MÜHL, M.D., 57 Sea Lane, La Jolla, California

BRIAN A. NORGARB, PH.D., 99 Pasteur Chambers, Jeppe Street, Johannesburg, South Africa

GERARD ODENCRANTS, M.D., Bragevägen 9–11, Stockholm, Sweden

S. J. VAN PELT, M.B., B.S., Harley Street, London, W. 1, England

PAUL J. REITER, M.D., Psychiatric Department, Copenhagen Municipal Hospital, Copenhagen, Denmark

J. B. RHINE, PH.D., Parapsychology Laboratory, Duke University, Durham, North Carolina

JEROME M. SCHNECK, M.D., 26 West Ninth Street, New York, New York

JOHN G. WATKINS, PH.D., Chief Clinical Psychologist, Mental Hygiene Clinic, Veterans Administration Regional Office, Chicago, Ill.

JOSEPH E. WHITLOW, M.D., 41 South Chestnut Street, Ventura, California

GRIFFITH W. WILLIAMS, PH.D., Associate Professor of Psychology, Rutgers University, New Brunswick, New Jersey

PAUL C. YOUNG, PH.D., Psychology Department, Louisiana State University, Baton Rouge, Louisiana

Experimental Hypnosis

CHAPTER ONE

Hypnosis in Perspective

Editor's Note

It is most fitting that the first article presented here should be one written by a student and associate of Hull, a participant in the experimental work in hypnosis which was begun at the University of Wisconsin and completed at Yale. Born in Wales, Dr. Williams has served on the faculties of various universities and, since 1937, has been located at Rutgers University where he specializes in abnormal psychology. His doctoral thesis was written on the effect of hypnosis on muscular fatigue (*J. Abnorm. & Social Psychol.*, 24:318, 1929) and on voluntary and hypnotic catalepsy (*Am. J. Psychol.*, 42:83, 1930). The results were included in Hull's book. Dr. Williams has maintained his interest in hypnosis and has lectured and published various other articles on hypnotism and abnormal psychology.

The popular conception of hypnotism as something to be regarded with superstitious awe and fear is almost universal. The word "trance" has connotations of mysticism, the psychic, and the supernatural. Dr. Williams shows that the trance state, in reality, is commonplace and ordinary, an experience which most people have had, though usually it is unrecognized as hypnosis or as a trance, these terms being almost synonymous. Hypnotism remains almost completely neglected because scientists have retained the popular conceptions about it or have a fear of public disapproval if they delve into it. If hypnotism can be "debunked" of misconceptions in the eyes of the public, it will then become scientifically more acceptable and undoubtedly will be extensively utilized in psychotherapy and in experimental psychology. "Debunking" will have been accomplished when it is fully realized how ordinary it is for one unwittingly to enter a trance state.

As Dr. Williams points out, the modern beginnings of hypnotism usually are ascribed to Franz Anton Mesmer in the last quarter of the eighteenth century. Actually, Dr. Mesmer only brought hypnotism, or "animal magnetism," to popular attention, since its history goes back to the early days of the human race.

In discussing some of the ancient and primitive peoples who have been familiar with hypnotism, Dr. Williams could have quoted many other references to be found in hypnotic and anthropological literature, but space has limited the number which can be mentioned. Among others which might have been included is the great epic poem of the Finns, the *Kalevala*,[1] * of uncertain date but hundreds of years old. Here is given a very detailed description of the hypnotic state. In his discussion of the psychological system of the Hawaiians, Max Long[2] has shown that the Polynesians used hypnosis as a psychotherapeutic measure in ways very closely resembling those of Mesmer. Their witch doctors, known as *kahunas*, were expert in the use of suggestion and hypnosis, even to the extent of causing death by means of "death wishes."

Few anthropologists are sufficiently familiar with hypnosis to mention it more than briefly in their reports on primitive peoples. Many of their reports are devoted to other matters, and hypnotism is overlooked or ignored even if its use was noticed.

REFERENCES

1. Satow, L.: *Hypnotism and Suggestion*, Dodd Mead & Company, Inc., New York, 1923.
2. Long, M.: *The Secret Behind Miracles*, Kosmon Press, Los Angeles, 1947.

* Superior numbers refer to the lists of books and articles following the sections in which the numbers appear.

Hypnosis in Perspective

BY GRIFFITH W. WILLIAMS, PH.D.

ASSOCIATE PROFESSOR OF PSYCHOLOGY,
RUTGERS UNIVERSITY, NEW BRUNSWICK, NEW JERSEY

INTRODUCTION

The attitude of Western science toward those experiences which are intensely personal is, in general, one of aloofness. When they are judged, they are usually dismissed as "odd," "primitive," or bordering on the "pathological," so that the commonplace, particularly when personal in nature, remains unobserved, as though there were a blind spot in our field of vision. This is the fate of hypnosis as it occurs in daily life.

The history of hypnosis is also a neglected field, despite the fact that throughout man's past history there runs the uninterrupted story of his experience with these phenomena.

Such is the background for this article. It attempts three things: to formulate a statement regarding the trance in our everyday lives; to trace its manifestations and use in man's early attempts to understand himself and the world around him; and to observe, and possibly to learn, from our contemporaries in other cultures the value and uses of this form of behavior.

EVERYDAY LIFE

What happens regularly and frequently often remains unobserved or unrecognized, so that trance states in daily life, especially light ones, occur, pass unnoticed, and remain unrecorded.

When a man is fishing, for example, there is little to distract him. The river washes over the rocks with a relaxing music. Gradually, the water seems to swell and creep up, while vision becomes slightly blurred. Often at this point, he will be seen to make a slight jerky motion of the head and to change his stance. While such an experience is frequently mentioned, it is seldom recognized that the antecedent conditions are ideal for mild self-hypnosis.

Much that is conducive to self-hypnosis in religious practice will similarly pass unnoticed. Consider the darkened interior of the church, the hush, the brightly illuminated altar as a point of fixation, the nature of the music—these and the ofttimes monotonous chant of the priest or minister, together with other factors, furnish ideal conditions for the trance. It may even be relevant to recall the tendency of many to "sleep" during religious observances! The practices in the religious meetings of certain sects, for example, the "Holy Rollers," and some revivalists cause definite trance behavior in many participants which is readily recognized as hypnosis.

Of greater significance is the possibility of entering the trance while driving. There is an impressive mass of evidence that the conditions of modern driving are conducive to hypnosis. A monotony similar to that of fishing and religious observances occurs again. A steady hum from the engine, an endless ribbon of concrete, a "wet" patch ahead at the point of visual fixation, grades and curves engineered for maximum smoothness, together with lack of distractions —all provide a setting for inducing hypnosis.

Many drivers who veer to the shoulder of the road are wakened to the situation when startled by the roughness of the shoulder. Others report having no recollection of covering long stretches, for example, between two towns. Some have developed an acute fear of such conditions and seek aid for what they consider to be recurrent attacks of amnesia.[1]

Perhaps the most common occurrence of the trance in everyday life is while daydreaming. It may vary from a light to a deep trance. On being hypnotized by a practitioner, these people will often comment that this is what has previously happened to them during prolonged daydreaming.

The list of trance-inducing stimuli in nature is long. The Japanese cultivated the art of listening to the drone of insects in the countryside; the Greeks deified the soughing of the wind in the trees into the Oracle of Dodona and interpreted the whispering of the trees as intelligible speech. Modern man is not immune. The tranquillity and repose that he associates with a lambent flame serve but to remind one that fire has been featured in the ceremonial rites of all ages.

Music has become such a commonplace that its effects may pass unnoticed, but when recordings of African or other unfamiliar music are listened to, it is realized that the rhythms are "fascinating." The repetition of phrase and motif, the complicated rhythm within a rhythm that is characteristic of much of this music, may explain why man throughout recorded history and in the multiplicity of modern cultures has used music, both instrumental and vocal, for inducing the trance. When these phenomena are subjected to experimental study, some forms of music will be found to be much more hypnogenetic than others, and some persons will be more susceptible than others. For example, Ravel's "Bolero" can hardly fail to induce definite trances in some listeners. Ancient man knew of the trance-inducing qualities of music and used it for this purpose. The Druids, at the beginning of the Christian Era, were versatile in their use of hypnosis, and music was one of their chief ways of inducing "magical sleep." [2] (MacCulloch reports that some of the "fairy" lullabies of the Scottish Highlands and of Ireland can be traced to these sources.) In their orgiastic rites, singing was continued until both priests and dancers fell into a deep sleep from which they awoke with amnesia and a feeling that many years had passed.

The hypnotic qualities of literature are well known. Many critics have called attention to the fact that not only is the form hypnogenetic, as in music, but the content of literature may also be used for this purpose. Gorgeous palaces seen beyond the shadows, ships seen through the half-light, and even phantom ships on phantom oceans can be experienced when the writer achieves his end. This is not the use of hypnosis as a literary theme but rather the inducing of a mild trance as an end in itself through the medium of literary form and content.

The trance-inducing qualities of poetry are similarly well known. Rhythm, form, and content may here be called into play. The role of form may be seen in Poe's "The Raven," where the narrative is improbable but the meter and refrain are complicated, smooth, and "catching." It is said that this poem left "a tremendous and lasting effect" when read by Poe himself.[3] Of its mechanical aspects it is said that "few poems, if any, in the English language tend so strongly to fix the listener's attention on the physical element of sound. . . . I find a climax of volume in next to the last stanza coincident with the climax of emotion."

Clearly, the hypnotic effect of poetry is not the deep, somnambulistic trance, despite the fact that the Druids were said to be able to "rime either a man or beast to death." In less proficient hands and a different cultural setting, a light, transitory hypnotic state is all that can be expected.

The poet is thoroughly familiar with the trance and, in some moments of insight, experiences an ecstasy resembling that of the mystic. As early as the era of Socrates it was realized that "the poets compose their songs not by virtue of any wisdom or skill but owing to a kind of natural inspiration like that of seers and prophets."[4] Expressed in the poet's own terms, this becomes:

For I dipt into the future far as human eye could see
Saw the vision of the world and all the wonder that would be.

Many poets skilled in inducing a hypnotic state in the hearers and readers of their poems were equally skilled in inducing the trance in themselves. Poe experienced an ecstasy which he describes as an "elevating excitement of the soul." Wordsworth speaks of "that serene and blessed mood in which . . . we are laid asleep in body . . ." while Tennyson describes this state as

. . . a kind of waking trance I have often had, quite from boyhood, when I have been all alone. This has generally come upon me by repeating my own name two or three times to myself silently, till all at once, out of the intensity of individuality, the individual itself seemed to dissolve and fade away into boundless being; and this is not a confused state, but the clearest of the clearest. . . .[5]

A similar state of "abstraction" or light trance seems to have been achieved by the creators of fiction, some of whom have described the creative process itself. There is, for example, the incident of the visitor to de Maupassant who heard the novelist in a heated discussion with someone. On inquiring, he was told that the "caller" was none other than d'Artagnan! Then, again, Flaubert tells of the strong taste of arsenic in his mouth when he was laboring with the description of the poisoning of Emma Bovary. That he could induce in himself such a hallucination is readily explained by what is now known of self-hypnosis. Flaubert refers in his "Correspondence" to other occasions when his degree of self-induced hypnosis approaches that of the mystics.

To most people, the writings of Gertrude Stein are no more than an oddity. Some, however, derive pleasure to a marked degree from a silent reading of her work, while others feel this way only when it is competently and sympathetically read aloud. As with Poe's "The Raven," a possible explanation lies in the hypnotic effect of sound, for while there is narrative embedded in the complex meters of "The Raven," there is an utter lack of content in Stein's

> Needs be needs be needs be near.
> Needs be needs be needs be.
> This is where they have their land astray.
> Two say,

Some of Swinburne's work is in many respects as puzzling as that of Stein, though it may have perfect metrical balance. The irritation that many experience when trying to understand Swinburne may be explained by the essentially hypnotic quality of much of his verse. It must be read aloud to be appreciated.

Sometimes a trance may be induced without deliberate intent when the psychologist is at work. In securing automatic writing from a laboratory subject, the conditions are identical with those for inducing a trance, as the following excerpt will show. "I have the subject relax and make his mind as nearly a 'blank' as possible— that is, I have him suspend active thinking as much as he can. . . . As a rule, if there is decided indication of the possibility of automatism . . . [this method] is almost sure to produce results." [6] These are the conditions for the induction of hypnosis also, and it might be mentioned, in view of what has been said of Gertrude Stein's writings, that she is reported to have served as a laboratory subject for William James when he was investigating this type of behavior.

Closely related to automatic (or trance) writing is trance drawing and painting. While in the trance, the artist projects his imagery to the paper or canvas. Frequently, the outcome may consist merely of monotonous lines and curves that are superficially without meaning but which may later prove to have symbolic meaning.[7]

There is but slight difference between this and the medium who claims to write messages while unaware of their content. It is not sufficient to dismiss these cases as untruthful or deluded. Among the mediums are those who go readily into a self-induced trance and this, together with automatic writing and subsequent amnesia, seems entirely adequate to explain what occurs.

The possibility of explaining too many phenomena as some form of hypnosis is always present, but we must also remember how scornfully hypnosis is neglected, which would lead to failure to observe it even when it is present. Furthermore, the validity of a hypothesis is always checked by experiment. The occurrence of trance conditions in normal activities of everyday life will furnish a broad and probably fertile field for investigation.

HISTORICAL PERSPECTIVE

Owing to neglect of historical perspective, hypnosis is uncritically assumed to begin with Franz Anton Mesmer (1733–1815), but to find its origin would necessitate peering into the gloom that precedes the dawn of history. Hypnosis, it seems, is as old as man.

In the half-light of earliest history, hypnosis appears as a fairly well developed art. There is evidence that "all the phenomena of apparitions, levitation, hypnotism, clairvoyance, etc., that are known to modern psychical research . . . were known to primitive [that is, ancient] man."[8] There is a record of the trance being practiced in China in the eighteenth century B.C. At this time, persons in a hypnotic or ecstatic condition, while seeking communion with the dead, would show convulsive motions of the face and limbs, shivering, uncontrollable jumping and running, etc. This was induced by singing and dancing, two methods of inducing the trance that have not only remained unchanged throughout the ages but which have been rediscovered by every culture. It is said that "the first evening was opened by them with bells and drums, the noise of which they alternated with music of stringed instruments and bamboo pipes . . . dancing with light steps and whirling round and round, they uttered a language of spirits." These statements of procedure from 1800 B.C. apply equally well to the much later whirling dervish, the medicine man, and others.

When the close connection between the trance and automatic writing is recalled, it is interesting to observe that such writing was known to the ancient Hebrews (II Chron. 21:12) as well as the Chinese at the opening of the Christian Era. With the aid of a forked stick held by two persons, it was possible for the Chinese to get information not otherwise available. Ten centuries later, by means of automatic writing, a girl was "able to write literary compositions of exquisite beauty. . . ." She wrote in several styles and manifested the greatest artistry in the use of the pencil, says Paton. We are reminded of the similar case of "Patience Worth" in our own times.

Another unequivocal instance of the trance in a highly elaborated form occurs in Chinese ancestor worship as described by Paton. The celebrant was required to fast and meditate for 3 days during which time he was also required to recall the looks of the deceased, how he stood and sat, smiled and spoke, what he liked to think and do. Finally, the ancestor appeared and spoke to the celebrant. In our terminology this is a positive hallucination hypnotically induced.

The Old Testament Hebrews were also familiar with hypnosis. The prophets of Baal "called on the name of Baal from morning even until noon," "leaped about the altar," and "cut themselves with knives till the blood gushed out upon them. . . . When midday was past, they prophesied" (I Kings 18:26–29). Here, again, the muscles were constricted, the limbs stiffened, and the subject remained motionless in a trancelike state.[9] The onlookers also participated in these activities until finally they became rhythmical. Modern counterparts of this ceremonial rite can be found today almost anywhere among primitive people.

The Celts of ancient Britain developed hypnotic practices to a high degree of excellence, from MacCulloch's description. Their priestly order, the Druids, knew the rudiments of stagecraft, ecstasy, and hypnotherapy. The subject would lie down as if to sleep while four Druids chanted over him until he fell into a "magic sleep." Then visions, for example, of the person to be elected king, would appear to him. It is very probable that the Druids resorted to hypnotic suggestion in this situation. Prophecy would occur when a state of ecstatic frenzy was reached by the seer, and out of his incoherent speech (speaking with tongues) would come the desired message.

The rudiments of hypnotherapy can be seen in the ability of the Druids (and nonpriestly practitioners) to assuage grief by making a person forget those he had loved dearly, while a wife could be made to forget her jealousy. A daughter suspected of lying could be cast into a Druidic sleep by her father and could then be made to reveal the truth. It seems like an anachronism to learn also that the Druids "could raise blotches on the face of the victim." Here we find the concept of psychomatics appearing at the beginning of the Christian Era.

Among the Greeks of approximately the same era, there is a wealth of material which shows a high development of the therapeutic phase of hypnosis. About the fourth century B.C., and for five centuries thereafter, the cult of Asclepius developed and flourished. At the various centers of healing dedicated to this god, the patient was instructed regarding the power of the god and about previous cures (prestige suggestion) and was then taken into the temple for the "temple sleep" which "seems to have been a combination of hypnosis and various lesser forms of suggestion." [10] The extent to which hypnotic or posthypnotic suggestion was used during the trance seems not too well established. "Some authors believe that it was entirely a matter of hypnotic suggestion; others think that the priests impersonated the divinity, perhaps themselves speaking the words of the god, or even performing surgical operations in his character." The record of alleviation of suffering is impressive and represents an important stage in the development and medical use of hypnosis.

Some writers have made reference to the use of the trance among the earliest Egyptians, but there is no indication that it was an integral part of their religious practices. However, across the pages of history to the Egypt of a century ago [11] and down to our day,[12] the ecstatic trance developed into a prominent feature of Egyptian life. The devotees are now called "whirling" or "howling dervishes," and the trance practices of these ascetics is a part of the cultural heritage of this country. Their mode of producing ecstasy is the familiar one of solitude, fasting, and the repeating of ritual prayers for 40 days. When the dances are performed, some of the spectators also experience ecstasy even though they do not dance. Lane says that, in the Egypt of a century ago, those who took part in the religious rites were even familiar with hypnotic analgesia (or anesthesia). This is shown in the practice of *doseh*, a ceremonial in which a mounted horse treads on the cataleptic bodies of the devotees. Those who did not prepare adequately for the observance "have on more than one occasion been either killed or severely injured," while those who had spent the previous day in preparation felt no pain and got up immediately to follow the procession.

Western culture customarily regards all hypnotic phenomena as abnormal, while an examination of the evidence would indicate their normality in certain settings. There is, however, a pathology of the trance itself which is illustrated by some of the events in medieval history, notably the dancing manias. This was a series of epidemics known variously as St. John's dance, St. Vitus's dance, Tigretier, tarantism, and others witnessed in Germany, the Netherlands, Italy, and Abyssinia. While the main events occur in the period from 1374 to 1819, "the dancing mania of the year 1374 was, in fact, no new disease, but a phenomenon well known in the Middle Ages. . . . In the year 1237, upwards of a hundred children were said to have been suddenly seized with this disease."[13] While the disease took different forms and was modified by local circumstances, its distinctive pattern was well defined. The advent of the mania in a given locality was anticipated. Then those who were afflicted

. . . formed circles hand-in-hand and appearing to have lost all control over their senses, continued dancing . . . for hours together, in wild delirium, until . . . they fell to the ground in a state of exhaustion. . . . While dancing they neither saw nor heard, being insensitive to external impressions . . . but were haunted by visions.

Such a syndrome can readily be explained as an involuntary hypnosis, while the particular form it assumed reflected the cultural setting of the period. Similar phenomena occurred in Paris during the Revolution and again at the close of the Franco-German War, and yet again in Madagascar as late as 1864.

The dispute over the role that hypnosis plays in the experience of the classic mystics of Western culture has been long and bitter, and the arguments have often been marked by the pleading of a cause. Only the outward forms of the behavior referred to as ecstasy, rapture, etc., need be considered here. In ends sought, the Western mystic achieves his purpose with his "union," the Hindu with his "release," the American Indian with his "locution," and the Gã with his "vision." The ends differ and are culturally determined, but the means are identical in all essentials.

The antecedents of a mystical experience are well known—fixation of gaze, fasting, meditation, solitude. This being so, the contemplative *should* go into a trance. The ecstasy which follows has been defined by Hastings as "an abnormal state of consciousness in which the reaction of the mind to external stimuli is either inhibited or altered in character. . . . As used in mystical theology, it is almost equivalent to trance. During ecstasy the visionary is impervious to messages from without and can even feel no pain" (Vol. V). In a textbook of psychology this could well serve as a description of self-induced hypnosis, provided the subject entered the trance with the expectation of becoming analgesic. From a psychological viewpoint the same writer describes ecstasy as "an extreme variety of monoideism." James, with his classical scholarship in both religious phenomena and psychology, associates the traditional ecstatic experience with fugues, automatic writing, and the mediumistic trance—all forms of behavior in which monoideism plays a part.[14] The similarity between these forms of behavior and hypnosis has already been described.

If the limitations set by a given culture and the expectations of a person in the light of what he knows about ecstasy or the trance are fully recognized, the behavior of the mystic seems to be adequately explained. The products of the experience may, however, be judged by their worth-whileness.

OTHER CULTURES

The preceding sections have shown the occurrence of hypnotic phenomena in the life of today as well as in the remote past of the human race. References have already been made to many races and cultures. There remains the task of looking for trance phenomena among contemporary cultures scattered throughout the world. Some of these are "primitive," others are highly developed. The need that is met by the trance varies greatly from one culture to another, as does the extent to which it is used. In its purpose, also, there is a variation from that of controlling the unknown (whether friendly or hostile) to seeking the ultimate in personal development. In this setting our own culture must be considered one which makes very little use of the trance and contrasts unfavorably with some of the "primitive" cultures in the extent of its knowledge of the trance. The list of possible references for this section is very long and uneven in quality. Nonetheless, even when doubtful cases are excluded, it is still possible to say that hypnosis in some form and to some extent is found among all peoples whose activities have been adequately reported.

In the northern reaches of the American continent, the Eskimos make extensive use of the trance. In an atmosphere of darkness, continuous drumming, dancing, and singing, the medicine man induces a voluntary self-hypnosis while curing a disease. Training for this type of work comes in the usual form of fasting and isolation, with one novel feature—grinding stones. While some have regarded the trances as pathological and hysterical in nature, others emphasize the essential normality of these practitioners, especially when judged by the criteria of contemporary American culture.[15]

Among the Greenlanders the trance assumes an unusual role. In describing his adventures in the Arctic, Freuchen says:

When the hunters row out in their kayaks on still water they are becalmed with the sun's bright glare reflected in their eyes as from a mirror. Suddenly as they wait patiently for seals to rise to the surface they are gripped with a paralysis which prevents their moving a muscle. They sit as if petrified and they say they have a feeling that the water is rising over them but they cannot lift a hand. . . .

I experienced the trance or "kayak disease" or whatever it is. I sat in my kayak day after day waiting for seals. . . . It is then that the mind begins to wander crazily. I dreamt without sleeping, resurrected forgotten episodes from my childhood. Suddenly great mysteries became for the moment plain to me. I realized I was in an abnormal state and reveled in it. I cannot explain the feeling exactly, but it seemed that my soul, or spirit, or what you will, was released from my body, my life and obligations, and it soared impersonally, viewing everything as a whole. . . . I approached a comprehension of mysteries otherwise denied me.[16]

This reference is unusual in two respects. It joins what has been mentioned about fishing and driving in our own culture with an experience that is as truly mystical as that of a medieval or modern mystic. The interpretation of the trance as a "disease" also approaches the popular concept of our American culture.

Among the Indians of the Arctic Circle there is evidence of the trance. Once more the rattle, singing, and dancing make up the essential procedure, the medicine man having been called into this profession through seizures that recur every few hours or days. While the trance is not fully described in the literature, the subsequent results of these cataleptic seizures justify the assumption that they are hypnotic.

From the Indians of the United States comes a wealth of material. The trance, in some form, has long been a feature of Indian life. Early travelers among the Sioux and Menominee in the middle of the eighteenth century found the trance then used for divination, according to Hastings (Vol. IV). Among the Paviotso of Western Nevada, the medicine man goes into a trance which is a therapeutic process if his patient is gravely ill, or, if life is not in danger, it will be used as an aid in diagnosis.[17] Among the Plains Indians, the vision (or trance) is sought by torture. Straps are inserted under the shoulder muscles and then attached to poles and "they hang suspended only by those cords without food or drink for two, three or four days, gazing into vacancy, their minds fixed intently upon the object in which they wish to be assisted by the deity and waiting for a vision from above." [18] The shamans of many tribes are chosen for the facility with which they can go into a trance. Once established, they maintain their position by further evidence of cataleptic proficiency.[19] In other tribes the trance is induced in the spectator or worshiper rather than in the priest or shaman. In peyote worship, the worshiper is exhorted to keep his eyes fixated on a peyote button used in the ceremonial. Concentration on this spot on the altar in a tepee lighted only by a flickering fire may well encourage self-hypnosis which would facilitate the ensuing vision.[20]

In South America the medicine men of the Araucanos of Southern Chile duplicate almost in detail the practices and experiences of their counterparts among the Eskimos.

Eskimo and Araucano medicine men alike are able to hypnotize their audience (white onlookers included!) to the extent that they see the medicine man open the body, handle the intestine and close the body again without (for good reasons) leaving any traces. This trick has made early white travellers describe the *machi* [medicine man] as a great abdominal surgeon. But he is no surgeon. He is a great hypnotist of the same calibre as the Hindu fakir who makes his white onlookers *see* him climb into the heaven on a rope which he has thrown into the air.[21]

Information regarding the shamans of Siberian tribes makes it clear that "the essential character of a shaman is a liability to nervous ecstasy and trances." [22] It is added that "all over Siberia, where there is a shaman, there is also a drum" and furthermore, "the shaman would invariably reply that he did not remember, that he forgot everything after the seance was over. . . ." In this remote culture all the familiar characteristics of hypnosis are again present.

The trance is again encountered in Japan. "At the present day, possession is represented by popular practices of which the principal element is hypnosis," says Hastings. "It is certain that this phenome-

non was the basis of primitive possession although the ancient docu-
ments do not describe it minutely. . . . In our day the hypnotic crisis
constitutes the essential point of the spiritual seances" (Vol. X).
The many and intricate cultures of Africa make use of the trance
in various ways. Among the Gã people of the west coast, hypnosis
has been developed to a very high level of proficiency. A special
stool and other paraphernalia are reserved for the exclusive purpose
of inducing a trance. In this manner all the advantages of prestige
suggestion are secured. When the patient is seated, a huge calabash
filled with water is placed on his head, thereby tending to fixate his
attention. Gong-gongs are beaten monotonously, and against this
background there emerges the singing and rhythmic shouting of
those who assist the medicine man. With the addition of stamping
of feet and clapping of hands, there emerges a method of trance
induction which is much more elaborate but probably equally as
effective as our own.[23]

An event of unusual interest occurred when the anthropologist
(M. J. Field) came upon a medicine man who was having great
difficulty in inducing the trance. She suggested to him "that he
should hold a plain copper finger-ring in front of her [the patient's]
face, make her fix her eyes and attention on it and [that he] also tell
the gong-gong beaters not to stop their beating for little rests. He did
this and by great good luck it was successful." Thus does Western
science invade the province of the medicine man!

From the east coast of Africa also comes evidence of familiarity
with the use of hypnosis, though, in this case, much less adequately
reported. Out of the experience of a Western physician in Abyssinia
comes the following statement:

In the field of mental diseases the native physician has achieved surprising
results through suggestion and hypnosis. The U. S. Technical Project
had opportunity to observe several cases of persons believing themselves
possessed by the devil. The methods used in curing these persons were
based on a psychological understanding which in no way could be called
primitive.[24]

There is also incidental evidence of trance practices among the
Bantu, Zulus, and Ashantis, as well as a concise but adequate state-

ment of a high development of trance uses among the Nuba.[25] Similar descriptions could doubtless be found for other tribes and cultures on this continent.

When attention is turned to the South Pacific and Indonesia, there are scattered references to hypnosis being used in a very large number of cultures. The practice of the trance in Bali has been recorded by photographs and descriptions that surpass any other current material. Here hypnosis has been integrated as an essential component of daily life. It is induced by incense, singing, and "by holding on to vibrating sticks connected by a string from which puppets are suspended." [26] The gods enter the puppets and set up a commotion in the string which then passes to the sticks and, finally, to the girl dancers. This method is distinctive, as is the unusual dissociation of parts of the body in these trances (as well as in their dances). There are "a variety of trance dances in some of which only the arm of the performer is in the trance." The differential relaxation and the fostering of separate awareness of various parts of the body are predominant aspects of their trance behavior. To quote further from Bateson and Mead:

There are villages where everyone has been a trancer; villages where no one has been in a trance. There are not, as far as I know, any Balinese who have not witnessed trance often. The trance itself approximates closely to the phenomenon of hypnosis and comparison of our trance films and records with materials on hypnotic subjects in this country has revealed no discrepancies except for the substitution of a formalized situation for the hypnotist.

To cite evidence of the existence of hypnosis and of the superb degree of perfection attained with it in Hindu culture is superfluous. To analyze the characteristics of its advanced stages with terms borrowed from Western science is, however, well-nigh impossible.

The problem is to discern the role that hypnosis plays in the various stages of Yoga experience. Part of the difficulty lies in the lack of equivalence of terms in Eastern and Western thought. In the West, for example, the term "concentration" denotes an intense preoccupation with a limited group of stimuli, but in Yoga literature it stands for "the elimination of all thought, getting behind thoughts, i.e., transcending the activities and fluctuations of *citta* or mind stuff." [27] In view of what is known of deep hypnosis, it is at least conceivable that the Yoga term "concentration" can best be approximated by the term "trance." It is, however, far from permissible to assume their equivalence even though the English term "concentration" is so clearly unsuitable. Behanan, a writer who is familiar with both Yoga and Western psychology, says that in Yoga, "attention is narrowed down to a vague, 'quality-less' point—a kind of mono-ideism claimed to be essential for auto-hypnosis . . . until at last by intense concentration even the steady mind and its single thought are surpassed."

The phenomenon known as "rapport" in hypnosis has its equivalent in Yoga sense withdrawal. To quote further from Behanan, the yogin "is responsive only to those stimuli that have a spiritual value." When it is recalled that Yoga trances are self-induced, there is no great discrepancy between this state and experimentally induced rapport on the one hand. On the other hand, the spiritual exercises of Western mystics closely resemble those of the yogin, for, having started "with the practice of self-hypnosis and removal of all sources of inner conflict, the [Hindu] mystic integrates all the forces of the mind into a unity and reconciles himself with the totality of experience as a spiritual system." If the determining conditions are right, "deep hypnosis may lead to an unexpected expansion of the faculties of the mind or the acquisition of supernormal powers." [28] (The fakir with his bizarre behavior is one who fails to progress from the initial stages to the ultimate.) If these statements, made by another writer who is also familiar with both Occidental and Oriental thought, can be confirmed, it would seem that the gap between the laboratory and the mystic can be bridged.

But the real problem of the relation of the trance to the ultimate experience of the yogin arises from statements to the effect that it is "mere speculation of doubtful value to affirm or deny that the two [Yoga and hypnosis] are essentially similar," as Behanan says, or that "the regular change of breathing in direct and then in reverse order, which . . . takes place more than 1,500 times in the course of the whole exercise completely excludes any notion of hypnotic trance" as Mukerjee affirms. The nature of the ultimate experience of the yogin will only be solved in the laboratory, and then only when much more is known about the nature of ideas and particularly of images.*

A realization of the extent and variety of trance practices in other cultures throughout the world should remove hypnosis from the realm of the abnormal. It should also stimulate research into the real nature of the trance and into the contribution it may make to life in our own culture.

* Dr. Behanan has been willing to modify his position considerably in personal conversation with the writer. He is willing to concede that, while yet unproved, the two may be essentially identical, the apparent differences arising from the cultural and psychological conditioning of those who embark on a trance state.

REFERENCES

1. Williams, G. W.: "Highway hypnosis," *Parade*, Aug. 28, 1949.
2. MacCulloch, J. A.: *Religion of the Ancient Celts*, T. & T. Clark, Edinburgh, 1911.
3. Snyder, E. G.: *Hypnotic Poetry*, University of Pennsylvania Press, Philadelphia, 1930.
4. Hastings, J.: *Encyclopedia of Religion and Ethics*, Charles Scribner's Sons, New York, 1908.
5. *Alfred Lord Tennyson. A Memoir by His Son*, Vol. 1, The Macmillan Company, New York, 1897.
6. Mühl, A. M.: *Automatic Writing*, T. Steinkopff, Dresden, 1930.
7. Benedict, R. F.: "Culture and the abnormal," *J. Gen. Psychol.*, Vol. 1, 1934.
8. Paton, L. B.: *Spiritism and the Cult of the Dead in Antiquity*, The Macmillan Company, New York, 1921.
9. Oesterley, W. O. E., and Robinson, T. H.: *Hebrew Religion*, The Macmillan Company, New York, 1937.
10. Rogers, S. L.: "Psychotherapy in the Greek and Roman world," *Ciba Symposia*, Vol. 9, 1947.
11. Lane, E. W.: *Manners and Customs of the Modern Egyptians*, E. P. Dutton & Co., Inc., New York, 1914.
12. Kelly, R. T.: *Egypt*, A. & C. Black, Ltd., London, 1904.
13. Hecker, I. F. K.: *The Epidemics of the Middle Ages*, Haswell, Barrington & Haswell, Philadelphia, 1837.
14. James, W.: *The Varieties of Religious Experience*, Longmans, Green & Co., Inc., New York, 1929.

15. Ackerknecht, E. A.: "Medicine and disease among Eskimos," *Ciba Symposia*, Vol. 10, 1948.
16. Freuchen, Peter: *Arctic Adventure*, Halcyon House, New York, 1938.
17. Rogers, S. L.: "Psychotherapeutic aspects of Shamanism," *Ciba Symposia*, Vol. 9, 1947.
18. Benedict, R. F. "The vision in plains culture," *Am. Anthrop.*, Vol. 24, 1922.
19. Benedict, R. F.: "Culture and the abnormal," *J. Gen. Psychol.*, Vol. 1, 1934.
20. LaBarre, W.: "Primitive psychotherapy in native American cultures: Peyotism and confession," *J. Abnorm. & Social Psychol.*, Vol. 42, 1947.
21. E. A.: "Arctic medicine in South America," *Ciba Symposia*, Vol. 10, 1948.
22. Czaplicka, M. A.: *Aboriginal Siberia*, Oxford University Press, New York, 1914.
23. Field, M. J.: *Religion and Medicine of the Gã People*, Oxford University Press, New York, 1937.
24. Barkhuus, A.: "Native medicine in Ethiopia," *Ciba Symposia*, Vol. 9, 1947.
25. Nadel, S. F.: *The Nuba*, Oxford University Press, New York, 1947.
26. Bateson, G., and Mead, M.: *Balinese Character*, New York Academy of Sciences, New York, 1942.
27. Behanan, K. T.: *Yoga: A Scientific Evaluation*, The Macmillan Company, New York, 1937.
28. Mukerjee, R.: *Theory and Art of Mysticism*, Longmans, Green & Co., Inc., New York, 1947.

CHAPTER TWO

Dynamics in Hypnotic Induction

Editor's Note

The methods of inducing the trance state have been adequately described in hypnotic literature, but little has been published regarding the actual psychodynamics which are involved. In order to bring about a trance state, the hypnotist adopts some procedure which he decides is likely to be appropriate to the subject and to the situation, and gives suggestions aimed at achieving the objective. Too often, it is merely a bit of "patter," which may or may not be successful in producing hypnosis. More adept hypnotists will carefully study the individual, perhaps test his suggestibility, and may ask some questions intended to uncover resistances to, and motivations against, hypnosis. The subject's behavior is closely watched for clues. For instance, if the hypnotist talks of relaxation, he may lift the subject's arm, seemingly to test relaxation. From the response, the information may be obtained that resistance is present. From all that is noted, a technique is selected which, it is hoped, will be most suited to that particular subject. Either strong domination, soft persuasion, or friendly cooperation may be the main factor in the chosen technique; less skillful hypnotists usually rely mainly on dominating the subject. Other decisions are formed as to the best methods of approach and what is to be said. Even the most experienced and adroit hypnotist finds that, in his approach, he must avoid the common tendency to fall into some habit pattern where he utilizes some technique which he particularly fancies or finds effective.

It must be remembered that no printed discussion of induction techniques and the words to be spoken can reveal the vocal intonations or the vital personal qualities which are involved. Such things as gestures or movements of the agent, his facial expression, the monotony of the spoken words, rhythm, accent or stressing of words or phrases, and many other matters all have effect on the subject. In discussing induction methods, such things cannot be adequately described.

Analysis of the psychodynamics of the inductive process is a progressive step toward a better understanding of the nature of hypnosis. Only with further knowledge will it be possible to formulate a workable, comprehensive theory as to its nature. A realization and understanding of the dynamics involved in the induction of hypnosis will also be of material advantage to the operator in selecting the most suitable technique for producing hypnosis in any particular subject. In the following chapter these dynamics are thoroughly analyzed, a single induction method having been employed in order to reach some basis for consideration.

This might well be called the "arm-levitation method," although it is not an actual method but rather the application of a technique which is adaptable to almost any procedure. When Dr. Christenson's description has been studied, the advantages of this technique become obvious. The main advantage is that, through ideomotor activity, both the subject and the hypnotist are given maximum awareness of the progress made toward the trance state. The technique may be varied in any number of ways, and any approach such as domination, persuasion, or cooperation, may be applied. It is even possible to use it in stage hypnosis or demonstrations in connection with the "rapid-fire" induction method, although not with so-called "instant induction."

Dr. Christenson's article was originally published in the February, 1949, issue of *Psychiatry*. It is so significant that it is reprinted here with some minor deletions and with the section on Procedure considerably amplified and expanded because it was felt that the chapter would be improved with the inclusion of more details as to this "arm-levitation" induction process.

In the article Dr. Christenson stresses the importance of clarity and the subject's understanding of the suggestions given him. He says: "It is essential that the agent be always definite . . . so that the subject knows specifically and without question what is expected of him." With some subjects, undoubtedly, the best results would be obtained in this way. For Christenson's research into dynamics, it was essential to use the method in this manner. However, it can also be applied in almost a reverse fashion and be just as successful in bringing the desired result of a deep trance. Erickson, who first formulated the technique, often varies it thus, adopting a confusion process instead of clarity and precision.* Most stage hypnotists, who *must* produce the trance in their volunteer subjects and who must obtain it very quickly, resort to a fast confusion technique which dominates and overwhelms the subject. Such a method is completely unsuited to hypnotherapy and usually to laboratory hypnosis as well, but it can be modified to a *slow* confusion technique which is safe and very efficient, and which would be contraindicated only with a patient suffering from intense anxiety. Obviously, any induction method must be very carefully handled with such an individual.

This slow confusion method involves giving the subject various suggestions *apparently* precise and clear, piled one upon another in a related way, but so that he becomes more and more uncertain as to just what the hypnotist desires or expects from him. As a result, his attention becomes intensely concentrated on trying to accomplish what has been suggested. He tries to focus it on some particular thing, but as he does so, he is called upon to shift it to something else, and yet he must keep his attention in a narrow range. For example, the suggestion may be given of his left hand levitating toward his face and, while it is still moving slowly upward, he is told that his right hand will move across his body until it has touched the left knee. Gradually, the subject becomes more and more confused, yet at the same time he is progressing deeper and deeper into hypnosis, and his subconsciousness is acting in an endeavor to carry out the various suggestions previously made. It is probable that this process results in a greater degree of dissociation, particularly with multiple activity required. As the subject finds himself responding involuntarily and automatically to the suggestions, while becoming more and more confused, he yields readily to the lethargy of the trance state and "lets go." He is glad to escape from the confusion into lethargy, mentally throwing up his hands

* See Chapter Four.

and sinking into hypnosis. Through the responses recognized as involuntary, he obtains a realization that he is hypnotized, and welcomes it as an escape, acceptance thus becoming complete.

It is by no means easy to formulate suggestions aimed at achieving this confusion. Only a skilled and experienced hypnotist will be able to utilize the method very successfully. Suggestions must be made at exactly the proper moment, and the responses of the subject and the state of his progress must be carefully noted at all times. Hints and implications are made; the more subtle, "insidious," and indirect the suggestions, the greater the confusion and the more the effect is enhanced. The agent keeps just one step ahead of the subject, obtaining the beginning of a response, then switching to something else in his attack. He must be "on his toes" and alert to take advantage of every opportunity to promote more confusion, yet his suggestions must always seem to be clear and precise, and at no time must the subject be allowed to suspect that the confusion is being deliberately fostered, for this would be fatal to obtaining hypnosis.

As a comment, the editor has observed Dr. Erickson apply this technique to a very difficult subject who had previously been hypnotized only lightly in several attempts made by others. This young woman was convinced that she would never be able to reach a deep state, though she was willing and eager to be hypnotized. Within a few moments she had been led to experience negative hallucinations, was disoriented so that she could not state where she was, and carried out a posthypnotic suggestion with complete amnesia after the trance. Certainly, the method is most effective when properly applied, though it requires considerable deftness and cleverness in its application.

There is one way to handle this type of technique which is much simpler and requires less skill, yet promotes dissociation in the same way. In utilizing it, the subject is required to begin counting backward aloud from 100, at a fairly slow tempo. He is told to pay as little attention as possible to what the operator will say as he continues his counting. When he has begun, the operator starts to give sleep suggestions, saying that the subject's eyes will soon become heavy and will close, that he will feel more and more relaxed and listless, that before he reaches zero he will be deep asleep. As the count progresses, arm levitation is suggested, adding motor activity to the subject's concentration on his backward counting. It is not easy for him to keep track of the count after a time, and confusion tends to develop as he begins to sink into hypnosis. His reactions are watched closely, and as the count falters, the subject is told he will lose track of it by the time he has counted 10 more numbers. The effect is excellent, and it can be enhanced by having the subject stand during the process with the operator directly in front of him, facing him. The operator's hands are placed on the shoulders of the subject, and, as he counts, his balance is disturbed by gently pulling his shoulders so that he is moving around in a circle, in a swaying motion. A chair should be placed just behind the subject into which he may sink when hypnosis has been obtained. There is a definite relationship between this method and the slower confusion technique.

Dr. Christenson is one of the relatively new researchers and writers in the field of hypnosis. As a psychological interne at Wayne County General Hospital, he received training under Dr. Erickson and, with several years service as Clinical Psychologist with the Army Air Force, the Army Service Forces, and the Veterans Administration, he has had considerable experience in the practical application of hypnosis as well as in research.

Dynamics in Hypnotic Induction*

By JAMES A. CHRISTENSON, JR., Ph.D.

CHIEF CLINICAL PSYCHOLOGIST, VETERANS ADMINISTRATION
MENTAL HYGIENE CLINIC, TAMPA, FLORIDA; CLINICAL PSYCHOLOGIST,
PINELLAS COUNTY CHILD GUIDANCE CLINIC, ST. PETERSBURG, FLORIDA

The present analysis is based primarily on observations made on 85 volunteer subjects, all of whom were hypnotized by the use of a single method of induction.† This procedure magnifies behavioral reactions to the process so that they may be observed with a good deal of acuteness and insight. The use of a single induction method permits some approach to a general description of the inductive process. Results have been summarized and used as a basis for discussing the psychodynamics of the process, first practically, then in terms of theoretical considerations.

PROCEDURE

The procedure adopted in the present study gives both hypnotist and subject maximum awareness of progress through its use of ideomotor activity. Although it is ordinarily best to adapt any method to the particular situation and to the subject's current reactions, attention has here been arbitrarily restricted to a single method of induction in order to give a uniform background for comparing the dynamics of individual reactions to hypnosis.

* Published with the permission of the Chief Medical Director, Department of Medicine and Surgery, Veterans Administration, who assumes no responsibility for the opinions expressed or conclusions drawn by the author. This article, in a somewhat different version, originally appeared in *Psychiatry*, 12:37–54, 1949.
† The essential features of this method were learned from Dr. Milton H. Erickson, Director of Psychiatric Research and Training, Wayne County General Hospital, Eloise, Mich.; now in practice at Phoenix, Ariz.

In practice, once a subject has volunteered, he is seated comfortably with his hands resting on his thighs or on the arms of the chair. He is told to watch one hand and to note all sensations in that hand: its weight, skin tension, the feel of the cloth beneath it, and whatever other sensations may appear. He is asked to continue to concentrate on the hand and all the sensations in it. Next he is told the hand will probably begin to feel a bit numb, or that it may feel different in other ways, for example, heavier or lighter, warmer or colder. In addition to the various sensations which he may observe, there may also be a growing feeling that something will happen, and he may find his fingers are beginning to feel restless and that they may start twitching.

When definite twitches are evident, the subject may be told that his fingers will probably begin straightening out, and time is allowed for this to happen. As the fingers begin to straighten, it is suggested that his hand will begin to rise and that the arm will float up into the air until eventually his fingers will touch his face.

If finger movements fail to occur, the same initial instructions are gone over again, with suggestions that these phenomena will probably occur as the subject begins to be hypnotized.

The hypnotist now begins direct suggestions of hypnosis, linking up the phenomena which have been induced and may be induced with progress into a hypnotic trance. He makes all phenomena as interdependent and contingent upon one another as possible, so that a building up of effect may be obtained. Thus, he tells the subject that he is going to count slowly in order to help him achieve deep hypnosis, and says that the higher he counts the more relaxed the subject will become. The agent then says that the more relaxed the subject becomes, the more his hand will lift, and that the degree to which it lifts will serve as an index to his degree of relaxation. The lifting, relaxing, and counting are all tied in, one to the other, and their interdependence is stressed.

Counting is begun in a slow tempo, usually in time with the subject's breathing, and in a soothing, monotonous tone. At intervals, suggestions for lifting the hand and arm and becoming more and more relaxed are interjected. The subject is also told, after his hand has raised appreciably, that he will probably find himself becoming more and more sleepy as his hand lifts, so that by the time his fingers reach his face, he will be ready to drop off into a deep, restful, dreamless, and refreshing sleep. The subject's reactions at this point will indicate his readiness for further induction. Thus, the hand may pause, or even begin to lower, or rise more slowly. The fact that a definite goal has been set at which the subject will fall asleep makes it imperative that he be allowed to set his own pace thereafter, with the agent refraining from forcing him. The agent should keep talking sufficiently to keep the subject's attention on his motor progress, but the agent must be careful not to distract or overdirect matters.

When the subject's fingers do touch his face, he is told that he will now go deeper and still deeper, until he is completely asleep. After an interval, he is told that by the count of 20 he will find that he can open his eyes, feel wide awake, and talk as usual, but that he will nevertheless be in the same deep state that he is in at the moment.

This procedure ordinarily takes half an hour or more. At all stages the subject is allowed tacitly to set his own pace, so that all effects will be grounded in his own reaction patterns and not imposed arbitrarily from the outside. Thus, by waiting for the subject to signal that he is asleep by dropping his arm to his side after his fingers have touched his face, the agent will avoid the common pitfalls of undue haste and inadequate preparation of the subject for the later stages of the process.

If the agent says that something may happen, he is on safer ground than if he says that it will happen, and it is much better to say that something will soon begin to happen, or must happen, and finally, has happened rather than to make a flat statement that something *is* happening.

The success of actual induction depends largely upon the extent to which the subject knows definitely what the agent means at all times, and upon the agent's ability to avoid techniques or effects which are unfavorable to hypnosis. It is essential that the agent be always definite, especially as to signals to be used, order of events, and so on, so that the subject knows specifically and without question what is expected of him. Care must also be taken not to say, do, or imply anything which opposes the subject's desires or beliefs, or which might reverse the process, for example, making an obvious overstatement, or expecting too much of the subject on the assumption that the process is more advanced than it is.

The outside conditions during hypnosis can be ignored to a great extent, provided the agent convinces the subject by his own indifference to minor distractions that the process is independent of such matters. However, physical discomfort, or the presence of some outside distraction with personal significance to the subject, will interfere unless the agent discovers the difficulty and cancels its effect. Outside interruptions must clearly be removed by the agent, but it will also be found that he must ordinarily guide the removal of personal discomfort to the subject. A subject will allow himself to become very uncomfortable without doing anything about it, partly because he expects the agent to discover and correct it, but also because he assumes tacitly that anything he does which was not directly suggested or allowed by the agent will interfere with the process.

Throughout the induction process, best results are ordinarily obtained when the subject is aware of the progress he is making. The hand-levitation technique gives continuous awareness; muscular-relaxation techniques give some subjective awareness; most other methods merely set up arbitrary landmarks for progress. In addition, it is essential to keep the subject aware of the agent. Counting is one means for securing attention and also gives a build-up effect when the number series is extended indefinitely. Patter, well used, is the stock in trade of many hypnotists.

CONDITIONS

The hand-levitation procedure was employed in the winter of 1943 44 on 85 volunteer subjects at a small lounge for soldiers where the atmosphere was informal and quiet. To most of the subjects the agent was simply an enlisted man who knew something about hypnosis, and there was no compulsion to cooperate because of any outside pressure, which he might have exerted if, for example, he had been a college professor or an army officer. About one half the people who watched the hypnosis volunteered as subjects; the number of girls who volunteered was definitely greater in proportion to their number. The entire group was of uniformly similar interests and background in the same general age group—late teens or early twenties.

DESCRIPTION

The process of hypnotic induction may be divided into three main stages: (1) achieving a state of readiness to be a hypnotic subject; (2) receptiveness to suggestion and development of the state of mind required for light hypnosis, with varying degrees of actual hypnosis; and (3) a full somnambulistic reaction or deep hypnotic trance. These stages are seldom discretely seen, since most methods of induction do not provide indications of moment-to-moment progress, and practice speeds up the process, so that they would be clearly observable only in the initial session or two.

Readiness. The state of readiness is best described as including both an interest in hypnosis and willingness to cooperate as a subject. Persons who fulfill these two conditions and show no distrust of the process or strong emotional reactions out of keeping with the situation may be considered ready for the inductive process.

Light hypnosis. Under this heading is included development of the state of mind required for being hypnotized, with intermediate degrees of effect up to and including stages in which it is evident that the subject has progressed beyond the point of simple cooperation or following out of the agent's wishes, until he does things he cannot stop himself from doing unless he interrupts the entire process. This involves bringing about a state of inner relaxation and such changes in the reactivity and awareness of the subject that he is highly susceptible to suggestions from the hypnotist and progressively more susceptible to the production of specialized hypnotic phenomena. This change appears to involve a special variety of concentration or attention which is not tense or focused but relaxed and receptive without specific direction or emphasis. Unless the agent calls them to attention, a number of environmental stimuli seem to be shut off, for example, noises in general, and awareness of or reaction to the presence of other persons not involved in the process. What those limitations of reactivity will be at any given moment depends on the suggestions given directly or implicitly by the agent and on the subject's expectations or desires concerning the trance.

Certain effects of pure waking suggestion, such as swaying, difficulty in unclasping the hands, or difficulty in opening the eyes, should ordinarily be taken as indices of readiness. However, once the inductive process has begun, they may be used in a manner characteristic of light hypnosis. The point of transition between simple waking suggestion and light hypnotic phenomena may be placed provisionally at the point where the subject displays either a reluctance to resist or an inability to resist despite evident efforts. Easily hypnotized subjects will telescope these effects, but the distinction is evident in most individuals when they are first hypnotized.

Deep hypnosis. This appears to be a distinct state, qualitatively different from earlier stages, with certain evident changes in behavior and a completeness in the various hypnotic phenomena which was not apparent earlier. Externally, the subject ordinarily exhibits relaxed muscular tonus, a reduced breathing rate which falls to a minimum of 12 to 15 respirations per minute when he is ignored, general body flush, and reduced reactivity to outer stimulation, all suggestive of a state of rest or sleep. There is a definite change in facial expression and voice, with an air of abstraction, indifference to surroundings, and a reduction of outwardly directed activity unless it is suggested by a hypnotist. Posthypnotic suggestions will be executed, usually with amnesia, and various other phenomena can be induced, for example, catalepsy, memory improvement, greater motor facility, heightened concentration, physiological and biochemical changes, and psychological dysfunctions such as delusions or hallucinations.

The most reliable single criterion for a full hypnotic state is that the subject can open his eyes and still remain in a trance. It is for this reason that the terms "deep trance" and "somnambulism" are used interchangeably. Doubts about depth of trance will most frequently arise if no attempt has been made to have the subject open his eyes.

The actual point at which a state of deep hypnosis is achieved is not always seen by the hypnotist, although it is often possible for one deeply hypnotized subject to tell the progress of induction in another and to indicate the point at which the other subject goes into a deep trance. Subjectively this point is often placed retrospectively by the subject as that at which he "let go" or his "waking" memory ceased. Since this change may occur without any awareness of the transition—as is likely when the eyes remain shut—he will frequently not be able to say when he is in a deep hypnotic state until he has experienced it a number of times. The simplest procedure for determining when deep hypnosis is reached is to use a motor signal; thus, the subject may be told that his left forefinger will lift if he is in a deep sleep.

The subject who is in a deep somnambulistic state will often not seem to be in a nonwaking state at all. One definite feature of resemblance to sleep is the fact that most subjects are not aware of the actual process of achieving the state. Posthypnotic questioning will show that they were not aware of any transition point or of any loss of continuity in mental process. The eyes-shut subject will accept the simile of being asleep fairly readily, but the subject who has been asked to open his eyes is not so ready to accept the idea that he is "asleep." To directed observation, however, there are a number of characteristic changes. The expression in the eyes will become somewhat vacant or inward-looking at the moment of induction, and may remain so. When not stimulated, the subject tends to lapse into a typical posture, head dropped slightly forward on the chest and attention apparently directed inwardly (the "hypnotic posture"). From the standpoint of ease of transition into a deep hypnotic state, the process ranges from a simple lapsing into a trance to a slow and often tedious development of the somnambulistic state. With all subjects who achieve successful somnambulisms, the transition becomes easier and faster with practice, except when conflicts develop. The better subjects almost entirely eliminate an observable process of induction, and they themselves notice the transition stages less and less.

In the somnambulist's speech and behavior there is a loss of socially imposed inhibitions and self-consciousness, with a corresponding increase in frankness and directness of response. The subject is no longer embarrassed or inhibited because he has been trained or "expected" to be; embarrassment and distress will still occur, but it is about matters which affect the subject's intrinsic ideals or concerns. In addition, the subject becames more literal in his thought processes; for example, a subject who was playing bridge while in a somnambulistic state, and was asked by her partner to show her hand, kept the cards in her left hand and extended her right hand to her partner.

With these sheddings of conventional ways of thinking there appears to be a shift back to earlier and more direct ways of perceiving and reacting, and the subject frequently displays greatly improved insight into his mental processes. These changes are not of the same nature as those observed in alcoholic intoxication or reactions to Sodium Amytal and Sodium Pentothal, for in those cases the subject appears to lose some degree of personal inhibition and control.

SUMMARY OF RESULTS

Of the 85 volunteer subjects on whom the hand-levitation technique was employed, about half went into deep somnambulistic trances during the first session. Most of these were in a state of readiness to be hypnotized, either spontaneously or through having watched others sufficiently to wish to try. The group was equally divided between soldiers and college girls. Those who did act as subjects may be divided into five main groups, according to their reactions:

Failures. Of the subjects, 13 per cent may be considered failures. One third of these failed to report any effects at all. Others had a merely frivolous interest and were not willing or able to settle down long enough to be hypnotized. Still others displayed a distinct antagonism and not only would not cooperate but often remained near by, whispering and otherwise trying to interfere. The common denominator of all these subjects seems to be strong inhibition or resistance to the idea of submitting to another's direction or to the demands of the process.·

Light trances. Light trances were achieved by 21 per cent, with eye shutting or other partial effects. They were either too slow in their progress for effective induction beyond this point in a single session, or they were overenthusiastic to the point of rushing their progress and attempting to simulate deep hypnotic effects.

Borderline states. A few spontaneous signs of deep hypnosis were displayed by 14 per cent of the subjects, but they failed to perform posthypnotic acts adequately or to develop amnesia. The impression gained was that they lapsed in and out of deep hypnotic states but were so unreliable as to be considered borderline cases. Two thirds of these subjects were women; in all the other groups, men and women were almost equally distributed.

Difficult somnambulisms. Twenty-two per cent of the subjects went into deep somnambulisms, but only after a delay or some struggle. Because of these signs they are listed separately from the final group.

Easy somnambulisms. Thirty per cent of the subjects went easily and readily into deep hypnosis without much dependence on the method adopted for induction. The clinical impression of this group was that it comprised the most normal and well-adjusted subjects.

In accepting these figures it should be noted that they represent percentages of a group of subjects who had already expressed willingness to be hypnotized and cannot therefore be considered an unselected sample from the general population. The precise figures are of no more than suggestive value because of the limited number of cases and the single set of conditions involved. Furthermore, the results achieved in this study cannot be applied even suggestively to the therapeutic situation. When the matter of ulterior employment of hypnosis becomes a consideration, all the factors of degree of maladjustment, type of therapy, subjective urgency of the situation, and the patient's reactions to psychotherapy are added to and qualify the patterns here described.

DYNAMICS

In the section on Procedure a statement was made of what is done in the process of hypnotic induction. At this point, some of the underlying psychodynamics will be analyzed. These fall under four headings: (1) the conditions determining the readiness to be hypnotized; (2) the determinants which can be isolated within the induction process as such; (3) methods of capitalizing on the trance; and (4) considerations of the relation between suggestion and hypnosis.

1. Conditions determining readiness. The *specificity of readiness* is a definitely observable fact. The same person may be ready or not ready to be hypnotized, depending on many intervening factors. Each act of hypnosis requires a separate decision on the part of the subject that he wants to be hypnotized, or a continuing desire to be hypnotized. It will be found, even with experienced subjects, that if they are not in the mood to be hypnotized, there is no point in going further. In fact, it is best to concede to the new subject that if he does not wish to be hypnotized, he cannot be forced.

A frequent variation in readiness which is usually not strong enough to prevent subsequent hypnosis is what may be called *second-session resistance.* Many subjects will prove to be harder to hypnotize in the second session, some to show their strength of will to the agent, and others to convince themselves that they can resist the process if they wish. Once they have shown that they can resist, this reaction ordinarily disappears.

The single most effective *test for readiness* is the sway test in which the subject is asked to stand up, and suggestions are made that he will sway forward, backward, or to either side. The directness or hesitancy of response, reversals, and overreactions to the suggestions will give good indices to the pattern and difficulty to be expected in induction. As the agent gains experience, he will also learn to correlate expressions, especially in the eyes, and to note other indications of conflict or readiness.

One of the most noticeable *initial reactions* to hypnosis is that of doubt about the process. Doubts will come out in a number of ways: embarrassed smiling when a prospective subject is asked if he wants to be hypnotized; statements that his will power is too strong or that he doesn't want to submit his will to another's domination; refusal to meet the agent's gaze; or occasional insistence that he be hypnotized under certain "favorable" conditions of solitude, lack of distraction, and the like. Most such subjects are not easily hypnotizable at any time, unless their attitudes are changed after a single demonstration or short period of reassurance about the process. Those who are not easily reassured will be resistant to direct attempts at induction, although indirect methods may work.

Other *factors unfavorable to hypnosis* are lack of confidence in or antagonism to the agent (lack of rapport), distrust of one's own reactions, frivolous attitude, overcuriosity, or resistance to the process. It is to cancel these effects that most subjects are encouraged to see a demonstration in advance. The person who is curious about the process and does not want to be hypnotized until he has seen it for himself will ordinarily be a better subject, once he knows what to expect; otherwise, his unsatisfied curiosity will be a deterrent to successful induction. On the other hand, those who evidence obvious conflict over the process are sometimes more readily hypnotized when they have been given no demonstration or explanation, since they are otherwise enabled to build up defenses against hypnosis. This effect is frequently seen when exposition and actual hypnosis have been separated by some hours or a day.

2. Determinants in the induction process as such. A successful and uncomplicated hypnotic induction is not the rule. The process will slow down, stop, or reverse for a number of reasons. Overcuriosity has already been mentioned. Inhibition and conflict of one sort or another will interfere. Reactions to the agent or the technique are also very important.

As in many psychological processes, *awareness* alters the nature of hypnosis and may easily destroy the state of mind which is favorable to effective hypnosis. Some subjects are so curious about what is happening, either critically or with the intention of remembering all that happens, that they have no time left over to be hypnotized. A few will appear to be going easily and quickly into a trance, then stop short with a shock of awareness that control is slipping away, after which they will react to the process with distrust and doubt; others simply show doubt or conflict from the very beginning.

Overenthusiasm is definitely responsible for a number of failures in deep hypnosis, since the subject tries to "force" progress and is accordingly overaware of the process. Such an attitude may lead to the assuming or simulation of hypnotic effects and can deceive the uncritical agent. Overcooperation is a variant of the same attitude. The former response seems to arise from the subject's distrust of the process or of his own reactions to it; thus, enthusiasm may well be a defense reaction. The latter response is more related to the agent than to the process. In the attempt to be a "good" subject, some subjects will even fake results in order not to disappoint an obviously hopeful agent who has given them sufficient clues to the desired response.

Conflict manifestations are especially important, since the agent must cancel or minimize them at once for effective hypnosis. The clinically untrained hypnotist, like the stage hypnotist, is well advised to terminate his efforts at the first sign of conflict, since he may find himself unable to manage the resulting phenomena. Obvious *physiological signs* of conflict are heavy breathing, excessive perspiration, trembling, and evident tenseness. Such *psychological indications* as undue emotion, including preoccupation and fascinated interest, as well as fear or terror, anger, excessive amusement, and the like, are all contraindications. Slowness of the process, some hesitancy, or fleeting emotional reactions are less likely to require clinical experience. Individual variations are to be expected in speed of hypnosis, reaction to the process, depth of effect obtainable within a reasonable period of time (say 2 hours), and usability of the trance, just as with any other psychological process.

In general, a subject who accepts the process matter-of-factly, and with interest, will present the least difficulty in hypnosis. If there are signs of *amusement* (attempts to depersonalize the process), it will facilitate matters to allow the subject to laugh it out. The ideomotor activity which is involved in levitation already represents a partial depersonalization which is acceptable as long as it offers no threat to the subject's security. If he begins to act as if the process were out of his control and becomes concerned, it is time for the unskilled agent to stop.

On the part of the agent, *haste* is probably the prime error. If he considers every suggestion as an experimental stimulus to the subject and waits until he is sure he has seen the subject's complete reaction to the suggestion, he can avoid major difficulties. It is only in this way that each agent can learn for himself the effects of his suggestions, both intended and unintended.

Many *suggestions* are implied in overtones of words or behavior, in vague statements, or even in the nature of the specific situation at the time, and they are seldom noticed by the agent except through study of the unexpected responses of his subjects. It is not too much to say that every variation in tone of voice, tempo, flicker of eyelid, and other expressive movement of the agent is carefully noted by the subject and as carefully interpreted, then frequently taken as a suggestion to be executed. Accordingly, an attitude of complete repose, with nothing said or done that is not specifically intended, is the ideal for which the hypnotist must strive. He must also avoid any impatience or attempts to hurry up the process, since such attempts will also alter the conditions and give hints as to his expectations.

The role of *expectation* cannot be overemphasized in the analysis of a process so subtle and subject to distortion as that of hypnosis. Many hypnotists have never considered that hypnosis can be a cooperative process, and for that reason all their results must be considered in terms of a dominance-submission relationship. Where the agent does not have definite expectations, the subject may himself tailor the form taken by the hypnotic trance to fit his speculations, prejudices, fears, or desires. Much of the confusion about the nature of hypnosis can properly be laid to inadequate assessment of the distorting factors introduced by agents' and subjects' preconceptions.

So many variables can affect hypnotic states that actually only a few are under the control of the hypnotist at any one time. He can isolate and control some consciously and note the effects of others, but a great many subtle variations are visible only in the contradictory and inexplicable difficulties which arise. Thus, if a subject fails to execute a suggested act, it may be because the agent has spoken too narrowly or too vaguely, because the subject is not at a deep enough stage of hypnosis, because he does not wish to respond, or for any of a number of individual reasons. For similar reasons, the execution may be different from what the agent expected. If these variations aid the process, they are seldom noted and hence do not serve as incentives to further study. The best antidote to such gaps in knowledge at the present time is to make the inductive process far more extensive and lengthy than seems necessary, for good as well as for slow subjects.

Once the process of hypnosis has been started, there is an *aural effect* which appears to continue up to several hours after the hypnosis but to disappear overnight, except when the subject fosters it as a means of controlling the agent. In keeping with this effect, it will be found that almost any interruption to the process of induction can be discounted, however disquieting it appears, and the stage of hypnosis already induced will be readily reinstated. Frequently, unwitting hypnosis takes place when induction has been abandoned with one subject, and hypnosis of others or discussion of the topic has been continued. Although there are no ill effects if hypnosis is not recognized, the agent can ensure recognition of such states by fixing a signal to be executed by each subject as soon as he is deeply hypnotized, for example, raising the right hand.

Apparently, interruption of the process furthers hypnosis in some cases, because the subject has assured himself that he can resist the process or decides that the "danger" is over—in either instance dropping his resistance. Other means for *fortifying hypnosis* are the use of irrelevant suggestions which condition the subject to execute any other unfulfilled suggestions, or of rapid alternation between suggestions of waking and sleeping. These likewise take advantage of the subject's lack of awareness or inability to reconstitute his defenses against a sudden change of policy. Any suggestion made during hypnosis which is not a source of conflict to the subject will reinforce the hypnosis. Similarly, irrelevant suggestions will fortify unexecuted suggestions, presumably by some process of association or contamination. The method of sudden reversals has a somewhat different basis—the more rapidly a person is hypnotized, the less time he has to erect specific defenses. Thus, a deep trance obtained quickly will be limited only by the basic attitudes and reactions of the person to hypnosis in general, whereas a slowly induced trance may be limited by all sorts of little qualifications introduced by the subject during the early self-conscious stages of induction.

As many subjects imply when they say that they "don't believe in hypnosis," there is a strong *mystical taint* attached to the name "hypnosis." The terms "animal magnetism" and "mesmerism" are suspected even more strongly on this ground. Because there has been so much charlatanry and mystery attached to the subject, it is placed in the same category as magic or spiritualism. Some effects during induction are obviously attributable to this preconception. Thus, subjects react more violently to the idea of being hypnotized than to the ideas of relaxing, sleeping, or going into a trance. A subject will fight over terminology as much as over suggested activities, as if he feels that the word used plays a dominant role in the effect to be obtained. That this mysticism is not always confined to the subject is seen in many agents' use of "passes," insistence on darkened rooms, silence, and the like.

An occasional reaction is that of subjects who like the hypnotic state so much that they lapse back into it spontaneously, often with *refusal to awaken* when the agent requests them to do so. This is probably best related to the question why the subject chose to be hypnotized in the first place, and to the needs served by hypnosis once it has been induced. People do not do anything idly, and they will consent to hypnosis only if it serves some acceptable purpose, whether therapy, being a "good fellow," or curiosity. A typical example is the frequent occurrence of "accidental" hypnosis, for example, hypnosis by a professor's eyeglasses or droning voice, and refusal to waken for several days. Undoubtedly, most such cases can be traced to a desire to escape from some unpleasant situation, such an an impending examination.

3. Capitalizing on the trance. The induction process can hardly be said to be complete until the agent is able to direct the subject in ways that are characteristic of deep hypnosis. In order for this to be possible, the subject must be deeply hypnotized, and the agent must recognize that fact and be able to utilize the hypnosis as planned. The major problem likely to arise at this stage centers about getting the subject to accept the fact that he is hypnotized. It is apparently from *lack of awareness* on both sides, as well as defects in technique, that borderline states arise and cannot be capitalized. Similarly, audience skepticism about hypnotic states is most frequently seen when the subject has given no overt signs of change in state. It is soon evident that the best hypnotic subjects are by no means so convincing to onlookers as those subjects who show conflict or resistance. Since the better subject has shown no real signs of change, it is usually felt by onlookers that he is still "awake" and faking, until demonstrable effects are seen.

Some difficulty will also arise in *convincing* some subjects that they are hypnotized, especially when a cooperative rather than assertive technique has been used for induction. This appears to be because the nondominating approach allows the subject to assume an active rather than passive attitude, which is out of the realm of his expectation for a state of "sleep." It has been found that both hypnotist and subject can alter the nature of the given hypnotic state by their particular preconceptions and expectations concerning the nature of the state to be achieved. One of the best means for convincing a subject that he is hypnotized is to induce inability to open the eyes or to move the arms.

A number of hypnotists leave their subjects in a so-called *passive state*, where they appear to be in a condition of ordinary sleep except that they will react to the agent's voice and will answer questions. In this state, of course, the subject is much more amenable to suggestions because he is deprived of the use of his vision and hence operates at only a small fraction of his normal spontaneity. Accordingly, it is easy to assume, as is often done, that these subjects are necessarily in a deep trance. For these reasons an exceedingly cautious, patient, and neutral (nonsteering) approach on the part of the agent is essential if he is to isolate the pure or nearly pure state of hypnosis. The observation of differing responses of subjects to the same wording of instructions and apparently identical situations, with questioning as to the reasons for particular responses, is the only safe basis for increased insight, improved technique, and removal of misconceptions about the nature of the process.

The subject who is in a passive eyes-shut trance is not likely to find difficulty in believing that he is asleep. If he is asked, however, to open his eyes and to feel just as he would when awake, he is forced immediately into an active attitude. Some subjects rebel, saying they cannot do it, and lose the air of relaxation and detachment which has characterized their behavior to this point. Those who do open their eyes without difficulty will generally be seen to continue to exhibit deep easy breathing, body flush, indifference to surroundings, and reduction in outwardly directed activity. That is, despite open eyes, they do not at once and automatically assume an attitude of spontaneous activity without suggestions to that effect. This initial pattern can then be obscured by positive suggestions that the subject will feel wide awake, active, and so on, and, with varying degrees of practice, subjects can learn to assume the *somnambulistic role* so readily that it is virtually impossible to detect anything other than normal waking activity.

Continued experiments with hypnosis will demonstrate to the agent that there are many times when he does not recognize the actual existence of a deep hypnotic state, whether because it is so fleeting, or because no obvious change has appeared in the behavior or attitude of the subject. It is safest, therefore, to assume that where any doubt arises, the subject may be hypnotized, and to seek decisive evidence. With borderline cases this effort is frequently sufficient to complete the induction process. It is important at this stage not to assume the reverse—that hypnosis is complete because the subject exhibits some changes—since a willing subject is not beyond manufacturing the effects he believes are expected. Sustained motor activity against gravity, execution of posthypnotic suggestions, lapse into a preoccupied trance, induction of compulsions, paralyses, and the like may all be considered as evidential, since they are difficult if not impossible to perform unless the subject is deeply hypnotized.

In cases where a subject is convinced that he is actually in a deep trance, and the question arises whether he is overcooperating to the extent of self-deception, a number of *devices* are useful for separating actual somnambulisms from lighter states. One convenient method is to teach the subject signals for waking and going into a trance, and suggesting a posthypnotic act, thereby using motor behavior as an index to progress. Spontaneous execution of a posthypnotic act with accompanying amnesia generally results from deep somnambulism. If the subject thereafter goes into a trance readily at signal, the prior state is further substantiated. When a subject is in a deep trance, such experiments as making people invisible, increased attention span or memory, and elaborate posthypnotic suggestions will be successful.

Other devices may be used for the purpose of testing and, if necessary, *furthering progress into a deep trance.* Thus, suppose a subject has been brought to a point which may or may not be a deep trance. He is then told that one finger will move automatically if he is in a deep trance, and another if he is not. The moving of either finger is clearly a sign that he is in a hypnotically receptive state of some sort. Accordingly, if he feels that he is not in a trance, this moving of his finger may be called to his attention as not typical of waking phenomena, and the question is brought up whether he could be asleep without realizing it, with the suggestion that if this is the case his finger movements will signal to that effect. After this point, the tests described above may be employed.

Other forms of *suggestion* appear in hypnosis, for example that of direct pressure, exerted by counting slowly to a predetermined number (20 or higher), by bringing the hands slowly together, or otherwise setting up a slow process at the end of which the subject knows he is to do something. In therapeutic probing this process speeds up memory recall, as will be seen in the verbalizations of the patients; but when deeper phenomena such as actual acceptance of memories or therapeutic insight are desired, it is necessary to wait for motor confirmation, as described above, in order to avoid the dangers of the traditional suggestive technique which is arbitrarily imposed from the outside.

4. *The role of suggestion in hypnosis.* At this point it would be well to examine the general nature of suggestion as it applies to hypnosis. There appear to be two main types, dynamically considered: *first*, the traditionally accepted use of imposed pressure; and *second*, internally assimilated suggestions. As judged by results, the two are not always easy to differentiate, since a given suggestion may be executed as a result of either or both of the processes involved. The former process is sometimes called *direct suggestion* and has been seen most often in so-called "suggestion therapy" in which symptoms are removed or, rather, suppressed, by the influence and authority of the hypnotist. As might be expected, when the hypnotist is absent or fails to reinforce the suggestion, its effects will wear off unless the second process has been called into play. This latter is closely tied up with the dynamics of *conviction.* In this case the process of conviction as it applies to the assimilation and acceptance of suggestions is consistent with the needs and desires of the subject.

Upon analysis it appears that there are intermediate stages between the making of a suggestion and its adoption or execution by the subject, regardless of the original nature of the suggestion. The complete *sequence* is: (*a*) *the suggestion* itself; (*b*) the process of "taking" or *assimilating* the suggestion; (*c*) "setting" or completion of that process, resulting in the *acceptance* of a belief, or conviction that a given course of action is desirable or necessary; and (*d*) *execution* of the suggestion where overt action is required. The usual hypnotic suggestion is so presented as to obscure stages (*b*) and (*c*).

With matters of subjective attitudes or psychological disturbances, the effect of suggestion lies more often in the field of motives. Accordingly, it is very difficult to assess the end results of any suggestion. If an externally imposed pressure technique should prove to have durable results, it can be assumed that the subject was somehow able to go through the fourfold process without external assistance. However, when the full process is kept in mind, and criteria for the different stages are known, results are more readily assessable.

Aside from the mechanics of acceptance, and more particularly of overcoming inhibitions, the effect of any pressure technique appears to lie largely in the arbitrary time delay which is imposed, coupled with the subject's realization that the agent is waiting specifically for him to respond. In deep hypnotic states complaisance is easier to detect, because results will fail in greater or lesser degree, and the subject will state his reactions more frankly if he has any objections to the suggestion. Of course, since the subject has never relinquished his rights in any deep sense, he must always be considered as capable of trying to skew results to serve his own purposes; the half-truth or near-truth is especially frequent in therapeutic probing.

THEORETICAL CONSIDERATIONS

In the literature on hypnosis there is frequent mention of *rapport* as a highly significant and essential factor. It does not seem desirable to abandon this term in favor of *transference*, since the observed dynamics of subject-agent interaction suggest that rapport is present regardless of whether transference is positive or negative, and may thus be considered a more comprehensive construct. Rapport is ordinarily described in terms of strength. Its absence is assumed to be sufficient to prevent any inductive process.

The inseparability of rapport and hypnosis is most evident in cases where the rapport has assumed such dependency-fostering functions that the subject will awaken spontaneously the moment the hypnotist ceases paying attention to him; the transference demands in such behavior are obvious. Here, as always, the hypnosis serves some specific purpose of the subject, who may even trick the inexperienced hypnotist into believing that he cannot be awakened as a means for prolonging contact with or controlling the hypnotist on a dependent basis. Some so-called "passive" subjects, on the other hand, will frequently turn out to be asserting their independence of the agent by an implicit refusal to do anything without prodding and by constant lapsing into sleep. This is best understood as a manifestation of negative transference, without loss of rapport, and should not be mistaken for the behavior in positive transference where the subject is actually waiting for coaxing or domination rather than resisting the process or the agent. Complete negative transference with loss of rapport would probably preclude hypnosis, but once the process of induction is well under way, definite negative factors seem to be capable of existing without disrupting the entire process. Most of these resistances arise where the subject has a definite antipathy to performing some hypnotic act or assuming a given attitude. Thus, one subject, who never moved her arm during induction and tried constantly to lapse into sleep, seemed to go into a state of reverie, with slow, contemplative movements of her hands and fingers which she denied emphatically at first, and which continued later in spite of strong countersuggestions. Another subject displayed the strongest objection to talking during hypnosis and finally rejected further hypnosis. The impression in each case was that the agent was running counter to attitudes and phenomena which the subject was not willing to relinquish, perhaps feeling that such a demand was an infringement on his integrity.

No subject ever willingly gives up his rights; this is especially evident with subjects such as the negativistic ones mentioned above, and will also be found true in cases where members of the audience want subjects to perform acts which are either not in good taste or not in accord with the subject's wishes. The story of the girl in Charcot's clinic, who woke up angrily when the students asked her to strip, is a typical example of how ego functions will turn active if threats arise to the integrity of the individual. Apparent exceptions will always be found to include such screening factors as trust in the discretion of the agent, or a feeling that the agent is assuming responsibility for the act so that the subject can disclaim personal responsibility. Similar dodges are used as excuse for irresponsible behavior while drunk. Drug intoxications are not comparable, since they definitely curtail the subject's ability to resist or uphold his "rights," that is, to act in accordance with his "superego" or "conscience." In narcosynthesis the subject cannot readily inhibit expression of thoughts or behavior which are suggested by the administrant, so that the subject is no longer a "free agent" and the question of coercion is a legitimate issue. In hypnosis as in drinking, the responsibility of the subject cannot be too strongly stressed; he assumes a role of his own free will, and he can reject it at any time. The individual who is already drunk may, of course, reach a point where the alcohol intoxication is comparable to drug intoxication. With hypnosis, the issue of antisocial acts suggested by the agent and executed by the subject thus reduces to the question of how willing the subject is to do something and then throw the blame on the agent, who unwittingly stands ready to assume the blame. Of course, in any legal capacity, the agent is coresponsible if he has encouraged the subject in thus taking advantage of him, but the contingency need never be allowed to arise.

An essential feature of the *hypnotic situation* is that another individual is involved, and hence all phenomena are conditioned by the subject's awareness of the agent's expectation that he shall do something. In *self-hypnosis* this separation is made when the subject plans in advance what he is to do; the fact that autohypnosis is harder to achieve is probably a function of the rapport situation. The dynamic difference between auto- and heterohypnosis appears to lie in this presence of an actual other person to guide the process, in contrast to the predecision of the lone individual concerning the procedure he will follow. Since constant correction and direction will make the process more effective, self-hypnosis can be expected to be less useful than interpersonal hypnosis. It is significant that typical autohypnotic states are seldom capitalized for their merits: the absent-minded reader of a book, attentive movie-goer, or daydreamer all exhibit such states of mind.

A corollary to the above distinction is that *pure hypnosis*, if there is such a state, is *reverie* only, and that all other hypnotic states involve a molding and alteration of the reverie state into patterns which are governed by the expectations of agent and subject and by the knowledge the hypnotist has of techniques and mental processes, but primarily by the existence of the rapport relation.

What happens in hypnosis, apparently, is that the ego gradually withdraws its various outwardly directed conscious perceptions, so that there is only a fringe of awareness of most outside phenomena, and the focus of direct awareness and reactivity is toward the agent and internal perceptions. With this development of increased introspective awareness, the ego finds it possible to recapture or perceive memories and experiences which have been preconscious. Thus, one subject recalled nearly verbatim a radio play he had heard 3 years previously, as checked by a member of the audience who had recently acted in the play. Phenomena which ordinarily occupy the center of awareness are likewise somewhat displaced, and the central focus seems to be in preconscious phenomena. When hypnosis is terminated, amnesia for previously preconscious or unconscious material may be expected unless there is some ego function served by recalling them.

According to this view, hypnosis does not produce *dissociation* of itself, but rather makes use of the existing dissociation between conscious and subconscious phenomena in the subject. Just as there is ordinarily a failure to attend to or be able to remember subconscious tendencies, the hypnotized person displays a lesser or greater tendency not to attend to usual waking phenomena and, when awakened, shows the same degree of awareness of the hypnotic state that he would show for other subconscious states.

This mechanism of what might be called "dissociative inheritance" seems to be adequate as a basis for explaining posthypnotic spontaneous amnesia: there is no need to infer that the subject has any sense of shame for having been hypnotized or for the acts done under hypnosis. Suggestions of amnesia would then simply reinforce this tendency which already exists in the nature of the process. Thus, the individual with a strongly integrated personality might be expected to achieve such dissociation by inattention or "neglect," instead of investing experiences with importance and then suppressing or repressing them. The fact that some subjects simply lapse into hypnosis, "adopting" the new state of mind spontaneously rather than depending on the mechanical process here used, indicates that hypnotic states are spontaneously generated far more frequently than we might suspect. A spectacular example of such a phenomenon was seen in the case of a subject who had been wakened, and suddenly walked over to a piano and sat at it as if he were about to play. When it became evident that he had re-entered a somnambulistic state, he was asked what he was doing and answered that he was playing the piano. It turned out that he heard a Chopin nocturne on the radio and fantasied himself playing it. Frequently, in the past he had undergone such autohypnotic states which ended when the music ceased and had never been detected. It is rather interesting that when this mechanism had been worked out and explained to the onlookers, two other somnambulists who had been hypnotized that evening lapsed into trances along with the original subject when another Chopin piece was played; this, of course, is an excellent example of contagion and of the fact that subjects can manufacture effects to order, unless the agent is exceedingly careful to rule out such possibilities. In contrast to dissociation by neglect, the dissociation of the hysteric is more a capsuling off of traumatizing experiences and may be distinguished from nonpathological responses by its high emotional tone and the extreme overreactivity shown toward hypnosis, which is dramatized to the utmost.

If the usual psychoanalytical analogy of the iceberg is kept in mind, the *scope of hypnotic phenomena* may be imagined more effectively. The portion of the iceberg out of water represents conscious perceptions and activity. Underneath the surface another third or quarter of the iceberg would cover the range of unrecalled fringe awareness, forgotten memories, and the like (preconscious phenomena). The remainder, which is not clearly differentiated from the intermediate portion, would include suppressed, repressed, or never-formulated awarenesses, as well as phenomena of which the individual has never been aware (unconscious or id functions). Deep trances may be assumed to fall within the preconscious areas, below the surface of directed awareness, and thus to share the amnesic quality of preconscious data. A very parallel state is that of the person who has become drunk to the degree where he recalls nothing the next day for a specific segment of his activities. On the basis of observation of several individuals who lapsed into this state for an hour or so and then out, with a consequent amnesia which was immediately determinable, it is possible to say that there, too, certain specific changes in behavior, mood, expression, and tone of voice will be seen. The spontaneous somnambulist or sleepwalker appears to fit this middle area also. Observation of three somnambulists who had fugue states suggests that the fugue is at a far deeper level and not so easily recoverable as a memory. It is well known, of course, that under hypnosis an individual may recall his activities when drunk, or absent-minded mislaying of articles, just as he may recall the activities of a prior trance. Ordinarily, then, the hypnotic state may be expected to lie within the preconscious area, and to be subject to the dynamics of subconscious activities which have been observed in psychoanalysis.

The characteristic simplicity, directness, and unaffectedness of *somnambulistic reactions* is reminiscent of the outlook of primitives and of children, in whom the complex patterns of civilization do not obscure spontaneous patterns of reaction. It is widely recognized that much drinking is used as a socially acceptable alibi for escaping temporarily from the restrictions of socially determined customs and restrictions to simpler reactions.

The posthypnotic state is subject to the aural effects previously noted, but it also includes *aftereffects* of one sort or another. If a subject has experienced strain either in the course of the inductive process or from the tasks performed during hypnosis proper, he will frequently suffer from a headache or other indication of tension. If that tendency is mentioned, he may even adopt the symptoms to himself. It is because of this possibility that most hypnotists assure their subjects that they will feel quite well and rested, with no ill effects or aftereffects. The specific aftermath of any given hypnosis will depend, then, on what both hypnotist and subject expect or want and on the subject's reactions to what was done and suggested. Amnesia, instead of being complete, is often selective, or variable from time to time, frequently being broken by the subject to assure himself that he can remember, after which amnesia may redevelop. During the posthypnotic period, ranging from several hours to overnight, the subject is ordinarily quite susceptible to reinduction of a somnambulistic state, whether by learned cues or by contagion, as in the case of the Chopin "playing" already described.

CONCLUSIONS

The general results of consistent application of a single method for hypnotic induction have here been used as a basis for analyzing the dynamics of the inductive process. A working theory concerning the nature of hypnosis has been advanced. The present observations and analysis are intended as a basis for evaluation and comparison of hypnotic results, regardless of the method and viewpoint adopted by the individual worker. It is recognized that adherence to a single method limits the scope of inference, but it has been felt that, without a clearly delimited study, no real beginning can be made toward proper study of hypnotic phenomena. No attempt was made to go beyond the limits of the inductive process except insofar as it was necessary for purposes of adequate presentation.

Advanced workers will find that the present observations can be checked and amplified more readily if several subjects are hypnotized at one time. However, such procedure requires a good deal of experience and working familiarity with some method for analysis and comparison of results. When more than one subject is utilized, the same wording of instructions will frequently arouse divergent behavior, so that the agent must analyze the situation immediately if he is to understand what has happened. This procedure is probably more suited to study of intratrance and posthypnotic phenomena; clear understanding of the inductive process requires more concentrated observation than is possible when the agent divides his attention between two or more subjects.

It will be desirable to test the present analysis against those of workers who employ divergent methods of induction, with a view to correction and amplification. In addition, the role of the type of situation within which hypnosis is attempted will need to be studied in relation to any given method of induction.

CHAPTER THREE

A Rapid Method for the Induction of Hypnosis

Editor's Note

Many physicians and dentists are well aware of the value and advantages of the use of hypnosis. A surprising number of them have become interested in and have studied the subject. It is frequently remarked by such practitioners that they would like to employ it more often, but that they are too busy and cannot spare the time usually necessary to obtain the trance state in a patient. The following article presents a solution to this problem, and it has been thoroughly tested in a busy clinic.

The question has arisen as to whether or not full information should be published as to an induction method which involves real danger to the subject (and to the hypnotist) if the operator is not skilled and careful. The method is one which might even be fatal and certainly is not one ever to be employed by the layman, no matter how expert a hypnotist he may be. Careful consideration was given this point, but it would appear that dissemination of information about the method is warranted, with due warning of the dangers. The main reason for this decision is that the procedure has been employed on the stage, both in this country and in England, in scores of exhibitions. Thousands of people have been hypnotized in this way without harm. It is rather remarkable that it should have been used so often without bad results. These stage hypnotists are skilled and careful, but they cannot know whether or not their volunteer subjects are healthy; some subjects would be expected to have physical conditions that would contraindicate the use of this method. Thus, it is apparent that, with care, the method is not dangerous in medical or dental practice. Since induction by this method has been witnessed by so many people, some of whom might feel inclined to experiment with it without knowing its dangers, it was decided to publish the article.

Practically, this procedure involves a physiological way of preparing the subject for the induction of hypnosis, the trance being produced by means of suggestion. Hypnosis is developed only because of the suggestions given, but, beforehand, the subject has been placed, within a few seconds, in a condition where he is confused, dazed, and almost unconscious, and is extremely responsive to suggestion; hence, the speed with which the trance is obtained. Controlled tests probably would show that, on the average, a deeper state is reached, though as yet this has not been definitely determined. The trance state produced in no wise differs from that reached through the ordinary induction methods.

A Rapid Method for the Induction of Hypnosis

BY JOSEPH E. WHITLOW, M.D.*

Depending on the susceptibility and the resistances of the subject, induction of hypnosis by ordinary methods may require a period of time ranging from a few seconds to several hours. With a person undergoing hypnosis for the first time, 20 to 30 minutes of induction probably will be the average. A timesaving technique often would be of great advantage to the practitioner or the researcher in hypnosis, and, of course, to the stage hypnotist brevity is an essential lest the audience become impatient and restless. Except with a few somnambulistic subjects, the busy physician or psychiatrist who may wish to employ hypnosis finds the length of time needed to obtain the trance a decided handicap. As a matter of fact, the operator who has finally conditioned a subject to enter hypnosis quickly through a signal usually finds a decided relief at escaping from the monotony and boredom of the ordinary induction process. Therefore an almost instant method is decidedly advantageous, even though it is sometimes contraindicated.

The technique to be described here is one which has been employed successfully for the past 3 years in the Whitlow Clinic with scores of patients, and in most cases it is the method of choice. Its origin is unknown to the writer, but the technique was first observed in stage exhibitions by John Calvert and by Hubert H. Wheeler and then demonstrated to the writer. It has been utilized by them with literally thousands of subjects over a period of years without bad

* 41 South Chestnut St., Ventura, Calif.

results of any kind, although it must be said that, in unskilled hands, the method is definitely dangerous, as will be discussed later.

As a prelude to induction the subject is told that this method will bring hypnosis almost instantly, and, in clinical use, one or two cases similar to this are described, with statements as to the favorable and beneficial results obtained. This places the subject in a receptive frame of mind so that acceptance of suggestions will follow. If it is thought desirable to allay possible anxiety, some description is made of what to expect. It is, of course, necessary for the operator to have the confidence and trust of the subject.

The best procedure is to seat the subject on the end of a treatment table so that he can fall backward in a supine position, his head to rest on a pillow. An ordinary couch is too low for the purpose. Otherwise, he may be asked to stand with his back to a heavy, comfortable chair which is placed just behind him, and he is told that he will be lowered into it. He is then instructed to clasp his hands loosely behind his back, to relax, and to look upward at a spot on the ceiling. Hyperventilation will serve to increase susceptibility to hypnosis, and the subject is therefore asked to breathe deeply a few times, holding his breath for a moment with each inhalation. Then he is told to make his mind as blank as possible, and that in a few seconds his eyes will close and he will soon be sleeping deeply.

The operator's left hand is now placed behind the subject's head at the top of the neck, in order to support the head and to prevent muscular "kinking," for any pain or discomfort will interfere with the induction process. The right hand gently pushes the subject's head back until he is gazing almost directly upward, but not to such an extent as to cause strain. Then the operator presses the right thumb and index finger against the vagus nerve and carotid artery on each side of the Adam's apple at about the level of the cricoid cartilage, leaving the larynx free from pressure so that breathing is not mechanically obstructed. The pressure is firm but should not be too strong.

At the same time that pressure is applied to the throat, the left thumb and second finger may be pressed firmly against the neck just below the mastoid, behind each ear. If the operator will experiment on himself, it will be found that pressure on a small spot just back of the lobe of the ear quickly produces a slight dazed feeling which it is the aim of the operator to utilize. However, this part of the procedure is not essential and may be omitted.

As pressure is applied with both hands at the same time, the operator whispers into the ear of the subject suggestions somewhat as follows: "Close your eyes and sleep, breathe deeply, relax and let yourself go; close your eyes and sleep. You are going to sleep now; within ten seconds you will be sound asleep, deep asleep. Now sleep, sleep; let go and sleep. Your mind is a complete blank; you will sleep soundly now. Sleep!" Of course this exact wording is not essential, but the operator should speak emphatically yet quietly, and with great rapidity, "pouring on" the suggestions and not allowing the subject time to think. The pressure of the hands is released as soon as the subject relaxes. Usually, it will be found that he goes limp rather suddenly, which is to be anticipated by the operator. Support is given as he falls backward, either on the table or into the chair. It is best to keep the right hand in position but without pressure for a few seconds thereafter, more as a psychic stimulant than for any other reason.

Just as soon as the subject is reclining, rapid suggestion is given that he will not awaken until told to do so; that he will do exactly as he is instructed; and at this time a posthypnotic suggestion for further trance induction should be given, something to the effect that a signal such as passing the operator's hand in front of the subject's eyes in future will always cause him to go to sleep instantly. Suggestions seem to be particularly effective when made immediately after induction, probably because the subject is dazed and confused.

When induction has been accomplished, having the subject listen to the sound of a metronome will distract his conscious attention. Suggestions aimed at producing deeper hypnosis, at making future induction easier and quicker, or therapeutic suggestions, are then more effective.

This procedure will usually bring hypnosis within 10 seconds, the degree varying, depending on factors such as susceptibility, previous experience with hypnosis, past experience with sedative or hypnotic drugs, etc. Subconscious motivations may be concerned. Involuntary resistances to hypnosis are often overcome with this technique, at least temporarily, some subjects entering a deep state but, on finding themselves in such a condition, partially bringing themselves out. Usually, further training and suggestions will enhance the depth of the hypnotic state obtained.

Tilting the head backward changes the angle of the semicircular canals, affecting the equilibrium and also helping to produce a state of mental confusion. The pressure on the vagus nerves tends to inhibit the heartbeat, and shutting off the carotid arteries produces rapid cerebral anemia and a fainting feeling which further "befogs" the mind and adds to the mental confusion. Strongly given suggestions then strike with full force into the subconscious, which takes over as consciousness fades. It is the purpose of the operator to bring the subject to the point of losing consciousness, but to release the pressure just before he "passes out." If lost, consciousness returns within a few seconds. In order to obtain a spectacular result, the stage hypnotist employing this method usually allows the subject to slump to the floor, then assists him into a chair.

Subjects with whom this technique is used describe their sensations as a feeling of confusion, faintness, and being dazed. Undoubtedly, at this time they become extremely suggestible. When barbiturates are given intravenously to obtain a state of narcosis (Sodium Pentothal being the usual choice), it has been found that the subject must be maintained at a level where he has almost, but not quite, lost consciousness. In this condition he is extremely suggestible, just as in hypnosis. It is probable that the brain anemia produced by carotid pressure creates the same or a similar state, and that the subject then is caused by rapid suggestion to pass into hypnosis.

With ordinary methods of induction there is often so little sensation experienced that the subject may be left wondering if he is hypnotized, unless convinced of it by challenging tests such as eye closure, handclasp, or the other common tests. With this method, subjects tend to accept more readily the fact that they are hypnotized because they have had definite sensations.

At first thought it might seem that the technique is one which the subject would find unpleasant. However, this is not the case, and subjects report no such reaction, invariably submitting willingly to further inductions. If it is found that the suggestion of entering the trance on signal has not been effective, as sometimes happens with ordinary methods, there is a possibility that the subject might awaken with a headache, so suggestions to prevent this are always given, and no patient has ever reported such discomfort.

It cannot be overemphasized that the method described here is one which is extremely dangerous for use by lay hypnotists. It is definitely one for the physician only. Brain damage from lack of blood and even death may result if the pressure is maintained too long on the vagi and carotids, and 15 seconds of such pressure is the very maximum which is safe. In skilled hands, however, the method is perfectly safe and is therefore worthy of being brought to the attention of physicians who wish to employ hypnosis.

It is also apparent that the method is not one which can be used indiscriminately, and subjects must be carefully selected. Only persons who would be considered good surgical risks should be subjected to this rapid method of induction. Generally speaking, there is contraindication with neurotic patients suffering from great anxiety, for the method is forceful, dominating, and confusing, so that the subject is rather overwhelmed and thus an anxiety attack might be precipitated. Certain types of hysterical patients also might be poor risks for the same reason. If anxiety or hysterical reactions should develop, firm, authoritative reassurance or an attention-distracting slap on the cheek is usually sufficient to correct the condition, or, if necessary, the subject can be awakened and reassured. Usually, proper preparation and explanations prior to induction are enough to prevent such reactions even with nervous, anxious, or highly excitable patients. With such persons, preliminary sedation may be of benefit, and perhaps Sodium Pentothal or other hypnotic drugs given intravenously may be used preparatory to induction.

This method has been successfully used in the Clinic on subjects ranging from 2½ to 77 years of age. A Wassermann was taken on a 2½-year-old girl, using a size 20 gauge needle, and suggestions of anesthesia brought freedom from pain. An abscess in the cheek of a 77-year-old woman was opened and incised similarly, and three tonsillectomies have been performed in this way without pain and with subsequent amnesia. In fact, it has been used repeatedly with suggestive anesthesia for repairing many lacerations and for other minor surgery, and the Clinic has had a number of childbirth cases where delivery was effected under hypnosis without pain and with employment of this method of induction.

Statistically, we have successfully obtained the trance state with this technique in approximately 90 per cent of the attempts made, 75 to 80 per cent of those who were hypnotizable reaching a light or medium state the first time, and deeper stages on subsequent inductions. In our experience it often is possible to obtain hypnosis with resistant subjects where slower methods fail entirely. The Clinic is one of general medical practice in a small city; hence, much of the treatment is of psychosomatic and neurotic patients, with rather superficial psychotherapy.

This technique is especially suitable to the busy private practitioner who must do some psychotherapy, but it should prove valuable also to the phychiatrist interested in brief treatment. With rising interest in hypnodontics, it should find much use in dental practice.

CHAPTER FOUR

Deep Hypnosis and Its Induction

Editor's Note

For hypnosis to be utilized to its greatest potentialities, induction of a deep trance state is necessary. Considerable space in this volume has been allotted to discussions of induction because of the importance of the subject. Although a lighter trance is sufficient for some of the procedures in hypnoanalysis, the most advantageous phenomena can be obtained only if a state of somnambulism has been produced. Somnambulism is usually an essential for purposes of experimentation in hypnosis.

Many psychotherapists who recognize the possible advantages of utilizing hypnosis fail to employ it because of the difficulty experienced in hypnotizing many people and in obtaining deep stages of hypnosis. This was one of the main reasons why Freud abandoned its use, and Freudian analysts have uncritically accepted Freud's rejection of hypnosis on the basis that he would have continued to employ it if any advantages were to be obtained. It is probable that Freud would have continued to work with it if he had known some of the techniques described in this and other modern books on hypnotism, for Freud was primarily an investigator.

In the following chapter Dr. Erickson approaches the problem of the induction of hypnosis and the obtaining of deep stages through a study of the personality of the subject, his behavior, his needs, motivations, etc., both conscious and unconscious. In hypnotic literature various induction methods and techniques have been described by many writers, although seldom in much detail. The editor and Jean Bordeaux, in *Hypnotism Today*, made an attempt to give in some detail a simple, uncomplicated induction "talk" which would be suitable for study by the beginner, though it was explained that this should be considered only as a sample for ordinary purposes, and that rigidity in method is inadvisable.

The techniques described by Dr. Erickson are far from simple and, in general, require a good knowledge of hypnosis and experience in its induction and use. Experienced hypnotists develop various procedures; few have described them in print. The editor believes that Erickson's contribution here will do much to extend the applications of hypnosis, because a study of his methods will lead to better results by any worker in hypnosis, experimental or therapeutic.

For theoretical purposes there have been many attempts to classify the various stages of hypnosis, although it is recognized that there are no definite steps and that it is difficult to say where one stage leaves off and another begins. The term "somnambulism" is usually employed to designate a deep stage of hypnosis. While Erickson does not consider it necessary to go into the matter to any extent in his article, the editor believes that some attempt should be made at further classification along the lines of Erickson's statements as to "deep or profound" hypnosis. While all experimenters have obtained such deep stages at times in inducing hypnosis, it is evident that there are differing degrees to "somnambulism." Thus, there should be recognition of a stage of deep somnambulism as distinguished from ordinary somnambulism. In the former the subject responds almost entirely at a subconscious level. Probably this means an almost complete dissociation; a dissociation greater in degree than is seen in the lighter somnambulistic state.

Erickson also mentions an even deeper state marked by lethargy. This has been noted by other writers, Burgess, for instance, calling it to attention in his chapter. It has been termed by the editor a "plenary" trance. The lethargy is not only physical but mental, marked by almost a cessation of thought—at least a minimum of mental activity.

It is probable that there is an even deeper state in which there is an approach to, or even an actual achieving of "suspended animation." Apparently, such a stage is reached by those yogins who have submitted to being "buried alive." Such trances should not be a matter of skepticism, for they have been attested to by competent British physicians in India who have examined the exponent before and after such burial. There has been reported some experimentation by Russian physicians of the use of a similar state induced by drugs, with claim of surprising elimination of some diseases when a patient was kept for 10 days to 2 weeks in such a condition. As a matter of fact, Wetterstrand, a Swedish physician and hypnotist of the late nineteenth century, obtained somewhat similar results at times by putting his subjects into an extremely deep hypnotic state and maintaining it for a number of days, during which time digestive processes and other bodily functions were largely inoperative. This should be a likely field for further modern hypnotic research.

Spontaneous states such as this have been reported from time to time. During the last century many people had great fear of being buried alive under such circumstances. One of the most famous cases of such burial, where the woman was rescued, was that of the mother of Robert E. Lee. In our time little is heard of this, perhaps because the methods of our morticians preclude burial while alive!

This writer has experimented as to extremely deep trance states with one excellent hypnotic subject. He is able to enter the usual somnambulistic stage very quickly. By carrying on the induction process over periods as long as 4 hours, he has reached much deeper states. Suggestions aimed at greater depth were given for 5 to 10 minutes, then silence maintained for a similar time, this being continued alternately. After some practice and with suggestion of speeding up the process, the same results can now be obtained in less than 1 hour. In the first attempt, after about 2 hours, he reached a stuporous trance in which he was unable to move a muscle or to make any response to suggestion, though he was conscious. This continued for about another hour. He then became somnambulistic again. Relying not only on his statements but on the behavior shown and on appearance, there seemed to be a complete dissociation in this state. In the stuporous state, respiration dropped to 8 breaths a minute, and the pulse fell from 80 beats to 60. It was not possible to determine whether the following somnambulistic stage was one deeper than the stuporous one or a return to the stage above the stupor.

Tentatively, it might be said that in our classification of stages of hypnosis we could adopt the following:

Light trance
Medium trance
Deep trance or somnambulistic trance
Deeper somnambulistic trance
Stuporous or plenary trance

Below this, perhaps, would come the stage of apparent suspended animation. Certainly research is needed further into these deep states.

For a quarter of a century Dr. Erickson has been one of the foremost researchers in the field of hypnosis. His work has been of the utmost value in establishing the validity of various hypnotic phenomena and in the field of hypnoanalysis. The painstaking thoroughness of his methods is shown in many of the articles he has published and is further evidenced in his present contribution. Some of his techniques and procedures are most original and unique. He is to be regarded as one of the world's leading authorities on hypnosis.

Much of Dr. Erickson's work has been in institutions and in the field of medical education. For many years he was connected simultaneously with Wayne County General Hospital at Eloise, Michigan, and the medical school of Wayne University in Detroit. For the past four years he has been located in Phoenix, Arizona, where he now is engaged in private psychiatric practice.

Deep Hypnosis and Its Induction

BY MILTON H. ERICKSON, M.D.*

GENERAL CONSIDERATIONS

A primary problem in all hypnotic work is the induction of satisfactory trance states. Especially is this true in any work based upon deep or profound hypnosis. Even the problem of inducing light trance states and maintaining them at a constant level is often a difficult task. Similarly, the securing of comparable degrees of hypnosis in different subjects and similar trance states in the same subject at different times frequently constitutes a major problem.

The reasons for these difficulties derive from the fact that hypnosis depends upon inter- and intrapersonal relationships. Such relationships are inconstant and alter in accord with personality reactions to each hypnotic development. Additionally, each individual personality is unique, and its patterns of spontaneous and responsive behavior necessarily vary in relation to time, situation, purposes served, and the personalities involved.

Statistically, certain averages may be obtained for hypnotic behavior, but such averages do not represent the performance of any one subject. Hence, they cannot be used to appraise either individual performances or even specific hypnotic phenomena. To judge trance depths and hypnotic responses, consideration must be given not only to average responses but to the various deviations and departures from the average that may be manifested by the individual. For example, catalepsy is a fairly standard form of hypnotic behavior, appearing usually in the light trance and persisting in the deep trance states. However, extensive experience will disclose that some subjects may never spontaneously develop catalepsy as a single

* 32 West Cypress St., Phoenix, Ariz.

phenomenon either in the light or deep trance. Others may manifest it only in the lighter stages of hypnosis, some only in the profound trances, and there are those who manifest it only in the transition from the light to the deeper levels of hypnosis. Even more confusing are those subjects who manifest it only in relation to other types of hypnotic behavior, such as amnesia. In other words, however good an indicator of trance states catalepsy may be on the average, its presence or absence for any one subject must be interpreted entirely in terms of that subject's total hypnotic behavior.

Efforts have been made to solve some of these difficulties by developing special techniques for the induction and regulation of hypnotic trances, sometimes with little regard for the nature of hypnotic behavior and its relationships. One of the most absurd of these endeavors, illustrative of a frequent tendency to disregard hypnosis as a phenomenon in favor of an induction technique as a rigidly controllable process apart from the subject's behavior, was the making of phonograph records. This was done on the assumption that identical suggestions would unquestionably and unvaryingly induce identical hypnotic responses in different subjects and at different times. There was a complete oversight of the individuality of subjects, their varying capacities to learn and to respond, and their differing attitudes, frames of reference, and purposes in engaging in hypnotic work. Additionally, there was an oversight of the importance of interpersonal relationships, however attenuated they may be in a given situation, and of the fact that these *interpersonal relationships* are both contingent and dependent upon the *intrapsychic* or *intrapersonal relationships* of the subject.

Even in so established a field as pharmacology, a standardized dose of a drug is actually an approximation as far as the individual's physiological response is concerned. When thought is given to the difficulty of "standardizing" such intangibles as inter- and intrapersonal relationships, the futility of a rigid hypnotic technique to secure controlled results is apparent. An awareness of the variability of human behavior and the need to meet it should be the basis of all hypnotic techniques.

In the problem of developing general techniques for the induc-

tion of trances and the eliciting of hypnotic behavior, there have
been numerous uncritical utilizations of traditional misconceptions
of hypnotic procedure. While the "eagle eye," the "crystal ball,"
strokings and passes, and similar aids as sources of mysterious force
have been discarded by the scientifically trained, the literature
abounds with reports of hypnotic techniques based upon the use
of apparatus intended to limit and restrict the subject's behavior, to
produce fatigue, and similar reactions as if they were the essential
desiderata of hypnosis. Crystal balls held at a certain distance from
the eyes, revolving mirrors, metronomes, and flashing lights are often
employed as the major considerations in the formulation of a hypnotic technique. As a result, too much emphasis is placed upon
external factors and the subject's responses to them. Primarily,
emphasis should be placed upon the intrapsychic behavior of the
subject rather than upon the relationship to externalities. At best,
apparatus is only an incidental aid, to be discarded at the earliest
possible moment in favor of the utilization of the subject's behavior
which may be initiated but not developed by the apparatus. However much staring at a crystal ball may be conducive to fatigue and
sleep, neither of these results constitutes an essential part of the hypnotic trance. To illustrate: A number of subjects were systematically
trained by a competent hypnotist to develop a trance by staring
fixedly at a crystal ball held at a distance of 6 in. and slightly
above the subject's eye level. As a result of this conditioning, efforts
to hypnotize them without a crystal ball were difficult and, in some
instances, ineffectual. Personal experimentation with these subjects
disclosed that the measure of having them simply imagine that they
were looking at a crystal ball resulted in more rapid trance induction and profounder trance states. Repetition of this procedure by
colleagues and students of the author yielded similar results. Return
to the actual crystal gazing resulted in the original slower and less
profound trances characterized by a greater dependency upon external factors than upon intrapsychic processes.

Numerous experiments by the author and his colleagues, in which
these experienced subjects watched silent pendulums or listened to
soft music or to metronomes, disclosed that imaginary aids were

much more effective than actual apparatus. The same findings were obtained with naïve subjects. Medical students were divided into two groups, one of which stared at a crystal ball and the other merely tried to visualize a crystal ball. The latter group gave the more rapid and better results. The experiment was repeated by having the second group listen to a metronome while the first group was instructed to depend upon auditory imagery of a metronome. Again, the imaginary aid proved the more effective. Numerous variations of this investigation yielded similar results. In brief, the utilization of imagery rather than actual apparatus gives the subject the advantage of utilizing his actual capabilities without being hampered by an adjustment to nonessential externalities. This has been found true with experienced subjects as well as naïve subjects, and in the whole range of imagery from visual to kinesthetic.

Additionally, utilization of imagery in trance induction almost always facilitates the development of similar or related more complex hypnotic behavior. For example, the subject who experiences much difficulty in developing hallucinations often learns to develop them when a trance is induced by utilization of imagery.

Subjective accounts from many subjects explaining these findings may be summarized as follows:

"When I listen to the imaginary metronome, it speeds up or slows down, gets louder or fainter, as I start to go into a trance, and I just drift along. With the real metronome it remains distractingly constant, and it keeps pulling me back to reality instead of letting me drift along into a trance. The imaginary metronome is changeable and always fits in with just the way I'm thinking and feeling, but I have to fit myself to the real one."

Similar subjective accounts were secured by the author and by his colleagues and students independently in relation to a wealth of other external apparatus.

In this same connection mention should be made of the author's findings in experimental and clinical work centering around hypnotically induced visual hallucinations. Originally, an actual crystal ball was employed, but experience soon disclosed that a hallucinated crystal ball was more easily available and completely variable and adaptable to the subject's needs. For example, a patient, greatly confused about her personal identity, was induced to visualize a number of crystal balls in which she could hallucinate a whole series of significant life experiences and make objective and subjective comparisons and, thus, to establish thereby the continuity of her life from one hallucinated experience to the next. With a real crystal ball the hallucinated experiences were physically limited in extent, and the changing and the superimposition of "scenes" were much less satisfactory.

Another important general consideration in trance induction concerns the appreciation of time as a factor in itself. Traditionally, the mystic force of a single glance from the eagle eye is sufficient to induce hypnosis. That this misconception has not really been properly discredited is readily realized when encounter is made in current literature of statements to the effect that 2 to 5 minutes' time is sufficient in which to induce any of the profound neuro- and psychophysiological changes of hypnosis. Nevertheless, these same writers would, in administering a powerful drug, wait a reasonable time for its effects. The expectation of practically instantaneous results from the spoken word indicates, at the least, an uncritical attitude and practice which militates against scientifically valid results. Unfortunately, much work has been published which has been based upon an unrecognized belief in the immediate omnipotence of hypnotic suggestions and a consequent failure to appreciate that responsive behavior in the hypnotic subject depends upon a time factor even as it does in the unhypnotized person. The hypnotic subject is often expected, in a few moments, to reorient himself completely psychologically and physiologically, and to perform complex tasks ordinarily impossible in the nonhypnotic state.

Just as subjects vary individually from statistical averages, so do they vary in respect to time requirements. Additionally, their time requirements vary greatly from one type of behavior to another, and also in relation to their immediate frame of reference. Some subjects, who can develop visual hallucinations promptly, may require a relatively prolonged time to develop auditory hallucinations. The presence of a certain mood may actually facilitate or hinder hypnotic responses, and even incidental considerations may interfere with the development of hypnotic phenomena ordinarily possible for the subject. Thus, the fact that the author is a psychiatrist has more than once militated against a subject readily developing auditory hallucinations.

Certain subjects can develop profound trances in a decidedly brief period of time and are capable of readily manifesting exceedingly complex hypnotic phenomena. However, critical study of such subjects frequently discloses a high incidence of "as if" behavior. That is, such a subject, instructed, for example, to develop negative hallucinations for observers present, will behave as if those persons were absent, accomplishing this primarily by avoidance reactions and inhibition of responses. If such behavior is accepted as valid and as the most that can be expected, the subject is likely to remain arrested at that level of functioning. If, however, such subjects are given adequate time to reorganize their neuro- and psychophysiological processes, negative hallucinations can be developed which will satisfactorily withstand searching test procedures.

Too often, the ease with which a deep trance can be induced in a subject is uncritically accepted as a valid criterion of subsequent trance performances. Experience, however, with many such subjects will disclose a frequent tendency to return to a lighter trance state when given complicated hypnotic tasks. Such subjects, for various reasons, are thereby endeavoring to ensure adequate functioning by enlisting the aid of conscious mental processes. Hence, unreliable and contradictory experimental findings are frequently obtained when apparently the experimental procedure was fully controlled.

Neither should the ease and rapidity of trance induction ever be mistaken as a valid indication of the ability to maintain a trance state. Rather, easy hypnotizability sometimes should be regarded as an indication of a need to allow adequate time for a reorientation of the subject's total behavior to permit full and sustained responses. To believe that the subject who readily develops a deep trance will remain deeply hypnotized indefinitely is a naïve assumption which can militate seriously against valid trance findings.

Also, there are those subjects who hypnotize easily, who develop a great variety of complex hypnotic behavior, and yet fail to learn to make some minor hypnotic adjustment. To illustrate, an excellent subject, capable of amazingly complex hypnotic behavior, was found to have extreme difficulty in relation to physical orientation. All experimental studies with him had to be done in a laboratory setting; otherwise, his functioning tended to be at an "as if" level. However, a hallucinatory laboratory situation was as satisfactory to him as a genuine laboratory. Another capable subject, easily hypnotized, could not develop dissociation and depersonalization states unless she were first induced to hallucinate herself elsewhere, preferably seeing herself reading a book at home. Once this was done, inconsistencies and contradictions in her dissociative behavior, otherwise present, disappeared. With both subjects, any effort to economize on time in establishing the laboratory or home situation, despite their rapid hypnotizability, resulted in faulty hypnotic responses. In other words, the general situation, even as time considerations, may be an essential factor in the development and maintenance of satisfactory trances.

The oversight and actual neglect of time as an important factor in hypnosis and the disregard of the individual needs of subjects account for much of the contradictoriness of hypnotic studies. Published estimates of the hypnotizability of the general population range from 5 to 70 per cent and even higher. The lower estimates are often due to a disregard of time as an important factor in the development of hypnotic behavior. Personal experience extending over 25 years with a total of well over 3,500 hypnotic subjects has been most convincing of the importance in hypnotic work of subject individuality and time values. One of the author's most capable subjects required less than 30 seconds to develop his first profound trance, with subsequent equally rapid and consistently reliable hypnotic behavior. A second remarkably competent subject required 300 hours of systematic labor before a trance was even induced. Thereafter, a 20- to 30-minute period of trance induction was requisite to secure valid hypnotic behavior from him.

Ordinarily, a total of 4 to 8 hours of initial training of the subject to go into a trance is sufficient. Then, since trance induction is one process and trance utilization is another, an allotment of time to permit the subject to reorganize behavioral processes in accord with the hypnotic work projected must necessarily be made, with full regard for the subject's capacities to learn and to respond. For example, muscular rigidity is usually produced in a few moments, but a satisfactory anesthesia or an analgesia for childbirth may take hours in divided training periods

The length of time that the subject has been engaged in hypnotic work and the variety of his hypnotic experience is also important in hypnotic research. Often subjects are, literally speaking, transients, serving in only one or two experimental studies. Personal experience, as well as that of colleagues, has demonstrated that the more extensive and varied a subject's hypnotic experience is, the more effectively he can function in complicated problems. For this reason, unless the project requirements are otherwise, the author prefers to do research with subjects who have experienced hypnosis repeatedly over a long period of time and who have been called upon to manifest a great variety of hypnotic phenomena. Lacking this, the subjects are systematically trained in different types of hypnotic behavior. In training a subject for hypnotic anesthesia for obstetrical purposes, she may be taught automatic writing and negative visual hallucinations as a preliminary foundation. The former is taught as a foundation for local dissociation of a body part and the latter as a means of instruction in not responding to stimuli. At first thought, such training might seem irrelevant, but experience has disclosed that it can be a highly effective procedure in securing the full utilization of the subject's capabilities. The goal sought is often infinitely more important than the apparent logic of the procedure, and the mere testing of a hypnotic procedure should not be regarded as a testing of the possibility of hypnotic phenomena.

The foregoing material has been presented as a general background pertinent to a discussion of the problems attendant upon the induction of profound or deep hypnosis. Now, more specific discussion will be offered concerning the nature of deep trances and their induction, but not with any view of trying to describe a specific technical procedure. The variability of subjects, the individuality of their general and immediate needs, their differences in time and situation requirements, the uniqueness of their personalities and capabilities, together with the demands made by the projected work, render impossible any absolutely rigid procedure. At best, a rigid procedure can be employed to determine its effectiveness in securing certain results, but, as such, it is a measure of itself primarily and not of the inherent nature of the results obtained. Even more apparent is this when it is recognized that trance induction for experimental work is actually a preliminary to trance utilization, which belongs to another category of behavior. Such utilization depends not upon the procedure employed to secure a trance but upon the behavior developments that arise subsequent to the induction and from the trance state itself. Furthermore, however controlled a trance induction may be, the development of hypnotic phenomena and of psychological reactions to those phenomena introduces variables for which no rigid procedure of induction can provide controls. As an analogy, however dependent upon a controlled anesthesia a surgical operation may be, the actual surgery and surgical results belong to another category of events, merely facilitated by the anesthesia.

DESCRIPTION OF DEEP HYPNOSIS

Before offering a discussion of deep-trance induction, an effort will be made to describe deep hypnosis itself. However, it must be recognized that a description, no matter how accurate and complete, will not substitute for actual experience, nor can it be made applicable for all subjects because of subject individual variability. Therefore, any description of a deep trance must necessarily vary in minor details from one subject to another. There can be no absolute listing of hypnotic phenomena as belonging to any one level of hypnosis. Some subjects will develop phenomena in the light trance usually associated with the deep trance, and others in a deep trance will show some of the behavior commonly regarded as characteristic of the light trance. Some subjects, who in light trances show behavior usually typical of the deep trance, may show a loss of that same behavior when deep hypnosis actually develops. For example, subjects who easily develop amnesias in the light trance may just as easily fail to develop amnesia in the deep trance. The reason for such apparent anomalies of behavior lies not in any inability of the subject to manifest generally characteristic behavior but in the entirely different psychological orientation of the deeply hypnotized person as contrasted to his orientation in lighter stages. At the lighter levels there is an admixture of conscious understandings and expectations and a certain amount of conscious participation. In the deeper stages, functioning is, more properly, at an unconscious level of awareness.

Hence, in the deep trance the subject behaves in accordance with unconscious patterns of awareness and response which frequently differ from his conscious patterns. Especially is this so in naïve subjects whose lack of experience with hypnosis and whose actual ignorance of hypnotic phenomena unwittingly interfere with the development of deep-trance phenomena, until experience permits a diffusion of understandings from the conscious to the unconscious mind.

The example of this most frequently encountered in inducing deep trances is the difficulty of teaching good naïve subjects to talk in the profound trance. In the light trance they can speak more or less readily, but in the deep trance, where their unconscious mind is functioning directly, they find themselves unable to talk without awakening. The reason is that they have had a lifetime of experience and understanding in which talking is done at a conscious level, and they have no realization that talking is possible at a purely unconscious level of awareness. Subjects often need to be taught to realize their capabilities to function adequately whether at a conscious or an unconscious level of awareness. It is for this reason that the author has emphasized so often the need, in hypnotic work, of spending 4 to 8 or even more hours in inducing trances and in training the subjects to function adequately, before attempting hypnotic experimentation or therapy.

Experimental work requiring deep hypnosis and in which verbalization by the subject is necessary has been observed in which the contradictory or unsatisfactory results obtained derived from the subject's need to return to a lighter stage of hypnosis in order to vocalize, without the experimenter realizing the subject's need and what was happening. Yet, the task of teaching the subject how to remain in a deep trance, and to talk and to function as adequately as at a conscious level of awareness, is relatively easy. The subject who seems unable to learn to talk while in the deep trance can be taught automatic writing, to read silently that writing, and to mouth silently as he reads; then it is a relatively simple step to equate the motor activity of writing and mouthing into actual speaking. A little practice, and speech, contrary to the subject's past experiential understandings, becomes possible at the unconscious level of functioning. The situation is similar in relationship to other types of hypnotic phenomena. Pain is a conscious experience, and analgesia or anesthesia often needs to be taught in a like fashion. The same may be true for hallucinations, regression, amnesia, or whatever phenomena may be desired. Some subjects require extensive instruction in a number of regards, and others can translate learnings in one field to a problem of another sort.

All of the above is essentially an introduction to a description of the nature of a deep trance. Stated briefly, *deep hypnosis is that level of hypnosis that permits the subject to function adequately and directly at an unconscious level of awareness without interference by the conscious mind.*

In other words, the subject in a deep trance functions in accord with unconscious understandings, is independent of those forces to which his conscious mind ordinarily responds, and behaves in the reality which exists in the given situation for his subconscious or unconscious mind. Conceptions, memories, and ideas constitute his world of reality, and the actual reality with which he is surrounded is useful only insofar as it can be utilized in the hypnotic situation. Such external reality does not constitute necessarily concrete objective matter possessed of intrinsic values. Thus, the subject can write automatically on paper and read what he has written. Also, he can hallucinate equally well the paper, the pencil, and the motor behavior of writing and read that "writing." The intrinsic significance of the actual pencil and paper derives from the subjective experiential processes within the subject, and, once used, they cease to be a reality part of his total hypnotic situation. In light trances or in the waking state, pencil and paper are reality objects possessed of inherent significances with which one must deal in addition to those significances peculiar to the individual mind.

A further elaboration warranted is that the reality of the deep trance must necessarily be in accord with the fundamental needs and structure of the total personality. Thus it is that the profoundly neurotic person in the deep trance can, in that situation, be freed from his otherwise overwhelming neurotic behavior, and thereby a foundation can be laid for his therapeutic re-education in accord with the fundamental personality. The overlay of neuroticism, however extensive, does not distort the central core of the personality, though it may disguise and cripple the manifestations of it. Similarly, any attempt to force upon the hypnotic subject, however deep the trance, suggestions not acceptable to the total personality leads either to a rejection of the suggestions or to a transformation of them so that they can be satisfied by pretense behavior so often accepted as valid in attempted studies of hypnotically induced antisocial behavior. The need of appreciating the subject as an individual possessed of a personality structure which must be respected cannot, indeed, be overemphasized. Such appreciation and respect constitute a foundation for recognizing and differentiating conscious and unconscious behavior. Only an awareness of what constitutes behavior deriving from the unconscious mind of the subject enables the hypnotist to induce and to maintain deep trances.

For convenience of conceptualization only, deep trances may be classified as (1) somnambulistic, and (2) stuporous. In the well-trained subject the former is that type of trance in which the subject is seemingly awake and functioning adequately, freely, and well in the total hypnotic situation in a manner similar to that of the nonhypnotized person. By a well-trained subject is not meant one laboriously taught to behave in a certain way, but rather a subject trained to rely completely upon his own unconscious patterns of response and behavior.

An example illustrative of this is the instance in which the author, as a teaching device for the audience, had a subject in a profound somnambulistic trance conduct a lecture and demonstration of hypnosis, unaided by the author, before a group of psychiatrists and psychologists. Although many in the audience had had experience with hypnosis, none detected that she was in a trance. A similar instance concerns a psychiatrist, a student and subject of the author's, who, without the author's previous knowledge and as a personal experiment in autohypnosis, conducted a staff meeting and presented a case history successfully without her trance state being detected. However, once apprised of the situation, the audience could readily recognize the tremendous differences between ordinary conscious behavior and trance behavior, and repetitions of this procedure were detected.

The stuporous trance is characterized by primarily passive responsive behavior, marked by both psychological and physiological retardation. Spontaneous behavior and initiative, so characteristic of the somnambulistic state if allowed to develop, are lacking. There is likely to be a marked perseveration of incomplete responsive behavior, and there is a definite loss of ability to appreciate the self. Medical colleagues asked by the author to examine subjects in a stuporous trance without knowledge of the hypnotic situation have repeatedly offered the tentative opinion of a narcotized state. In the author's experience the stuporous trance is difficult to obtain in many subjects, apparently because of their objection to losing their awareness of themselves as persons. Its use by the author has been limited primarily to the study of physiological behavior and to its therapeutic application in certain types of profoundly neurotic patients.

PROBLEMS OF DEEP-TRANCE INDUCTION

An exposition of the numerous problems of deep-trance induction will be presented by means of a discussion of the major considerations involved, with a detailing of procedures that may be used and the purposes to be served. Although the author is presenting his own experience, this has been confirmed by the experience and practice of his students and colleagues. These considerations will be listed and discussed separately.

1. Trance induction versus trance utilization. Foremost among the major considerations in any work with deep hypnosis is the need to recognize that trance induction is one thing, and trance utilization is another, even as surgical preparation and anesthesia is one thing, and the surgery is another. This has been mentioned before and is repeated here for emphasis. Unless the work projected is no more than a study of trance induction itself, this differentiation must be made by both the subject and the hypnotist. Otherwise, there can be a continuance of trance-induction behavior into the trance state with the result that trance activities become an admixture of partial and incomplete induction responses, elements of conscious behavior, and actual trance behavior.

2. Differentiation of trance behavior from ordinary conscious behavior. Directly related to the first consideration is the recognition and differentiation of conscious behavior from the behavior arising from the unconscious. In this matter, experience is the only teacher, and careful study of behavior manifestations is necessary. This is best accomplished in relationship to reality objects. The subject in profound hypnosis can be instructed to note well and thoroughly an actual chair. Secret removal of that chair does not necessarily interfere with his task. He can continue to see it hallucinatorily in its original position, and sometimes to see it at the same time in a new position as a duplicate chair. Each image is then possessed of the same reality values to him. In the ordinary conscious state such behavior would be impossible or a pretense. Or, if the subject discovers that the chair has been moved, searching study will disclose other mental adjustments. Thus, he may develop a different orientation. For example, a chair specified as in the northeast corner, secretly moved to the southwest corner, may result in a new spatial orientation of the subject so that, to him, the chair remains unmoved in the northeast corner, his sense of direction having altered to meet the situational need.

Similarly, the induced hallucination of a person by a comparable procedure, resulting in two visual images, confronts the subject with the question of which visual image is real. Such a development could not occur in the ordinary conscious state. Neither could there be the spontaneous solution, witnessed by the author on several occasions, achieved especially by psychology and medical students, in which the subject would silently wish that a certain movement would be made by the two figures. The figure responding to that silent wish could then be recognized as hallucinatory. The reality to the self of the subject's hypnotic behavior and its recognition by the hypnotist is essential to induce and to permit adequate functioning in the trance state. Failure of such recognition permits the acceptance of inadequate responses as valid manifestations and causes oversight of the prolonged and intensive effort required for various types of hypnotic phenomena.

3. Orientation of all hypnotic procedure about the subject. All techniques of procedure should be oriented about the subject and his needs in order to secure his full cooperation. The actual projected hypnotic work should be no more than a part of the total hypnotic situation, and it should be adapted to the subject, not the subject to the work. These needs may range from the important to the insignificant, but, in the hypnotic situation, an inconsequential matter may become crucial.

As an illustrative example, a subject, repeatedly used by another hypnotist with equivocal and unsatisfactory results in an experiment involving the use of a plethysmograph on one hand, gave good experimental cooperation and results when the author recognized his unconscious need to have his left-handedness recognized by placing the plethysmograph on his left rather than his right hand. This done, it was found that he could then also cooperate when his right hand was used. An ambidextrous subject, in an experiment involving automatic writing and drawing, was found to insist unconsciously upon the privilege of using either hand at will. Other subjects, especially medical and psychology students, have often insisted at an unconscious level upon the satisfaction of mere whims or the performance of other hypnotic work before their full cooperation could be secured for the experimental project for which they had volunteered.

A patient with a circumscribed neurotic disability was both unable and unwilling to pay for therapy. Also, he was unwilling to receive treatment without first making payment. Accordingly, he was induced to act as a volunteer subject for a long series of experiments, with no attempt at therapy, which was at his insistence. After more than a year of experimental work, he unconsciously reached the conclusion that his volunteered hypnotic services constituted adequate payment for therapy, which he then accepted fully.

In brief, a subject's psychological needs, no matter how trivial and irrelevant, need to be met as fully as possible in hypnosis where inter- and intrapersonal relationships are so vital. Oversight or neglect of this consideration will often lead to unsatisfactory, equivocal, and even contradictory results. Indeed, when contradictory results are obtained from a subject, there is a need to review the entire hypnotic situation from this point of view.

4. *Recognition of the need to protect the subject.* A subject needs to be protected at all times as a personality possessed of rights, privileges, and privacies and recognized as being placed in a seemingly vulnerable position.

Regardless of how well informed and intelligent a subject may be, there exists always, whether recognized or not, a general questioning uncertainty about what will happen or what may or may not be said or done. Even subjects who have unburdened themselves freely and without inhibition to the author as a psychiatrist have manifested this need to protect the self and to put the best foot forward no matter how freely the wrong foot has been exposed.

This protection should properly be given the subject in both the waking and the trance states. It is best given in an indirect way in the ordinary waking state and more directly in the trance state.

For example, a 20-year-old girl volunteered as an experimental subject but always reported for work in the company of a tactless sharp-tongued associate who constituted a serious obstacle to hypnotic work. After a considerable amount of work the subject began reporting alone, and some time later she explained with mixed amusement and embarrassment, "I used to bring Ruth with me because she is so awfully catty that I knew I wouldn't do or say anything I didn't want to." She then told of her desire for therapy for some concealed phobic reactions she had originally been unwilling to disclose to anyone. Her experimental work both before and after therapy was excellently done.

In working with new subjects, and always when planning to induce deep trances, a systematic effort is made to demonstrate to the subjects that they are in a fully protected situation. Measures to this end are relatively simple and seemingly absurdly inadequate. Nevertheless, personality reactions make them effective. For example, a psychology graduate volunteered as a demonstration subject for a seminar group. A light trance was induced with some difficulty, and her behavior suggested her need for assurance of protection. Under the pretext of teaching her automatic writing, she was instructed to write some interesting sentence and, having written it, not to show it until after automatic writing as a topic had been discussed. Hesitantly, she wrote briefly. She was told to turn the paper face down so that not even she could read what she had written. Handed a new sheet of paper, she was asked to write automatically her conscious and unconscious answers to the question, "Are you willing to have me read what you wrote?" Both written replies were "yes," to which was added, also automatically, "anybody."

The suggestion was offered that there was no urgency about reading her sentence since it was her first effort at automatic writing, that it might be more interesting to fold it up and put it away in her purse and at some later time to compare the script with further automatic writing she might do. Following this, a deep trance was easily and readily induced.

Some time later she explained, "I really wanted to go into a trance but I didn't know if I could trust you, which was silly because everything was being done in front of the whole class. When you asked me to write, my hand just impulsively wrote, 'Do I love Jerry?' and then I wrote that you or anybody else could read it. But when you just told me to put it away and later just examine it for the handwriting, without even hinting about a possible meaning of the writing, I knew then that I had no reason whatever for any hesitation. And I also knew that I could answer my own question later instead of doing it all at once and wondering if I was right."

This type of example has been encountered many times, and this general method of handling the need for ego protection has been found remarkably effective in securing deep, unconscious cooperation in inducing deep trances.

Another measure frequently employed in this same connection is that of instructing the subject in a light trance to dream a very vivid, pleasing dream, to enjoy it, and, upon its completion, to forget it and not to recall it until so desired at some later date in a suitable situation. Such instruction is manifold in its effects. It gives the subject a sense of liberty which is entirely safe and yet can be in accord with any unconscious ideas of license and freedom in hypnosis. It utilizes familiar experiences in forgetting and repression. It gives a sense of security and confidence in the self, and it also constitutes a posthypnotic suggestion to be executed only at the subject's desire. Thus, a broad foundation is laid conducive to the development of profound trances.

This type of comprehensive suggestion is employed extensively by the author since it serves to initiate a wealth of hypnotic responses, pleasing to the subject and constructive for the hypnotist, in a fashion fully protective of the subject and thereby insuring cooperation.

Another measure, of a somewhat negative character, is that of instructing the lightly hypnotized subject to withhold some item of information from the hypnotist. This item should, preferably, be one of a definitely personal character not fully recognized by the subject as such. It might be his middle name, what member of his family he resembles most, or the first name of his best girl friend when he was a little boy. Thus, the subject discovers, by actual experience, that he is not a helpless automaton, that he can actually enjoy cooperating with the hypnotist, that he can succeed in executing hypnotic suggestions, and that it is his behavior rather than the hypnotist's that leads to success. All of these reactions are essential in securing deep trances. Also, the subject learns unwittingly that, if he can act successfully upon a negative suggestion, the converse is true.

Another frequently overlooked form of protection for the subject as a personality is the expression of appreciation for the subject's services. Full regard must be given to the human need to succeed and to the desire for recognition by the self and by others of that success. Deprivation of the subject of success and of its recognition constitutes a failure to protect the subject as a sentient being. Such failure may imperil the validity of hypnotic work since the subject may feel that his efforts are not appreciated, and this may result in lesser degrees of cooperation. Even more can this be recognized when it is realized that emotional reactions are not necessarily rational, especially so at an unconscious level of reaction. Experience has shown that appreciation must be definitely expressed in some manner, preferably first in the trance state and later in the ordinary waking state. In projects where expressed appreciation is precluded, the subject can be taught in other situations full confidence in the hypnotist's appreciation of services rendered. In any hypnotic work, careful attention must be given to the full protection of the subject's ego by meeting readily his needs as an individual.

5. The utilization of all of the subject's responsive and spontaneous behavior during trance induction. Often, techniques of hypnosis center primarily about what the hypnotist does or says to secure trances, with too little attention directed to what the subject is doing and experiencing. Actually, the development of a trance state is an intrapsychic phenomenon, dependent upon internal processes, and the activity of the hypnotist serves only to create a favorable situation. As an analogy, an incubator supplies a favorable environment for the hatching of eggs, but the actual hatching derives from the development of life processes within the egg.

In trance induction the inexperienced hypnotist often tries to direct or to bend the subject's behavior to fit the hypnotist's conception of how the subject should behave. There should be a constant minimization of the role of the hypnotist and a constantly increasing enlargement of the subject's role. An example may be cited of a volunteer subject, used later to teach hypnosis to medical students. After a general discussion of hypnosis she expressed a willingness to go into a trance immediately. The suggestion was offered that she select the chair and position she felt would be most comfortable. When she had settled herself to her satisfaction, she remarked that she would like to smoke a cigarette. She was immediately given one, and she proceeded to smoke lazily, meditatively watching the smoke drifting upward. Casual conversational remarks were offered about the pleasure of smoking, of watching the curling smoke, the feeling of ease in lifting the cigarette to her mouth, the inner sense of satisfaction of becoming entirely absorbed just in smoking comfortably and without need to attend to any external things. Shortly, casual remarks were made about inhaling and exhaling, these words timed to fit in with her actual breathing behavior. Others were made about the ease with which she could almost automatically lift her cigarette to her mouth and then lower her hand to the arm of the chair. These remarks were also timed to coincide with her actual behavior. Soon, the words "inhale," "exhale," "lift," and "lower" acquired a conditioning value of which she was unaware because of the seemingly conversational character of the suggestions. Similarly, casual suggestions were offered in which the words sleep, sleepy, and sleeping were timed to her eyelid behavior.

Before she had finished the cigarette she had developed a light trance. Then the suggestion was made that she might continue to enjoy smoking as she slept more and more soundly; that the cigarette would be looked after by the hypnotist while she absorbed herself more and more completely in deep sleep; that, as she slept, she would continue to experience the satisfying feelings and sensations of smoking. A satisfactory profound trance resulted, and she was given extensive training to teach her to respond in accord with her own unconscious pattern of behavior.

Thereafter, she was presented on a number of occasions to groups of medical students as a volunteer subject with whom they might work. Her behavior with them was essentially the same as with the author. However, her request to smoke a cigarette was variously handled by the students. Some tactfully dissuaded her from thus postponing the trance induction, some joined her in smoking, and some patiently waited for her to finish. Only after the cigarette question was disposed of in some manner was she allowed to settle down to the task of being hypnotized. The result in every instance was a failure. At a final session with all of the students who had participated, two other students were brought in separately to attempt to hypnotize her. Both of these had been given independently the above account of the author's utilization of the subject's behavior. Both induced profound trances. Then the other students, following the examples set them, also succeeded.

This case has been cited in some detail since it illustrates so clearly the importance of the hypnotist adapting whatever technique he may be employing to the behavioral activities of the subject. To interpret that subject's desire to smoke as an active resistance to trance induction would be incorrect; rather, it was an expression of an actual willingness to cooperate in a way fitting to her needs. It needed to be utilized as such rather than to be overcome or abolished as resistance.

Many times the apparent active resistance encountered in subjects is no more than an unconscious measure of testing the hypnotist's willingness to meet them halfway instead of trying to get then to act entirely in accord with his ideas. Thus, one subject, who had been worked with unsuccessfully by several hypnotists, volunteered to act as a demonstration subject. When her offer was accepted, she seated herself in a stiffly upright, challenging position on the chair facing the audience. This apparently unpropitious behavior was met by a casual conversational remark to the audience that hypnosis was not necessarily dependent upon complete relaxation or automatism, but that hypnosis could be induced in a willing subject if the hypnotist was willing himself to accept the subject's behavior fully. She responded to this by rising and asking if she could be hypnotized standing up. Her inquiry was countered by the suggestion, "Why not demonstrate that it can be?" A series of suggestions resulted in the rapid development of a deep trance. Inquiries by the audience developed that she had read extensively on hypnosis and that she objected strenuously to the frequently encountered misconception of the hypnotized person as a passively responsive automaton, incapable of self-expression. She explained further that it should be made clear that spontaneous behavior was fully as feasible as responsive activity, and that utilization of hypnosis could be made effectively by recognition of this fact.

It should be noted that the reply, "Why not demonstrate that it can be?" constituted an absolute acceptance of her behavior, committed her fully to the experience of being hypnotized, and ensured her full cooperation in achieving her own purposes as well as those of the hypnotist.

Throughout the demonstration, she frequently offered suggestions to the author about what next he might ask her to demonstrate, sometimes actually altering the suggested task. At other times she was completely passive in her responses.

Another subject, a graduate in psychology with whom extensive work requiring a deep trance was projected, experienced great difficulty in going into one. After several hours of intensive effort, she timidly inquired if she could advise on technique, even though she had no other experience with hypnosis. Her offer was gladly accepted, whereupon she gave counsel: "You're talking too fast on that point; you should say that very slowly and emphatically and keep repeating it. Say that very rapidly and wait awhile and then repeat it slowly, and please, pause now and then to let me rest, and please don't split your infinitives."

With her aid, a profound, almost stuporous trance was secured in less then 30 minutes. Thereafter she was employed extensively in a great variety of experimental work and was used to teach others how to induce deep trances.

Acceptance of such help is an expression neither of ignorance nor of incompetence; rather, it is an honest recognition that deep hypnosis is a joint endeavor in which the subject does the work and the hypnotist tries to stimulate the subject to make the necessary effort. It is an acknowledgment that no person can really understand the individual patterns of learning and response of another. While this measure works best with highly intelligent, seriously interested subjects, it is also effective with others. Rightly handled, it establishes a feeling of trust, confidence, and active participation in a joint task. Moreover, it serves to dispel misconceptions of the mystical powers of the hypnotist and to define indirectly the respective roles of the subject and the hypnotist.

Fortunately, this experience occurred early in the author's work and has been found of immense value ever since in inducing hypnosis of every degree and in the eliciting of highly complex hypnotic behavior.

One often reads in the literature about subject resistance and the techniques employed to circumvent or overcome it. In the author's experience the most satisfactory procedure is that of accepting and utilizing the resistance as well as any other type of behavior, since, properly used, they can all favor the development of hypnosis. This can be done by wording suggestions in such a fashion that a positive or a negative response or an absence of response are all actually responsive behavior. For example, a resistive subject who is not receptive to suggestions for hand levitation can be told, "Shortly your right hand, or it may be your left hand, will begin to lift up, or it may press down, or it may not move at all, but we will wait to see just what happens. Maybe the thumb will be first, or you may feel something happening in your little finger, but the really important thing is not whether your hand lifts up or presses down or just remains still; rather, it is your ability to sense fully whatever feelings may develop in your hand."

With such wording, absence of motion, lifting up, and pressing down are all covered, and any of the three possibilities constitutes responsive behavior. Thus, a situation is created in which the subject can express his resistance in a constructive, cooperative fashion. Indeed, the manifestation of resistance by a subject is best utilized by developing a situation in which resistance serves a purpose. Hypnosis cannot be resisted if there is no hypnosis attempted. The hypnotist, recognizing this, should so develop the situation that any opportunity to manifest resistance becomes contingent upon hypnotic responses, with a localization of all resistance upon irrelevant possibilities. The subject whose resistance is manifested by failure of hand levitation can be given suggestions that his right hand will levitate, his left hand will not. To resist successfully, contrary behavior must be manifested. The result is that the subject finds himself responding to suggestion, but to his own satisfaction. In the scores of instances where this measure has been employed, less than a half dozen subjects realized that a situation had been created in which their ambivalence had been resolved. One writer on hypnosis naïvely employed a similar procedure in which he asked subjects to resist going into a trance in an effort to demonstrate that they could not resist hypnotic suggestion. The subjects cooperatively and willingly proved that they could readily accept suggestions to prove that they could not. The study was published in entire innocence of its actual meaning.

Whatever the behavior offered by the subject, it should be accepted and utilized to develop further responsive behavior. Any attempt to "correct" or alter the subject's behavior, or to force him to do things he is not interested in, militates against trance induction and certainly against deep trances. The very fact that a subject volunteers to be hypnotized and then offers resistance indicates an ambivalence which, recognized, can be utilized to serve successfully the purposes of both the subject and the hypnotist. Such recognition and concession to the needs of the subject and the utilization of his behavior do not constitute, as some authors have declared, an "unorthodox technique" based upon "clinical intuition"; instead, they constitute a simple recognition of existing conditions, based upon full respect for the subject as a functioning personality.

6. *The basing of each progressive step of trance induction upon actual accomplishments by the subject.* These accomplishments may be those of the hypnotic situation, or they may belong to the subject's everyday experience. Merely volunteering to act as a subject may be the outcome of a severe inner struggle. Relaxing comfortably in a chair and disregarding external distractions is an accomplishment. Absence of response to land-levitation suggestions is not necessarily a failure, since the very immobility of the hands is, in itself, an accomplishment. Willingness to sit quietly while the hypnotist laboriously offers numerous suggestions, apparently futilely, is still another accomplishment. Each of these constitutes a

form of behavior that may be emphasized as an initial successful step toward a greater development in the trance state.

To illustrate, a Ph.D. in psychology, extremely scornful and skeptical of hypnosis, challenged the author to "try to work your little fad" on her in the presence of witnesses who would be able to attest to the author's failure. However, she did state that if it could be demonstrated to her that there were such a phenomenon as hypnosis, she would lend herself to any studies the author might plan. Her challenge and conditions were accepted. Her promise to act as a subject, if convinced, was carefully and quietly emphasized since it constituted behavior of her own and could become the foundation for future trance behavior. Next, a technique of suggestion was employed which was believed certain to fail, which it did. Thus, the subject was given a feeling of success, gratifying to her, but carrying an admixture of some regret over the author's discomfiture. This regret constituted a foundation stone for future trances. Then, apparently as a face-saving device for the author, the topic of ideomotor activity was raised. After some discussion, indirect suggestion led her to express a willingness to cooperate in experimentation of ideomotor activity. She qualified this by stating, "Don't try to tell me that ideomotor activity is hypnosis, because I know it isn't." This was countered by the observation that ideomotor activity could undoubtedly be achieved in hypnosis even as in the waking state. Thus, another foundation stone was laid for future trance activity.

Hand levitation was selected as a good example of ideomotor activity, and she acceded readily, since she was unacquainted with the author's frequent use of hand levitation as an initial trance-induction procedure.

In the guise of a pedantic discussion, a series of hand-levitation suggestions was offered. She responded quickly and delightedly. This was followed by the suggestion that, as a preliminary to experimental work, it might be well if she absorbed herself completely in the subjective aspects of the experience, disregarding, as she did so, all external stimuli except the author's remarks. Thus, a further stone was laid. Within 10 minutes she developed a profound somnambulistic trance. After some minutes of further suggestion of variations in her ideomotor responses, the remark was made that she might like to discontinue and to return to another point in the original discussion. Thus, she was given a suggestion to awaken from the trance, safe from any autocritical understandings. She agreed and wakened easily, and the author immediately resumed the original discussion. Shortly, a second trance was induced by the same procedure, followed in the course of 4 hours by 4 more.

During the third trance she was tested for catalepsy, which was present. This alarmed and distressed her, but before she could awaken, it was described to her satisfaction as "arrested ideomotor activity," and this not only reassured her but stimulated further interest.

In the next two trances she willingly undertook to experience "other associated phenomena of ideomotor activity." Thus, she was instructed to glance at the witnesses and then to note that, as her attention to the others waned and she became more absorbed subjectively in the ideomotor behavior of her hands, she would cease to see the others. In this way she was taught to develop negative hallucinations by extending her interest in ideomotor activity to an exclusion of other behavior. By a comparable measure she was taught positive hallucinations by visualizing her levitated hand so clearly in two different positions that she would not be able to distinguish her hand from its visual image in another position. This done, the specious argument was offered that, as her attention to her ideomotor activity waxed and waned, she would variously see and not see, hear and not hear the others present, that she might visualize in duplicate others present, and that she could forget the presence of others and even ideas about them or any other thing. By this means, she was induced to experience a wealth of hypnotic phenomena.

There followed the more difficult task of informing her that she had been hypnotized. This was done by suggesting, in the sixth trance, that she recall her feelings "during the first demonstration of ideomotor activity." As she did so, it was pointed out that her self-absorption might possibly be compared to a somewhat similar state that was manifested in hypnosis. Proceeding to the "second demonstration," the suggestion was offered that her behavior was almost trancelike. She was then asked to visualize herself as she must have appeared in the "third demonstration." As she did so, she was asked to comment on her cataleptic behavior, to develop auditory imagery of what had been said to her, and to note the responses made. This time, hypnosis was hinted at as a definite probability, and she was tactfully praised for her ability to develop the imagery, visual and auditory, that enabled her to view so clearly her behavior. Immediately, she was asked to consider the fourth instance. As she did so, she asked hesitantly if, in that demonstration, she were not really in a trance. Assured that she could understand freely, comfortably, and with a most pleasing sense of actual accomplishment, she declared, "Then I must really be in a trance right now." The author agreed and rapidly reminded her of every success she had achieved and how excellently she had been able to utilize her ideomotor activity to expand her field of personal experience. She was further instructed to review mentally the entire evening and to give the author any counsel she wished.

After quiet meditation she asked the author not to tell her, after she had awakened, that she had been hypnotized, but to give her time to reorganize her general attitudes toward hypnosis and toward the author as an exponent of hypnosis, and time to get used to the error of her previous thinking.

It was agreed, and she was told she would awaken with an amnesia for her trance experience and with a pleased feeling that both she and the author were interested in ideomotor phenomena. Suggestion was then given that her unconscious mind would take much pleasure in keeping awareness away from her consciousness of the fact that she had been hypnotized, and that this secret could be shared by her unconscious with the author. She was instructed that her unconscious could and would so govern her conscious mind that she could learn about hypnosis and her hypnotic experience in any way that was satisfying and informative to her as a total personality. By this posthypnotic suggestion the subject was given still further hypnotic training in relation to the independent functioning of the unconscious and conscious mind, the development of a hypnotic amnesia, and the execution of posthypnotic work. In addition, she was made aware at a deep level that she, as a personality, was fully protected, that her functioning rather than the hypnotist's was the primary consideration in trance induction, and that utilization of one process of behavior could be made a steppingstone to development of a similar but more complex form.

The outcome was most interesting. Two days later the subject offered her apologies for her "flippant skepticism" about hypnosis and her "unwarranted" disparagement of the author's work. She added that she was much amused by her need to apologize. A few days later she volunteered to act as a subject, stating she was now seriously interested and would like to participate in some investigative studies. She proved to be a most productive subject over a period of years.

This lengthy example illustrates many of the considerations this author has found of tremendous importance in inducing deep trances. The little item of having a "secret understanding" between the subject's unconscious mind and the hypnotist has many times proved to be remarkably effective as a means of securing deep trances in otherwise aggressively resistant subjects. By virtue of this, they could make conscious and express freely and safely their resistances. At the same time they could have a profound feeling that they were cooperating fully, securely, and effectively. The satisfaction so derived by the subject leads to a desire for continued successful accomplishment, and active resistances are rapidly dispelled, resolved, or constructively utilized.

In brief, whatever the behavior manifested by the subject, it should be accepted and regarded as grist for the mill. Acceptance of her need for the author to fail led to ideomotor activity. This led progressively to a wealth of hypnotic phenomena based either directly or indirectly upon ideomotor responses and culminated in a success pleasing to her as well as to the hypnotist. Had any effort been made to get that subject to conform to some rigid technique of trance induction, failure would have undoubtedly ensued, and rightly so, since the development of a trance was not to prove the author's ability but to secure experiential values and understandings by the subject.

Much of the foregoing material constitutes an exposition of the major considerations involved in the securing of deep trances. Some special hypnotic procedures which are usually successful will now be summarized. Full details are omitted due to space limitations and because of the constant shifting from one orientation to another which they require.

THE CONFUSION TECHNIQUE

For want of a better term, one of these special procedures may be termed the "confusion technique." It has been employed extensively for the induction of specific phenomena as well as deep trances. Usually, it is best employed with highly intelligent subjects interested in the hypnotic process, or with those consciously unwilling to go into a trance despite an unconscious willingness.

In essence, it is no more than a presentation of a whole series of individually differing, contradictory suggestions, apparently all at variance with each other, differently directed, and requiring a constant shift in orientation by the subject. For example, in producing hand levitation, emphatic suggestions directed to the levitation of the right hand are offered together with suggestions of the immobility of the left hand. Shortly, the subject becomes aware that the hypnotist is apparently misspeaking, since levitation of the left hand and immobility of the right are then suggested. As the subject accommodates himself to the seeming confusion of the hypnotist, thereby unwittingly cooperating in a significant fashion, suggestions of immobility of both hands are given, together with others of the simultaneous lifting of one and pressing down of the other. These are followed by a return to the initial suggestions.

As the subject tries, conditioned by his early cooperative response to the hypnotist's apparent misspeaking, to accommodate himself to the welter of confused, contradictory responses apparently sought, he finds himself at such a loss that he welcomes any positive suggestion that will permit a retreat from so unsatisfying and confusing a situation. The rapidity, insistence, and confidence with which the suggestions are given serve to prevent the subject from making any effort to bring about a semblance of order. At best, he can only try to accommodate himself and, thus, yield to the over-all significance of the total series of suggestions.

Or, while successfully inducing levitation, one may systematically build up a state of confusion as to which hand is moving, which more rapidly or more laterally, which will become arrested in movement, and which will continue and in what direction, until a retreat from the confusion by a complete acceptance of the suggestions of the moment becomes a greatly desired goal.

In inducing an extensive amnesia with a regression of the subject to earlier patterns of behavior, the "confusion technique" has been found extremely valuable and effective. It is based upon the utilization of everyday experiences familiar to everyone. To regress a subject to an earlier time in his life, a beginning is made with casual conversational suggestions about how easy it is sometimes to become confused as to the day of the week, to misremember an appointment as of tomorrow instead of yesterday, and to give the date as the old year instead of the new. As the subject correlates these suggestions with his actual past experiences, the remark is made that, although today is Tuesday, one might think of it as Thursday, but, since today is Wednesday and, since it is not important for the present situation whether it is Wednesday or Monday, one can call to mind vividly an experience of one week ago on Monday, that constituted a repetition of an experience of the previous Wednesday. This, in turn, is reminiscent of an event which occurred on the subject's birthday in 1948, at which time he could only speculate upon but not know about what would happen on the 1949 birthday and, even less so, about the events of the 1950 birthday, since they had not yet occurred. Further, since they had not occurred, there could be no memory of them in his thinking in 1948.

As the subject receives these suggestions, he can recognize that they carry a weight of meaningfulness. However, in order to grasp it, his tendency is to try to think in terms of his birthday of 1948, but to do so he has to disregard 1949 and 1950. Barely has he begun to so orient his thinking when he is presented with another series of suggestions to the effect that one may remember some things and forget others, that often one forgets things he is certain he will remember but which he does not, that certain childhood memories stand out even more vividly than memories of 1947, '46, '45, that actually every day he is forgetting something of this year as well as last year or of 1945 or '44, and even more so of '42, '41, and '40. As for 1935, only certain things are remembered identifiably as of that year and yet, as time goes on, still more will be forgotten.

These suggestions are also recognized as carrying a weight of acceptable meaningfulness, and every effort the subject makes to understand it leads to acceptance of them. In addition, suggestions of amnesia have been offered, emphasis has been placed upon the remembering of childhood memories, and the processes of reorientation to an earlier age level are initiated.

These suggestions are given not in the form of commands or instructions but as thought-provoking comments, at first. Then, as the subject begins to respond, a slow, progressive shift is made to direct suggestions to recall more and more vividly the experiences of 1935 or 1930. As this is done, suggestions to forget the experiences subsequent to the selected age are given directly, but slowly, unnoticeably, and these suggestions are soon reworded to "forget many things, as naturally as one does, many things, events of the past, speculations about the future, but of course, forgotten things are of no importance—only those things belonging to the present—thoughts, feelings, events, only these are vivid and meaningful." Thus, a beginning order of ideas is suggested, needed by the subject but requiring a certain type of response.

Next, suggestions are offered emphatically, with increasing intensity, that certain events of 1930 will be remembered so vividly that the subject finds himself in the middle of the development of a life experience, one not yet completed. For example, one subject, reoriented to his sixth birthday, responded by experiencing himself sitting at the table anxiously waiting to see if his mother would give him one or two frankfurters. The Ph.D. previously mentioned was reoriented to an earlier childhood level and responded by experiencing herself sitting in the schoolroom awaiting a lesson assignment.

It is at this point that an incredible error is made by many serious workers in hypnosis. This lies in the unthinking assumption that the subject, reoriented to a period previous to the meeting with the hypnotist, can engage in conversation with the hypnotist, literally a nonexistent person. Yet, critical appreciation of this permits the hypnotist to accept seriously and not as a mere pretense a necessary transformation of his identity. The Ph.D., reliving her school experience, would not meet the author until more than 15 years later. So she spontaneously transformed his identity into that of her teacher, and her description as she perceived him in that situation, later checked, was found to be a valid description of the real teacher. For Dr. Erickson to talk to her in the schoolroom would be a ridiculous anachronism which would falsify the entire reorientation. With him seen as Miss Brown and responded to in the manner appropriate to the time, the schoolroom, and to Miss Brown, the situation became valid, a revivification of the past.

Perhaps the most absurd example of uncriticalness in this regard is the example of the psychiatrist who reported at length upon his experimental regression of a subject to the intrauterine stage, at which he secured a subjective account of intrauterine experiences. He disregarded the fact that the infant *in utero* neither speaks nor understands the spoken word. He did not realize that his findings were the outcome of a subject's compliant effort to please an uncritical, unthinking worker.

This need for the hypnotist to fit into the regression situation is imperative for valid results, and it can easily be accomplished. A patient under therapy was regressed to the age level of 4 years. Information obtained independently about the patient revealed that, at that time in her life, she had been entertained by a neighbor's gold hunting-case watch, a fact she had long forgotten. In regressing her, as she approached the 4-year level, the author's gold hunting-case watch was gently introduced visually and without suggestion. His recognition as that neighbor was readily and spontaneously achieved.

This transformation of the hypnotist into another person is not peculiar only in regression work. Many times, in inducing a deep trance in a newly met subject, the author has encountered difficulty until he recognized that, as Dr. Erickson, he was only a meaningless stranger and that the full development of a deep trance was contingent upon accepting a transformation of his identity into that of another person. Thus, a subject wishing for hypnotic anesthesia for childbirth consistently identified the author as a former psychology professor, and it was not until shortly before delivery that he was accorded his true identity. Failure to accept seriously the situation would have militated greatly against the development of a deep trance and the training for anesthesia.

Regardless of a hypnotist's experience and ability, a paramount consideration in inducing deep trances and securing valid responses is a recognition of the subject as a personality, the meeting of his needs, and an awareness and a recognition of his patterns of unconscious functioning. The hypnotist, not the subject, should be made to fit himself into the hypnotic situation.

THE REHEARSAL TECHNIQUE

Another type of deep-trance induction may be termed the rehearsal or repetition technique. This can and often should be used for deep hypnosis and for individual phenomena. It can be employed in a variety of ways both experimentally and in therapeutic work, especially the latter. It consists of no more than seizing upon some one form of behavior that apparently gives a promise of good development and having the subject rehearse it and then repeat it in actuality.

Thus, a subject who makes little response to hypnosis but who seems clinically to be potentially a good subject may make abortive responses to suggestions of automatic writing. This partial tentative response can be seized upon as an instance of actual success by the subject. Then, a series of suggestions is given leading the subject to rehearse mentally what must have been done to achieve that particular success. Then he is asked to rehearse mentally how it could be done on plain paper, on ruled paper, with a pen, a pencil, or a crayon. Next, he is asked to perform what has been rehearsed mentally in the various permutations possible with that equipment. This can be followed by further rehearsals and repetitions, introducing as new variables hallucinatory paper and writing instruments, and new letters, words, and sentences. As this procedure is followed, the subject progressively develops a deeper and deeper trance, especially if the rehearsal and repetition are applied to other forms of hypnotic behavior.

Sometimes this technique can be applied in an entirely different fashion. For example, before a class of senior medical students, the author undertook to produce amnesia in a volunteer subject who wished both to go into a trance and to disappoint the author. The student expressed the opinion that he doubted if he could develop amnesia, and declared that he himself would propose his own proof of amnesia, namely the removal of his right shoe. Should this occur, he explained, it would constitute proof to him that he had developed an amnesia.

He developed a fairly good trance, and a whole series of instructions was given him, emphatically and repetitiously, that he perform several acts such as borrowing one student's cigarettes, another's glasses, etc. Repetitious command was also given to forget each simple task. Slipped unobtrusively into these suggestions was the statement that, after awakening, while discussing with the class the presence or absence of an amnesia for the assigned tasks, he would cross the room, write a sentence on the blackboard, and sign his name, still continuing his discussion.

Upon awakening, he declared that he recollected everything said to him and that he had done. His statement was challenged, whereupon he heatedly gave a running account of the tasks and his performance of them. Without interrupting his argument, he wrote the sentence and signed his name. After he had returned to his seat, his attention was called to the writing which he disclaimed, emphasizing that his narration proved his remembrance, and he extended his right foot with the shoe on to prove conclusively that he had no amnesia. He then continued his remarks, absent-mindedly removing his shoe as he did so. This he did not discover until the class was dismissed. Systematically appraising the situation, he recognized that he had developed an amnesia with no conscious knowledge of the fact. The class was reconvened, and he was asked to duplicate the writing. As he was doing this, a few suggestions elicited a profound trance, and an extensive demonstration of the psychopathology of everyday life was conducted.

Thus, the subject had been given a long, repetitious list of simple performances, apparently to lead to amnesia but actually to permit him to succeed over and over in accord with his personal needs. Hence, the failures were really successful performances which could actually favor another successful performance, namely the development of amnesia. The unobtrusive slipping in of the suggestion of writing permitted him to set it apart from the other more urgent suggestions. Then, as he achieved his numerous successes of no amnesia, the pattern of response was completed for more successes by his proving the lack of amnesia, by exhibiting his shoe on his foot. This however, left unsatisfied his actual desire for still more success, namely his demonstration of an amnesia by the removal of his shoe, an item of behavior he himself had selected. This he achieved by a double amnesia for the writing and the shoe removal, an even greater success than he had anticipated. Then, as he repeated the writing, he found himself again in the situation that had led to his most satisfying accomplishment. The situation led easily to a deep trance state by virtue of a repetition or rehearsal procedure.

Still another form of this technique has been found useful in inducing deep trances and in studies of motivation, association of ideas, regression, symbol analysis, repression, and the development of insight. It has proved a most effective therapeutic procedure.

This technique is primarily a matter of having the subject repeat over and over a dream, or, less preferably, a fantasy, in constantly differing guises. That is, he repeats a spontaneous dream or an induced dream with a different cast of characters, perhaps in a different setting, but with the same meaning. After the second dreaming the same instructions are given again, and this continues until the purposes to be served are accomplished. To illustrate, a patient offered this spontaneous dream of the previous night: "I was alone in a grass-covered meadow. There were knolls and curving rises in the ground. It was warm and comfortable. I wanted something dreadfully—I don't know what. But I was scared—paralyzed with fear. It was horrible. I woke up trembling."

Repeated, the dream was: "I was walking up a narrow valley. I was looking for something I had to find, but I didn't want it. I didn't know what I was looking for, but I knew something was forcing me to look for it and I was afraid of it, whatever it was. Then I came to the end of the valley where the walls came together and there was a little stream of water flowing from under a thick bush. That bush was covered with horrible thorns. It was poisonous. Something was pushing me closer and I kept getting smaller and smaller and I still feel scared."

The next repetition was: "This seems to have something to do with part of the last dream. It was spring and the logs were in the river and all the lumberjacks and all the men were there. Everybody owned one of the logs, me too. All the others had big hardwood logs but mine, when I got it, was a little rotten stick. I hoped nobody noticed and I claimed another, but when I got it, it was just like the first."

Again repeated: "I was in a rowboat fishing. Everybody was fishing. Each of the others caught a great big fish. I fished and fished and all I got was a little sickly fish. I didn't want it, but I had to keep it. I felt horribly depressed."

Again: "I went fishing again. There were lots of big fish shooting around in the water, but I caught only miserable little fish that would fall off the hook and float dead on the water. But I had to have a fish so I kept on fishing and got one that seemed to have a little life in it. So I put it in a gunny sack because I knew everybody should put his fish in a gunny sack. Everybody else did, and their fish always filled their gunny sacks completely. But my fish was just lost in the gunny sack, and then I noticed my gunny sack was all rotten and there was a hole in it, and a lot of slime and filth gushed out and my fish floated away in that horrible slime, belly up, dead. And I looked around and I was on that meadow I told you about and the gunny sack was under that bush with all those thorns and my good-for-nothing fish was floating down that stream of water I told you about, and it looked just like a rotten stick of wood."

A series of further repetitions finally resulted in the breaking down of extensive amnesias and blockings and his disclosure that, at puberty, under circumstances of extreme poverty, he had acted as a nurse for his mother, who had rejected him completely since infancy and who had died of an extensive neglected cancer of the genitals. Additionally, he told for the first time of his profound feelings of inferiority deriving from his lack of phallic development, his strong homosexual inclinations, and his feeling that his only protection from homosexuality would be a yielding to the "horrible pressure and force society uses to shove you to heterosexuality."

This instance from a case history has been cited, in part, since it lends itself to summarization and illustrates unconscious processes so clearly. Each succeeding dream resulted in a more easily induced and more easily maintained trance, at the same time giving the patient greater freedom in his thinking and in his use of less and less abstruse symbolism.

A necessary caution in this regard is that, in utilizing this type of procedure for experimental or demonstration hypnosis, dreams of a pleasant character should be employed if possible. If not, the implantation of an artificial complex, thereby limiting the extent of unpleasant emotions, is desirable. In all instances care should be taken to discontinue the work should it tend to lead to a situation which the hypnotist is not competent to handle. Otherwise, acute emotional disturbances and active repressions may result, causing a loss to the hypnotist of the subject's good regard and services, in addition to causing emotional distress to the subject.

Another variation of the rehearsal method is that of having the subject visualize himself carrying out some hypnotic task and then adding to the visualization other forms of imagery such as auditory, kinesthetic, etc. For example, a patient under therapy for neurotic maladjustment had great difficulty in developing and maintaining a deep trance. By having her, as an induction procedure, mentally rehearse the probable general course of events for each exploratory or therapeutic session and then to hallucinate as fully as possible the probable experiences for that occasion, it was possible to elicit and maintain satisfactorily deep trances. By giving her "previews," she was able to develop and maintain a profound trance. After exploration of the underlying causes of her problem, the next step in therapy was to outline in great detail, with her help, the exact course of activity that she would have to follow to free herself from past rigidly established habitual patterns of behavior. Then she was reoriented to a time actually 3 months in the future. Then the patient was able to offer a "reminiscent" account of her therapy and recovery. A wealth of details was given, affording an abundance of new material which could be incorporated in the final therapeutic procedure.

A comparable instance is that of a girl who was a most competent subject except before an audience. Then it was impossible to induce a deep trance or to maintain one induced in private. By having her rehearse a fantasied public demonstration for the future and then reorienting her to a date several weeks further in the future, she was able to regard the fantasy as an actual successful accomplishment of the past, much to her satisfaction. Immediately, she was asked to "repeat" her demonstration before a student group, which she willingly and successfully did. There was no recurrence of the difficulty even after she was given a full understanding of how she had been manipulated.

Subjects reoriented from the present to the actual future, instructed to look back upon proposed hypnotic work as actually accomplished, can often, by their "reminiscence," provide the hypnotist with understandings that can readily lead to much sounder work in deep trances. Certainly in therapy, as well as experimentally, the author has found this measure highly effective, since it permits elaboration of hypnotic work in fuller accord with the subject's total personality and unconscious needs and capabilities. It often permits the correction of errors and oversights before they can be made, and it furnishes a better understanding of how to develop suitable techniques. A subject employed in this manner can often render invaluable service in mapping out procedures and techniques to be employed in experimentation and therapy.

MULTIPLE-DISSOCIATION TECHNIQUE

Another measure is frequently employed by the author in inducing deep trances, maintaining them, or utilizing them for extensive complex work. It is the induction of multiple visual hallucinations in which different but related things are visualized. (Many subjects can be taught "crystal gazing" in the light trance.) One patient, in a profoundly depressed, discouraged mood, readily seized the opportunity to intensify by contrast her unhappy mood by accepting the suggestion that she see in action in a crystal ball a happy incident of her childhood consciously forgotten. Utilizing her masochistic response to this, a second crystal ball was suggested in which she could see, simultaneously with the first, an incident belonging to another age level. Soon there was a total of a dozen hallucinatory crystals in each of which a life scene of a different age level was being portrayed by hallucinatory figures belonging to her experiential past. Thus, a combined experimental investigative and therapeutic situation was created in which her limited immediate willingness for a brief trance served to carry her into an extensive development hours long that served therapeutically her total personality needs.

This procedure is not limited to induced hallucinatory behavior. A musician, unresponsive to direct hypnotic suggestion, was induced to recall the experience of having his "thoughts haunted by a strain of music." This led to a suggested search for other similar experiences. Soon he became so absorbed in trying to recall forgotten memories and beating time as a kinesthetic aid that a deep trance developed. In other words, dissociation phenomena, whether spontaneous or induced, can be used in a repetitious manner to establish a psychological momentum to which the subject easily and readily yields.

POSTHYPNOTIC TECHNIQUES

In a previous paper in collaboration with E. M. Erickson, attention was directed to the spontaneous hypnotic trance developed in relation to the execution of posthypnotic tasks. In inducing hypnosis, light or deep, the hypnotist may introduce unobtrusively some form of posthypnotic suggestion that will permit the development subsequently of a spontaneous trance. This trance can then be utilized as a point of departure in developing a new trance state. Not all subjects respond to this procedure, but it often proves of immense value.

Sometimes a subject who is in only a light trance can be given a simple posthypnotic suggestion. As he develops a spontaneous trance in executing the posthypnotic act, suggestions may be given to deepen it. The procedure can be repeated, and a third trance, still deeper, can result, until sufficient repetitions bring a deep hypnosis.

Concerning unobtrusive posthypnotic suggestions, the author resorts to such measures as saying, "Each time I take hold of your wrist and move your arm gently in this way [demonstrating], it will be a signal to you to do something—perhaps to move your other hand, perhaps to nod your head, perhaps to sleep more soundly, but each time you receive the signal, you will become ready to carry out the task." Repeated several times in the first trance, the subject, in his immediate thinking, applies the suggestion only to that trance session. However, weeks later, in an appropriate setting the repetition of the signal may result in a rapid induction of hypnosis. This method has been used extensively as a timesaving procedure in teaching medical students to become both hypnotists and hypnotic subjects.

As to posthypnotic acts for the subject to execute, some simple casual activity is much better than some attention-compelling overt act. Watching the hypnotist light a cigarette, noting whether the match tossed toward the wastebasket falls in, or observing that the book on the desk is about two inches away from the edge, are all infinitely better than having the subject clap his hands when the word "pencil" is spoken. The more casually hypnotic work can be done, the easier it is for the subject to adapt to it. Casualness permits ready utilization of the behavioral developments of the total hypnotic situation.

COMMENTS

In presenting this material, the intention has not been to outline specific or exact techniques of procedure for hypnosis; rather, it has been to demonstrate that hypnosis should primarily be the outcome of a situation in which interpersonal and intrapersonal relationships are developed constructively to serve the purpose of both the hypnotist and the subject. This cannot be done by following rigid procedures and fixed methods, nor by a striving to reach a single specific goal. The complexity of human behavior and its underlying motivations makes necessary a cognizance of the multitude of factors existing in any situation arising between two personalities engaged in a joint activity. Whatever the part played by the hypnotist may be, the role of the subject involves the greater amount of active functioning—functioning which derives from the capabilities, learning, and experiential history of the total personality.

Primarily, the hypnotist can only guide, direct, supervise, and provide the opportunity for the subject to do the productive work. To accomplish this the hypnotist must understand the situation and its needs. He must protect the subject fully in that total situation. He must be able to recognize the work accomplished. He must accept and utilize the behavior that develops, and he must be able to create opportunities and situations favorable for adequate functioning of the subject.

In the effort to clarify problems of deep-trance induction, the author has relied upon his experience over a long period of time with a large number of subjects, many of whom were hypnotized hundreds of times. Additionally, that experience was supplemented by the teaching of hypnosis to several hundred students, psychologists, and medical men. Many of them served also as subjects, and all served in various ways to test the validity of the author's experience. Hence, the major part of any credit the author may receive properly belongs to those workers who so willingly contributed to his understandings.

BIBLIOGRAPHY

The following is a selected list of articles by the author containing previously published material pertinent to various points elaborated in this paper, and appended as they indicate the variety of his experience upon which this paper is based.

1. "The investigation of a specific amnesia," *Brit. J. M. Psychol.*, **13** (Pt. 2):143, 1933.
2. "A study of an experimental neurosis hypnotically induced in a case of ejaculatio praecox," *Brit. J. M. Psychol.*, **15** (Pt. 1):34, 1935.
3. "Development of apparent unconsciousness during hypnotic re-living of a traumatic experience," *Arch. Neurol. & Psychiat.*, **38** (6): 1282, 1937.
4. "The use of automatic drawing in the interpretation and relief of a state of acute obsessional depression," *Psychoanalyt. Quart.*, **7** (4):443, 1938. (With L. S. Kubie.)
5. "Experimental demonstrations of the psychopathology of everyday life," *Psychoanalyt. Quart.*, **8** (3):338, 1939.
6. "An experimental investigation of the possible anti-social use of hypnosis," *Psychiatry*, **2** (3):391, 1939.
7. "The permanent relief of an obsessional phobia by means of communication with an unsuspected dual personality," *Psychoanalyt. Quart.*, **8** (4):471. 1939. (With L. S. Kubie.)
8. "The translation of the cryptic automatic writing of one hypnotic subject by another in a trance-like dissociated state," *Psychoanalyt. Quart.*, **9** (1):51, 1940. (With L. S. Kubie.)
9. "Concerning the nature and character of post-hypnotic behavior," *J. Gen. Psychol.*, **24** (1):95, 1941. (With E. M. Erickson.)
10. "The successful treatment of a case of acute hysterical depression by a return under hypnosis to a critical phase of childhood," *Psychoanalyt. Quart.*, **10** (4):583, 1941.
11. "Hypnotic investigation of psychosomatic phenomena: Psychosomatic interrelationships studied by experimental hypnosis," *Psychosom. Med.*, **5** (1):51, 1943.
12. "Experimentally elicited salivary and related responses to hypnotic visual hallucinations confirmed by personality reactions," *Psychosom. Med.*, **5** (2):185. 1943.
13. "Unconscious mental activity in hypnosis—psychoanalytic implications," *Psychoanalyt. Quart.*, **13** (1):60, 1944. (With L. B. Hill.)
14. "Hypnosis in medicine," *M. Clin. North America*, **28**:639, 1944.

15. "The method employed to formulate a complex story for the induction of an experimental neurosis in a hypnotic subject," *J. Gen. Psychol.*, **31**:67, 1944.
16. "An experimental investigation of the hypnotic subject's apparent ability to become unaware of stimuli," *J. Gen. Psychol.*, **31**:191, 1944.
17. "Hypnotic psychotherapy," *M. Clin. North America*, May, 1948, New York Number, 571.

CHAPTER FIVE

Hypnotic Susceptibility as a Function of Waking Suggestibility

Editor's Note

Hypnosis has been said to be a state of heightened suggestibility, and suggestion and hypnotism are certainly closely related topics. Hence, it is important for us to know as much as possible about suggestibility and susceptibility to hypnosis. Both are frequently confused with gullibility, and resistance to hypnosis may arise as a result, for the subject may believe he would show gullibility and be considered "weak-minded" if he yielded to hypnosis.

Many of the tests conducted in the Hull series of experiments were as to suggestibility and susceptibility to hypnosis, and work in this field has continued. More recently, Furneaux and Eysenck, of the University of London, have been interested. Sometimes working together and sometimes separately, they have investigated and reported on different phases of these matters. The paper which follows, by Furneaux, is a continuation of their research. Concluding it is an excellent bibliography which includes most of the previous reports that have been published on these subjects.

Professor Furneaux is the Senior Investigator of the Nuffield Foundation project on the selection of University students, which is being carried out by the Institute of Psychiatry of the University of London. Before turning to psychology, he was a research worker in the field of radio physics. He has published mainly in the fields of suggestibility and hypnosis.

Hypnotic Susceptibility as a Function of Waking Suggestibility

By W. D. FURNEAUX, A.I.P., B.Sc.

PSYCHOLOGY DEPARTMENT, INSTITUTE OF PSYCHIATRY,
UNIVERSITY OF LONDON, ENGLAND

The formulation of an acceptable theory of hypnosis, adequately supported by experimental evidence of high quality, is a matter of crucial importance for the further development of hypnotic procedures for use in therapy and would be of the greatest possible significance for the whole of psychology. It is impossible to spend any great amount of time working with subjects in the hypnotic state without coming to feel that, if the mechanisms underlying the phenomena that are obtainable were in any real sense understood, we should have available to us techniques for carefully controlled experiment which would open up entirely new possibilities over a very wide field. Unfortunately, however, in spite of some brilliant experimental work, we are as yet hardly in a position even to define the hypnotic state.[1, 2] Certainly, it is impossible to be dogmatic as to the significance of the various induction techniques that are used, to be sure that there is a unitary state of "hypnosis" that underlies all the often highly individual changes in behavior that commonly follow the induction, or to define more than a very few phenomena that are fundamental to the hypnotic state as such, as opposed to those unessential artefacts that arise from the expectation of the subject or the half-concealed implications of statements made by the operator.

In developing an adequate theory of the subject, it is clearly of great importance to relate hypnosis to other aspects of behavior.

We must, if we can, define the personality traits which most persistently characterize the normal states of those who prove to be most susceptible to hypnotic procedures. Such knowledge would immediately provide a very important yardstick against which the validity of a theory could be assessed.

The main object of this paper is to review the evidence which links suggestibility as a normal personality trait with susceptibility to hypnotic procedures. One of the main inadequacies of nearly all attempts to evolve a theoretical framework for hypnosis lies in the fact that no attempt is made to give an operational definition either of hypnosis or of the concepts in terms of which it is to be explained. It is commonly assumed, for example, that a similar end state results from all the manifold induction procedures that are used, that the active, responding phase of hypnosis forms part of a continuum which includes also the passive stage which usually arises during induction, that there are high correlations between the extents to which the varying stimulus-response mechanisms may be brought under control, etc.; in short, that there is a single, unitary state of hypnosis. Our present knowledge of the facts simply does not justify such a range of assumptions.

The confusion that may arise from such lack of definition is well illustrated by the state of affairs which, until recently, obtained in relation to suggestibility, one of the concepts most frequently employed in attempting to explain hypnotic phenomena. In the past, a suggestible person would have been defined as "an individual in whom ideas, actions, beliefs, decisions, etc., could be induced by another through stimulation, whether verbal or otherwise, but exclusive of argument or command" (Warren), or in similar terms. In an attempt to bring the phenomena of suggestion into the field of experimental psychology, a number of tests of suggestibility have been devised, each designed to make it possible to give an individual a score in terms of the extent to which he reacts positively to the attempt to induce such "ideas, actions, beliefs, decisions, etc." Attempts to use measures thus derived to relate suggestibility to other aspects of behavior, including hypnosis, led, until about 1920, to a mass of inconsistent and contradictory results. The cause of the confusion had been diagnosed by W. Brown as early as 1916,[3] when he produced evidence in favor of the thesis that there was no general trait of suggestibility but rather several more or less independent suggestibilities—those who were suggestible in one way not necessarily being so in others. In 1919 Prideaux put forward a similar hypothesis,[4] but general acceptance of these views was delayed, partly by the apparent demonstration of a general trait of suggestibility by Aveling and Hargreaves [5] in 1921, and again by Otis [6] in 1923, and partly by the fact that the concept of a general trait had been so firmly built into both clinical and general psychology that to abandon it would have called for a good deal more evidence than was at that time available.

However, from 1929 onward, the idea that suggestibility was not a unitary trait again began to make headway. With the publication of his *Hypnosis and Suggestibility* in 1933, Hull [7] made a distinction between prestige and nonprestige suggestion. Most of the evidence favoring such a distinction was drawn from the table of suggestibility test correlations that was obtained by Aveling and Hargreaves in 1921 and on the basis of which they argued for a general factor. Hull pointed out that, although all the correlations were positive, two of the tests, one involving the suggestion of hand rigidity, the other that of arm levitation, stood out from the rest, having a correlation of 0.55 one with the other, whereas no other two tests correlated more than 0.3, with several values approaching zero. He further pointed out that Jenness [8] had reported correlations of 0.63 between susceptibility to arm-levitation suggestion and susceptibility to hypnosis, and that this result indicated a rather close relationship between arm levitation (and thus hand rigidity) with the waking postural-suggestion test which had also been found to correlate with hypnotizability.[9] He suggested that the administration of all these three tests involved what he called direct prestige heterosuggestion, and that in this they differed from the other tests used by Aveling and Hargreaves (Binet's progressive weights and progressive lines, a warmth illusion, and a fidelity-of-report test). He suggested, therefore, a division of suggestibility tests into those that did and did not involve prestige. Murphy [10] and Bird [11] also reviewed the available evidence, in 1937 and in 1940, respectively, and attempted to define different types of suggestibility, without having available to them, however, very many facts additional to those considered by Hull.

The question was clearly one that could only be settled by a suitable research program. In 1942 Eysenck opened his attack upon the problem by giving eight tests of suggestibility to each of 60 neurotic subjects, 30 men and 30 women.[12] If suggestibility were a general trait, then it would follow that those who are very suggestible according to one test would be highly reactive to all the tests, and vice versa. On the other hand, if there exist several unrelated types of suggestibility, then a person having a high score on a test involving one type could have any possible score on tests involving other types. The results of the experiment strongly favored the latter hypothesis, in that there were several tests having reasonably high intercorrelations which seemed to define one type of suggestibility (Chevreul pendulum, arm-levitation, body-sway), tentatively called "primary suggestibility," while the remaining tests (progressive weights, progressive lines, personal and impersonal forms) also showed a tendency to hang together. They were adjudged to define a trait of "secondary suggestibility." Intercorrelations between the two groups were all extremely low, indicating that the two suggestibilities were relatively independent. (Table 5–1, Appendix 2.) * The division thus made accorded very well with that suggested by Hull in that the resulting grouping of tests was very similar in the two cases, but Eysenck was of the opinion that prestige was not the differentiating factor. He preferred to adopt the terms "primary" and "secondary" in that they were free from etiological suppositions, while yet advancing the view that in primary suggestibility some form of ideomotor tendency was active.

In order to confirm and extend the results of this inquiry, Eysenck and Furneaux [13] carried out a rather similar experiment in 1944, using a group of 60 patients at a war emergency hospital. All the subjects had been referred to the hospital as having neurotic symptoms. With the exception that cases so severely ill as to be

* See page 134.

unduly difficult to test were omitted, the sample used was quite unselected save for the factor of intelligence. In this last respect the
group was composed only of individuals whose score on the Raven
Matrices put them roughly between I.Q. 90 and 110, so that the
effect of differences of intelligence on test responses was minimized.

Each individual involved was given 10 suggestibility tests which
will be described in detail in Appendix 1. They were:

1. Picture-report test
2. Ink-blot suggestion test
3. Odor suggestion
4. Progressive weights, impersonal
5. Progressive weights, personal
6. Heat illusion
7. Body sway (postural suggestion)
8. Press and (9) release test
10. Chevreul pendulum.

In addition, an attempt was made to hypnotize each subject; this
part of the experiment will be considered separately.

As in the previous investigation, analysis of the table of correlations between test scores clearly separated one group of tests from
the rest. The tests involved again included the body-sway test and
the Chevreul pendulum, and it seemed reasonably clear that the
underlying trait could be identified as the primary suggestibility
isolated in the previous study. As the other tests in this group were
the press and release tests, it followed that these, too, were tests of
primary suggestibility, as had been hypothesized.

Of the remaining tests, three (2, 3, and 5) seemed to be sufficiently
closely related to define an independent factor which was clearly
identical with the secondary suggestibility previously defined. In
fact, all the remaining tests could reasonably be considered to belong
to ·this group, although with the exception of 2, 3, and 5, the relevant intercorrelations were too low to justify excluding the possibility that they were in reality concerned with yet other types of
suggestibility which were essentially distinct from both primary and
secondary types (Table 5–2, Appendix 2). From a consideration of

the nature of the tests involved in primary suggestibility, it appeared that they all involved an overt motor response to an idea involving muscular activity, a fact that confirmed Eysenck's previous suggestion that a form of ideomotor mechanism was involved.

In 1945 Furneaux [15] carried out an investigation on a precisely similar population at the same hospital, using 50 subjects. Each took the body-sway test as a measure of primary suggestibility, the odor-suggestion and ink-blot tests as measures of secondary suggestibility, and the test of heat illusion. This last test had been assigned no clear position by the previous studies and seemed to have an interesting relationship with susceptibility to hypnosis, so that its inclusion seemed to be called for. In addition, an attempt was made to hypnotize each subject, the main object of the investigation being to learn the usefulness of the various test procedures in predicting susceptibility to hypnosis. Consideration of this aspect of the research will be deferred; for the moment, the interest of the results obtained lies in the fact that once again the intercorrelations of the three types of test proved to be extremely low (Table 5–3, Appendix 2). The evidence of the existence of unrelated traits of primary and secondary suggestibility was thus further strengthened, while there seemed to be a distinct probability that yet another independent trait was active in the heat illusion.

It was not quite certain, however, that these results could be extended to apply to a normal population, as the experiments involved had all been carried out on neurotics. It is extremely difficult to obtain an unselected normal population for research of this nature, but in 1946 Furneaux [16] was able to obtain the cooperation of 26 subjects, parents and friends of students attending part-time courses in science and arts at a London college, ranging in age from 20 to 60 years. All subjects were told that they could contribute to a research program by taking tests designed to measure balance, sensitivity to heat, and weight-discrimination ability, and were then given the body-sway test, progresive weights, and heat illusion. No one was tested who had at any time taken a course in psychology. The results (Table 5–4, Appendix 2) showed the same absence of relationship between the tests as emerged from the previous studies.

Further evidence tending to justify the extension of the results to a normal population is contained in an unpublished paper by S. Rostal. She found a correlation of 0.05 between response to the body-sway test and to the heat illusion in a group of 100 normal soldiers, thus clearly establishing the independence of the two traits involved.

It is therefore meaningless to discuss the relationship between suggestibility and hypnosis without making an explicit statement as to the type of suggestibility that is being considered, particularly as there may be yet other types than those discussed here, for example, the prestige type involving change of attitude or opinion in a direction to conform to that expressed by individuals having prestige.[17, 18, 19] As the relationship of this trait to other suggestibilities and to hypnosis has not formed the subject of investigation, it cannot be further considered at this stage.

Provided that the necessary distinctions are made, we find that, in discussing the relationship of suggestibility and hypnosis, we are dealing with a mass of evidence that is reasonably free from contradictions and which makes possible a number of fairly dogmatic statements. At first sight this seems somewhat remarkable in that, as has been pointed out, no operational definition of hypnosis exists. It turns out, however, that all the investigators concerned have implicitly defined hypnosis in much the same terms, in that they have assessed its depth with reference to the extent to which the subject makes overt response to simple suggestions of motor activity, and also, in some cases, verbally reports that he has experienced a number of suggested sensory hallucinations of a simple type.

To consider first primary suggestibility, the evidence may be summarized briefly. White,[20] in 1930, found a correlation of 0.75 between a form of body-sway test and susceptibility to hypnosis in a young adult population of 22 subjects. Susceptibility was measured on a point scale similar to that of Barry, Mackinnon, and Murray.[21] In 1933 Jenness[8] found rank difference correlations of from 0.33 to 0.63 between response to a suggested arm movement and susceptibility as measured by the time needed for lid closure to be induced. The magnitude of the correlation varied with the exact conditions under which the experiment was performed. Unfortunately, in this study only 8 subjects were used. However, Williams and Kreuger, in an unpublished study quoted by Hull,[9] found a coefficient of 0.6 in a similar experiment involving a group of 18 males. Again, the Barry, Mackinnon, and Murray report showed that under some conditions of experiment a correlation of 0.52 was obtained between body-sway response and susceptibility in a group of 73 subjects. Finally, Eysenck and Furneaux, in their 1945 study,[13] obtained correlations of 0.57, 0.73, 0.24, and 0.64 between response to Chevreul's pendulum, the body-sway test, Eysenck's press test, and his release test, respectively, and hypnotic susceptibility. Furneaux[15] found the body-sway test to correlate with susceptibility to the extent of 0.64. There can, thus, be no doubt that primary suggestibility is intimately connected with hypnosis as defined by the scales used for assessing its depth.[21, 13]

The other forms of suggestibility have received rather less study, and the only direct evidence regarding their relationship to hypnosis seems to be contained in the papers by Eysenck and Furneaux, and Furneaux, already mentioned. In the former, correlations with hypnotizability of −0.1, 0.13, 0.12, −0.17, and −0.10 are quoted for the picture-report test, ink blot, odors, progressive weights (impersonal), and progressive weights (personal), respectively. In the latter, the figures are 0.08 and −0.22 for odors and ink blot. None of these relationships approaches statistical significance, and it may be concluded that neither secondary suggestibility nor the traits underlying response to those tests which cannot yet be assigned any definite position are active in determining susceptibility.

One important exception must be made, however, in the case of the test of heat illusion. It will be remembered that this test does not seem to be related to either primary or secondary suggestibility nor yet to any other unplaced test that has so far been considered. It was, however, found[13, 15] that it was significantly related to hypnotic susceptibility, the correlation in the first study being 0.51, in the second, 0.59. It would appear, then, that those two quite unrelated traits, primary suggestibility and that underlying response to the heat illusion, play an important role in the etiology of hypnosis. The question immediately arises as to whether these traits are themselves simple or whether they can each be split up into a number of components. From a consideration of the introspections of subjects taking the body-sway test, and from a study of their overt responses, Eysenck [12] was led to the view that primary suggestibility involves two components, attitude and aptitude. "Aptitude" may be defined as strength of ideomotor tendency, involving the automatic translation of an implanted idea of movement into the efferent impulses which would normally bring about the movement itself. "Attitude" covers the subject's reactions to the resulting experienced tendencies including any efforts he may make to inhibit them. The fact that the injection of drugs such as Sodium Amytal greatly increases the press-release test response of those who show some degree of reaction in the absence of the drug while yet failing to initiate response in those who are nonreactive in its absence [22, 23] strongly favors this view. Such drugs are known to decrease voluntary control and must therefore reduce a subject's ability to disguise his aptitude; however, a change of attitude will naturally of itself be unable to initiate response.

On the available evidence it is not possible to be sure that these two components are alone sufficient to provide an explanation of the phenomena of primary suggestibility. Baudouin [14] distinguished a factor of "acceptivity" as being active in suggestion where the term may be defined as the extent to which an individual introjects the idea which forms the basis of the suggestion, and it would seem that a strong case can be made out for including this concept in our theoretical framework, particularly since its validity can rather easily be examined experimentally. In the first place the experiment involving the injection of Sodium Amytal which provides support for the two-component theory may also call for the introduction of the additional factor. Nothing is known regarding the distribution of ideomotor tendency, as such, within the general population. It would seem unlikely, however, that it can be completely absent from an individual's make-up unless he is in some real sense abnormal. If this is the case, then the fact that in one of the experiments quoted [23] not one of the individuals failing to respond to suggestion in the absence of the drug showed any increase of response following injection may need to be explained on the basis that, although the ideomotor mechanism was ready to operate, the suggestions given were not introjected.

At the moment, the strongest evidence against the need for the concept is provided by an experiment quoted by Eysenck and Furneaux [13] in which a correlation of 0.93 was found between response to heterosuggestions of falling and response to autosuggestions of the same nature, the amount of sway resulting being almost exactly the same under the two conditions. It would seem that differences should be expected in the subject's acceptivity under the two sets of circumstances, and the result seems therefore to minimize the role of this factor in determining response. However, it would seem that acceptivity will be determined to a far greater extent by the whole context of the experimental situation than by its individual details. The instruction "imagine as vividly as you can that you are falling forward" does not automatically result in a vivid imagining on the part of the subject, and the factors determining acceptance of the instruction may perhaps be related to those determining response to frank heterosuggestion.

The evidence favoring the inclusion of the concept lies in the fact that response to body-sway suggestion has been shown to depend to a variable extent on such factors as the sex of the operator, and whether suggestions are given in person or by a phonograph record.[24] As primary suggestibility correlates with susceptibility to hypnosis, the demonstration by White [25] that susceptibility can be predicted with moderate success by a consideration of the subject's attitude to the idea of hypnosis may also be relevant.

The question as to the need for the concept of acceptivity can be settled with the aid of experiments involving a study of the change in response to suggestibility tests with change of the content and method of presentation of the tests. By changing the operator, by using tests such that the subject is unaware that he is responding,[26] by controlling attitude by drugs, and by measuring the action potentials to the relevant muscles to reveal inhibited response, it should be possible to disentangle the effects of the several factors involved.

As nearly all practicing hypnotists assert that acceptivity is important, and as the psychoanalytical schools base their entire theory of hypnosis on subject-operator relationships and thus lean heavily on the concept, it would seem that the component should, at least for the time being, be included in any theoretical framework intended to cover the phenomena of primary suggestibility.

To consider now response to the heat illusion, we may assume that a similar analysis can be made, although no experimental data seem to exist which have any bearing on the question. Stage one would be the same—the introjection of the idea that heat is being felt. Stage two would involve the automatic translation of the idea into impulses to the relevant sensory analyzers. It would seem useful to use the term "conversion" to cover this process in this case and also to designate the same stage in primary suggestion.

Stage three raises a point of some interest. One would expect that a subject who felt himself begin to fall forward in response to suggestion would quite automatically tend to resist the development of the response. It seems extremely unlikely, however, that an individual will have any tendency to resist the development of a hallucination which is quite appropriate in the context of the test involved, as is the case with the heat illusion. It thus seems very unlikely that "attitude" plays any part in response to this test. The correlations reported between response to this illusion and response to tests of primary suggestibility so nearly approach zero that it is very unlikely that the two tests have any common ground. It would, however, seem wise to bear in mind the slight possibility that the conversion mechanisms involved in the two traits have some degree of overlap which is disguised, when we consider only overt responses, by the lack of attitude in the one case and its action in the other.

It is now possible to consider some of the implications of the demonstrated relationship between these two forms of suggestibility and susceptibility to hypnosis. As far as primary suggestibility goes, the evidence suggests that it is entirely concerned with response to suggestions of motor activity. It has been suggested [24] that response to the heat illusion is a measure of a type of sensory suggestibility. Now the impression most hypnotists have is that both motor and sensory activity come increasingly under the control of the operator as the trance deepens. If this is, in fact, true, then in the trance there must be some substantial common basis to the two types of suggestibility in that, as one type of suggestibility is increased, so is the other. If adequate experiment should, in fact, confirm such covariation during hypnosis, then, granting the initial premise, there would appear to be only two possible explanations for the lack of covariation in the normal state. As one possibility we should have to consider the two types of suggestibility as both depending on some third attribute that was present in all unhypnotized individuals to a substantially equal extent but which became distributed as a result of the induction processes. All that we know about the distribution of mental and physical characteristics in the general population argues strongly against such a possibility. The only other explanation, however, would involve the assertion that a complete and radical reorganization of stimulus-response mechanisms results from hypnotic procedures and is responsible for setting up connections between aspects of behavior which, in the normal state, are quite distinct.

Another possibility, of course, is that the impression of an over-all increase in suggestibility is mistaken, and that experiment will reveal that there is no relationship between the two types of response (motor and sensory) in hypnosis. If this should prove to be the case, then we should have to define motor, sensory, and mixed types of hypnosis, and, possibly, as the evidence accumulated, several other types as well. There are a few experimental results, however, which do seem to argue in favor of the existence of a fairly unitary state which includes at least some of the phenomena commonly held to define hypnosis. For example, there is a substantial relationship between score on a susceptibility scale, such as is detailed in Appendix 1, and the tendency to carry out posthypnotic suggestions of a fairly complicated type.[13] Again, there is a strong tendency for a spontaneous amnesia, covering the events of the trance, to develop in subjects making a high score on such a scale.[15] Although, therefore, the relationship of sensory and motor suggestibility in the hypnotic state urgently requires experimental examination, it is the writer's impression that the concept of hypnosis as a unitary state will be substantially justified.

The most probable solution to the difficulties which arise on considering the implications of the independence of motor and sensory suggestibilities would seem to involve the abandonment of the initial premise that the heat illusion should be regarded in any special sense as a measure of a generalized sensory suggestibility. There would seem to be little justification for concentrating on the sensory nature of the response to this test, which is related to hypnosis, while yet neglecting the equal involvement of sensory aspects in response to the odors test, which is not so related; rather, it would seem profitable to concentrate attention on the actual procedure of the test. Much further experimental work is needed before attempts to explain the predictive usefulness of the heat illusion can be anything but highly speculative. It does seem possible that this test provides what is essentially a conditioning situation. The subject's actual experience of heat is associated with an integrated set of kinesthetic and visual cues by virtue of the fact that he himself turns the knob controlling the current of the heating element, and himself reads off the pointer reading when heat is felt. Moreover, the association occurs under conditions of maximum attention (Appendix 1). To redesignate the test as one of conditioning rather than of suggestibility does not, of course, in any real sense "explain" anything, for in the last resort either concept can be extended to cover all the phenomena normally embraced by the other. The change of phrase does, however, serve to direct attention to the fact that it might be very profitable to investigate the relationship between response to suggestibility tests and to the classical conditioning procedures, and to relate susceptibility to conditioning to susceptibility to hypnosis. In particular, the effect of giving the heat-illusion test in forms having more and less in common with other conditioning procedures requires to be studied. It is of interest to note that Berreman and Hilgard [27] have produced evidence tending to show that there is no correlation between body-sway suggestibility and susceptibility to a form of conditioning involving eyelid response. This fact does not, of course, prove that the heat illusion, because it shows a similar lack of relationship to body sway, involves a form of conditioning, but it does strongly argue for further exploration in this direction.

We come now to the question of whether these two mechanisms, primary suggestibility and heat-illusion suggestibility, are alone active in determining response to hypnotic procedures. If the multiple correlation between them taken together and hypnotizability were unity, it would follow either that only these two causative factors were active in promoting hypnosis or that these two traits were the only ones of the several responsible for hypnotization which were present in different individuals to different degrees. Of these two alternatives, the former would seem infinitely more probable. In actual fact, Eysenck and Furneaux reported that this multiple correlation was 0.96, while Furneaux subsequently reported a figure of 0.92. It is very difficult to know just what weight to give to these figures, however, in view of the fact that the standard error of a multiple correlation is rather large and difficult to assess.

Again, the reliability of the scale used for scoring the depth of hypnosis was about 0.85, so that no great stress can be laid upon any value for the multiple correlation that is higher than this, while the fact that no figure at all was obtained for the reliability of the heat-illusion test increases the uncertainty. But the question can be considered in a slightly different light. It was found that all the individuals who responded strongly both to the body-sway test and to the heat illusion achieved reasonably high scores on the hypnosis scale (that is, were markedly susceptible), while all those who failed to respond to either test achieved uniformly low scores. This would seem to imply that all the individuals in this group, who in the test situation exhibited acceptivity and the two types of conversion to a reasonable degree, and who did not display negative attitude, were susceptible to hypnosis. Does the evidence indicate that, in the absence of any one of these features, hypnosis is impossible? It is certainly true that none of those who failed to respond to both tests was more than mildly susceptible; 45 per cent of them failed to respond even slightly to the hypnotic procedures. On the evidence available it is impossible to know which of the components that have been suggested was responsible in any particular case for failure either in the test situation or in hypnosis. By examining the correlations between hypnotic susceptibility and response to a range of tests of primary suggestibility arousing varying degrees of ego involvement, by examining the role of the test situation in determining response, by separating out the conflicting effects of aptitude and attitude, etc., it should not be difficult to arrive at an understanding of the relative importance of these several mechanisms. It should also be possible to decide whether or not they can, between them, account for all the factors that are involved in determining hypnotic susceptibility.

One point can perhaps be made with reasonable assurance. The demonstration that susceptibility can be predicted with considerable accuracy from a consideration of response to tests which are administered in a context very different from that obtaining during the attempt to induce hypnosis would seem very strongly to limit the role that can be assigned in the theory of hypnosis to relationships between subject and operator which are specific to the hypnotic situation. We must assume that the tendency to form those types of relationship, if any, which are active in the genesis of the hypnotic state characterizes an individual fairly constantly and is active in situations having little relationship to the hypnotic one. Most psychoanalytically oriented explanations of hypnosis seem rather to stress the special nature of the hypnotic situation, and it seems possible that, in this respect at least, they will prove to need reformulating.

Finally, a degree of caution must be exercised when generalizing from the degree of predictability found possible with a neurotic population to that which may be expected with normals. It is possible that the rather dramatic success obtained by considering performance in only two tests may be due partly to the fact that a neurotic population is rather highly selected with regard to some of the traits operating to determine susceptibility. Let it be assumed, for example, that in the normal population three traits—primary suggestibility, heat-illusion suggestibility, and X—are equally and completely responsible for determining susceptibility. Then the true multiple correlation between primary suggestibility and heat illusion together and susceptibility would be approximately 0.81. Suppose now that trait X were highly active in the genesis of neuroticism; then nearly all neurotics would show this trait in sufficient degree to be hypnotizable if they also showed the requisite primary and heat-illusion suggestibilities. Under these circumstances the same multiple correlation calculated for the neurotic population would rise to a figure approaching 1.0, and experiments made on this population would give no hint of the importance of X. It is very unlikely that the position with regard to the researches that have been mentioned here is as extreme as this, for the neurotic groups involved contained substantial numbers of rather mild cases, and a fair number of incorrect diagnoses, the true diagnosis not involving neurosis at all. Nevertheless, it is a matter of some importance that the experiments quoted should be repeated on a normal population.

That the concepts put forward will need to be greatly extended before the phenomena of active deep hypnosis can be successfully accounted for seems certain. Under some circumstances the hypnotized subject manifests behavior that is at least as complex as that of a normal individual. We can hardly hope that the theoretical framework needed to cover such phenomena will be less intricate than that required to explain normal behavior. There may, however, be relatively few factors which, between them, are responsible for the change under appropriate conditions from the normal to the hypnotic state. It is suggested that among these the most important is ideomotor tendency, whatever mechanisms underlie response to the heat illusion, attitude, and possibly acceptivity, as they operate in the test situations that have been described.

APPENDIX 1

Description of Tests Mentioned in This Chapter

1. Body-sway test. This test consists in the measurement of the effect of verbal suggestions that the subject is falling forward, continuing for 2½ minutes, on the posture of the subject who is trying to stand still and relaxed, with his eyes closed. The amount of sway induced is measured in inches through inspection of a pointer on a scale which is activated by a thread fastened to the subject's clothing. The score on this test is the maximum amount of sway induced, in inches. Complete falls are arbitrarily scored as 12 in.

2. *Chevreul pendulum test.* The subject is shown a small pendulum made of a bob suspended by a thread about 1 ft long. He is told that if he holds the pendulum over a ruler and looks fixedly at the bob, he will quickly notice that the bob starts to swing along the ruler, even though he himself remains quite passive and is careful not to produce a movement deliberately. This is demonstrated, and the pendulum is then handed to the subject with the instruction to hold it steady and look fixedly at the bob. Continuous strong suggestion is then given to the effect that the bob is beginning to swing, that the swing is increasing, etc. The actual swing of the pendulum in inches constitutes the score on this test.

3. *Press and (4) release tests.* This measures the effect of verbal suggestion that the subject is either releasing his hold on, or is grasping more firmly, a rubber ball. This ball is connected through rubber tubes with a particularly large tambour, which in turn activates a lever which writes on a kymograph, thus making a complete record of the pressure exerted on the ball. The subject is fully aware that he is expected to keep his pressure steady, just as in the body-sway test he knows that he is expected to stand still. In the press test the subject starts by holding the ball so that he exerts just a small amount of pressure (in order to enable him to give a negative reaction to the suggestion). In the release test he starts by squeezing the ball hard so that he should be able to relax to a considerable extent. (Here, also, a negative response is possible.) Scores are calculated in terms of maximum excursion of the lever.

5. *Arm levitation, up and (6) down.* Here the subject is seated on a chair and told to hold out his right arm sideways at the level of his shoulder. Then, with his eyes shut, the same recording device as in the body-sway test is attached to his cuffs by means of the thread and needle. After his tremors and involuntary movements have been studied for 30 seconds, suggestions are made for 2½ minutes that his arm is feeling lighter and is rising. Again the extent of the rise is measured on the scale.

A few minutes after the completion of this test, the same procedure is repeated, with the suggestion that the arm is getting heavier and is falling.

7. *Ink-blot test.* One of the Rorschach ink blots is shown to the subject and he is told that some people think it looks like (here follow two common responses to the blot). Then he is given four quite inapplicable responses and asked if he can see something resembling these in the ink blot. The number of suggestions accepted constitutes his score.

8. *Odor-suggestion test.* The subject is told that his sense of smell is to be tested. Six dark-green bottles are placed before him, labeled, in

order, pineapple, banana, vanilla, rose, jasmine, and coffee. He is told that the cork will be removed from each bottle in turn and that the bottle will then be brought slowly up to his nose from a distance. He is to report as soon as he can detect the smell. The cork is removed from the first bottle (pineapple essence) while it is some 2 ft from the subject's nose, this distance then being decreased until either the subject reports that he can detect the smell, or the bottle is in contact with his nose. The procedure is repeated with each of the other bottles in turn, the subject being told each time what odor to expect. The last three bottles contain only water, and each claim to detect an odor from these bottles scores one point. The first three odors are selected in such a way that they decrease in strength, pineapple being the strongest, vanilla the weakest.

9. Picture-report test. The subject is shown a photograph for 30 seconds. It is then removed and 14 questions are asked regarding various details in it. Five of these contain suggestions that certain details are present in the picture which actually are not there. The number of these suggestions accepted constitutes the score on this test.

10. Progressive weights, impersonal. Twelve identical boxes are placed in front of the subject, who is told that they all differ in weight. He is to compare box 1 with box 2, 2 with 3, 3 with 4, and so on, saying each time which of the two is heavier. The first 5 boxes increase in weight by identical amounts, the next 7 are identical in weight with the fifth box. The score is the number of identical boxes called "heavier" minus the number of identical boxes called "lighter."

11. Progressive weights, personal. Here the raw data from test 10 are used, but the scoring is such that the number of times the identical boxes are called "heavier" and the number of times they are called "lighter" are added. Thus, the scoring consists in counting in test 11 the effect of the personal suggestion that the weights are all going to be different, and in test 10 the effect of the impersonal suggestion emanating from the arrangement of the material that the weights will continue to get heavier.

12. Progressive lines. This test is similar in every way to the progressive weights save that the comparison has to be made between the lengths of successively presented lines. Typical material would be 15 white cards, 3 by 5 in. On each a line is drawn, somewhat off center to make judgment more difficult. The line lengths increase from ½ to 1, 1½, 2, 2½ in., and then remain constant at 2½ in. The test can be scored in both personal and impersonal forms.

13. Heat-illusion test. A small heating element is applied to the forehead of the subject, the element being connected through a variable resistance, an invisible switch, and a transformed to the electric mains.

The subject is shown how the element becomes hot as he turns a cali-
brated knob connected with the variable resistance. He is asked to turn
the knob slowly until he can just detect the first sign of heat in the
element, when he is to remove the element from his forehead immediately and call out the reading on the dial. He is then asked to repeat the
procedure, and on this occasion the secret switch is silently opened, so
that no current passes through the element. As the dial reading approaches
that at which heat has been reported previously, the subject's attention is
drawn to this fact, and he is told: "Be on the alert now, you should soon
feel the heat." Those who report feeling the heat when the switch is
open are scored as suggestible.

Typical susceptibility scale used for assessing depth of hypnosis:
List of Verbal Suggestions Given during and after the
Induction of Hypnosis, in the Order Given

1. Your eyes are tired.
2. Your eyelids are heavy.
3. Your eyes close irresistibly.
4. You feel completely relaxed.
5. You feel a sensation of pleasant warmth.
6. You feel quite incapable of any activity.
7. You feel miles away.
8. You are unable to hold your arm up; it falls irresistibly.
9. It is impossible to raise your arm; it is held down.
10. Both your arms have become stiff and rigid.
11. Suggestion of complete catalepsy.
12. Suggestion of "glove" anesthesia.
13. A kinesthetic delusion (of leg movement) is suggested.
14. Hallucination of electric bell ringing.
15. The buzzer (a constant tone used for auditory fixation) is asserted
    to be getting softer. (At this state the subject is told to open his
    eyes but to remain in the hypnotic condition.)
16. You are unable to hold your arm up. (This is a check on the con-
    tinuance of the hypnosis following the opening of the eyes.)
17. Subject is shown a torch that he has previously seen switched on
    and is told that the filament of the bulb is glowing a dull red.

A subject's score for the hypnosis is obtained by weighting the degree
of his reaction to each suggestion (assessed on a three-point scale) by a
factor that is inversely proportional to the frequency of acceptance of
that suggestion among the whole test population, and then adding to
obtain his total score.

APPENDIX 2

Intercorrelations of Suggestibility Tests

Table 5-1.   Eysenck [12]   60 Neurotics

Test	1	2	3	4	5	6	7	8
1. Weights, personal	—	0.610	0.230	0.121	−0.256	−0.090	−0.159	−0.216
2. Lines, personal		—	0.295	0.194	0.095	0.133	−0.103	−0.127
3. Weights, impersonal			—	0.308	0.144	−0.070	−0.186	0.187
4. Lines, impersonal				—	0.156	−0.090	0.032	−0.076
5. Pendulum					—	0.329	0.107	0.174
6. Body sway						—	0.257	0.410
7. Levitation, up							—	0.351
8. Levitation, down								—

Table 5-2.   Eysenck and Furneaux [13]   60 Neurotics

Tetrachoric Correlations among the 12 Tests

Test	1	2	3	4	5	6	7	8	9	10	11	12
1. Hypnosis	—	0.72	0.57	0.73	0.24	0.64	0.51	−0.10	0.13	0.12	−0.17	−0.10
2. Posthypnotic		—	0.54	0.57	0.24	0.54	0.29	0.06	−0.04	−0.17	0.09	0.30
3. Pendulum			—	0.75	0.00	0.38	−0.07	−0.07	0.22	0.06	0.24	−0.04
4. Body sway				—	0.47	0.45	−0.16	−0.21	−0.12	0.18	0.05	−0.25
5. Press					—	0.47	0.10	0.18	−0.22	−0.19	0.27	−0.16
6 Release						—	0.02	0.10	−0.18	−0.03	−0.22	−0.23
7. Heat illusion							—	0.31	0.22	0.18	0.05	−0.25
8. Picture								—	0.31	0.07	−0.23	0.10
9. Ink blot									—	0.24	−0.02	0.48
10. Odors										—	0.24	0.38
11. Weights, impersonal											—	0.11
12. Weights, personal												—

Table 5-3.   Furneaux [15]   100 Neurotics

	A	B	C	D	E
A. Hypnosis	—	0.73	0.59	0.08	−0.22
B. Body sway		—	0.04	−0.24	−0.28
C. Heat illusion			—	−0.24	0.03
D. Odors				—	0.29
E. Ink blot					—

Table 5-4.   Furneaux [16]   26 Normals

	A	B	C	D
A. Body sway	—	−0.12	−0.22	−0.05
B. Heat illusion		—	0.25	0.21
C. Weights, personal			—	0.14
D. Weights, impersonal				—

REFERENCES

1. Young, P. C.: "A general review of the literature of hypnotism," *Psychol. Bull.*, **24**:540, 1927.
2. Young, P. C.: "A general review of the literature on hypnotism and suggestion," *Psychol. Bull.*, **28**:367, 1931.
3. Brown, W.: "Individual and sex differences in suggestibility," *Univ. California Publ., Psychol.*, **2**:291, 1916.
4. Prideaux, B.: "Suggestion and suggestibility," *Brit. J. Psychol.*, **10**:228, 1919.
5. Aveling, F., and Hargreaves, H. L.: "Suggestibility with and without prestige in children," *Brit. J. Psychol.*, **13**:53, 1921.
6. Otis, M.: "A study of suggestibility in children," *Arch. Psychol.*, **70**:5, 1923.
7. Hull, C.: *Hypnosis and Suggestibility*, Appleton-Century-Crofts, Inc., New York, 1933.
8. Jenness, A. F.: "Facilitation of response to suggestion by response to previous suggestion of a different type," *J. Exper. Psychol.*, **16**:55, 1933.
9. Williams and Kreuger: Unpublished. Quoted by Hull, p. 77. (See Ref. No. 7.)
10. Murphy G.; Murphy, L. B.; and Newcomb, T. M.: *Experimental and Social Psychology*, Harper & Brothers, New York, 1937.
11. Bird, C.: *Social Psychology*, Appleton-Century-Crofts, Inc., New York, 1940.
12. Eysenck, H. J.: "Suggestibility and hysteria," *J. Neurol., Neurosurg. & Psychiat.*, **6**:22, 1943.
13. Eysenck, H. J., and Furneaux, W. D.: "Primary and secondary suggestibility," *J. Exper. Psychol.*, **35**:485, 1945.
14. Baudouin, C.: *Suggestion and Autosuggestion*, George Allen & Unwin, Ltd., London, 1920.
15. Furneaux, W. D.: "The prediction of susceptibility to hypnosis," *J. Pers.*, **14**:282, 1946.
16. Furneaux, W. D.: "Three types of suggestibility in a normal population." (To be published.)
17. Bowden, *et al.*: "A study in prestige," *Am. J. Sociol.*, **40**:193, 1934.
18. Ferguson, L. W.: "An analysis of the generality of suggestibility to group opinion," *Char. & Pers.*, **12**:237, 1944.
19. Moore, H. T.: "The comparative influence of majority and expert opinion," *Am. J. Psychol.*, **32**:16, 1921.
20. White, M. M.: "The physical and mental traits of individuals susceptible to hypnosis," *J. Abnorm. & Social Psychol.*, **25**:293, 1930.

21. Barry, H.; Mackinnon, D. W.; and Murray, H. A.: "Hypnotizability as a personality trait and its typological relations." *Human Biol.,* **3**:1, 1931.

22. Baernstein, L. H.: "An experimental study of the effect on waking suggestibility of small doses of scopolamine hydrobromide," Thesis Univ. Wis., quoted by Hull (Ref. No. 7).

23. Eysenck, H. J., and Rees, W. L.: "States of heightened suggestibility: narcosis," *J. Ment. Sc.,* **91**:301, 1945.

24. Eysenck, H. J., *Dimensions of Personality*, Routledge and Kegan Paul, Ltd., London, 1947. The Macmillan Company, New York, 1948.

25. White, R. W.: "Prediction of hypnotic susceptibility from a knowledge of subjects' attitudes," *J. Psychol.,* **3**:265, 1937.

26. Hull, C.: *Hypnosis and Suggestibility*, Appleton-Century-Crofts, Inc., New York, 1933, p. 43.

27. Berreman, J. V., and Hilgard, E. R.: "The effects of personal heterosuggestion and two forms of autosuggestion upon postural movement," *J. Social Psychol.,* **7**:289, 1936.

CHAPTER SIX

Narcotic Hypnosis

Editor's Note

Dr. J. Stephen Horsley, prominent British psychiatrist and author of this chapter, is one of the discoverers of barbiturate narcosis and a pioneer in the field of narcoanalysis. He is undoubtedly the world's foremost authority on the subject and his book *Narco-analysis* [1] is the standard text. The article which follows is to appear also in an early issue of the quarterly *British Journal of Medical Hypnosis*, following publication here.

During World War II there was urgent necessity to develop brief methods of psychotherapy to alleviate "battle fatigue," and British psychiatrists in the armed services quickly adopted Dr. Horsley's narcoanalysis and narcosynthesis as the most advantageous method, since few were trained in hypnotic techniques, and Sodium Pentothal could be employed by any physician. Horsley himself first used it in the early 1930's and continued it in his war work, and general adoption soon followed his successful applications. When the United States entered the war, our service psychiatrists also took up the use of the barbiturate drugs in narcosis, and they were employed on a large scale.

After the war, psychiatrists returning to civil life attempted to continue the use of Sodium Pentothal in their civilian practices. The results were very disappointing. The conclusion was reached that narcoanalysis is of real value only when a neurosis is of recent origin, and particularly if it is of traumatic type (as is often the case in war neuroses) where ventilation and abreaction provide a catharsis. Its use, therefore, has declined very considerably.

From Dr. Horsley's article, it is apparent that these conclusions are entirely unwarranted. The real reason for lack of success was that psychotherapists have been ignorant of the proper techniques in its employment and have endeavored to make simple narcosis a substitute for the hypnotic state—a definite error.

For instance, the Menninger Clinic experimented in an attempt to use Sodium Pentothal as an aid in breaking down resistant hypnotic subjects and, by postnarcotic suggestions given under Sodium Pentothal, to make them good subjects for hypnosis. The results were almost nil, and it was concluded that narcosis had no value for such a purpose. It would seem that hypnosis was not superinduced on the narcotic state, and the subjects therefore did not respond to the suggestions. Many psychiatrists have reported the same lack of results.

Yet Dr. Horsley, with proper techniques, uses narcosis for this purpose with a very large percentage of successful results. Wholesale adoption of Sodium Pentothal narcosis with no knowledge of hypnotic techniques and a lack of understanding of narcosis are very evidently the reasons for the difference in results. Those who have failed where Horsley has succeeded should review the facts and follow the leads he indicates in his article.

There has also been a custom with psychiatrists who have used Sodium Pentothal to rely on it and to continue its use in most of their sessions with a patient, for a physician is familiar with the use of drugs, and Sodium Pentothal is easy to administer and rapid in action. Injections would be given time after time, the patient being drugged at every session. It was the easiest way, and no knowledge of hypnosis seemed necessary. With war neuroses, where the trauma was recent and the neurosis newly developed, this method was successful, but it failed in civilian practice. Dr. Horsley's discussion indicates the reason. His explanation should revive use of this valuable technique, which greatly shortens the time involved in psychotherapy.

As Horsley points out, prior to this article there has been a total lack of laboratory investigation of narcosis or any comparative study of narcosis and hypnosis. This indicates the regrettable and, indeed, reprehensible lack of interest in brief psychotherapy by most psychiatrists, though there is such a crying need for such brevity. Here is a field where intensive research is vitally necessary. With the understanding of the proper employment of narcosis and of the relationships between the two states, and knowledge of how to use them in combination, narcoanalysis will assume its proper position as a psychotherapeutic tool of value. Essentially, its value is in shortening the time for conditioning the patient to deep states of hypnosis and in overcoming resistances to hypnosis. It is an adjunct to hypno-analysis, not a substitute for it.

REFERENCE

1. Horsley, J. S.: *Narco-analysis*, Oxford University Press, New York, 1943.

Narcotic Hypnosis

By J. STEPHEN HORSLEY, M.D.*

*A CRITICAL DISCUSSION OF THE RELATIONSHIP
BETWEEN HYPNOSIS AND NARCOSIS, AND OF THE VALUE
OF THESE STATES IN PSYCHOLOGICAL MEDICINE*

Narcotic Hypnosis is a paradoxical title chosen to describe the psychosomatic state in which the phenomena of simple or verbally induced hypnosis are produced by means of seminarcosis with a drug.

In former times such attempts usually failed because of the uncertain action of the drugs then available. This objection is applicable to alcohol, to the volatile anesthetics, to opium, to cocaine, hashish, and mescaline, and even to scopolamine. The discovery of the new barbiturate drugs, however, provided physicians with narcotics of greater reliability in psychiatry. As aids to hypnosis, the barbiturates have been used for nearly 20 years, and many papers have been published on the possibility of inducing hypnosis in this manner in those individuals who could not be hypnotized by other methods.

In 1932 Hauptmann in Germany and the author in Great Britain, working quite independently, simultaneously demonstrated that the then new barbiturate Evipan injected intravenously could be used to induce a state indistinguishable from verbally induced hypnosis.

In 1936 Sodium Pentothal was first used in psychiatry by the author [1] and was shown to be the most effective of the barbiturates for use as an aid to hypnosis as in narcoanalysis and narcosynthesis. Nine years later Grinker and Spiegel, repeating my technique, claimed that all the phenomena of hypnosis could be secured in narcosing without inducing hypnosis. If these gifted writers had

* St. Margarets, Wimborne, Dorset, England.

referred more carefully to my earlier papers on narcoanalysis and narcosynthesis, they would perhaps have been more guarded in their claims. The point might even have been made that the psychosomatic state which occurs during seminarcosis is not simply a chemical condition but is probably dependent in part on the personality of the physician giving the Sodium Pentothal. In other words, there is a possibility of the experimenter overlooking himself as hypnotist, if his conscious intention is to do no more than inject a soothing or an exciting drug.

In attempting to clarify the problem, it is necessary to ask whether narcosis and hypnosis are identical, whether they are quite distinct, whether they are more or less similar, and, if so, whether this similarity is automatic or whether it appears only when it has been suggested. If, as seems probable, the states of hypnosis and narcosis are only similar, then it may be useful to postulate three distinct states—simple narcosis, drug hypnosis, and ordinary hypnosis—and to these might be added a fourth state, namely, narcosis given in an already hypnotized subject.

In comparing narcosis with hypnosis, it is obviously important to differentiate between these states and simple narcosis due to a drug without any additional effect by the experimenter (and I would emphasize that any such effect may be deliberate, as in hypnotic suggestion, or accidental and even unconscious, as when the doctor unwittingly suggests to his patient that certain reactions are to be expected from the injection of the drug). That this could happen purely by chance became obvious to me in 1933 when, during the induction of intravenous anesthesia, several patients, on experiencing the consequent subjective sensations, sometimes spontaneously asked whether they were being hypnotized. It was observed that many patients in this state responded to suggestion in exactly the same way as do those who have been hypnotized.

And now, before discussing the application of these states in psychological medicine, it is advisable to attempt to define their limitations and their meaning. Hypnosis has been defined as a psychosomatic phenomenon in which thought and action are controlled by suggestion. Simple narcosis is a state of sleepiness in which, according to the dose, there are varying degrees of drowsiness with confusion, disorientation, and incoherence. Drug hypnosis, on the other hand, is a state in which suggestion has been superimposed on semi-narcosis with the result that the subject becomes responsive to the commands of the therapist.

The question has been asked whether it is correct that all the phenomena of hypnosis can be secured in narcosis without the induction of hypnosis. My answer is, emphatically, no. If the patient under narcosis is left quietly alone, he is likely to sleep without exhibiting any of the manifestations of hypnosis. Again, the question has been asked, *"How can it be decided that hypnosis has been induced on top of narcosis?"* It may be suspected that hypnosis has been superimposed on narcosis if one observes the usual signs of hypnosis such as immediate relaxation and drowsiness, fluttering of the eyelids, partial loss of power with either contraction or relaxation of specified muscle groups, and, commonly, a pronounced lassitude with disinclination to move or speak. At this stage, analgesia and anesthesia are often present if suggested. But one can only decide with certainty that a state of drug hypnosis has been induced by demonstrating at least some of the phenomena which are unquestionably of the variety accepted as being hypnotic, such as, for example, posthypnotic suggestion and alterations of memory including both hypermnesia and amnesia.

Writers who claim that there is no practical distinction between the hypnotized patient and the narcotized patient are just as inaccurate as those like Maclay, who claim that in the use of narcoanalysis "no links with hypnotherapy are made." Wolberg rightly emphasizes that if narcosis is to be successful as a means of inducing posthypnotic suggestion, it is important to give attention to details and to ask the patient if he understands thoroughly what he is to do at every stage and in every aspect of the induction process. The taboo against hypnosis still exists in many hospitals; moreover, the more conventional approach by intravenous injection is nowadays acceptable to a number of patients who regard verbally induced hypnosis with suspicion. The main advantage of the intravenous method of inducing hypnosis is its speed. In a matter of minutes, the doctor obtains results which would take weeks of patient work if they were to be achieved by verbal hypnosis in a subject who had not been hypnotized previously.

This factor of speed in inducing hypnosis for the first time in any individual is the main distinguishing feature of narcotic hypnosis. As Wells has stated, the first hypnotizing of somnambulistic subjects is almost always a slow and difficult process possible with only a small percentage of persons, while the rehypnotizing of these same subjects can be done easily and quickly. Narcotic hypnosis is rapid, and the technique is far simpler than that of verbal hypnosis. Narcotic hypnosis has the immense value of almost immediate results which are comparable only with the results of many hours of hard work by verbal methods. Moreover, during a single session of narcotic hypnosis it is possible to give posthypnotic suggestion that the patient will subsequently respond identically with verbal methods of induction.

The technique of utilizing seminarcosis for the induction of major hypnotic phenomena must be based on complete understanding by both doctor and patient of what is to be done. Perhaps one of the most important things in teaching a patient how to be hypnotized is the utilization of known physiological trends, and it is just here that we find a common factor between seminarcosis and verbally induced drowsiness. And, in comparing narcosis with sleep, we note in particular the general suspension of the higher brain centers with simultaneous release of simpler, perhaps more primitive, reactions. This may occur spontaneously when it is most difficult to differentiate and to say whether the state is one of simple narcosis or whether hypnosis has been superimposed. If this question is to be answered adequately, it may be necessary to redefine our conception of the hypnotic state. In simple narcosis, without any suggestion whatever of hypnosis, there is often, owing to the removal of repressive controls, a sudden release of emotion and of behavior (abreaction). At this stage the narcosis may prove a veritable obstacle to hypnosis, because of the intensity of suddenly released and possibly overwhelming emotions. Abreaction such as just described, although of very great therapeutic value, is distinct from hypnosis. Abreaction, although it has nothing to do with hypnosis, can be altered by it. Abreaction of the most dramatic kind may occur when a narcotic is given to a patient who is already under hypnosis, and in such cases the patient shows a striking difference in reaction, becoming more emotional, as though responding from a subthalamic level.

The importance of psychotherapeutic preparation for narcosis was stressed by Rennie, who, in describing the treatment of war neuroses, said that Amytal alone did not always permit immediate release of emotion and that Amytal alone could not be considered as the sole therapy, the pre-Amytal psychotherapy being important in preparing the way for Amytal catharsis. The more closely we study this relationship between hypnosis and narcosis, the more clearly can we see that the characteristics of both depend upon the same principles of physiology and of mental activity. In view of the closeness of this relationship it is surprising that so many physicians still go so far as to deny the use of any form of hypnotherapy in their hospitals. This ostrichlike attitude is amusing to anyone with the slightest knowledge of hypnotherapy, as it is obvious that those physicians who describe their modification of narcoanalysis in which they deny any link with hypnotherapy are nevertheless utilizing a state of artificially increased suggestibility which is clinically identical with hypnosis, although they may call it by another name.

The technique which has been found most useful in utilizing one session of narcotic hypnosis for the subsequent production of posthypnotic suggestion is one based on Vogt's method of fractionation in which the patient is repeatedly hypnotized, awakened, and then immediately hypnotized again. If narcosis is to be successful as a means of inducing posthypnotic suggestion, it is necessary for the suggestions to be both detailed and specific and, if the patient seems at all confused, these suggestions must be repeated as the effect of the drug diminishes, when the patient can be asked to repeat what he will do at the next session. This is really a form of intensive training in hypnosis in which the patient is taught how to be hypnotized and in which it is useful to stress three features of hypnosis, namely, the ability to enter the hypnotic trance quickly on the appropriate suggestion, the ability to perform posthypnotic suggestions, and the ability to regress. In a patient who wishes to co-operate, this initial trance can be induced with as little as 2 cc of Sodium Pentothal injected intravenously. On the other hand, in overanxious patients it is sometimes helpful to inject twice this dose. Again, in resistant patients it is sometimes useful to give a full narcotic dose and to induce hypnosis during the stage of confusion while the subject is still half-asleep. In these latter cases it is particularly important to use fractionation, waking the patient and rehypnotizing him again and again until the effects of the drug have quite ceased. Attention to this detail is essential if one is to avoid the criticism that physiological alterations in the patient may make it impossible to bridge the amnesic gap caused by the narcosis. This process of conditioning by large doses of drugs, counteracted by Methedrine if the patient becomes too drowsy to think clearly, is mainly of theoretical interest, but its possibilities are sinister. In ordinary psychiatric practice it is nearly always possible to achieve as good, or better, results with minimal doses of Sodium Pentothal which provides an excellent opening for fractionation with progressive deepening of hypnosis.

Reviewing the numerous books, special chapters, and clinical reports on barbiturate narcosis which have appeared during the last 20 years, one is impressed by the almost complete absence of any laboratory research regarding narcohypnotic states. A solitary article appearing in the *Medical Press* [2] (1937) seems to be the only published record of the reactions of normal controls to narcotic hypnosis. One of the most interesting features of this article was the fact of the consistent response of the normal controls. Several of the controls laughingly asserted that they would never be made to talk freely as my patients had done, and others ridiculed the suggestion that even by the aid of a drug they could be hypnotized. These opinions were changed quickly by the test.

Twenty nurses were each given an experimental injection of 2 cc Sodium Pentothal, and all but two exhibited good hypnotic rapport. One of the exceptions, a girl of average ability and a good mixer, was resistive to all verbal suggestions but finally developed catalepsy. Of these 20 "normal" girls, 18 found themselves unable to refuse to answer questions, and several who were ordinarily reserved exhibited dissociation of consciousness with spontaneous garrulity. One of these reactions is of particular interest as it illustrates the effect of a quick, small dose of intravenous barbital. This control chatted gaily for some time, describing numerous indiscretions, whereupon her "confession" was terminated by a peremptory order to wake up. This resulted in an immediate return of her usual personality with a vehement denial that she had been sleeping at all. Nevertheless, she was quite unable to remember anything that she had said. The amnesia was complete. A point of greater interest in regard to the use of Sodium Pentothal for hypnosis is the fact that the day following the initial experiments every one of the control subjects made an immediate response to purely verbal suggestion and, on retesting 10 of them, posthypnotic suggestion was effective in 9, with complete amnesia in 6. This is a very small series, but it merits further investigation.

A further question of importance in understanding the nature of hypnosis and its relationship to narcosis is, "What makes a person susceptible to the induction of hypnosis?" Hypnotizability is a characteristic of all normal people, and it is, therefore, distinct from any artificially induced state of narcosis. Susceptibility to hypnosis is a matter for psychiatric and philosophical inquiry, but it is also a problem suitable for laboratory investigation. This will establish the facts of the extent to which susceptibility to hypnosis can be increased by the use of drugs; it will support the argument in favor of adequate preparation (psychologically) for any narcotic procedure; and it will determine whether the barbiturates have some specific *hypnosislike* effect which other narcotics do not possess. There is a good deal of experimental evidence to support the view that the barbiturates, in small doses, have a selective subcortical action. It seems probable that this action is primarily on the thalamus and corpus striatum, and it is a fact that doses insufficient to produce any measurable effect on cortical efficiency will nevertheless facilitate the induction of hypnosis.

One of the most interesting features of hypnosis, whether of the verbally induced or drug-induced variety, is the willingness and even eagerness with which the subject enters into a relationship of dependency upon the hypnotist with unquestioning surrender to his commands. This state of surrender was regarded by McDougall as a response to a submissive instinct, the degree of hypnotizability depending on the quantity of this instinct. Psychoanalysts have contended that hypnosis is a reactivation of the infantile state of blind faith and implicit obedience based on both love and fear of the parents. On this hypothesis they describe two methods of hypnotizing. The first of these methods corresponds with Ferenczi's "paternal way," the method of command, the use of authority, and the assumption of mysterious power. The second method corresponds with Ferenczi's "maternal way," the method of coaxing, soothing, and encouraging the patient's intelligent cooperation.

The second of these two methods is usually the more successful when used in conjunction with seminarcosis. This fact can be explained by the observation that both hypnosis and suggestibility are essentially erotic in nature. Hypnosis appears to satisfy a desire for erotic gratification and, apart from the specific suggestions by the hypnotist of well-being, it commonly causes euphoria and even elation. This tendency to elation through seeking erotic gratification is particularly characteristic of first experiences with hypnosis, but when hypnosis is repeated for therapeutic purposes, the motivation should change as the patient acquires insight. A discussion of the analysis of this motivation is outside the scope of this paper.

In conclusion, I would emphasize that the main advantage of narcotic hypnosis over verbally induced hypnosis is the speed with which hypnosis of sufficient depth can be reached. Most normal persons respond only gradually to verbally induced hypnosis, and, as a general rule, only a light degree of hypnosis is induced during the first session. In most normal persons the depth of hypnosis can be increased at subsequent sessions, but many hours of hard work are required to produce complete amnesia and somnambulism. Once this has been achieved, however, any normal person can be rehypnotized quickly and easily. The value of narcosis is, then, that it practically eliminates the necessity for hours of preliminary sessions of instruction in how to be hypnotized. And, after a single session of narcotic hypnosis, posthypnotic suggestion is effective for the subsequent induction of hypnosis by verbal methods alone. Rarely, in patients whose psychopathology makes relaxation difficult, it is useful to repeat the full technique, combining the use of Sodium Pentothal with training in posthypnotic suggestion on several successive days. And I would emphasize that narcosis is not a substitute for hypnosis; it is only a means of facilitating its induction.

Finally, for the sake of completeness, I must mention an alternative technique which is seldom used but is of value in the rare instances of patients who refuse to have any form of injection. Any of the quick-acting barbiturates may be given by mouth, when they will produce a similar effect but of delayed and more gradual onset. This alternative to the usual technique of narcoanalysis is used infrequently because the intravenous method possesses the considerable advantages of speed, accuracy of dose, and greater force of suggestibility. However, for these exceptional cases, the oral administration of a rapidly acting barbiturate is a valuable aid to the induction of hypnosis. Moreover, it seems that inhibited and mute individuals who refuse injection will respond to the suggestion of automatic writing within half an hour of taking 3 gr of Nembutal by mouth.

An interesting question would be, "How successful are attempts to induce hypnosis after a previously refractory subject has had suggestion under narcosis that he will be amenable thereafter to hypnosis?" My impression from my personal experience is that this method is completely successful in some 60 per cent of normal subjects, and partially successful in a very large part of the remainder. But this is a question which needs full and detailed laboratory investigations if it is to be answered with conviction.

REFERENCES

The following articles are by the author of this chapter.

1. "Pentothal sodium in mental hospital practice," *Brit. M. J.*, **1**:938, May 9, 1936.
2. "Narco-analysis: A method of investigating normal and morbid mentality," *M. Press*, **194**:5109, 1937.

CHAPTER SEVEN

A Study of Age Regression under Hypnosis

Introductory Note

One of the most interesting and also most highly controversial topics in the field of hypnosis is that of age regression. Investigators in this area have tended to divide themselves into two camps. The first point of view, held by a number of able and skilled experimenters, contends that age regression is merely an artefact, a kind of almost-conscious acting out by the subject in order to please the hypnotist. The second group maintains that age regression is real, involving the actual blocking off or inhibiting of recent behavior patterns. This permits earlier patterns of behavior to become once more operative, and, within the limits of the present physical structure of the subject, these are relived and experienced just as they were many years before.

In this chapter LeCron presents experimental evidence which has been published by people representing both points of view. He summarizes the most important studies in this area. In addition, he presents the results of newer and previously unpublished studies, by both himself and others, which clearly support the second hypothesis; namely, that age regression is actual and not merely apparent. It becomes evident that the author of this chapter, like many others, has approached this subject from an unbiased and objective viewpoint and has become convinced of the reality of the phenomenon of age regression through his studies.

In this chapter he has described some of these studies to us quite clearly, pointing out their limitations and the restrictions of experimental method that inhered in their design. The reader is urged to approach this paper with the same objective attitude, weighing the pros and cons, and to arrive at his conclusions after careful consideration of the evidence.

Although much more evidence has been made available concerning the reality of age regression, the controversy is by no means a closed one at the present time. It is to be hoped that the discussion presented in this chapter will stimulate other scientific workers to initiate further carefully controlled studies and to report their findings in order that we may know not only if these phenomena are real, but, if so, under what conditions they can operate and what are their limitations.

No fully adequate theories exist today to explain the phenomenon of regression. There are those who hold that conditioned reflexes, once developed, do not disappear completely but leave organic traces in the nervous system. The word suggestions given by the hypnotist then become the stimuli adequate to reinvoke these reflexes.

Those who believe that age regression can be actual usually note that it often is not complete; that frequently it is only partial, and sometimes the investigator does obtain only a kind of acting. They feel that regression may or may not be *true*, depending upon the hypnotizability of the subject and the skill of the hypnotist. This would account for the negative results reported by some investigators.

Establishing the true status, values, and limitations of age regression is a vital need in the advancement of hypnotherapy. Psychoanalysis claims its most therapeutic results by means of a type of regression. The associations of the patient are worked through back to early childhood levels. The amnesia for this period is lifted, and early pathogenic experiences are revivified in the transference situation so that they may be beneficially resolved by an emotionally corrective experience. This revivification within the transference to the analyst is a very time-consuming procedure, frequently requiring a year or more of preliminary work.

If emotionally corrective experiences can be administered to an age-regressed patient under hypnosis, this reliving through, which is the heart of analytical therapy, can perhaps be achieved in a fraction of the time ordinarily required without hypnosis. In this way deep therapy can be made available to many more people. It is possible that investigators in the field of hypnotic age regression may be able to present the psychoanalysts with a new and very powerful therapeutic weapon.

This symposium, bringing together as it does new contributions by a large group of recognized specialists in the field of hypnosis, is indeed indicative of the recently increased scientific and professional interest in the area. No volume has ever been published before which presents the pooled thinking and experiences of such a sizable number of the world's hypnotic specialists. The editor (and writer of this chapter) is to be congratulated on this monumental undertaking.

Leslie M. LeCron is well fitted to integrate these various contributions. As joint author with Jean Bordeaux, he has already summarized the field of hypnosis in a recent volume.[1] This is an excellent survey and probably the best which has been published in recent times. It can be recommended both to a beginner in the field who wishes to become informed of the current status of hypnotism, and to the more experienced scientist or clinician who would like to acquire greater flexibility in his techniques for inducing trance states. This chapter is a welcome addition to the literature on the vital topic of age regression under hypnosis.

JOHN G. WATKINS *

REFERENCE

1. LeCron, L. M., and Bordeaux, J.: *Hypnotism Today*, Grune & Stratton, Inc., New York, 1947.

* 5742 South Kensington, La Grange, Ill.

A Study of Age Regression under Hypnosis

By LESLIE M. LeCRON, B.A.*

Read before the Society for Clinical and
Experimental Hypnosis, March, 1950.

Workers in the field of hypnosis usually find age regression to be one of the most interesting of all hypnotic phenomena. Such regression is an apparent return to any particular age suggested by the operator, even to some definite date in the subject's past. The regression may be directed to a specific birthday or a certain Christmas or other holiday. The time may be left indefinite, perhaps stated as prior to a certain age or event.

Ordinarily, regression is produced by suggestions of becoming progressively younger, though success is more certain if mental confusion and a disorientation as to time and place are instigated. An excellent description of the process has been given by Erickson and Kubie.[1]

Their paper also points out two types of age regression, either of which may occur. In one, the subject describes a former experience or time as though witnessing it or remembering it, but he relates it in terms of the past. Such memory recall may be only partial and rather vague; at other times it may be clear and remarkably redundant.

The more genuine type of regression is one in which the subject seems to be actually reliving some episode of his life. He relates it as though veritably experiencing it, speaking in the present tense. Told he is 3 years old and that it is his birthday, a subject may recall many of the day's events. If he had a birthday party, he may tell the names of the children present and remember just what food was

* 8217 Beverly Blvd., Los Angeles 48, Calif.

served and what presents were received. Sometimes the material obtained in this way can be verified through a parent.

In this type of regression apparently all time subsequent to the suggested period or event, including the present, is blotted from the mind. It is, therefore, necessary for the operator to fit himself into the regression, otherwise the subject might fail to recognize him and rapport might be lost. Hence, the hypnotist must ostensibly transform himself into someone known to the subject at the earlier period, such as a teacher or relative. Failing this, the subject may himself assign the operator such a role as will conform to the situation.

Regressed in this way, the subject employs language such as would be expected of a person of the regressed age. Often his voice becomes childlike; at other times he retains normal tone but uses only simple words and phrases. His other behavior will also conform to the suggested age. If told he is 6 years old and given a suitable toy to play with, there may be protests and tears if it is suddenly snatched away. Instructed to draw or paint a picture, it will be childish and grotesque, corresponding to what such a picture would be if executed by a child of 6 years. This will be true even if the subject is an accomplished artist.

Handwriting also changes and seems to be almost identical when compared with actual specimens of the subject's childhood writing. (It would be of interest to have a handwriting expert make a scientific comparison and study of such writings.) Sarbin[2] regressed a 20-year-old girl to various ages. Giving her a piece of chalk, he placed her at a blackboard with instructions to write. At a 6-year level, she changed the chalk to her left hand, then used it with dexterity suitable to the age. When questioned later, she stated that she could no longer write left-handed, for she had been changed over in the second grade.

A third form of age regression has recently been publicized. In 1950 L. Ron Hubbard, a science fiction writer, published *Dianetics*,[3] a book which aroused considerable public interest, though it was coldly received and ignored by the medical and psychological professions. In his therapy, Hubbard uses a form of regression which he labels "return." Although he denies that hypnosis is involved, this is definitely a hypnotic technique. It seems to be a form of regression between the two types previously described. The subject relives an experience with great vividness and may have perception with all five senses. Some regressed behavior may be betrayed. But he is in both the present and the past. He speaks in the present tense, though he may comment about and analyze the experience he is describing as if also in the present time. His speech is normal to his real age.

Dianetic return can be obtained with surprising ease with most people. Only a very light trance state is needed. The regression is then obtained merely by directing the subject to go back in time to a particular age, date, or event. To facilitate this, frequent use is made of association to words.

While Hubbard has called attention to this form of regression, a good description of it was given by Freud [4] as long ago as 1892.

Hubbard claims, with no proof of his contention, that subjects may thus be returned to the prenatal period, even to the moment of conception! Subjects can easily be led to describe a prenatal happening, usually one where pain was experienced. But whether this is fact or fantasy would be difficult of scientific proof. Yet others, Fodor,[5] for instance, have maintained that prenatal events are registered in memory, citing the study of dreams as verification. Stekel [6] is another who accepts this hypothesis, also stating that patients in analysis sometimes recall the experience of being born.

While dianetics has had no scientific acceptance, this form of regression does provide a technique valuable for analytical exploration. It is easily obtained, whereas true regression requires a deep trance and can be induced with a much smaller percentage of people.

Various attempts have been made by experimenters to demonstrate the actuality of age regression. Working with Dr. D. B. Klein, the writer prepared a list of words for a word-association test, including among them a number of recent origin or significance such as radio, Pearl Harbor, etc., and others beyond the comprehension of a 10-year-old child. A list of questions along this same line was also prepared. A male subject of 35 was then regressed to the 10-

year level, asked the questions, and given the word test. He was unaware of the purpose of the test. While such an experiment is far from conclusive, it is indicative, since the subject did not once fail to maintain the suggested level and was unable to answer the question or associate to a word which he could not have known at 10 years old. Prior to this, Dr. Klein had felt that so-called "regression" might be explained on the basis of memory and role playing, but he was less convinced of the tenability of this explanation after working with this particular subject.

Erickson, in a personal communication, has told the writer of regressing a male subject 30 years old, with the intention of studying his behavior at a regressed level. The subject was seated in a chair arranged so that release of a latch would cause the back to fall into a horizontal position. With the man regressed to an infantile level of prior to 1 year, the latch was suddenly released so that the chair back fell flat. An adult or an older child, as an involuntary reaction, would extend both arms and legs in an effort to maintain balance. The regressed subject squalled in fright, made no movement of the limbs, and fell backward with the chair. A reaction quite unexpected and embarrassing to both Erickson and the subject was an accompanying urination which soaked the man's trousers! Certainly such behavior is not acting and is an impressive indication of the actuality of regression.

Hakebush, Blinkowski, and Foundillere [7] have reported making intelligence tests at various regressed age levels, finding that the tests conformed to these ages. Platenow [8] regressed subjects to 4, 6, and 10 years and gave them Binet-Simon intelligence tests with corresponding results. He also found that word stimuli reanimated in the subjects earlier conditioned reflexes which had been lost.

Bergman, Graham and Leavitt,[9] as well as Sarbin,[10] state that significant changes corresponding to the suggested age occurred when Rorschach tests were given at consecutive age-level regressions. This is further confirmed by Norgarb in the next article in this volume.

A most interesting experiment in age regression was conducted by J. G. Watkins and B. J. Showalter.[11] In an unpublished paper they report an investigation of hypnotic regression through the measurement of academic skills which are subject to objective evaluation and for which age norms are available. Since reading represents such a skill and standardized tests of reading are available with established norms, this was selected for their tests. With a young woman subject, tests of trance depth showed deep somnambulism attained, with complete amnesia, negative visual hallucinations, and complete anesthesia obtained.

Their summary of the study is as follows:

A superior college student, age 19–5, was regressed through hypnotic trance to the following grade-age levels: grade 1.9, age 6–10; grade 3.9, age 8–10; grade 6.9, age 11–10; grade 10.9, age 15–10. At each level she was given a battery of oral- and silent-reading tests. Her eye movements were also photographed on the ophthalmograph. Reading-test scores and opthalmographic records of eye movements were also secured at three subsequent levels: trance unregressed; normal, not in trance; and trance, accelerated. In this last she was informed while under hypnotic trance that she had a doctor's degree, was 29 years of age, and could read with enormous speed and accuracy. [This might be called *age progression*.] All scores were compared with each other and with norms at each level to determine whether true regression or acceleration had taken place. The following results were obtained:

1. Regression was satisfactorily established to the 1.9 and 3.9 grade levels.
2. Scores secured at the lowest level, grade 1.9, showed that the subject was about normal for her grade in some reading skills, accelerated in others, and retarded in still others, being near the grade norm in the average of her abilities. Most noticeable was subnormal reading speed and large number of eye regressions.
3. At the 3.9 level the subject had fallen in her average reading abilities about half a grade behind norms. This might have been symptomatic of poor teaching in the primary grades.
4. Results secured when regression was attempted to the 6.9 and the 10.9 grade levels were contradictory. On a reading survey the subject made scores at or somewhat above normal reading abilities for her grade. However, photographs of eye movements showed reading ability only slightly below her normal college level.

5. The subject made slightly lower scores during an unregressed trance than when completely normal, thus indicating that trance itself, without regressive suggestions, has a retarding effect. This retarding effect, however, was not sufficient to account for the regressed scores made at the early levels.

6. An attempt to accelerate reading skills through hypnotic suggestion to a supernormal level resulted in an increase of reading speed of 63 per cent without loss of comprehension, as recorded by ophthalmographic record. The number of eye regressions was at the same time reduced 40 per cent. No increase was apparent, though, when the subject took a college-level reading-comprehension examination calling for analytic skills.

One of the most unusual factors in these tests was the evidence seen in photographing the eye movements at grade 1.9, age 6–10. Here the film showed considerable lack of ocular coordination and stability. At the beginning of each line there occurred the typical V slants in the first fixations which evidence the need for pulling the eyes together to secure adequate convergence. The movements seem typical of a child in the first grade who lacks adequate motor control.

From W. H. Roberts and D. Black [12] of Morningside College there is a report, also unpublished, of another experiment in age regression. It was carried out with Black's wife as the subject. Her eyesight had been defective since early childhood, and she had begun wearing glasses at the age of 12 years.

When regressed during a demonstration, it was noted that she found her glasses uncomfortable and complained of diminished vision. Without her glasses her vision improved as she was regressed to earlier and earlier levels. This obviously called for investigation. A local optometrist agreed to participate in a further test. A check of her vision was made in the waking state and again while hypnotized and regressed to a 7-year level. A table of the results follows:

Near Vision

Uncorrected	Normal	Regressed
R eye	14/28	14/21
L eye	14/21	14/14
Both	14/14	14/14

Near Vision—Cont'd

Corrected	Normal	Regressed
R eye	14/14	14/35
L eye	14/14	14/55
Both	14/14	14/24

Far Vision

Uncorrected	Normal	Regressed
R eye	Finger vision at 10 ft less than 20/400	20/200, 20/200
L eye	Finger vision at 13 ft less than 20/400	20/200, 20/200 plus
Both	20/400	20/200 plus
Corrected		
R eye	20/15	20/50
L eye	20/15	20/70
Both	20/15	Patient complained of discomfort and headache

RETINOSCOPY

R eye	−3.50, −0.50 cyl.	The same
L eye	−2.00, −1.00 cyl.	The same

Two conclusions seem justified: (1) hypnotic regression to the age of 7 years resulted in a small but measurable improvement of both near and far vision; (2) the strong glasses worn by the subject provided excellent vision in the waking state, but, when regressed, they markedly impaired near vision and improved far vision but to a much smaller degree than in the waking state. In both cases the subject complained of discomfort and headache. It should be added that direct suggestion under hypnosis but unregressed did not produce any improvement. During the tests she was instructed to make no intense effort to see and no straining was evidenced.

Conclusions cannot be drawn from one such case, of course.

Another alteration in vision accompanying age regression was noted by Ford and Yeager.[13] In January, 1943, their subject had had a colloid cyst removed from the floor of the third ventricle, prior to this suffering from blindness in the left half of the right eye (homonymous hemianopsia). Vision had become normal again after this operation. In 1947 Ford and Yeager regressed the subject to a time shortly before the operation, and the right homonymous hemianopsia reappeared during the regression.

The most convincing proofs of the actuality of age regression would probably be found in tests of a physiological or neurophysiological nature where the response could not be simulated. A most convincing test of this nature has been reported by Gidro-Frank and Bowersbuch [14] as to the Babinski reflex. With a normal adult, stroking the sole of the foot causes the great toe to turn down—flexion. In certain pathological conditions the response to this stimulus is dorsiflexion, or upturning of the toe. In infants up to approximately 7 months of age, the reflexive response to this stimulation is also dorsiflexion. After that age it reverses.

To quote from Gorton's [15] digest of the literature on the physiology of hypnosis:

> With these facts in mind [as above], the startling nature of the experiments of Gidro-Frank and Bowersbuch can be appreciated. These authors were able to achieve the recovery of the Babinski sign during hypnotic age regression in three adult subjects.

In the experiment, the subjects were unaware of the purpose of the test. They were regressed to less than six months of age by suggestions directed to that end, but otherwise nonspecific chronologically. Neither the hypnotic state itself, nor direct suggestion, produced the change. These authors say:

> A month-by-month study of the regression showed the alteration of the response from plantar flexion to dorsiflexion to take place at the regressed age of five or six months. Reversal of the response to its adult form occurred at the same age in progression.

The experimenters found, too, that changes in peripheral chronaxie accompanied the change in plantar reflex. With the same tests made in the waking state, the response was always plantar flexion, nor could voluntary efforts by the subjects produce dorsiflexion when the stimulus was given.

These findings have been confirmed by the writer, using three different subjects. At the regressed age of 5 months it was also found that the sucking reflex of infancy revived. When the lips were stroked with the end of a fountain pen, the subjects seized it avidly between the lips with facial expressions of anticipatory enjoyment. The prehensile movement of the lips was most pronounced.

R. M. True [16] worked out a most convincing test for the validity of age regression. In his experiment he used 50 subjects ranging from 20 to 24 years old, 40 men and 10 women. Quoting his article:

They were then regressed year by year, using memorable dates as chronological landmarks. On such dates they were asked "What day is this?" and their answers were scored. . . . 82.3 per cent gave entirely accurate answers to these questions, while the remaining 17.7 per cent answered less than half the questions correctly.

In these tests, regression was made to the ages of 10, 7, and 4, to Christmas and their birthdays of those years. They were then merely asked what day of the week it was. Of the answers, 93 per cent were correct at the age level of 10, 82 per cent at age 7, and 69 per cent at age 4. The last figure is remarkable because not many 4-year-olds would be expected to identify the days of the week.

Before hypnosis was induced, as a control experiment the subjects were asked on what day of the week some relatively recent events had happened. Only a small percentage gave any correct answers, the results apparently being largely owing to chance.

As an experiment where results may accurately be measured, this seems highly conclusive and significant. It also demonstrates the accuracy and extent of human memory for trivial matters and shows the manner in which hypnosis may be used for recall of lost memories.

To determine further as to the reality of hypnotic regression, this writer has tried to test behavior results which cannot be simulated. To do this, conditioned reflexes were set up in subjects in the waking state. They were then tested for their continuation during hypnosis and again tested after age regression had been induced. It was thought possible that the reflex might be lost during regression, the investigator's attitude at the beginning of the test being quite neutral as to whether or not this would occur. If anything, it was negative, because a conditioned reflex has not only psychological aspects but also neurological.

As the investigator is in private psychological practice, laboratory equipment is not easily available to him, and it was necessary to depend on visual observation of the results rather than to measure them. In all the tests, witnesses watched closely and were unanimous in agreement as to the results they observed.

It has already been determined by Scott [17] that a conditioned reflex set up in the waking state is retained under hypnosis. Nevertheless, in the tests reported here, after the subject was hypnotized, the conditioned reflex which had been set up in the waking state was stimulated to make sure it was established and present with the subject under hypnosis. In each case the proper response was made to the stimulus (a buzzer).

The tests were given in two separate sessions, two subjects being used in each, and the tests made on each separately. The subjects were two males and two females, all exceptional hypnotic subjects, well informed on hypnotism, and very intelligent; the two men and one of the women also are experienced as hypnotists. All were aware of the purpose of the tests. Each was able to reach a deep state of hypnosis, with subsequent amnesia and other somnambulistic phenomena obtainable.

At the first session the two subjects were a young businessman and his wife, in their early 30's. To set up a conditioned reflex, each was given a number of light electric shocks to the accompaniment of the sound of a buzzer, the shock being sufficiently strong to cause the subject's hand to jerk away from the electric terminals. After the reflex had been established, the subject hypnotized, and the reflex tested, each was regressed to a 10-year level. The tests were conducted separately throughout. The subject was then led to converse, and the buzzer was sounded several times at irregular intervals. Neither betrayed any sign of flinching. When returned to normal age level and instructed to remember everything after being awakened, they were asked to discuss what had occurred. Both expressed surprise that they had not flinched, and both stated that they had not expected the experiment to prove successful. In the case of the girl the buzzer had evoked no sensation of any kind when it had been sounded. The man reported having had a feeling that the sound meant something to him, but he could not identify it, and the thought had been only a fleeting one. Both subjects were positive that they had neither flinched nor felt any such inclination. During the discussion, the buzzer was sounded twice in each case, and the subjects again responded to the stimulus by flinching, a definite hand jerk.

In the second session it was decided to use a different reflex, the corneal, which causes a wink of the eyelid when the cornea is touched with a soft cotton twill. The first subject of this experiment was the Mrs. S. who is again mentioned in Case 3 further on in this chapter. The second subject was the man who is mentioned in Case 1. With both, 15 minutes were devoted to securing a very deep trance, although each could attain the ordinary somnambulistic trance in a few seconds and had previously been conditioned to very deep states.

While the reflex was being established, Mrs. S. found the stimulation of the cornea unpleasant and had developed a flinch away from the experimenter as well as the eyewink response. After being hypnotized and the conditioned reflex tested, she was regressed 10 years to the age of 32. The buzzer was sounded three times, at intervals, and she neither winked nor flinched.

With the man subject, the suggestion was made that he should return to any age or any pleasant experience which he himself should select. After a moment he announced that he was 23 years old and was on a ship at sea. He described the ship and the ocean, and later stated that he had had a very vivid hallucination of both. As he talked, the buzzer was again sounded repeatedly with no wink evidenced by him.

After being awakened, with suggestion of full remembrance the sound of the buzzer again brought the eyewink response from both subjects. In the posttrance discussion both said that they had heard the buzzer but gave it no significance and were unaware of any tendency to wink. It should be noted that in all the tests the subject *heard* the buzzer, otherwise there might be the possibility that a selective anesthesia for the sound of the buzzer could have been spontaneously produced which would have prevented the reflex from "working."

These two subjects were aware of the success of the test with the first two subjects and expected it to be successful also with themselves.

Discussion. The results of this experiment with only four subjects is merely indicative rather than conclusive. It should be repeated with a larger group and with utilization of a conditioned reflex which can be mechanically measured for response. It is also barely possible that foreknowledge of the nature of the test might influence the result, though this is believed unlikely for the reason that a conditioned reflex is theoretically uncontrollable. However, a further test should be made to prove that under hypnotic suggestion with regression a conditioned reflex cannot be inhibited. A repetition of the experiment in the waking state as a control would seem to be unnecessary, as the subjects could not be regressed.

In consideration of the results of the experiment, much weight should be given to the posttrance statements of the four subjects as to the fact that the buzzer evoked no sensation and that they felt no response.

Young [18] has questioned whether regression is "fact or artifact." He believes it to be entirely a simulation on the part of the subject. The material reported by previous writers was criticized by Young as inconclusive because of utilizing too few subjects. Young regressed 14 subjects to the third birthday and found intelligence tests indicated an average mental age of 6 years. Behavior also did not conform properly to what should be expected if regression were real. Control tests with seven unhypnotized subjects, who were told to simulate as best they could the age of 3, gave performances nearer that level than did the hypnotized subjects. Young therefore believes he proved regression to be nonfactual.

However, his conclusions are open to question. The fact that the tests of his hypnotized subjects showed different results from those of the control group who were unhypnotized is in itself significant.

If they were simulating, the tests of the hypnotized group should have averaged about the same as those of the control group. Apparently, Young did not consider the significance of this. It would seem that he merely proved age regression to be incomplete and perhaps fluctuant in this particular group of subjects.

There may, perhaps, be reasons for his lack of success. If Young's report correctly describes the wording of the suggestions used in his tests to produce regression, they would seem to be quite inadequate to bring complete regression. With very little repetition, he merely stated that the subjects were now 3 years old. Certainly this is insufficient to stimulate actual regression of the reliving type. True regression is not often obtained so easily. Nor can we judge the depth of trance obtained in his various subjects.

In Young's experiment the matter of operator attitude is involved, for Young apparently made his tests believing that regression is only simulated. Estabrooks [19] emphasizes the importance of operator attitude and its effect on the results of investigation, thus bringing differences of opinion between researchers who obtain opposite results from their tests. Subjects have a remarkable ability in hypnosis to sense the attitude of the hypnotist through minimal cues and will respond accordingly. If the operator believes a negative result will ensue, the subject will probably respond negatively.

Some other workers in hypnosis are apparently not convinced of the reality of regression. Gill,[20] in reporting a case of spontaneous regression, accepts the recall type of regression but not the reliving type. He even questions whether Erickson and Kubie could have meant what they say in their description of this type of regression and seems astounded that they could accept it as real. Since Gill has had much experience in hypnoanalysis, it seems even more astounding that he would not have encountered patients who could be regressed in this way during hypnoanalysis.

Almost every other authority is of the opinion that regression is actual. Those using hypnosis in the practice of psychotherapy see continual evidence of the reality. Traumatic events repressed from conscious memory are brought out with such display of emotion and accompanying childlike behavior as to preclude the possibility of acting. Often, it is possible to check the validity of the material thus recalled, which may date back to 2 years or even to infancy.

A matter greatly needing clarification through research is the question as to how far back regression may be carried. If a very good subject is regressed to an early age and then is told to return further to the time just before he was born, he will sometimes curl up in the fetal position. Imagination, fantasy, hallucination, or mere simulation may be involved in regressions to early periods of life.

Several authorities, including Wolberg,[21] believe some subjects can be returned to the neonatal period. Wolberg reports one subject regressed so that he made sucking and grasping movements and was unable to speak. When told to remember the experience, after being awakened he said:

"I was very small. I didn't understand anything.* Everything was new. . . . I was trying to get hold of things . . . somebody was leaning over me—mother. She picked me up and held me. . . . I saw mother, the different things, the walls."

Lindner [22] also has reported regression in a psychopath to an age between 6 months and 1 year. In the writer's experience regression to infancy is not difficult to obtain with a good subject.

Aside from being a fascinating phenomenon, age regression is of the greatest practical value to the psychotherapist utilizing hypnosis. It is one of the most important techniques in hypnoanalysis, facilitating the exploration of childhood, particularly in seeking traumatic material and in obtaining catharsis. Regression can be one of the main factors contributing to the brevity of treatment possible with hypnoanalysis.

Another very practical use of age regression which seems to have been completely overlooked is the opportunity it affords for research into the mind. Freud has made much of the various stages of child development, oral, anal, etc., and of the complexes which arise, such as the Oedipus situation. It should be possible, by means of regression, to check many of his contentions, which many psychotherapists regard as far from the true facts.

* Actually, he heard and obeyed the operator's instructions.

SOME UNUSUAL PHASES OF AGE REGRESSION

Engaged in a practice of psychotherapy with the use of hypnosis, the writer has encountered three cases in which unusual and surprising aspects of age regression have been noted.

Case 1. While lecturing and demonstrating hypnosis to a group of physicians, a male subject 45 years of age was used. After placing him in a deep trance, he was regressed progressively to his third birthday. Thereupon, the subject began to gasp for breath, wheezing violently, coughing, and choking. His face and neck became markedly flushed, and he displayed signs of acute distress. It was obvious to all that he was undergoing an attack of asthma. One of the physicians made a quick stethoscopic examination and reported rales present, with a high rate of pulse. No extensive examination was made because the subject was obviously suffering. Therefore, he was quickly returned to his proper age and awakened, whereupon the attack ceased. Inquiry revealed that he had had severe asthma during his childhood. His mother remembered his third birthday as the occasion of a bad attack. Of course the exactitude of her memory of an event 42 years ago could not be verified.

A few weeks later this subject was again regressed in an attempt to duplicate the former episode. This was with his permission, and a physician was present to study the case. An asthmatic attack was again produced, but it was much less violent. The stethoscope showed neither rales nor any significant increase in heartbeat, and his face was only slightly flushed. The conclusion was reached that this time the attack was simulated as a defense against the actual suffering experienced during the former regression. The subject attempted to carry out the suggestion of regression, but subconsciously he resisted. This person is not only a somnambulistic subject but is also a competent hypnotist. Thus, he can report both objectively and subjectively. He related that he had felt a definite resistance to carrying out the instructions to regress to the 3-year level. His experience this time seemed to be only a partial regression and to some extent was an acting out of the part required of him, though this was not done consciously.

Case 2. The patient was a 34-year-old male, an alcoholic undergoing hypnoanalysis. The referring physician was present at the event described. Involved in the alcoholic pattern of the patient was a hatred for his mother and a wish to cause her pain and distress through his excessive drinking and accompanying escapades.

A somnambulist, the subject entered a deep trance at the first induction of hypnosis. At the second session, hypnosis was induced again. While the operator was still giving sleep suggestions, the patient began to sob brokenly and to display other signs of emotion. The analyst made comforting suggestions, but the subject wept all the more. Asked why he was crying, he spoke brokenly in childlike terminology and tone.

"Ma is being mean to me," he wailed.

"How old are you?" asked the operator, suspecting by now what had happened.

"Why, I'm five," was the reply. "It's my birthday today."

Under further questioning, he told where he lived and answered other inquiries aimed at eliciting more information.

Asked again why he cried, he replied that his father had given him a much-desired goat as a birthday present. Once more he burst into tears and exclaimed,

"His name is Billy, but Ma won't let me bring him in the house 'cause he stinks. She says I can't keep him. She is so mean!"

This regression was entirely spontaneous. Such automatic regressions were repeated a number of times during this patient's treatment, always with reversion to some minor traumatic event which had occurred through the range of age levels from 5 to 15. Each time, regression came immediately after the trance state was entered. This happened often, but not invariably. If it was desired to work along different lines, the operator prevented regression by appropriate suggestion during the induction talk.

Such a spontaneous regression seems to be very unusual. To the writer's knowledge it has not been mentioned in the literature, aside from Gill's report, in which case the regression was of memory-recall type rather than reliving the episode. Inquiry among others working with hypnosis confirms its rarity, though such spontaneous, unsuggested regression has sometimes been noted.

Case 3. Formerly a psychiatric social worker, Mrs. S. is an intelligent married woman of 42, well informed on abnormal psychology and psychotherapy. For as long as she can remember, she had suffered from recurrent asthmatic attacks, greater in intensity and frequency during childhood but still persistent. In her work it was sometimes necessary for her to enter a hospital. In such a situation she always experienced strong fear reactions which she recognized as phobic. Another phobia was the sight of the bare, hairy arms of a man. Still another was knives, and as a child she had run from the dining table when her father carved. Sometimes she experienced nightmares. Other than for these symptoms she was well adjusted, happy, in excellent health, and competent in her work.

During her study of psychotherapy, Mrs. S. read Horney's *Self Analysis*. Lacking finances for treatment, she undertook analysis of herself, intending to secure guidance later from a professional analyst. From her reading she was able to acquire a better understanding of herself and of her motivations. Part of her analytic work was accomplished in bed at night before going to sleep. One night she determined to explore her childhood systematically, and she began searching back in memory, starting at the age of 14. Her attempt was to recall anything pertinent, particularly as to traumas, because of a "feeling" that a traumatic episode might be involved.

She worked through a number of minor emotional events of childhood but with the impression that they were unimportant. One completely forgotten incident at the age of 5 was recalled with unusual clarity. Then, very suddenly, she seemed to be lying on a table, clothed in a white gown and under brilliant lights. She could see a man standing beside her holding a small knife. Above her head was a vague, threatening object which was settling down over her face. Terror-stricken, she struggled to rise, but two hairy arms seized her and roughly forced her back. She continued to struggle and was grasped violently and shaken; then a hand slapped her sharply and repeatedly. The object came down over her face, smothering her. At this point she began to scream, waking her husband. She was in extreme panic, trembling and sobbing, and he had great difficulty quieting her.

Next day Mrs. S. questioned her mother for light on the experience. She learned that, at the age of 16 months, a mastoidectomy had been performed on her and that she had been very sick afterward, with severe shock complications. Two of the nurses at the hospital had informed the mother of the brutality displayed toward the child by the anesthetist, and they had resigned in protest. For some time the child had experienced nightmares and had been emotionally disturbed. Following the operation, her first attacks of asthma had been manifested.

As a result of the catharsis obtained from this regressive experience, Mrs. S. felt a relief and has been entirely free of asthma ever since (3 years). She has lost her fear of hairy arms, though they continue to bring mild feelings of repugnance. The phobias for knives and hospitals have entirely disappeared.

At the time of this episode Mrs. S. knew nothing of hypnosis and had never heard of age regression. Now experienced as a subject, she is certain she entered a self-induced trance during her mental exploration. There is the possibility that she experienced a dream, but a dream associated with a trauma is much more likely to appear in disguised form and with symbolism rather than to be relived so vividly. Therefore, it would seem that she had probably entered a trance and, having deliberately fixed her attention on memory recall, had actually regressed to the age of 16 months, re-experiencing the traumatic event. This is her own conclusion, with which the writer is in accord. It should be added that she has since been regressed, with various age levels easily obtained.

SUMMARY

Age regression under hypnosis is a phenomenon readily obtained in a somnambulistic subject by suggestions of progressive return to some certain age or time, or perhaps through disorientation. The phenomenon has great practical value in hypnoanalysis and could be used to advantage in various studies of the mind.

Researchers have reported intelligence and Rorschach tests, reading tests, patterns of behavior, reanimation of former conditioned reflexes, changes in handwriting, reversal of the Babinski reflex, and changes of vision during age regression as confirmatory of its actuality. Accurate recall of lost memories has also been reported. Most authorities regard hypnotic regression as actual.

A report is made on tests tentatively showing that a conditioned reflex set up in the waking state is lost during regression, then is evidenced again on return to the real age.

Three unusual instances of regression are cited. In Case 1 a subject was regressed to his third birthday and experienced a severe asthmatic attack, with rales and a fast pulse. Case 2 was a subject undergoing hypnoanalysis who spontaneously regressed to various minor traumatic events at different ages after induction of hypnosis. Case 3 was a woman who, in apparent autohypnosis, unwittingly regressed herself to the age of 16 months and relived a severe trauma, subsequently recovering from asthma and losing certain phobias.

REFERENCES

1. Erickson, M. H., and Kubie, L. S.: "The successful treatment of a case of acute hysterical depression by a return under hypnosis to a critical phase of childhood," *Psychoanalyt. Quart.*, **10**:592, 1941.
2. Sarbin, T. R.: Unpublished—an occurrence during a demonstration to a college psychology class.
3. Hubbard, L. R.: *Dianetics.* Hermitage Press, Inc., New York, 1950.
4. Freud, S., and Breuer, J.: *Studies in Hysteria.* Nervous & Mental Disease Publishing Co., Washington, 1912.
5. Fodor, N.: *The Search for the Beloved.* Hermitage Press, Inc., New York, 1949.
6. Stekel, W.: *Conditions of Nervous Anxiety and Their Treatment,* Liveright Publishing Corp., New York, 1950.
7. Hakebush, Blinkowski and Foundillere: "An attempt at a study of development of personality with the aid of hypnosis," *Trud. Inst. Psikhonevr. Kiev*, **2**:236, 1930.
8. Platenow, K. I., "On the objective proof of the experimental personality age regression," *J. Gen. Psychol.*, **9**:190, 1933.

9. Bergman, M. S.; Graham, H.; and Leavitt, H. C.: "Rorschach exploration of consecutive hypnotic age level regressions," *Psychosom. Med.*, **9**(1):20, January–February, 1947.

10. Sarbin, T. R.: "Rorschach patterns under hypnosis," *Am. J. Orthopsychiat.*, **9**:315, 1939.

11. Watkins, J. G., and Showalter, B. J.: Unpublished paper on reading tests given a hypnotized subject while regressed to various age levels.

12. Roberts, W. H., and Black, D.: Unpublished paper on a measured change in vision in a regressed myopic subject.

13. Ford, L. F., and Yeager, C. L.: "Changes in the electroencephalogram in subjects under hypnosis," *Dis. Nerv. System*, **9**:190, 1948.

14. Gidro-Frank, L., and Bowersbuch, M. K.: "A study of the plantar response in hypnotic age regression," *J. Nerv. & Ment. Dis.*, **107**:443, 1948.

15. Gorton, B. E.: "The physiology of hypnosis," *Psychiatric Quart.*, **23**:317, April, 1949, and 457, July, 1949.

16. True, R. M.: "Experimental control in hypnotic age regression states," *Science*, **110** (2866):583, Dec. 2, 1949.

17. Scott, H. D.: "Hypnosis and the conditioned reflex," *J. Gen. Psychol.*, **4**:113, 1930.

18. Young, P. C.: "Hypnotic regression—fact or artifact," *J. Abnorm. & Social Psychol.*, **35**:273, 1940.

19. Estabrooks, G. H.: *Hypnotism*, E. P. Dutton & Co., Inc., New York, 1943.

20. Gill, M.: "Spontaneous regression on the induction of hypnosis," *Bull. Menninger Clin.*, **12** (2):41, March, 1948.

21. Wolberg, L. R.: *Medical Hypnosis*, Grune & Stratton, Inc., New York, 1948.

22. Lindner, R. M.: *Rebel without a Cause*, Grune & Stratton, Inc., New York, 1944.

Rorschach Psychodiagnosis in
Hypnotic Regression

Editor's Note

As has been mentioned in the previous chapter, Rorschach tests offer an excellent means of judging the actuality of hypnotic age regression, for reaction to such a test is difficult if not impossible to simulate. Any real alteration of personality produced by age regression should be adequately indicated in the responses. While it would be possible voluntarily to alter responses, basic patterns would still appear in the analysis, and a mere attempt to behave and respond like a child while undergoing the test would fail to produce basic changes in patterns.

The following article tends to confirm the genuineness of hypnotic regression. Dr. Norgarb's investigation is along the lines of a previous study by Bergman, Graham, and Leavitt,[1] and his findings agree in every particular with theirs. As these writers concluded: "The Rorschach findings reflected . . . changes at the various regressed age levels and followed closely the clinical data. This technique of longitudinal personality analysis by the Rorschach may have diagnostic and therapeutic value. It also shows promise of throwing increased light on the growth and development of personality." The advantages of the method demonstrated by this article and by Norgarb's are so obvious that Rorschach exploration during regression should be adopted by psychotherapists as standard procedure with any patient who can be hypnotized sufficiently to be regressed.

Rorschach technicians also might well adopt the policy of giving the test under hypnosis whenever this is possible. The end results of the test would present a somewhat truer picture if this were done. Bergman, Graham, and Leavitt; Norgarb; and also Sarbin[2] and Wolberg[3] have all found that the responses to the test when made under hypnosis are less repressed. The subject is then "intellectually inert" as Norgarb puts it, more egocentric, and is closer to his repressed conflicts.

For the benefit of readers who are unfamiliar with the Rorschach test, it is a projective type of personality test of diagnostic value. It consists of 10 standard cards on which are printed, some in color, ink blots which have been formed by folding a piece of paper over a patch of ink. Each blot has been carefully chosen and the responses of thousands of people have been tabulated and analyzed so that definite conclusions may be drawn from them. The person to be tested is required to look at each card and to tell what he sees in the blots—what he is reminded of, either considering the blot as a whole or its details. His replies, with timing and some other things taken into account, are tabulated and analyzed.

Readers who know nothing of the test will find the following article highly technical. The tabulations are full of scoring symbols and abbreviations as used by Rorschach technicians. However, in general, the explanations will make the text understandable. Clinical psychologists and other Rorschach examiners will find the completeness of the tests and the detailed analyses to be of the utmost interest.

Dr. Norgarb is a practicing psychologist of Johannesburg and is South Africa's leading authority on hypnosis, having begun his work in this field while studying for his degrees. His master's thesis was on narcotic hypnosis and was followed by a doctoral thesis on the Rorschach test.

REFERENCES

1. Bergman, M. S.; Graham, H.; and Leavitt, H. C.: "Rorschach exploration of consecutive hypnotic age level regressions," *Psychosom. Med.*, **9** (1):20, January–February, 1947.
2. Sarbin, T. R.: "Rorschach patterns under hypnosis," *Am. J. Orthopsychiat.*, **9**:315, 1939.
3. Wolberg, L. R., *Medical Hypnosis*, Grune & Stratton, Inc., New York, 1948.

Rorschach Psychodiagnosis in Hypnotic Regression

By BRIAN A. NORGARB, Ph.D.*

Alexander and French, introducing their book *Psychoanalytic Therapy*,[1] state that

. . . like most psychoanalysts, we have been puzzled by the unpredictability of therapeutic results, by the baffling discrepancy between the length and intensity of treatment and the degree of therapeutic success. It is not unusual for a patient to get well as the result of a few consultations; for even a severe neurotic condition with psychotic elements to yield to brief therapeutic work. Yet another case which seems comparatively mild may not respond to a systematic treatment of many years. That there is no simple correlation between therapeutic results and the length and intensity of treatment has been recognized, tacitly or explicitly, by most experienced psychoanalysts and is an old source of dissatisfaction among them.

This publication contains the results of investigative work by members of the Chicago Institute of Psychoanalysis on the crucial practical problem of every clinical psychotherapist, namely that of formulating the basic principles of and possible specific techniques for effective and, whenever possible, more economic treatment. The resultant suggestions are that psychotherapy should be planned in each case as far as possible a priori, the plan being based upon the specific psychodynamics of each individual case.

While Alexander and French do not stress brief treatment, recent work on hypnoanalysis, such as that of Wolberg,[2, 3] Watkins,[4] and others is largely directed toward this end, namely, abbreviation of

* 99 Pasteur Chambers, Jeppe St., Johannesburg, South Africa.

the extraordinarily attenuated time usually required for deep psychotherapy.

Adverting to the paragraph quoted above, it is clear that the difficulties of the clinician are almost insuperable when required to answer the patient's usual query, "How long will it take?" The choice of therapy, for example, whether suppressive or expressive, the duration of the treatment period, the number of sessions indicated, and the prognosis are all dependent upon factors which are difficult to evaluate from the clinical history alone (usually given by the patient himself). These factors include the nature of the syndrome, the strength and stability of the ego, the date of the onset of the neurosis, the environmental conditions which confront the patient and proved beyond his adaptive capacities, and other personality factors such as intelligence, age, self-objectification, and insight.

Of the various clinical psychodiagnostic methods, the Rorschach test has proved "that it is beyond doubt the most potent single diagnostic instrument clinical psychology possesses." [5] By means of this projective technique we are able to arrive at a more dynamic diagnosis, a more objective appraisal of the patient's adjustment, and a more direct insight into the underlying personality structure.

In combining the method of Rorschach examination with hypnotically induced regression, it is possible to study retroactively the psychogenesis of the patient's personality pattern, the stability or lability of his development, to determine the probable period of onset of the neurosis, the choice, duration, and intensity of therapy indicated, and, by inference, the prognosis. By means of this method it should be possible to plan the therapeutic procedure with a more objective understanding of the underlying psychodynamics and pathogenesis, and hence probably abbreviate the time otherwise required.

TECHNICAL PROCEDURE

In the following illustrative study, the subject, a 20-year-old male, was given a Rorschach test in the ordinary manner. He was then hypnotized a few days later, and the test was repeated under hypnosis *after he had been given the suggestion of complete amnesia for the previous test.* (The purpose of this was to endeavor to eliminate the influence of previous experience with the test by means of hypnotic repression. This procedure is, however, not without objection, as it would naturally tend to inhibit the production of responses associated with the initial test and affect the psychogram accordingly, and therefore be an uncontrolled factor in estimating the influence of hypnosis per se on the subject's Rorschach performance.)

Various more or less arbitrary age levels are then decided upon for the subsequent tests, it having been already ascertained that the subject is capable of adequate trance depth to secure regression. In this case the ages chosen for testing were 17 (adolescence), 14 (puberty), 11 (prepuberty), 8, and 5 years—in that order of sequence. Prior to inducing hypnosis, it is desirable to obtain certain factual data from the subject regarding his general circumstances at the particular age to which it is desired to regress him, for example, home conditions, occupation, persons closely associated with him at the time, and so forth. Such data often prove useful in helping to orient the subject to the time period when he is in the regressed stage. Such orientation by means of discussion is not only valuable but *necessary* to assure as total a regression as possible. For example, should the subject be regressed to an early school period, discussion at the regressed level would center around his activities and experiences at school during that day, his intentions for the "forthcoming" week end, etc.

The method of induction is more or less immaterial, but in this particular case Wolberg's excellent technique of hand levitation was used in conjunction with a metronome. Slow, systematic induction seems most important in obtaining the necessary depth of trance state. When the subject is deeply hypnotized, I proceed to produce regression by using, *mutatis mutandis,* the following formula: "Now concentrate very carefully on what I am going to say to you; I am going to take you back in time to when you were a little boy of five years of age. I am going to turn the clock back and you are going to go back in time. Now imagine that you are looking at the dial of a big clock. (Pause.) When you see the clock clearly in your mind's eye, just tell me. (The subject indicates that he does.) Good. Now as you concentrate on that clock you begin to notice a strange thing happening: you notice that the hands of the clock are moving in an *anticlockwise* direction. Do you notice that? Right! Now you see that they begin to move faster and faster and faster, and you can feel how you are rapidly slipping back in time, sliding back in time, back, back, back—hours and hours are rushing past backwards, days and nights—weeks—months—and you are getting younger and younger. Now I want you to tell me every time you pass a birthday. Every year younger you will announce your age to me, do you understand?"

During this entire period I make use of a gramophone recording of a single high-frequency note which appears to have a valuable suggestive effect on the subject (probably due to Hollywood dramatizations). The purpose of requiring the subject to announce his age at each year level is twofold: (1) he can choose his own time for the regressive process which facilitates the degree of regression; and (2) it can be clinically instructive to use a stop watch to time the subject in his progressive backward movement, observing time fluctuations which could indicate possible blocking or reluctance to return to certain periods or a desire to pass a particular phase as rapidly as possible. Having arrived at the age at which it is desired to test him, he is oriented to the period by means of discussion, as previously described. It should be noted that it is, of course, necessary for the hypnotist to reintroduce himself to the subject, preferably presenting himself as some appropriate person such as a friend whom the subject trusts. After the preliminary discussion, he is asked whether he minds doing the test, and the usual test instructions are given. The tests are done at intervals of a few days between each.

ILLUSTRATIVE CASE

The subject of this experimental study was an individual of relatively normal and uncomplicated personality. He was chosen for study because he was readily hypnotizable and capable of "genuine" rather than "dramatized" regression (compare Erickson and Kubie [6]) and was prepared to give enough of his time for the purpose of the research. For the sake of brevity we shall refer to him as Ken.

The subject and his father were both in the Navy, and the latter was absent from home for the larger part of the time. That Ken has a strong ego identification with his father very soon became manifest and is illustrated by his response in the Tendler Emotional Inquiry (sentence-completion test) where to the item "My hero is ————" the immediate response was the word "Dad." The paternal-filial relationship was one of rather sentimental mutual affection.

Ken's mother, judging from her history and his own description, appears to be an unstable, frigid, and emotionally inhibited woman whose treatment of her son, and only child, was marked by a strict oversolicitous discipline. He was often brutally beaten for minor offenses, was confined to the house as a matter of principle, and consequently deprived of opportunity for normal socialization through friendships.

The following is a verbatim transcript of the subject's autobiographical outline given in the usual psychoanalytic manner. It provides a clear impression of his diction and cultural status as well as the domestic atmosphere of his younger days.

Well, first of all, one thing you *must* know, is this: at the age of 8 I found out I was illegitimate and from an early age I had thought that I was, because Mother and Dad always used to have big arguments, and Mother always tried to keep me out of it, because Dad always used to say, "he is not mine"—meaning me. I never thought anything of it. Mother used to say, "it's all a pack of lies" but eventually I saw my Birth Certificate, which was a special one for adopted and illegitimate children.

At 5 I started school and enjoyed it. I had friends and Mother was very strict on who I went with, when and where. She would never allow me to go out and play, and I could only play on the way to or from school. She used to take me to school and see I went straight in and very often came to fetch me and take me straight home when I wanted to go out with the boys. Dad was away at sea, and when he came home he gave me some money for the pictures and some sweets, and of course I always liked him more than Mother, and as soon as he went off again, she'd ask me what I did with it. When he gave me some money, he'd never show Mother how much it was, but Mother would follow me upstairs and in a nice kind of way ask me how much it was. He had told me not to tell her but I had to tell her because I didn't know what to expect if I didn't. Often she took the money off me.

Mother never went to a cinema, but would go about once in six months to a theater to see some special show such as a pantomime. Eventually I started stepping out. I was *never* late for school. When I came out of school I often had a game with the kids, but soon they would say "You'd better be going home or your mother will be coming down the street," when she'd give me a bloody good hiding. The other kids didn't like me because of Mother. For instance, once I was the one who kicked a football through a school window and she tried to stand up for me when the headmaster came to the house to demand that I pay for it. The same thing happened once before but then the kids clubbed together and all paid for it, but I was nobody to them. One thing I will say for Mother is that she always took my part before strangers.

When I was seven, Dad decided not to go to sea any more, and got a job, but after about a month he was fed-up and went on the trawlers again. He started right at the bottom and worked right up to Chief Engineer. He used to earn plenty of money, but Mother could *never* save. She was always spotlessly clean—*too* clean because she'd say "Don't go in there!" because she'd just cleaned that room.

At 7½ or 8 I left home one day. I walked around the town all day and had nowhere to go but eventually I met an old friend of Mother who took me to her house. She know what Mother was to me, gave me something to eat, and advised me to go home again. Mother was waiting for me, but gave me food and was glad to see me and *didn't* give me a hiding.

Just before I ran away that day Dad had come home blind drunk and had an argument with Mother. He often came home drunk and one night she wouldn't let him in. So he smashed a window and got in. Then about 2 or 3 days afterwards, Dad was at home, a Sunday, and Dad was reading the paper. Mother was clearing the table, and she suddenly and for no reason picked a milk jug up and threw it at Dad, and split his forehead open, and there I saw Dad bleeding like a pig. I got up and started shouting, "You've killed Dad! You've killed Dad!" and I ran out into the street. Mother told me to shut-up and just lit a cigarette as if nothing had happened. The woman next-door asked what had happened and Mother calmly and without feeling said, "I have just smashed a jug on him." The woman advised him to go to the Infirmary where they bandaged him up and he came home again. He soon afterwards decided to go to sea again. He was always coming back, soon having an argument with Mother and going to sea again.

I knew that Mother refused sexual relations with Dad and that he afterwards went to live with another woman. [Ken says he has known this from about age 11.] I often heard them talking in the next bedroom and would hear Mother saying "No!" . . . She would often go downstairs and sleep in a chair whenever Dad approached her sexually. Later when I was about 14, she told me that when I was born she had not even seen Dad yet, and that I was left in a Maternity Home as she was single and had nowhere to take me. About a year afterwards she met Dad and married him in a registry office after knowing him a *very* short while. She says that as they came out of the registry office she looked in a big mirror there; he also turned round, looked in the mirror and said, "Why the hell have I married you?"

A week later she decided to tell him about me, and he immediately said, "Let's go and fetch him." Later, when the arguments started, he always brought it up. In other words, he adopted me, so he was only responsible for me up to the age of 14, but he has always said that if I need a home he'll look after me, and I know he would.

At school I was never too high, about tenth out of thirty. I was always interested in engines—Meccanos, trains, little cars and so on, and Mother says I used to take things to pieces as soon as I got them and put them perfectly together again. At 14 the headmaster asked what job I wanted and straight-away I said, "Engineering," so he told me he could get me a job but I said I'd get it myself.

During the war Mother always looked after me, for example during the air raids she'd see I was in the shelter. In 1944 Hull was very badly bombarded and we were not allowed to go back home by the police on account of unexploded bombs. One night, without any air-raid warning, bombs just started dropping and I missed being killed by inches. The next day we found that a lot of stuff had been stolen from our home, and that we were bombed-out. We then had to get rooms, and got our furniture into them. Mother got a job in a hotel and I also got a job as a cellar-boy and worked there three weeks, but Mother kept on arguing with the manager about the sort of jobs he gave me. I didn't like it nor did he. So I left and looked for a job which I got with an engineering firm with fairly good pay. After about a year I was *really* good at the job and the foreman developed confidence in me, so when I had been there for 3½ years and got to be 17½ and I was at an age to get into the Navy, they didn't want me to leave, but I joined the Navy all the same.

Apart from the foregoing, the following specific data were obtained: Until the age of 10 he used to sleep in a double bed with his mother. He recalls that on one occasion she said to him, "If you do what you were doing last night again, you'll sleep with gloves on!" Questioned on this, he replied, "I think she meant I was masturbating in my sleep," and then added "because I didn't know enough to have tried doing anything to her at that age. . . ." He declared that he had never masturbated until he was 14 years old. At the factory he got to know certain girls through a friend and had sexual intercourse rather regularly, about every three nights. As he said, "Then I met Joan, but she would never let me. I used to be very much in love with her and thought a lot about marrying her."

During his younger days the mother had had a serious motor accident, was taken to a mortuary, and was reported killed in the local daily paper. She had been thrown through a plate-glass window.

Asked what he considered the most important aspect of his early life, he immediately referred to the lack of freedom and "too many good hidings" which, he said, caused him not to be as interested in school as he might have been.

The father had on several occasions sought a divorce which the mother stubbornly refused. The domestic status has always been a major concern to Ken and is manifestly still his major area of preoccupation, although he has been stationed in South Africa for nearly 2 years. He does not know where his father now is and has received no tidings from his mother for over 6 months.

THE TESTS

The scoring technique here used * is an eclectic combination of those of both Dr. Samuel Beck [7] and Drs. Klopfer and Kelley.[8]

a. Areas are those delineated and numbered by Dr. Beck.
b. The scoring of chiaroscuro follows Beck (that is, V and Y).
c. The scores for animal movement (FM) and inanimate motion (m) are used.

* I am indebted to Professor H. A. Reyburn of the Department of Psychology, University of Cape Town, South Africa, for this system of scoring.

d. C′ is used for the achromatic responses (using black, white, and gray as colors).

e. c is used for texture.

f. R% VIII–X refers to the percentage of responses on the last three plates.

g. P (popular) responses are those listed by Beck.

h. White-space responses are differentiated into those where the S is primary (SX) involving a reversal of figure and background, and those in which S is secondary (XS). An example of the former would be "ballet dancer" for the center white space on Card II, and of the latter "A cat's face" on Card I. (The importance of the differentiation lies in the interpretative significance of SX compared with XS; the former is interpreted as assertiveness, aggressiveness, which can go all the way to negativism, whereas secondary white spaces appear to be related to self-criticism and inferiority feelings.)

i. (f) following upon the score for any response indicates that the subject is *fabulizing* the response; for example, "somebody laughing"; "a man contemplating suicide."

The tests follow in the sequence in which they were administered, and the tabulations of scores are given in Table 8–1 at the end of the series.

TEST 1 (Under normal conditions)

Card No.	Timing		RESPONSE	SCORING
I. 1.	∧	40″	I could see something like an albatross. (dW; d21 "the wing span").	dW F− A
2.	V		Could be the back of a car (W).	W F− Tr
3.	><		(Shakes head) Well . . . like looking at an aeroplane from the tailend (W).	W F+ Tr
4.			I don't think I could say anything else. A poodle dog with very long ears and it's looking at its image in a pond (D2).	E FV− A; Ls
		3′ 30″		

Card No.		Timing		RESPONSE	SCORING
II.	5. 6.	∧>	30″	I see a bulldog and it is leaning backwards . . . as if someone has thrown a piece of meat in front of it and it is frightened . . . its image is in water again (D1; D2 "because it's red and streaky").	D FMV A P D C Fd
	7.	∧V		The head and shoulders of two bears . . . their noses are touching.	D F+ A
		<V 4′ 00″		I can't see anything else in it.	
III.	8. 9.	∧	10″	(Smiles.) I can see two old men here trying to catch a butterfly or something.	D M H P D F+ A P
	10.	V		Two girls kissing. (D1; facial detail very minute.)	D M H
		> 3′ 00″		No, I can't see anything more in this one.	
IV.	11.	∧V	20″	A frog (W).	W F+ A
	12.	∧		Could be a man on a motor-bike, showing his front wheel and boots (W).	W M H Tr; Cg; P
	13.	V><		I see a countryside—a lake, and a dark cloud (D2) coming over a hill (reflected in a lake).	W FVY Ls
		∧ 4′ 00″		That's all.	
V.	14.	∧	10″	A bat.	W F+ A P
	15.			Two girls leaning up against a bush or a tree (D4). (Arms folded looking up into the sky.)	D M H
		2′ 30″		That's all.	

TEST 1 (Under normal conditions)—*Cont'd*

Card No.	Timing	RESPONSE	SCORING

VI. 16.   ∧   20″   Could see a lighthouse. (D8;   D FVYm Ar
"light flashing; it's high; light
because it's dark in the center
and then goes paler.")

17.   V<   A submarine—on top of the   S FV Tr. (Ma)
water. (W; incl. reflection.)

∧   Pause V

18.   Somebody is drilling a shaft   D Fm Imp.
right down into the earth. (D5;
"It's working now.")

4′ 00″   That's all.

VII. 19.   ∧V   10″   Two girls jitterbugging (W).   W M H

20.   <∧   Twins—they are looking at one   D M H P
another and all the time they're
waving at somebody (D2).

21.   >   A girl diving into the water—   D M H
22.   she looks as if she has just   d F+ Rock
banged her head on a rock
(D2) + (d22) or something.

No I can't see anything else.

VIII. 23.   ∧<   25″   A big dog (D1) on some rocks   D F+ A P
24.   (D2 + D5). It's at the side of   D FV Ls
a pool. (Reflection in water.)

V
2′ 00″   Pause. I can't see anything else.

IX.   ∧   Hm! What a mess!
25.   V<∧> 2′ 30″   I can see a man (d4) looking up   D F+ H P
26.   into a tree (D1; CF: "more the   D CF− Bt
color").

∧   I can't see anything in this
really.

Card No.	Timing	RESPONSE	SCORING
27.		Hm! A person's skull with a	ds F+ Dh
28.	4' 00"	sword pushed right through it from top to bottom (d22 and D5).	D F— Sword
X. 29.	∧ 10" ∨ 40"	I can see two men trying to	D M H
30.		climb a mountain (D6 and D9).	D FV Ls
31.	< 2' 10" ∧	It reminds me of the bed of the	W F+ Ma
32.		sea, with all sorts of fishes (D2)	D F— A
33.		and snails (D4).	D F+ A
34.		I see two crabs (D1).	D F+ A P
35.		Something like a crayfish (D8).	D F+ A
	3' 30"	Hm! Nothing else.	

TEST 2 [Actual age level (20), under hypnosis]

Ever see this before? "No." (Amnesia has been suggested.)

I. 1.	∧>∨ 40"	A child of about four years. She's pointing. It's only the head and the shoulders, just down to the waist. The child has hellish big eyes. (D2; d28 the face; D21 the arm.)	D M H
2.	∧	Two people (D2)—they're pulling at a woman (D4). Both are pulling in the opposite way.	D M H
3.		The woman hasn't got a head. (She has a frock on but you can see her legs right through it.)	D F+ H
	>∧	No. I can't see any more.	
4.	<∨	Hm! I can see a bear (D4) in	D F— A
5.		between two rocks (D2).	D F— Ls
	6' 45"	No. I can't see anything else.	

TEST 2 [Actual age level (20), under hypnosis]—*Cont'd*

Card No.	Timing	RESPONSE	SCORING

II. 6.   ∧   55″   I can see a jet-propelled "Fly-   SD F+ Tr
    7.   ing Wing"—a new sort of plane.   D CFm Fi
                       (S5 plus D3; "Jet" because it's
                       red.)

    8.   <V   A ship . . . the upper deck   S F— Tr
                       seems to have blown up.
    9.   (S5 plus D3.)   D CFm Fi

           4′ 50″   No. I can't see anything else.

       >V

III. 10.   ∧   30″   Two people here—they seem to   D M H P
    11.   be frightened to touch this but-   D F+ A P
                       terfly (D3) or something. (They
                       are drawing back from it.)

    12.   This is a governor—a thing you   D F+ Mech.
                       have in a motorcar. A thing that
                       spins around on a spindle, but
                       you can't see the spindle. This
                       (D3) is the governor, two
                       blades that spin around but they
                       are not spinning around now—
                       you would say the machine has
                       stopped. (Looks much like it.)

       V>∧
           6′ 00″   I can't see any more.

IV. 13.   ∧>   60″   This center piece could be a   W F — Imp.
                       drill and the side pieces blades
                       that spin around with it. (W,
                       no motion sensed. "It is station-
                       ary.")

       V<
           3′ 45″   I don't think there's anything
                       else.

V. 14.   ∧   8″   A bat (W).   W F+ A P

    >V<∧
           2′ 10″   No. I think that's all here.

Card No.	Timing	RESPONSE	SCORING
VI. 15. 16.	∧> 18″	An underground tube, like in London. Here (D2) is a train coming into the station here (s30; Motion Fm; "A cross-section picture. Its lights are shining." "Lights" d23).	D Fm Tr. Fi Ds FV Ar.
17.	V<∧	This looks like a body inside a mummy's case (D2).	D F+ H Dh
18.		It's on top of a plateau or hill (D1).	D FV Ls
19.		This looks like a very long narrow passage or tunnel and you can just see the opening at the other end (d22).	d FV Ar.
	5′ 40″	I can't see any more there.	
VII. 20.	∧>V> 90″	This looks like some kind of tool (W) which is used to cut away something down here (i.e. at D6).	W F− Imp.
21. 22.		A Scotch terrier here (D2) and another dog here of which you see only the head and shoulders (d22).	D F+ A d F+ Ad.
	4′ 45″	That's all.	
VIII. 23. 24.	∧> 32″	An animal here (D1)—a tiger or something, on top of the rocks and you have a reflection of it in a river or some kind of stream here.	D F+ A P D FV Ls
	∧ 2′ 12″	No. I can't see anything else in that.	
IX. 25. 26.	∧ 20″	A speed boat here (D8) and it's throwing up waves (D3) on either side of it as it races along.	D Fm Tr. D Fm Waves

TEST 2 [Actual age level (20), under hypnosis]—*Cont'd*

Card No.	Timing	RESPONSE	SCORING
27.		You have a path on the edge of a stream here (D5) and you have a tree over it. (D1; "A tree	D FV Ls.
28.	<	because it's green; there's no particular shape to it.")	D CF— Bt.
	V>∧		
	3′ 00″	No. I can't see anything else in this.	
X. 29.	∧>∧ 60″	All I can see here is some kind of design for wallpaper or something. (W; "seems to be for a nursery with all these colors. It might interest a child.")	W CF+ Art
	2′ 6″	No. . . . That's all I can see here.	

The following factual data were obtained from the subject prior to inducing hypnosis: At the age of 17 he was living with his mother in Britain. His father was away in Mombassa on an assignment in the Merchant Navy. There had been trouble between the parents. The subject was then occupied in a fitter's shop.

TEST 3 (Subject hypnotically regressed to age 17)

Card No.	Timing	RESPONSE	SCORING
I.		∧ "Do you want me to say what I see in all this, or just in pieces?" *Just as you like.*	
1.	15″	I can see a woman here in a shawl (s30).	s F H
2.		There is somebody's head here —laughing about something—I don't know what it is (di in D2 opposite d28).	di F— Hd (f)
3.		Two people here—they are trying to look at something, and they don't like what they are looking at. (Tiny detail of profile facing into s30.)	d F+ Hd; (f)

Card No.	Timing	RESPONSE	SCORING
4.	>V	I can see a girl's face here . . . smiling (d28).	d F+ Hd (f)
5. 6. 7.	V	Here is fat chap here (d28) spinning a coin (d23)—he's trying to make up his mind whether he will jump over this cliff here (d21). (His hand is small projection from d25.)	d M H (f) d Fm Obj. d F V Ls
	< 6′ 00″	I can't see any more here.	
II. 8.	∧ 18″	I can see a fat lady here . . . and another fat lady here. They are arguing the point or something. They have big top-hats on—big high caps. (D2 "Just the head and shoulders." Noses are tiny under details.)	D F+ Hd (f)
9.	>	There's an electric motor here; it hasn't got the armature. Just the casing. One bearing is burnt out (d24); it hasn't got any oil. It's in a hell of a mess. It's an easy job—there's nothing wrong with the casing (D6). A Yankee job. ("Burnt out because it is all red" i.e. at D3.)	D FC Imp. Fi.
10.	V	There's an outline of a man here—a big fattish chap with a bit of a paunch. He's standing and waiting for something. ("Head" at d22; "feet" at D13.)	D M H
11.		Here's a chicken here (d22 the head; the body extends to the horizontal line at the beginning of DS5). There's a chap here—	d F+ A
	<	an elderly chap with a brown coat and flannels. There's a woman too, and he's mad with	
12.		her because she's done some-	di MFC H (f)

TEST 3 (Subject hypnotically regressed to age 17)—*Cont'd*

Card No.	Timing	RESPONSE	SCORING
13.		thing he doesn't like. There's a boy here at the side and he's just watching. (Vague inner details in D1; the man seems to be in some sort of aggressive	di F— H
14.		attitude.)	di F-- H
	8′ 50″	I can't see anything more.	
III. 15.	ʌV 20″	I can see something like a wheel-spanner here (D2). It's bent over a bit, but it is something like a wheel-spanner.	D F— Imp.
16.	<ʌ	Two real old chaps with long noses (D1). ("They are standing with their hands behind their backs or something.")	D M H
17.	>	We've got some kind of a bearing here again (D8). It has an oil-ring in the middle and a groove. It could be a wooden bearing they use on a ship. It's all cracked at one end.	D F+ Mech.
	4′ 45″	I think that's everything.	

IV. (Before receiving the card he says he has to be at work tomorrow at 7:30: "New orders of the foreman." This spontaneous remark reflects his regressed status.)

	ʌ	They couldn't have made any worse a mess of it, now could they? (Smiles.)	
18.	Vʌ 60″	A pair of old boots here, all ragged and torn (D6).	D F+ Cg P.
19.	<	All I can see is a storm at night or something. A big dark cloud coming over the hill. (D7 hill; D2 cloud.)	D Y.V F. Cl; Ls

Card No.	Timing	RESPONSE	SCORING
20.		A chap here on top of a stone or something—trying to do acrobats (D4).	D M H
21.	V	You have a kind of pump here, a three-way pump with 3 cylinders inside ("cylinders" are inner dark lines in D1). It has all these little cooling fins on the sides like on a motor bike.	D F+ Mech.
	<	No, that's all on that.	
V. 22.	∧ 50″	A big moth or bird (W).	W F+ A P
	><∧ 2′ 30″	I don't see much. No. I can't see anything on that.	
VI. 23.	∧> 40″	There's a tank with a gun-turret on it (D4).	D F+ Tank
24.	V	You've got an engine here—like a big electric fan. (W. "It's revolving now.")	W Fm. Mech.
25.	V∧<∧	Hm! Some kind of a lighthouse and the light is flashing on and off. . . . Not exactly a lighthouse, but one of those buoy-ships that's anchored out (W).	W Fm Obj. Fi.
	4′ 30″	Nothing else.	
VII. 26.	∧ 40″	Two baby boys and they're pulling faces at one another or something (D2).	D F+ Hd. (f)
27.	>V	A roundabout on a fun-fair. (W. "It spins around this shaft here" d26, "with chairs or something"—lower edge of D1.)	W F+ Rec.
	<∧ 2′ 45″	No. There's nothing. I can't see anything on this one.	

TEST 3 (Subject hypnotically regressed to age 17)—*Cont'd*

Card No.	Timing	RESPONSE	SCORING
VIII.	∧>	Looks bonny anyway.	
28.	∧ 50″	A Christmas tree. (D8. F.)	D F+ Bt. Rec.
29.		People standing aside it putting toys up (D1).	D M— H
30.	>V∧	An aeroplane here in the middle (s32)—firing a gun (d27).	s F— Tr.
31.		("There is smoke or gas as it fires." d30).	d Fm Fi.
	V∧ 3′ 30″	Hm! Can't make head or tail out of it.	
IX. 32.	∧ 36″	One of these water fountains (D5; FC: "The color makes it look like water. There could be some lights shining through from the bottom to make it look greenish.")	D FCm Fountain
33.	>	A crocodile (D5; d30 the head).	d F— A
	∧ 2′ 55″	No, nothing on this one.	
X. 34.	∧ 15″	A rabbit . . . a rabbit looking out from behind some bushes (D5 and D4).	D FV A
35.			D CF— Bt.
36.	<	A cat lying down (d21).	d F— A
37.	V	Two men fixing the wires on a telegraph pole. (D8 and D24.)	D M H
38.			d F+ Obj.
39.		A man hanging from two pieces of rope (D5 and D4).	D M H
40.			d F+ Obj.
	<∧ 3′ 15″	No, that's all on that.	

Immediately after the test he looked at the clock and commented with manifest concern that it was 11:30 P.M. Thereupon the following conversation took place, with the subject still under hypnosis and at the regressed age level.

Does the time matter? Yes, because of my mother.
What is your mother going to say when you get home? She'll meet me at the door and I'll get a bloody good hiding! (Smiles.)
When last did you have one? Hm! About four hours ago!
What about? Because I didn't come straight home from work. I went to see my mate and seems she didn't like it.
Where's your dad? Away in Mombassa.
How does your mother feel about it? Indifferent.
How long has he been away? Now? About a month or six weeks.
Is she unreasonable at times? At times!
Wouldn't you like to get away from home? I intend to.
Where do you intend going? Join the navy. Definitely!
Do you think there'll be big trouble tonight when you get home? I'm sure of it. . . . But I couldn't worry.
Are you looking forward to seeing your dad again? Yes, but I don't know when.
How does he feel about your mother lately? He doesn't!
Was there trouble before he went away? Yes. That's the reason why he went.
What happened? Oh, Mother told him off about something. She argues the point about the slightest thing. One cannot expect him to keep quiet.
What do you think about it? I don't know what to think. But I think Dad's done the right thing by going away. Maybe that will teach her a lesson.
How do you feel about it? Mother knows.
What? She knows I like Dad, and that I'm not so fond of her.

TEST 4 (Subject hypnotically regressed to age 14)

Card No.	Timing	RESPONSE	SCORING
I. Oh yes, I see what you mean by "ink blot" now. (Note amnesia)			
1.	∧ 25″	Like you have at school—a desk for books on either side (de21).	de F— Voc.
		Is that all? (*Just whatever else you may see.*)	
2.	>∧	This is a big bird. (Upper half of card only.) It's got big claws (D1).	d F+ A

TEST 4 (Subject hypnotically regressed to age 14)—*Cont'd*

Card No.	Timing	RESPONSE	SCORING
3.	>∧	A sailor, just his head and shoulders—this pale gray. (Gray detail adjacent to s29, left side. A profile.)	d F— Hd
	3′ 45″	That's all I can see.	
II. 4.	∧V 60″	Pause. Two animals here (D1) like wolves . . . and a sunset or something behind them (D3) ("sunset because it's red and because of these rays from it" d25).	D F— A D CFVm Fi
6.	<	A face of a woman here (de ot d21) and her nose is bleeding (at d26).	de CF+ Hd; Bt
	2′ 38″	That's all.	
III. 7.	∧ 25″	Two men . . . looking at something (D1).	D M H P
8.	V	Two women here having an argument (D4). (Because this little white part makes me think of looking daggers at each other; like a flash of white from each other's eyes. i.e. s in D8. Heads only.)	Ds Fm Hd Fi (f)
9.	>	Fish there (D5) . . . and one here too (homologous area).	D F+ A
10.	V	A butterfly (D3; E).	D F+ A P
	4′ 5″	That's all.	
IV. 11.	∧ 12″	A tortoise. (W; Head at D3; legs are D4 and D6.)	D F+ A
	1′ 15″	Nought else.	

Card No.	Timing	RESPONSE	SCORING
V. 12.	∧ 18″	A bat (W).	W F+ A P
13.	1′ 30″	A policeman's helmet here (d30).	d F+ Cg
VI. 14.	∧ 30″	The bar counter with the pumps on for pulling beer. (W excluding flared portion at top; D1 the counter and D11 the pump.) (At this age S was working in a public bar. Cf. Also next response.)	W F+ Voc.
15.	∨ 2′ 5″	A tap for a barrel. (W; this (D8) goes into the barrel.)	W F— Voc.
VII. 16.	∧> 60″ ∨ 1′ 55″	A dog (D2; F only).	D F+ A
VIII.	∧	(Asks: "Where's this rig from?" Referring to his naval uniform. I reply that he had tried that on for a fancy-dress party. He asks. "Which one?" I tell him that there is to be a fancy-dress party and he is going as a sailor. This appeared to satisfy him.)	
17.	∨ 3′ 00″	Looks like a bowl with a big flower in it—like a big rose. (W; D2 the flower; mostly the shape but also the pink.)	W FC Hh Bt.
	3′ 20″	(The prolonged delay on this plate was caused by his confusion at the discovery that he was in uniform—a fact that he could not reconcile with his level of hypnotic age regression which was prior to his having joined the Navy.)	
IX. 18.	∧ 20″	Looks something like a big flower (W; "an opening at the top, a stem inside it and perhaps the color").	W FC+ Bt.
	1′ 20″		

TEST 4 (Subject hypnotically regressed to age 14)—*Cont'd*

Card No.	Timing	RESPONSE	SCORING
X.	∧V> 1' 45"	I can't see nothing in particular. It's just a lot of colors.	Rejection
	1' 50"		

Shortly after completing the test, he looked at the clock and said spontaneously: "I'd better be getting home now; Mother will be waiting on the doorstep to lather me because I'm late."

TEST 5 (Subject hypnotically regressed to age 11)

Card No.	Timing	RESPONSE	SCORING
I. 1.	∧> 45"	A pig (D2; d21 are "its long ears").	D F+ A
	∧	I can't see no else.	
	1' 58"		
II. 2.	∧ 22"	It looks like two dogs (D1).	D F+ A P
	V<∧ 1' 51"	That's all.	
III. 3.	∧>∧ 65"	A face here (s between D6 and d22 right side).	s F+ Hd
4.		Two men (D11; *Not* D1; i.e. excluding D5).	D F+ H
	2' 15"		
IV. 5.	∧ 18"	A train (D1) coming through	D F— Tr.
6.		a tunnel (W excl. D1 is "tunnel").	W FV Ar.
7.		And a man up on top of the bridge looking over it (d25).	d F+ Hd
	1' 25"	Nought else.	
V. 8.	∧ 35"	Something like a butterfly (W).	W F+ A P

Card No.	*Timing*	RESPONSE	SCORING
9.		A little girl's face here (d21).	d F+ Hd
	2' 00"	No, no more else.	
VI. 10.	∧ 20"	A big crown (W).	W F— Cer
11.	>V	A man sitting in a big chair (D4).	D F+ H Hh
	2' 10"	That's all.	
VII. 12.	∧ 20"	A woman laughing (D3).	D F+ Hd (f)
13.	V	Another face here, see? (D3)— And a big nose (d29).	D F+ Hd
14.	>V 3' 30"	Two people dancing here (D2).	D M H
VIII. 15.	∧ 20"	A bull's head here (S3).	S F— Ad
16.	>	A dog here (d26+) sitting on top of a rock.	d F+ A
17. 18.		An old woman (d22) tipping a cupboard (D5) into the water here.	d M— H D F— Hh
19.		A dog there (D1).	D F+ A P
	3' 57"	That's all.	
IX. 20.	∧ 22"	Two devils or something. (D3; mouth at d27.)	D F+ (H) P
21.		An aeroplane (D5 + d22).	d F— Tr
	1' 35"	That's all.	
X. 22.	∧ 15"	A little dragon here (D7)—also there (homologous area).	D F— A
23.		Two funny fishes here (D8)— with four legs.	D F— A
24.		And crabs here (D1).	D F+ A P

TEST 5 (Subject hypnotically regressed to age 11)—*Cont'd*

Card No.	Timing	RESPONSE	SCORING
25.		And seaweed (D10), because it's green; (CF).	D Cf Ma
26.		Some more little fish here (D2; F only).	D F— A
27.		A big cup here (s29) with the top on. ("Like those silver cups for prizes.")	s F Rec.
28.		And a castle (s surrounded by D9 and D6).	s F+ Ar.
	3' 21"	That's all.	

TEST 6 (Subject hypnotically regressed to age 8)

I.	1.	∧V 4' 00"	A big Cheshire cat—its face—he's smiling and showing his teeth (Ws).	Ws F+ Ad (f)
	2.		The whole lot looks like a spinning top. (Query: "Yes, it's spinning now.")	W Fm Rec.
II.	3.	∧ 50"	A big face here, real big eyes (s30) and he's got his mouth (S5) open.	Sᵈ F— Hd
	4.		A little dog here (D1) begging. And another here.	D FM A P
	5.	V<V	Two men looking at one another (D2; position only. Not M.)	D F+ Hd
		2' 38"	Nothing else.	
III.	6.	∧V 1' 20"	Two girls here (D4 and D11)	D F+ H
	7.		and a mask (D8) between them. (Noses inwards, viz. tiny projection from D4.)	Ds F+ Mask

Card No.	Timing	RESPONSE	SCORING
8.		Two birds falling out of a tree or the sky.	D Fm A
9.		Two men with big noses and a long neck (D11; N.B. Legs are d30, NOT D5).	D F+ H
	3' 30"		
IV. 10.	∧ 30"	Reminds you something of a little man; with a hunchback or something like that. (W; excl. D1. Hunchback "because he's bowing forwards.")	W M H
11.	V>	A crocodile (D1) moving out of some bushes.	D FM— A
12.		("Bushes" also on account of shading. Hence FY.)	D FY Bt
V. 13.	∧V< 30"	A gun (D1) on top of a hill	D F— Imp
14.		(D4; vista).	D FV Ls
15.	V 1' 14"	A bird (W).	W F+ A P
VI. 16.	∧ 28"	Looks like a knife (D5).	D F+ Imp
17.	2' 10"	Like a ferry boat (W).	W F— Tr
VII. 18.	∧ 30" V 1' 15"	Two rabbits (D1 and D5 "ears").	D F+ A
VIII. 19.	∧> 55" 1' 38"	A sheep's head here (D2)—I think that's what it is.	D F+ Ad
IX. 20.	∧ 35"	An old man (D4) carving a big wooden statue—a big face, here (D1).	D M H
21.			D F+ (Hd) Art.
	>V∧ 1' 50"		
X. 22.	∧V> 1' 40"	Some rocks here (D9) like steps —leading up to a statue of a lion (D6).	D FV Ls
23.			D F— (A)

TEST 6 (Subject hypnotically regressed to age 8)—*Cont'd*

Card No.	Timing	RESPONSE	SCORING
24.	2' 30"	And a person lying down here (d36). ("He's resting on his chin and has a peak cap on.")	d M H

TEST 7 (Subject hypnotically regressed to age 5)

I.	1.	∧ 10"	A big cat (Ws; head only).	Ws F+ Ad
		∨ 1' 30"	There ain't anything else.	
II.	2.	∧>∨ 1' 15"	A dog . . . and another dog here (D1, noses at junction adjoining D3).	D F+ A
		∧ 2' 25"	Nothing else in that one either.	
III.	3.	∧ 5"	A butterfly (D3; F).	D F+ A P
	4.	∨	A snowman. (Inner white space; "because he's white.")	s FC' Rec.
		1' 57"	I can't see anything else in that.	
IV.		∧∨>∨∧ 2' 18"	I can't see anything on this one.	Rejection
V.	5.	∧ 10"	A butterfly (W).	W F+ A P
	6.	>∨	A man's head (D4; "nose" at d21).	D F+ Hd
		∧< 1' 35"	Nothing else in that.	
VI.	7.	∧ 25"	A big carriage with big wheels (D1).	D F+ Tr.
	8.		. . . and a big stick on top.	D F− Stick
		1' 25"	I can't see anything else.	
VII.	9.	∧ 12"	A man's face here (D3).	D F+ Hd

Card No.	Timing	RESPONSE	SCORING
10.	>V	A dog's head (D1).	D F+ Ad
	2' 5"	Nothing else there.	
VIII. 11.	∧V 54"	A ship (Ws).	Ws F+ Tr
	1' 25"	That's all.	
IX. 12.	∧ 16"	Like a fountain. (W; "because it's all colored and it is spouting.")	W CFm Fountain
13.	V	A turkey (D3 and D2).	d F— A
	2' 30"		
X. 14.	∧V 35"	A big flower (W; "because it's pink and it's got a little stalk:" CF).	W CF Bt
15.		Two bees (D7).	D F— A
	1' 35"	That's all.	

ANALYSIS OF RESULTS

The objective of the experimental procedure described was to investigate the hypothecated possibility of obtaining information regarding the subject's personality development and, insofar as *clinical* rather than purely *scientific* purpose may be involved, to ascertain or infer from the accumulated data the period of onset of observed abnormalities. Detailed analyses of the individual tests would be beyond the scope of this paper, and only those features of the material which have illustrative significance relative to the formulated experimental objective will be treated here.

Tests 1 and 2. Differential analysis of the first and second Rorschach tests, namely, under normal conditions and under hypnosis, respectively, reveals that in the latter state there is a decrease in drive (W%), spontaneous creative imagination (M), responsivity to color (R% VIII–X), respect for the objective configuration of the blots (F+%), stereotypy (A%), and conformity (P).

TABLE 8-1   TABLE OF RORSCHACH PSYCHOGRAMS

TEST NUMBER	1	2	3	4	5	6	7
AGE LEVEL	20a	20b	17	14	11	8	5
R – TOTAL	35	29	40	18	28	24	15
APPROACH %	29:66:5	14:79:7	10:50:40	28:44:28	11:60:29	21:71:8	33:53:14
SEQUENCE	REG.	REG.	IRREG.	REG.	REG.	IRREG.	REG.
SX : XS	0:1	2:1	2:0	0:1	4:0	1:2	1:2
NON – F%	51	51	45	33	14	42	20
F + %	77	64	66	67	65	71	75
M	8	3	8	1	2	3	0
W:M	10:8	4:3	4:8	5:1	3:2	5:3	5:0
SUMC	2.5	4	2.5	3	1	0	2
M : C	8:2½	3:4	8:2½	1:3	2:1	3:0	0:2
FM+m:C'+c	1+2:0+0	0+5:0+0	0+5:0+0	0+2:0+0	0+0:0+0	2+2:0+0	0+1:1+0
R% VIII–X	37	24	33	11	50	25	33
CF+C:FC	1+1:0	4+0:0	1+0:3	2+0:2	1+0:0	0+0:0	2+0:0
V+Y	7+2	5+0	3+1	1+0	1+0	2+1	0+0
A : Ad	12+0	5:1	5:0	7:0	9:1	6:2	5:2
H : Hd	9:0	5:0	11:5	1:3	5:5	5:3	0:2
A : H	4:3	6:5	1:3	7:4	1:1	1:1	7:2
A%	34	21	13	39	36	33	47
P	9	4	2	3	5	2	2
(f)	0	0	7	1	1	1	0
TOTAL TIME	34'00"	41'15"	44'10"	23'20"	23'15"	24'00"	19'50"
Avg. T/R	60"	85"	66"	77"	50"	60"	76"
Avg. T/R 1	36"	41"	40"	48"	28"	68"	27"

There is an *increase* in the color sum from 2.5 to 4, and, whereas he made use of color only twice in the first test, under hypnosis he does so four times (on a CF level). There is also an increase in his score for inanimate motion (Fm).

The following conclusions can be drawn from these data:

1. He becomes more intellectually inert under hypnosis (decreased W, M, and F+%).
2. He is less inhibited in his emotional expression (increased use of color).
3. Under hypnosis the subject becomes more egocentric (decreased A%, F+%, and diminution of the most conformable percepts, namely P).
4. Hypnosis brings him closer to his repressed conflicts, his "hostile inner forces," [9] and his sense of frustration (increased Fm).

Regarding the content of his responses in these two tests, the following seem noteworthy: In the first test he projects in R21 "a girl diving into the water—she looks as if she has just banged her head on a rock or something." Could this unusual percept relate to his conception of the motor accident his own mother had when she went headfirst through a plate-glass window? (See case history.)

On Card III he sees in the first test "two old men here trying to catch a butterfly," but in the second test (under hypnosis) the two people "seem to be frightened to touch this butterfly." In the former the attitude is aggressive; in the latter there is a withdrawal. The butterfly (a red one) probably symbolizes a desired object with emotional significance—we may surmise that it relates to his inner need for a warm and tender love object, but that there is an anxiety present in respect to such emotional gratification. This interpretation is supported by his R5 in the first test where he projects "a bulldog . . . leaning backwards . . . as if someone has thrown a piece of meat in front of it and it is frightened." Here, on a more primitive level (FM), is again withdrawal from a desired object—a piece of red meat.

R8 in the second test is "a ship . . . the upper deck seems to have blown up." Perhaps this is a perfectly normal response for a "lower deck *matelot!*"

Test 3. It is in this test where the subject was regressed to the age of 17 (he actually declared his age 16½) that we see the most marked Rorschach signs of deviation from normality. The approach is disrupted (deficient W and D, and an excessive attention to minor details), his sequence is more irregular than usual, there is a significant (although single) response involving chiaroscuro diffusion. (That is, R19, namely, *"All I can see* is a storm at night *or something.* A big dark cloud coming over the hill." The scoring of determinants is YVF, the formal delineation being secondary to the shading factor.) Such a response is an indication of strong "free-floating" anxiety, and this is emphasized by his gray-black shock on this plate (Card IV) revealed by his initial remark: "They couldn't have made any worse a mess of it, now could they?"

There is a seriously deficient animal percentage (only 13 per cent), and his "popular" score is only 2 out of a total of 40 responses. Moreover, his approach shows a deficient attention to normal details. All this points toward a divorce from practical reality: M:C=8:2½, and when *all* the introversive factors (Fm+FM+M+f) are summated and compared with the extratensive factors (C+CF+FC+V+Y+C'+c) we find a strong introversive bias (namely 17:8), emphasizing the *tendency to turn inward* and away from the outer environmental reality.

The W:M ratio is in the wrong direction (namely 4:8, whereas the norm is 2–4:1). Here again we see avoidance.

His nonconformity is also shown in his responses involving the white spaces—a sign of oppositional attitudes. This is more significant than the score of only 2 space details would seem to show, as both are unusual or minor details, and moreover his very first response to the test is one in which the white space is the area chosen.

Although there is so much fantasy living at this age, he nevertheless produces no single FM response despite 8 M and 5 Fm. Where M and Fm are produced in such profusion and FM is absent, it can safely be concluded that *he is repressing his more instinctual drives.*

His outgoing emotional expression also points in the direction of control; in this test he produces 3 FC and only 1 CF—an indication of emotionally mature self-expression, but also indicating inhibition and self-discipline. He dilutes his expression of feeling.

From this Rorschach psychogram it is manifestly patent that he suffered considerable anxiety at the age of 17, and, when examined against the background of the other tests, it is clear that his personality configuration was discrepantly deviant at that age.

An examination of the content of the protocols reveals several interesting features. His introductory query (whether he is to react to wholes or parts) illustrates the amnesia for the previous tests. His comment before receiving Card IV reflects the genuineness or reliability of the regression. Here it should be noted that Ken is by no means a man of many words, and therefore such a spontaneous comment (to the effect that his foreman of several years ago had changed the working hours) carries considerable weight. Both his lack of spontaneity and his regressed status are well illustrated in the conversation reported immediately after the test. This discussion also provides a key to the circumstances with which he found himself faced at that age and which underlie the disturbance reflected in his Rorschach performance.

At this age he was preoccupied with the problem of whether or not to resign his job and join the Navy. Both his mother and his employer pleaded with him not to do so, but he was finding it almost untenable to live with his mother any longer and, moreover, being deeply identified with his father, there was the potent ambition to "follow in Dad's footsteps," so he eventually forced the issue and joined what his father had described as "the finest service in the world." It seems highly probable that his R5 on this test ("a fat chap here spinning a coin—he's trying to make up his mind whether he will jump over this cliff here") related to this major decision with which he found himself faced.

He was working in a "fitter's shop" at that time, and his vocational preoccupation is reflected in E9 where he actually completely loses distance from the card (compare Rapaport [10]). This same interest is found in R17 and R24.

Rivaling in personal importance the problem of enlisting in the

Navy was Ken's concern about the relationship between his mother and foster father. The quarrel between them had resulted in his father's leaving home again. There can be little doubt that the almost entirely subjective inner-detail percepts of R12, R13, and R14—submerged as they are in the chiaroscuro interior of Card II—relate to the domestic scene: "an elderly chap with a brown coat and flannels. There's a woman too, and he's mad with her because she's done something he doesn't like. There's a boy here at the side, and he's just watching." Such inner-detail percepts reveal a need to penetrate into the nature of some anxiety-laden topic, and this single response which is so strongly subjective that it could be considered almost hallucinatory, and which is so strongly reminiscent of projective hypnoanalytical procedures such as the "crystal-gazing" technique that it can be safely inferred this response was possible only under hypnosis, is most revelatory of the emotional setup then obtaining.

Test 4.   The Rorschach test performed at the hypnotically regressed age of 14 also shows considerable anxiety; *he reacts to this anxiety with constriction.*

The anxiety is reflected *inter alia* in neurotic shock in the face of the strong colors of Card X, to which he reacts by complete rejection: "I can't see nothing in particular. It's just a lot of colors." (Note the diction which reflects his less mature grammatical control.)

The constrictive defense against anxiety is seen in his underproduction (R-total only 18), the approach shows very deficient attention to D and emphasis on d, and this is the only test in which he evades the problem by turning to the auter edge of the blots (de). There are only 1 M, 0 FM, and 2 Fm; he is repressing natural basically instinctive reactions, as well as his more mature inner promptings. He constricts himself when faced with the all-color plates (R% VIII–X only 11 per cent) in which he produces only 2 responses both unusually controlled for a 14-year-old, namely FC, and the content is a perseveration (both to Cards VIII and IX he responds with a "flower" in which the form dominates). This is also the only test in the series in which he shows an intrapsychic constriction, a lack of self-confident assertion, revealed in his 3 human details to 1 whole human form. Sixty-seven per cent of his responses in this test are produced by the formal characteristic alone, indicating his constrictive crude control.

Examination of the content of the protocols is again most illuminating: Again at the beginning of the test he responds to the instructions with a remark which reveals his amnesia for previous performances: "Oh yes, I see what you mean by 'ink blot' now." His regressed interests are reflected in his very first response where he perceives "a desk like you have at school," and on Card VI he projects two reactions relating to his erstwhile occupation as an assistant in a public bar, namely, "a bar counter with the pumps on for pulling beer" and "a tap for a barrel."

His confusion upon arriving at Card VIII when he became aware of being dressed in naval uniform also indicates his regression. This point is stressed, as the validity of the entire experimental procedure depends upon the reliability of the regression. In this connection his spontaneous remark after the experiment, when he looked at the clock and said, "I'd better be getting home now; Mother will be on the doorstep to lather me because I'm late," also supplies positive evidence of his regression.

It was at this age that his father struck his mother in the face on an occasion. Could the woman with the bleeding nose in R6 relate to this experience?

His conception of women as querulous creatures is projected in R8 where he produces "two women here having an argument"—the minute white space in D8 representing their "looking daggers at each other."

In summary, there is much disturbance reflected in this test. At the ages of both 14 and 17 we see Rorschach indications of anxiety and maladjustment. *At the age of 14 he defends himself by means of constriction; at 17 he has turned inward.*

Test 5. The most important aspect of this test, the subject having been regressed to the age of 11, is that the constrictive process noted previously in the analysis of Test 4 is already marked at this age.

His coarctative defense can be dated around this age, as he produced a non-F score of 42 per cent at the age of 8, whereas the same score here is only 14 per cent. There is also some avoidance at this age (W% only 11 and emphasis on d, namely 29 per cent where 9 to 10 per cent would be nearer normal).

His hypersensitivity to the color plates (50 per cent of his responses are found in the last three cards here) does not lead to active use of color. His sum C is only 1, consisting of a single CF response. Whereas at the age of 14 he contracts in the face of the brighter emotions (only 11 per cent responses on the all-color plates), he reacts to these at the age of 11 with a profusion of formal reactions (12/14 pure F). Moreover, he produces 4 white-space (or "negativistic") answers in this test, and all of these are on color cards—3 on the all-color plates and 1 on Card II involving the bright-red areas.

The content throughout is most unsophisticated and what one would expect at the 11-year level.

Test 6.   Regressed to the age of 8, his Rorschach performance begins to approach normality. But for the complete absence of emotional expression (C sum is zero) and the somewhat deficient responsivity to the bright color cards, this test is reasonably normal. Here he produces 2 FM; *it is after this age that he became alienated from his instinctual life.*

The content is what one would expect. His very first response at this age on the test is "a big Cheshire Cat—its face—he's smiling and showing his teeth." When subsequently questioned whether he had read *Alice in Wonderland* he said: "Yes, when I was about seven or eight."

Test 7.   This test seems typically 5-year-old. The content is childish, the primitive crude control (F%) is about what should be expected (namely 80 per cent), the responses are to a large extent stereotypical animal forms (A% is 47), M is entirely absent, and he only produces 2 human details and no whole human forms. His rejection of Card IV is probably due to the difficulty this blot presents for a 5-year-old.

His performance is generally normal for this age level.

PSYCHOGENESIS

1. Non-F% : There is a developmental progression toward greater emotional spontaneity.

2. F+% : The form-quality level remains reasonably constant; his ego stability shows very little fluctuation.

3. M : There is a gradual increase in M potential.

4. C sum : Remains constant at a low level: he has always been rather inhibited in his emotional expression.

5. FC:CF : His development in respect to emotional adjustment to the social environment has been retarded. (This should be expected in view of his case history, Ken having been isolated in his childhood from the company of other children.) At 14 and 17 he showed signs of a more mature emotional adaptation, but at 20 he has regressed to a more egocentric level.

6. FM : After the age of 8 he repressed his more childish attitudes and more primary drives.

7. V : There is an increasing introspective preoccupation revealed in a gradual increase in his "vista" percepts. This may indicate that he has developed insight into his anxieties and brought them into rational perspective.

SUMMARY

A series of Rorschach tests were administered to a 20-year-old man at various hypnotically regressed age levels, namely 20, 17, 14, 11, 8, and 5. This procedure rendered it possible to trace his psychogenetic development and to determine at what ages he was most disturbed in his adjustment, how he has reacted to his anxieties, the nature of his ego defenses at various periods, and the time of onset of libidinal repressions.

It is postulated that this procedure could contribute materially toward the clinical problem of briefer psychotherapy.

REFERENCES

1. Alexander, F., and French, T. M.: *Psychoanalytic Therapy*, The Ronald Press Company, New York, 1946.
2. Wolberg, L. R.: *Hypnoanalysis*, William Heinemann, Ltd., London (Grune & Stratton, Inc., New York), 1946.
3. Wolberg, L. R.: *Medical Hypnosis*, Grune & Stratton, Inc., New York, 1948.
4. Watkins, J. G.: *The Hypnotherapy of War Neuroses*, The Ronald Press Company, New York, 1949.
5. Rapaport, D., and Schafer, R.: "The Rorschach test: a clinical evaluation," *Bull. Menninger Clin.*, Vol. 9 (3), May, 1945.
6. Erickson, M. H., and Kubie, L. S.: "A successful treatment of a case of acute hysterical depression by a return under hypnosis to a critical phase of childhood," *Psychoanalyt. Quart.*, **10:**592, 1941.
7. Beck, S. J.: *Rorschach's Test*, Vol. I, Grune & Stratton, Inc., New York, 1944.
8. Klopfer, B., and Kelley, D. M.: *The Rorschach Technique*, World Book Company, Yonkers, N.Y., 1946.
9. Mons, W.: *Principles and Practice of the Rorschach Personality Test*, J. B. Lippincott Company, London, 1948.
10. Rapaport, R.: *Diagnostic Psychological Testing*, Vol. II, Year Book Publishers, Inc., Chicago, 1946.

CHAPTER NINE

Time Distortion in Hypnosis

Editor's Note

It has been said, too positively, that all of the phenomena of hypnosis had become known more than a century ago. It has remained for Dr. Linn F. Cooper to demonstrate otherwise. In the following chapter he reports a most unique experiment where he found that, under hypnosis, a young woman could produce some amazing results in accelerated mental activities owing to a great alteration in time perception. She was able greatly to transcend her normal mental capacities in a contraction of elapsed time.

Cooper's initial article was published in April, 1948, and is reprinted here in full. It concerns a single subject. Hence, the test left uncertainty as to whether the results were an attribute of hypnosis. It was possible that the subject happened to possess some unusual ability within herself which permitted such a distortion of time perception. Collaborating with Dr. Milton H. Erickson, Cooper later set out to check his results through more extensive experiments. Using six more subjects, the original findings were fully confirmed. Their report, supplementing the first one, was published in the winter of 1950. A digest of this article follows the original one.

Other experiments have been made as to time and hypnosis, but these have been as to the appreciation of the lapse of time. The subject was given a posthypnotic suggestion to the effect that some certain action would be performed a definite number of minutes later, perhaps in the thousands. Cooper's effect was to slow the subject's perception of time so that as much was accomplished in a second as ordinarily could be done in a minute.

Dr. Cooper is a physician residing in Washington, D.C.

Time Distortion in Hypnosis*

By LINN F. COOPER, M.D.†

Despite the fact that time perception is one of the most basic of human experiences, it is subject to wide variations. The commonest of these is observed in the dream, where the subject may experience many hours, or even days, of dream life in the course of but a few minutes of solar time. Another instance of the distortion of time perception is found in cases where persons in danger have related how the scenes of their life passed slowly before their eyes in a matter of seconds or minutes. Such experiences are encountered by near-drowning persons or those having falls. Time passes more rapidly for the aging than for the young, and certain drugs, notably marijuana, are said to alter time perception. Disorders of time modality as a personal experience are found in organic brain lesions, the psychoses and psychoneuroses, delirium, and toxic states. Pleasure may shorten the sensation of time, and pain increase it. "Time flies on Love's wings," and yet, "The watched pot never boils."

The following studies were begun in an attempt to determine whether or not time sense could be deliberately distorted in the hypnotized subject, and, if so, whether the subject could utilize his "slowed" time by engaging in mental activity. As will be seen, an affirmative answer was obtained in both instances.

ABBREVIATIONS AND DEFINITIONS

W.T.—world time—solar time as measured by watch or metronome.
P.T.—personal time—subjective, experiential, or psychological time.

* Reprinted by permission from The Bulletin, Georgetown University Medical Center, 1 (6): 214–221, 1948.
† 2222 Q St., N.W., Washington, D. C.

E.P.T.—estimated personal time—estimate, by the subject, of the length of an interval of his experiential time.

S.P.T.—suggested personal time—a time interval suggested to the subject under hypnosis as in, "There will be ten minutes between the two signals," or, "You will have ten minutes for this."

A.T.—allotted time—the time, in world time, that is allotted to a test by the operator. It is not told to the subject. Thus, it may be suggested to the subject that he will have 10 minutes for a problem, while the actual interval between signals is only 10 seconds.

D.R.—demonstrated rate—in the counting experiments the subject was frequently asked to demonstrate, by counting aloud, the rate at which he counted hallucinated objects. This was done both during trance and posthypnotically. In the former instances the subject had finished the test and was presumably not in a phase of response to suggestion.

(D.R) (E.P.T.)—demonstrated rate multiplied by estimated personal time—a product used in the counting tests. It indicates the count that would be reached if the subject counted at the demonstrated rate for a period equal to the estimated personal time.

A description of a test will illustrate the use of these terms. Example:

The following suggestions were given:

"You're back on the farm and are going to churn some butter.

"Tell me what you see." [Subject described the scene in some detail. She was sitting on the back porch, with a crockery churn half full of milk. She mentioned the paddle with the "crosspiece on it," and the hole in the top of the churn through which the paddle passes.]

She was interrupted at this point by the observer, who continued:

"Now just stay there for a while, and listen carefully. You're going to churn that milk, and it's going to take you ten minutes, which will be plenty of time. While churning, you're going to count the strokes. I shall give you a signal to start, and another signal, at the end of ten minutes, to stop. Here comes the signal—start."

Three seconds later, by world time, the "stop" signal was given as follows:

"Now stop. The ten minutes are up.

"Now make your mind a blank. Your mind is a blank.

"Now tell me about it. Tell me what you did, how high you counted, and how long you were churning."

She reported that she counted 114 strokes, and churned for 10 minutes. Everything was very real to her. The churning became more difficult toward the end as the butter formed, and this slowed things down. She heard the churning, and had plenty of time. At the "stop" signal the entire scene faded from view.

When asked to demonstrate, by counting aloud, the rate at which she operated the churn, she counted to 60 in 1 minute, adding that toward the end the strokes became slower because of the increased resistance from the butter.

Continuing:

"I'm going to wake you up by counting to ten. You will remember all about this experience and tell me about it."

On waking, she was again asked to give a report. Her story was similar to the above, including the number of strokes counted, the time estimate, and the demonstrated rate.

In this example, then, the world time (W.T.) and the allotted time (A.T.) was 3 seconds, the suggested personal time (S.P.T.) 10 minutes, the estimated personal time (E.P.T.) 10 minutes, and the demonstrated rate (D.R.) 60 strokes per minute.

The product of the demonstrated rate times the estimated personal time (D.R.) (E.P.T.) is 600, yet the subject insisted that she took only 114 strokes, that she counted each stroke individually, and that she was occupied for the full ten minutes. When asked posthypnotically about the discrepancy, she had no explanation to offer.

METHOD

In brief, an inquiry was made into the relations between the "world time" and the "subjective" or "experiential" time involved in various experiences suggested to the hypnotized subject. The "experiences" were listening to a metronome, counting hallucinated objects, and a diverse group of familiar activities. In some cases a time interval (S.P.T.) was suggested; in others, none. An "allotment of world time" (A.T.) was employed in many of the tests.

The subject was a young woman of 36 years, of unimpeachable integrity, and known to the writer for 10 years. She had had a high-school education, and worked as a secretary-stenographer. During the earlier tests she had no idea as to the purpose of the experiment, and she accepted the suggested time intervals as real. Later she was told the truth, and she expressed great surprise. It was her first experience with hypnosis. The experiments were done daily for eight days and were consecutive except for an interval of 1 day between the first and second sessions. Hypnosis was induced 33 times, the trances lasting from 5 minutes to 45 minutes. Induction was very easy, and suggested experiences were clear and "very real." She not only "saw" clearly, but could "hear" conversations and other sounds, and could "feel" things she handled. She was unaware of odors or tastes. Emotions were "felt," sometimes spontaneously, and she was always aware of the passage of time. In comparing her suggested experiences to dreams, she described them as "making more sense," and added: "I lived them, whereas in a dream, I'm more of an onlooker." It was noted that the simplest suggestions caused a rich and detailed hallucinatory production on all occasions. For this reason, simple suggestions such as "You're standing in the street in Memphis," were generally employed, the subject spontaneously supplying details.

Invariably, there was amnesia concerning the trance unless the suggestion was given under hypnosis that recollection would be retained posthypnotically. Such a suggestion was frequently given and is to be inferred wherever the subject is reported to have described her trance experiences while awake.

World time was measured by a stop watch or a metronome.

Personal time was determined by asking the subject to estimate it.

Hypnosis was deep enough to produce amnesia, and catalepsy if suggested, but light enough to permit free discussion by the subject, who lay quietly on a divan with her eyes closed throughout the experiments.

Because of the very nature of the experiments, mathematical

analysis cannot be applied to the results. The tabulation of measurements and calculations is done merely to show general trends.

METRONOME EXPERIMENT

A metronome was started at 1 stroke per second, and the hypnotized subject was told the rate. The suggestion was then made that the metronome was being gradually "slowed down" to 1 stroke per minute. The subject confirmed this apparent slowing. She was then told that she would be given a signal (tap on the forearm) at which time she would start to review in her "mind's eye" some of her school days during the fifth grade, seeing in her imagination the school, the teacher, and her companions. She would do this for 10 minutes, that is, 10 strokes of the metronome, at the end of which time she would be notified to stop.

The metronome was stopped after 10 beats—10 *seconds*, world time—and the subject was waked up. On questioning, the following significant experiences were recounted:

1. The metronome was most certainly "slowed down."

2. A good 10 minutes had elapsed between signals.

3. She had "lots of time" and saw clearly the school and her classmates.

4. She expressed great surprise when told that the metronome had not changed rate and that, actually, her experience had taken only 10 seconds.

Observations similar to the above were repeated on numerous occasions, and subsequent studies showed the following:

1. With the "suggested rate" of the metronome at 1 stroke per minute, the subject, asked to count the strokes aloud, did so at a rate of about 1 every 5 seconds rather than one every 60 seconds.

2. When the "slowed" metronome was stopped without the subject's knowledge, she continued to "hear" it and count the beats.

From this it was concluded that the "slowing" of the metronome experienced by the subject was a hallucination of hearing, and that during this hallucination the actual striking of the instrument was inaudible.

EXPERIMENTS IN COUNTING

There were two groups, an earlier one, Group A, made up of some 15 tests, and a later one, Group B, consisting of 4 tests, which will be considered first. Usually, a group of objects was suggested to the subject, and she was directed to count them.

Group B. The technique employed is similar to that illustrated in the example given in the section on abbreviations. Table 9–2 shows the results of four tests run at one session. The following comments are in order:

1. It is probably quite impossible for the average waking person to count 137 objects, "one by one," in 3 seconds of world time, much less 862 objects. Not only did the subject allege just this, but she insists that she did not hurry. For instance, in counting the cows she "walked around the edge of the field. They were very close together." With the cotton—"I used both hands, and moved the bag accordingly. I picked only the ripe bolls, leaving the green ones alone. Sometimes I stopped and looked under the leaves to make sure that I had not missed any." We have already mentioned how the churning slowed down as the butter formed. It is quite obvious that the subject truly "lived" these experiences.

2. The product (D.R.) (E.P.T.) is invariably larger than the count. In other words, if the subject had counted at the demonstrated rate for the estimated time, she would have counted far higher, yet she insisted that she kept busy throughout. She had no explanation to offer for the discrepancy, nor do we.

Group A. Prior to the above, many tests on counting had been run, but a different form of suggestion and different signals were used. Table 9–1 shows the results of four of these. An example follows:

"You now see a bushel basket of potatoes.

"Now tell me what you see. [Subject here described the scene.]

"When I give you the signal, those potatoes are going to be turned out onto the floor and you're going to count them. Take your time about it.

"I now raise your left arm. It will stay raised until you have finished counting, when it will drop to your side.

"Here's the signal—start counting."

And as the arm dropped, "All right, make your mind a blank. Now your mind's a blank."

The time between the signals was noted and recorded.

The essential difference in the technique is that here, in Group A, no time interval was either allotted or suggested to the subject. She merely counted until the task was finished. Furthermore, whereas the signal to start was given by the operator in both groups, in Group A there was no true stopping signal, although the subject did indicate when she had finished by dropping her arm.

But why is there such a vast difference in rate of counting? It will be noted that in Group B the allotted time (A.T.) was rather short —3 seconds. This figure was chosen because in other tests, that is, taking walks, with a suggested personal time of 1 hour, the task was completed in an allotted time of 5 and 3 seconds. When the allotted time was cut much below 3 seconds, however, the subject reported that she had been interrupted before her hour was up. Now it is of great interest to note that in the Group B tests, 3 seconds of allotted time (A.T.) sufficed, whether the suggested time (S.P.T.) was 10 minutes or 1 hour and 20 minutes. This makes one wonder whether, for a given individual, a suggested experience may not be "lived" within a more or less fixed interval of world time—3 seconds in this case.

We were unable to induce our subject simply to count at a specified rate. In response to the suggestion, "In the ten minutes following the signal, you will count to 800. I'll let you know when time is up," the subject counted merely to 29 in 10 seconds, world time.

Group A included a number of counting tests. Objects counted other than those mentioned were books in bookcases, persons passing in a crowded street, sheep, houses passed while walking or driving, freight cars, sewing-machine stitches, etc. There was almost always a marked discrepancy between the estimated personal time and the number of objects counted in that time. When asked about this, the subject not infrequently explained her slow counting by reporting: "I had to move the potatoes in the top layer before I could count the ones below," or "The cattle got in each other's way at the gate," or, "I had to get down on my knees to count the books on the lower shelves." or "I had to lift the chicks out of the incubator and set them down on the floor as I counted, and that took time." These reports were all obtained while the subject was awake. Special precautions were taken, incidentally, in all the reporting, to make certain that the subject was no unconsciously adding new "experiences" to those she was supposed to be recalling from her trance. On repeated occasions reports taken during the trance were compared with those taken posthypnotically, and there were never any appreciable differences.

TABLE 9–1

Group A	W.T.	S.P.T.	Count	E.P.T.	D.R.	(D.R.) × (E.P.T.)
Counting cows	65 sec	...	664	30 min	36/min	1,080
Counting soldiers	82 sec	...	90	10 min	72/min	720
Counting churn strokes	100 sec	...	115	10 min	76/min	760
Counting cotton bolls	217 sec	...	719	80 min	56/min	4,480
	464 sec		1,588	130 min	240/min	7,040

Average rate of counting (world time) ... count/W.T., 3.4/sec, 204/min
Average rate of counting (subject's time) ... count/E.P.T., 12/min
Average demonstrated rate (world time) ... 60/min

TABLE 9–2

Group B	A.T.	S.P.T.	Count	E.P.T.	D.R.	(D.R.) × (E.P.T.)
Counting cows	3 sec	30 min	137	30 min	60/min	1,800
Counting soldiers	3 sec	10 min	112	10 min	80/min	800
Counting churn strokes	3 sec	10 min	114	10 min	60/min	600
Counting cotton bolls	3 sec	80 min	862	80 min	68/min	5,440
	12 sec	130 min	1,225	130 min	268/min	8,640

Average rate of counting (world time) ... count/W.T., 102/sec, 6120/min
Average rate of counting (subject's time) ... count/E.P.T., 9.4/min
Average demonstrated rate (world time) ... 67/min

W.T.—world time   E.P.T.—estimated personal time
A.T.—allotted time   D.R.—demonstrated rate
S.P.T.—suggested personal time

Notes concerning the counting tests:

1. Where there was no allotted time or suggested personal time, that is, in Group A (Table 9–1), the counting rate in world time was slower than in Group B (Table 9–2), where there was an allotted time of only 3 seconds.

2. As shown by the demonstrated rates, 36 to 76 for Group A, and 60 to 80 for Group B, the subject thought that she was counting fairly slowly. Yet actually she was often "counting" very rapidly, the average rates being 204 and 6,120 per minute for Groups A and B, respectively.

3. She "lived" these experiences, and they were, to her, very real. At no time was she aware of hurrying.

4. On posthypnotic interview she stated that the "counting" and the "thinking" she did during trance differed in no way from normal counting and thinking.

PROBLEMS

In these tests the subject was presented with a problem to consider, and given both an allotted time (10 seconds, world time) and a suggested personal time (10 minutes) for its completion. The following example will illustrate the technique:

"I'm going to give you a problem to solve in ten minutes. After I tell you the problem you will receive a signal, at which you will start working on it. At the end of ten minutes I shall give you the signal to stop. You will have plenty of time.

"Now here is the problem. A young girl is in love with a young man who wants to marry her. However, the girl has an invalid mother who is dependent upon her, and to whom she feels obligated. She hesitates to marry because she does not wish to burden her fiance with her mother, and yet she is very anxious to get married and does not wish to sacrifice her entire life to her mother. These young people want your advice.

"When I give you the signal, you're going to think this situation over from all points of view and afterward tell me what conclusion you came to.

"Here comes the signal—start."

Ten seconds, world time, later she was told, "Time is up. Now tell me about the problem."

The subject reported that she saw and talked to a young man and girl about this, their problem. She discussed the matter at length with them, asking the girl various questions and receiving answers. She suggested that the girl work after marriage in order to support her mother, who, she felt, should not live with the young people but rather with some friend her own age. She did not think that the girl should give up her life to her mother, but on the other hand, she shouldn't shirk her responsibility. She should marry by all means. She talked mostly to the girl. "The boy didn't have much to say."

Her account of this experience was amazing in the fullness of detail and the amount of reflection that it apparently indicated. This was especially surprising in view of the fact that in waking life the subject was not prone to speculate on matters. When told that she had thought the problem through, not in 10 minutes but in 10 seconds, she was astounded.

Numerous other problems were presented from time to time, among them the following:

Should a young girl, daughter of well-to-do parents, seek a job?

What are the relative merits of government and private-industry employment?

Are you in favor of compulsory military training?

What do you think about segregation of the Negro in the South?

In every case the reports gave evidence of careful and thorough consideration, and the estimated personal time interval was always the same as the suggested one. She didn't have to hurry. She always "saw" something, that is, she saw and talked to the young couple; she saw the girl who was discussing the job; she saw a government office building and a factory; in considering the Negro problem, she was watching a group of poor and shabby Negroes in a small Southern town. A fish bowl with names in it appeared while she was considering compulsory military training.

The last test done was given a suggested personal time of 10 minutes, but an allotted time of only 3 seconds. The subject reported that she seemed to be working on it for 10 minutes, and gave a very complete account of her "thoughts."

OTHER EXPERIENCES

All sorts of activities were suggested to the subject, among them the following:

Reviewing previous periods of her life in her "mind's eye"

Listening to a band

Taking walks

Going on picnics

"Reliving" periods of her life

Dreaming

Sometimes she would be told to engage in a given activity for a suggested length of time and to signal by dropping her raised arm, when the time was up. Table 9–3 shows the relation between suggested personal time and world time in some of these cases.

Usually, there was both an allotted time (A.T.) and a suggested personal time (S.P.T.), the interval being designated by signals. Almost without exception the subject's estimate of the interval was the one that had been suggested to her. However, where the A.T. was too short, the estimated personal time would be less than the suggested one "because you interrupted me before the hour was up." This led to a series of "1-hour walks" with gradually decreasing allotted times. "The walks," incidentally, were over the same "route" each time. Table 9–4 shows the results.

In one test the subject was simply told that a band was playing and that she was to listen to it. She was interrupted after 30 seconds and reported that she had been listening for 9 minutes. No time had been suggested to her.

On several occasions dreams were experienced as the result of suggestion. Time in these dreams showed the same sort of distortion that is seen in normal ones. Their duration was indicated by the subject dropping her arm when the dream was over.

TABLE 9-3

Activity	W.T.	S.P.T.	E.P.T.
Walking	65 sec	30 min	30 min
Picnic	130 sec	"all day"	9 hr
Day's activities	115 sec	day	9½ hr
Walking	10 sec	none	30 min

TABLE 9-4

Activity	S.P.T.	A.T.	E.P.T.
Walk a	1 hr	5 sec	1 hr
Walk b	1 hr	3 sec	1 hr
Walk c	1 hr	1 sec	"30 or 40 min"

DISCUSSION

We do not feel qualified to say what the nature of hypnotically induced experience is. What, if any, relation does the "counting" and the "thinking" of this subject, under hypnosis, bear to such activities carried out by her while awake? What is this amazing state of affairs that permitted this subject, "in her mind," of course, but with complete sense of participating, to pick and count 862 cotton bolls in 3 seconds, carefully selecting each one, and occasionally looking beneath the leaves "to make sure that I had not missed any"? We do not know.

We are certain, however, that our subject's sense of time was altered, more or less at the will of the operator, and that in this altered time which he bestowed upon her she had experiences that were very real to her. These, while occurring at a normal rate as far as she was concerned, actually moved incredibly fast according to world time. Furthermore, they were experiences that, to a considerable degree at least, "made sense." This in itself is indeed intriguing and causes one to wonder if, under hypnosis, judgments may not be made, and decisions arrived at, in a mere fraction of the world time ordinarily required. Also, it makes one wish that ideas could somehow be introduced into the human mind with a speed proportional to that of the mental activity of this hypnotized subject.

REFERENCE

1. Schilder, P.: "Psychopathology of Time," *Imago* **21**:261–278; also *J. Nerv. & Ment. Dis.*, **83**:530–546, May, 1936.

(A DIGEST)

Time Distortion in Hypnosis II

By LINN F. COOPER, M.D.

AND MILTON H. ERICKSON, M.D.*

The experiments reported here were undertaken to determine if the findings in the previous research could be confirmed in a further and more extensive series of tests with a group of subjects.

The subjects were divided into two groups, an earlier one of 4, which worked for a period of 7 weeks, and a later one of 2, which worked a little over a week. All except one had a college education. All were much interested in the experiments, cooperative, and eager to improve their performance They were paid by the hour.

Subjects A, B, C, and D were not informed concerning the nature of the problem until the end. With Subjects E and F, on the other hand, this was discussed at the start.

In essence, the experiments consisted in suggesting to the hypnotized subjects that they perform certain hallucinated activities and in studying the relationship between the experiential and the physical time involved. In the majority of tests an allotted time (A.T.) was used. In a few instances the hallucinated activity was explored by means of injected sound signals.

There follows a partial list of the activities used: buying various things, counseling, counting various objects, dancing, dreaming, free association, group discussion, housework, listening to a metronome, listening to music, making decisions, mathematics, painting, sewing, seeing movies and plays, thinking, walking and riding, watching games, writing letters.

Induction of a simple trance state was effected by suggestions of

* 32 West Cypress St., Phoenix, Ariz.

sleep. Posthypnotic amnesia was routinely suggested with the earlier group of subjects but was only partially successful. The later group was told that they could remember the trance experience if they so desired.

As a rule the suggestions were read from cards to ensure uniformity. Timing was done with a stop watch. During trance the subjects lay supine on a bed, with their eyes closed. After a test activity was finished, the subject was asked to report on his experience.

The degree of time distortion and the amount of subjective experience occurring within the experiential time interval depend upon the various factors. Important among these are the absence or presence of an allotted time and its duration, the assigning of an incomplete or a completed activity, and the absence or presence of a suggested personal time and its magnitude.

RESULTS

The following generalizations can be made on the basis of our results.

There is a marked difference between subjects regarding their ability to produce the various phenomena under study. This is to be expected, and it is mentioned here in order to call attention to the fact that the amount of training required is variable within wide limits. Thus, one subject may require only 3 hours' training while another may require 20.

In all cases the reports were simple, narrative accounts of a recent experience.

All subjects showed the phenomenon of time distortion, and all were able to engage in mental activity during the prolonged subjective time intervals. This activity proceeded at a rate considered normal or usual as far as the subject was concerned, yet its amount was greatly in excess of what the world time interval would ordinarily permit.

In all cases, performance improved with practice. All four subjects who worked with the metronome were able to effect marked slowing of the instrument. With two of these, practice was required.

Of the 5 subjects who practiced counting activities during time distortion, 4 achieved satisfactory results. The fifth had difficulty but showed progressive improvement.

All subjects were astonished by the things they did, some of them strikingly so, when informed of the facts.

Sound signals could be introduced into hallucinated experiences in all cases in which this was tried with sufficient care. Their position in the experiential interval corresponded fairly well to that in the world time interval.

By far the most dramatic results were those obtained in the counting experiments.

Initially, a metronome was started at 60 strokes per minute, and the following suggestion was then given: "You now hear a special variable-speed electric metronome striking at sixty strokes per minute. Please listen to it. I'm soon going to slow it down gradually. When it's going very slowly, please let me know by saying 'Now.' "

The metronome, of course, continued at its initial rate of 60. Three of the four subjects who were thus tested reported marked slowing. However, for one of these, the slowing did not always occur.

A few pilot experiments were run in an effort to learn whether our subjects could review for a history examination in distorted time. The results were inconclusive, but it led one of them, a professional violinist, to attempt to review certain pieces and to practice these while in a self-induced trance, using her "special time" for this purpose. Thus, she was able to practice and review long pieces over and over in very brief world time periods, and she found that not only did her memory improve strikingly, but also her technical performance was better. This remarkable result is attested to by her husband, himself a musician.

It is impossible at present to evaluate these reports which, if confirmed, carry important implications for facilitation of the learning process. They suggest at least two possibilities for making use of distorted time in the hypnotized subject. The first is that the memorizing of new material might be speeded up by hallucinating the frequent repetition, either in visual or auditory form, of whatever is to be learned. The second is that hallucinated practice and review be used to aid in the acquiring of new motor skills.

One who hears a number of the reports of the subjects soon becomes convinced of their truth and of the actual existence, for the subject, of the alleged experiences. The subjects were honest individuals, interested in the research, and their waking reports agreed with those given under hypnosis. They all insisted that they did not elaborate. Questions directed to the "subconscious" concerning the presence of falsification were invariably answered in the negative.

For successful "utilization" of experiential time by increased mental activity, it is probably mandatory that the subject be totally unaware of his surroundings and of world time. With some subjects this is difficult at first; with others it is easy.

ANALYSIS OF RESULTS

If we simply assign a completed type of activity to a subject and ask him to let us know when he has finished it, we shall find the following to be true:

1. He will complete the activity.
2. It will appear to proceed at the usual rate.
3. It will probably take less than 3 minutes by world time.
4. It will seem, to the subject, to take much longer.

In other words, there will be definite time distortion, even though the suggestion made no stipulation whatever concerning time. It is thus seen that, in hallucinatory activity in hypnosis, there is apparently an inherent tendency for time distortion to occur.

Another basic consideration is the fact that the subject will try his best to carry out whatever is suggested—to "obey orders," in other words. He will learn somehow to adjust his hallucinated action to the short world time interval.

A third consideration, and a most effective one, is the direct suggestion of a subjective time interval—the use of a suggested personal time (S.P.T.)

Time distortion, as effected in these experiments, is accompanied by a marked increase in the ratio E.P.T./W.T. It is usually accompanied by an appropriate increase in hallucinated activity.

CONCLUSION

The following statements are probably true:

1. The results reported in an earlier communication on time distortion in hypnosis can be duplicated in the majority of subjects. Time sense can be deliberately altered to a predetermined degree by hypnotic suggestion, and subjects can have an amount of subjective experience under these conditions that is more nearly commensurate with the subjective time involved than with the world time. This activity, while seeming to proceed at a natural rate as far as the subject is concerned, actually takes place with great rapidity.

2. Retrospective falsification does not enter into the subject's reports.

3. The continuity of these subjective experiences during distorted time is good.

4. Thought, under time distortion, while apparently proceeding at a normal rate from the subject's point of view, can take place with extreme rapidity relative to world time. Such thought may be superior, in certain respects, to waking thought.

Special Discussion of Psychological and Psychiatric Implications

BY MILTON H. ERICKSON

The discovery or development of every new concept in science poses the difficult question of what will be its eventual significance and application. The findings made in the original study and confirmed by this second report suggest the definite possibility of new, readily available avenues for the examination of those inner experiences that constitute so large a part of life and which are so difficult to study in a rigorously scientific manner. No attempt will be made to offer an elaborate discussion of the psychological and psychiatric implications of these two studies. Rather, a number of them will be mentioned briefly.

Foremost to this writer are the implications of time distortion in the field of psychotherapy. Certainly no one questions the importance of the subjective experiential life of the individual, nor the present unsatisfactory, laborious time-consuming, and unscientific methods of studying it.

What constitutes a subjective reality? Of what seemingly pertinent and irrelevant elements is it comprised? In what way is it integrated into the total life of the person? What self-expressive purposes does it serve for the personality? What determines its validity? How does it differ from a memory, a dream, a fantasy, and from retrospective falsification? In what way is it distorted by present methods of concurrent or retrospective reporting, and how much time does it require? All of these considerations are touched upon either directly or indirectly in this study, and each of them constitutes a significant problem in psychotherapy, to say nothing of psychology in general.

The girl who, in an allotted 10 seconds, subjectively experienced in voluminous detail a 30-minute automobile ride upon which a report could be made with "stills" of the scenes, demonstrated a challenging possibility of a new approach to the exploration of the experiential past of the individual.

The subject who found it impossible to demonstrate in the waking state her experiential behavior in picking flowers because it was under a "different" time limit and work limit, and yet, weeks later in a trance state, was able to demonstrate in actual accord with the previous findings, discloses the possibility of controlled studies of subjective realities.

Delusions and hallucinations have long constituted intriguing problems. They are subjective realities accepted by the person as objective realities. Experimental studies patterned from this and the other similar findings above might lead to a better understanding of pathological delusions and hallucinations.

Theories of learning and memory are constantly in need of revision with each new development in experimental studies in these fields. In this regard the findings pose definite problems for research on learning, memory, and conditioning.

In this same connection one may speculate upon the role of motor functioning in mental learning, since the violinist subjectively experienced the total process of playing the violin, studying the written music, and memorizing it, while lying supine and inactive, and yet demonstrated the actual effects of reality practice.

Time, and its relationship, constitutes a significant element in all psychological functioning, no matter from what school of thought it is viewed. Hence, any study dealing with the element of time itself in psychological functioning must necessarily have important bearing upon every school of thought, and this concept of time distortion offers a new approach to many psychological problems.

A final item of special interest to this writer centers around the problem so pertinent in research in clinical psychology and psychotherapy, namely, the problem of how to create for a subject or a patient a situation in which to respond with valid subjective reality. Certainly, this study indicates the possibility of much more rigorous controlled research with time as an aid rather than a barrier.

To conclude, this writer, in all modesty, since the conception, plan, and organization of this study was entirely original with the senior author, can express the opinion that the experimental findings reported in this paper offer a wealth of highly significant ideas and concepts for extensive psychological research and clinical psychiatric application.

CHAPTER TEN

The Influence of Hypnosis on
Somatic Fields of Function

Editor's Note

Many old-time hypnotic practitioners and a few modern ones have reported that some of the physiological processes of the body can be controlled or influenced through hypnotic suggestion. It has been claimed that these effects can be brought about by direct suggestion as well as by stimulating emotions through suggestion. According to these claims, most of the organs and some of the glands, such as the mammary, can be so influenced. However, there has been an incredible lack of investigation of such important assertions. Yet, experimentation as to some of these matters would present little difficulty.

In the chapters herein on the use of hypnosis in dentistry, it is stated that the circulation of the blood can be regulated and the flow inhibited, at least as to the gums. As a matter of fact, dentists who use hypnosis in dental surgery witness direct proof of this phenomenon, but no attempt has ever been made to verify it in any measurable way.

Such a simple matter to test as the question of whether or not the heart and pulse rate can be controlled has long been a matter of controversy. It has been recognized that suggestion of emotion could cause a speeding up of the heart rate (with or without hypnosis), but it has been stated that direct suggestion cannot cause such a change. In Chapter Eleven van Pelt shows by cardiograms that this is possible.

The present renaissance of interest in hypnosis has been largely confined to its utilization in psychotherapy. Possibilities of beneficial results from direct suggestion in treating organic conditions are entirely disregarded. In medical research it is necessarily standard procedure, when testing the effect of any drug on a disease, to use a control group of subjects who are given only a placebo. It is recognized that otherwise the effect may result from suggestion rather than from the drug or treatment. Usually, some of the control group show a positive effect, sometimes a large percentage being benefited. One would expect this to arouse interest and inquiry, but suggestion is not regarded as legitimate. Its escutcheon carries the bar sinister through its close connection with hypnosis.

Strangely, the nineteenth-century physicians who used hypnosis and treated disease by direct suggestion all reported cures of various organic diseases. The reports of such men as Libeault, Bernheim, Moll, Wetterstrand, Quackenbos, and many others are arbitrarily dismissed as having been descriptions of cases where the diagnosis was in error. The disease must, therefore, have been functional. However, many of these physicians were very competent. Bernheim, for instance, was one of the foremost physicians of his time. He reported having cured by hypnotic suggestion multiple sclerosis and other diseases where there was little question of proper diagnosis. Quackenbos, working in New York in the early twentieth century, claimed to have cured several cases of diabetes mellitus. Liebeault claimed success with anemia, pulmonary tuberculosis, and even lead poisoning. Others mentioned Parkinson's disease and organic paralyses.

If hypnotic suggestion can influence the action of organs and glands, it may be that the old-timers were right in their claims. Certainly the matter is worthy of modern scientific investigation. Research should first concern what functions can be influenced, and then experimental applications to various diseases might be attempted. Medicine has yet to offer cure for some of the conditions reported in the past as relieved by hypnotic suggestion (and also through faith cures), such as diabetes and multiple sclerosis.

Such investigation as to somatic functions affected by hypnosis as has been made has been carried out mostly in Europe. Researchers in the United States have neglected this field. Recently Gorton [1] reported at length, summarizing a long list of such investigations and their results. The next three chapters in this book report some recent experiments in the somatic field. The following paper by Dr. Paul J. Reiter of Copenhagen, Denmark, like Gorton's, summarizes a number of articles, mostly by Europeans. Some of these were also considered by Gorton; others are additional. Reiter's article and Gorton's between them describe practically all research that has been conducted along this line, with the exception of possible Russian experiments.

The results of the tests which Reiter reports are not conclusive, as he points out. However, his method of reporting is so excellent that it is possible to indicate some sources of error, or rather some shortcomings. He not only gives the exact wording of his suggestions (translated into English) but also states the time intervals involved. If these points are correctly given, it is evident that Dr. Reiter hardly made his suggestions strong enough, and failed to repeat them sufficiently. Also, the tests followed one another too closely, so that the subject hardly had time to reorient himself, and the effects of the previous suggestion were not eliminated. If enough time for the experiment could have been allowed, and only one or two tests made at one session, the results might have been much more definite and positive. However, if successful, they would only prove that suggestion of emotion can induce certain reactions. Other than to cause the subject to become more suggestible, hypnosis has nothing to do with the results. Emotions can also be aroused in the waking state by either suggestion or imagination. A comparative study would be needed to judge the results. Whether direct suggestion under hypnosis can cause such changes as were tested should also be a matter of inquiry.

Dr. Reiter is a psychiatrist connected with the Municipal Hospital of Copenhagen. He is recognized as one of the leading authorities on hypnosis and hypnotherapy. As most of the literature on the subject of his article is in German and other European languages, Dr. Reiter was requested to prepare this chapter, and he has spent much time and effort not only in digesting this literature but in the research which he reports.

REFERENCE

1. Gorton, B. E.: "The physiology of hypnosis," *Psychiatric Quart.*, **23** (2):317, and (3):457, 1949.

The Influence of Hypnosis on Somatic Fields of Function

By PAUL J. REITER, M.D.

PSYCHIATRIC DEPARTMENT, COPENHAGEN
MUNICIPAL HOSPITAL, COPENHAGEN, DENMARK

It is a generally recognized fact in principle that, by means of hypnosis, it is practicable, in individual varying measure, to influence both mentally and physically the functioning of any reactive system within the organism. Insofar as the physical phase is concerned, it is, of course, a question of an emotional or sensory influence that partly may affect directly through the vegetative nervous system the individual organs or vegetatively innervated systems of organs. Although it is still limited, the sphere of operations which can thus be affected by hypnosis is very great.

The first phenomena which appear, even under light hypnosis, are the spontaneous tonus and motility changes in musculature. To begin with, every spontaneous movement ceases completely. It is an almost sure criterion of beginning hypnosis that the subject remains lying motionless, though with full, regular, lethargic respiration as the last remaining muscle activity.

Then, varying according to the profundity of hypnosis, all the motor functions, isolated and primitive as well as complicated and undifferentiated, come under the influence of the hypnotist. It is thereby possible to provoke muscular work which the subject is unable to perform voluntarily when awake, and without experiencing fatigue either during or after the hypnosis.

During hypnosis, relaxation may become flexibilitas cerea, which often appears spontaneously, and there may be catalepsy. If the limbs of the subject are placed in an uncomfortable position, they will so remain for a long time, many times longer than would be possible in the waking state. The muscles, for example of an arm, may, without the patient feeling it, be so rigorously tensed that it is like a real ankylosis in the shoulder and elbow joint. This may be illustrated by the old classic "bridge experiment" of placing the subject across two chairs, while he remains so rigid that a heavy weight on his abdomen will not press his body down.

It is possible to provoke paralysis, contractions, limping, and other changes of gait. If a chalk line is drawn on the floor and it is suggested that the subject cannot cross the line, he will walk to it and, as though confronted by a wall, will be incapable of proceeding until the hypnosis is lifted. It is also possible to induce local or universal automatisms, for example, fine or strong tremors, or compulsory movements such as clapping the hands in rhythm.

The motor phenomena which may be provoked through hypnosis are, in principle, realized in conformity with Schiller's body scheme. Thus a hand, an arm, a leg may be paralyzed, but not an isolated ulnaris or peronaeus paralysis. But nothing prevents the artificial provocation, by means of adequate suggestions, of phenomena corresponding to lesional disturbances of the system, such as hemiplegia, motor aphasia, dysarthria, or paralysis agitans.

Quite similarly, one may bring about changes of sensitivity through hypnosis. One may suggest a complete analgesia in any part of the body. Technically, it is easiest to begin with the back of the hand or the lower arm, suggesting increasing coldness of the skin and numbness, and ending with complete analgesia. This may be tested by piercing a fold of the skin with a needle. After the subject has had this experience, anesthesia may be suggested elsewhere. If suggested for one side of the face, the nasal septum may be pricked on one side without it being felt, while there would be reaction to a prick from the other side of the septum.

On the other hand, it is possible to stimulate dissociate hyperesthesia or increased sensitivity to touch, pain, temperature, muscle, or joint feeling, etc. The other senses—smell, sight, hearing, and taste—may be affected in an analogous way. Thus, if a person smells only a glass of water, it may be suggested that he perceives perfume or ammonia.

It is practicable to suggest any sort of hallucination of vision such as color perception, form or object perception, mist sight, double sight, or even absolute blindness. The purely psychological character of this blindness can easily be illustrated by making it selective through the suggestion that some particular person in the room cannot be seen, or that all persons present, except their heads, can be seen ("negative hallucinations").

Complete deafness can be suggested, in which case it is necessary to take measures for an adequate signal to remove it, and one may then fire a pistol immediately behind the subject without his reacting. Correspondingly, a hyperacuity of hearing may be suggested, enabling the subject to hear the sound of a needle dropped on the floor at the opposite end of a large room.

Equally well known is the possibility of hallucinating the sense of taste, suggesting that a piece of potato tastes like chocolate or an apple, or water may be tasted as whisky.

These facts have been observed since the earliest days of hypnotism, and most of them are frequently resorted to in stage hypnosis.

Even more surprising is the influence of hypnosis upon the vegetative nervous system and its functions. This field has been the subject of modern hypnotic research with a series of interesting investigations. Some of these will be cited in brief, for many of them have been carried out in European countries and have not been made available for readers in English.

Baumler[1] observed with a subject that at the beginning of hypnosis there was an increased pulse, and at the same time the subject was excited and restless.

Max Löwy[2] found, in a similar experiment, the same result, though his subject was calm, suggestion reducing the pulse. In the case of a cardiac neurosis with paroxysmal tachycardia, he was able through hypnotic suggestion to reduce the heartbeat to normal value.

Deutsch and Kauf[3] made the following test with four subjects. They were led to perform easy work, awake and under hypnosis, with the suggestion in the latter case that the work would be easy.

Under hypnosis an increased frequency of heartbeat was intermittently experienced. In heavy work, without and under hypnosis, increased heartbeat was experienced in both situations. With suggestion under hypnosis (easy work) with a resting subject, an increase of heartbeat was noted but less than in the case of real work. Increased frequency of pulsation in the case of easy work is ascribed to expectant emotion and disappears under suitable hypnotic suggestions. With heavy work the increased frequency is ascribed to organic factors. With five cardiac neurotics, these authors were able to provoke increased pulsation through suggestions and post-hypnotic suggestions of emotions.

Paul Astruck [4] was able, by means of adequate suggestions under hypnosis, to cause both an increase and a decline of the pulse frequency. With increase, double P dents, glimmer, or flare would appear on the electrocardiogram; with retardation there was a disappearance of P dents or bigemini (pulse marked by two beats close together followed by a pause).

Cramer and Wittkower [5] found with eight subjects frequency increases of up to 60 beats per minute during hypnotically suggested emotional states. There were no electrocardiographic changes. In some cases an X-ray examination showed slight enlargements of the heart under hypnotically stimulated emotion.

Walther Bier [6] finds that the pulse rate falls under hypnotic suggestions about tranquillity and rises moderately after suggestions about agitation. On the electrocardiograms are found P.R.T. somewhat higher in the case of suggestions about delight.

Jenness and Wible [7] investigated the difference between heart action during sleep and hypnosis, using four men and four women. During sleep there was lower pulsation than during ordinary rest; under hypnosis the same frequency as during rest without sleep. Electrocardiographic changes were not evidenced during either sleep or hypnosis.

Berthold Stokvis [8] tested 10 normal and 10 hypertensive subjects and found a slight decline at the start of hypnosis and an increase to normal after awakening. Suggestions of tranquillity gave a slight decline, whereas suggestions of anxiety produced an increase of up to 52 beats per minute. Suggestions of wrath, pain, or work gave smaller increases than those of anxiety. Direct suggestion of palpitation produced no effect on the pulse.

Kleinsorge and Klumbies [9] made a thorough and careful investigation of a series of suggested emotions and sensations upon pulse and electrocardiogram (coldness, heat, anxiety, delight over fulfillment of wishes, delight over expectations of fulfillment, pain, love, fury, disgust, yearning, bracing oneself, and fright). The electrocardiograms were not definite and clear. The figures for pulse beat, however, were in almost all cases more or less influenced by the varying emotions, strongest in those of heat, coldness, disgust, and fright, though in no case remarkably great. The records of the tests are thorough, and one can follow collaterally with the curves the results of the verbal suggestions, which are quoted verbatim.

In their work, Deutsch and Kauf also reported the effect of hypnosis on blood pressure. By suggestion of work, a slight increase was seen, smaller in the case of easy work. In Cramer and Wittkower's test they also studied changes in blood pressure and under emotion registered an increase up to 40 mm. In the Bier experiments, in testing 14 subjects under various conditions, a slight decrease in blood pressure was seen just after hypnosis began, though sometimes there was no change. Suggestion of anxiety produced a slight increase, the maximum being 15 mm.

In the experiments of Jenness and Wible, which included work on respiration under hypnosis, there was a tendency toward less frequency and amplitude during sleep, but no difference in respiration between ordinary rest and hypnosis.

A number of authors have examined the influence of hypnosis on the stomach and digestive processes. Heyer [10] made mock feeding tests under hypnosis and by posthypnotic suggestion. The stomach was emptied, and then pretended feeding suggestions were given for 2 or 3 minutes. The results were quantitative according to the nature of the suggestions (of broth, bread, milk), and there was a rather strong secretion of gastric juice, increasing, dependent on the suggestion for 25 minutes, then decreasing again. The secretion was strongly peptic, the acid content varying.

If hypnosis was repeated at short intervals, the secretion became smaller but increased again strongly if there was a 1-week pause between inductions. If emotions of delight or fright were suggested following the simulated feeding, a decrease of secretion was observed. Atropine injection before and after the suggestions caused a reduced secretion and a decline of acidity. Pilocarpine injection caused increased secretion regardless of mock feeding.

Heilig and Hoff,[11] like Heyer, made simulated feeding tests. If the hallucinatory feeding was accompanied by suggestions that the subject liked the food, an increase of quantity of gastric juice as well as its acid content was observed; in the opposite case there was reduced quantity and less bile. The oscillations were generally small. With X-ray examination after a contrast meal, increased motility was observed if it was simultaneously suggested that it was savory. Disgust suggestions caused reduction in peristaltic movement.

Langheinrich[13] examined the stomach and duodenal function after hallucinatory suggestions of eating butter. He found as a result a rather strong secretion of pronounced peptic gastric juice. With suggestions of eating broth, insofar as the duodenum was concerned, after the lapse of a half hour there was a small secretion of bile and slight amount of trypsin.

Luckardt and Johnston[12] produced increased acidity in a 21-year-old male subject, after Ewald's test meal, by hypnosis alone with special suggestions. With hypnosis alone a weaker secretion appeared than after the test meal. A suggestion of eating Ewald's test meal during hypnosis provoked a secretion in quantity and composition similar to that which succeeds the actual test meal without a primary fall in the secretion curve, despite the fact that no real consumption of food took place. The suggested stomach secretion lasted 1 to 2 hours, and a repetition of the feeding suggestions produced another increase as before. Suggestions of fullness gave no further changes in the curve of secretion.

Wittkower,[14] in 20 conformable experiments, found increased secretion of bile when delight, grief, or anxiety was suggested, but a reduced secretion if annoyance was suggested. The quantity of bile remained unchanged when atropine was given. He believes the cause of the reduced bile secretion in the case of annoyance was because of spasms in the bile ducts, and he ventures the surmise that psychical factors play a part in bowel obstruction and formation of biliary calculus (stones).

Delhaugne and Hansen [15] used a single subject and tested the gastric and duodenal secretion during mock feeding suggestions, after first draining the stomach. Suggestions were given of eating biscuits spread heavily with butter, chocolate, marchpane, and "schnitzel." This produced a strong increase of acid, pepsin, and lipase in the stomach secretion. In the duodenum there was a corresponding increase of trypsin, lipase, and diatase. Everything considered, they believe suggestions about food produce a quantitatively as well as qualitatively corresponding increase as with a real meal.

The kidney functions during hypnosis have been examined by Heilig and Hoff.[16] Ten subjects were used. Their weights were taken before and after the experiments and diuresis, specific gravity, sodium chlorine (Volhard), and total phosphate (Neumann) were determined. There were three series of experiments on each subject, each without suggestion and with suggestion of inclination and disinclination, respectively. A somnambulistic state was obtained with each subject. The suggested disposition was continued for 2 to 4 hours, and urine samples were examined every half hour. The preceding day, 1,500 cc of liquid and food containing 8 gm of sodium chlorine were given.

The authors ascertained that a hypnotically suggested feeling of inclination caused retention of water, chlorine, and phosphorus. The feeling of disinclination gave the opposite effect, and corresponding changes of weight were proved.

Marx [17] tested subjects after 12 hours of fasting and abstinence from liquid. The specific gravity and quantity of the morning urine were measured just before hypnosis was induced. Before, during, and 2 to 3 hours after the trance, hemoglobin examinations were made.

Under hypnosis suggestions of drinking were given, though the subject held only an empty glass. A half hour later the subject was awakened with amnesia suggested. Twelve experiments gave uniform results, showing an increase of urine (400–500 gm) and a fall of specific gravity from about 1.025 to about 1.002. Simultaneously, a few moments after the suggestion, there was a hemoglobin fall with secondary increase. After the hypnosis there was again a fall and increase. The subject felt a spontaneous thirst after the drinking-suggestion experiments.

Control tests with hypnosis without the suggestion of drinking, but with suggestion of anxiety, produced no changes.

Marcus and Sahlgren [18] made pharmadynamic tests by injection of adrenaline, pilocarpine, and atropine on three hypnotized subjects. It was possible to provoke a weakening of the reactions through suggestion, except after pilocarpine.

Glaser [19] examined the alimentary leukocytosis with five persons. Under hypnosis, leukocyte counting was made until he found fairly stable figures. Suggestions of eating a meal were made, with a pause until the leukocyte figures had reached the starting values. Thereafter, a real meal was given with subsequent leukocyte counting. As a rule, a rise of the leukocyte figures was ascertained with hypnotic hallucinatory feeding as well as with the real meal without hypnosis. With the same person there was a uniform reaction toward the mock and the real meal. The author decided that the alimentary oscillations in the leukocyte figures are to be ascribed to vegetative tonus oscillations.

Wittkower [20] tested emotional leukocytoses with and without hypnosis with determination of the leukocyte figures and differential counting every 5 minutes. There were 30 tests. Examination was made during hypnotically induced emotions, posthypnotic emotional dreams, and with genuine emotion while awake. The emotions were delight, grief, anxiety, wrath, with and without motor discharge.

Under hypnosis without emotional suggestion, as well as during sleep, normal or slightly subnormal leukocyte figures were found. Under emotion—regardless whether with or without hypnosis—a remarkable increase of the leukocyte figure (up to 5,000 per milli-meter) was ascertained. There was no change at differential count-ing. The increase was strongest in the case of emotions without motor reaction.

Altenburger and Kroll [21] tested 15 subjects as to chronaxy (a number expressing the sensitiveness of a nerve to electrical stimula-tion). Hypnotic suggestion of increased sensitiveness caused a fall in chronaxy (constant rheobase); from 0.24 to 0.1 was observed. There was an increase to 0.28 with suggestion of reduced sensitive-ness. It is the authors' opinion that the vegetative changes due to psychical influence take place peripherally through the sympathetic nervous system.

Opinions concerning affectability of the blood sugar content un-der hypnosis are divided. Marcus and Sahlgren [22] tested four sub-jects and, with sugar charging, an increase was noted despite the suggestion that they were drinking only water. Crystallose dosing with the suggestion that the subject had taken a sugar dissolution produced no rise. Adrenaline was injected, with and without hyp-nosis, in the latter case with the suggestion that pure water was injected. The reaction was normal with three of the subjects. One showed a perceptibly smaller blood-sugar increase under hypnosis.

Gigon [23] made the suggestion of increased pancreas function with decreasing blood-sugar percentage to four somnambulistic dia-betics. He also suggested an injection of adrenaline. The result was an unmistakable fall of blood-sugar percentage, sometimes to one half of the prehypnosis value.

Nielsen and Geert-Jorgensen [24] were unable to cause any change in blood sugar by hypnotic suggestion of taste hallucinations or of anxiety shock.

Glaser [25] experimented with four subjects, three suffering from hysteria. High serum-calcium values were detected (deWaardt's method) when they were emotionally agitated, and the values de-clined to normal through suggestion either awake or under hypnosis.

Kretschmer and Krüger [26] were unable to influence by suggestion the blood calcium content with five normal subjects. Three who showed abnormal blood calcium showed a fall of the calcium values under ordinary hypnosis and a renewed increase under hypnotically suggested emotion.

Schazillo and Ambramov [27] found that hypnosis influences potassium as well as calcium with neurotic subjects. Under ordinary hypnosis with emotional tranquillity, the K/Ca quotient remains constant. Suggested pleasure produced increased activity of the sympathetic nervous system, reduced activity of the vagus; grief has the opposite effect. The conclusions of the authors seem too far reaching since the changes were small.

Kirschenberg,[28] an hour after induction, examined blood viscosity under hypnosis and found a spontaneous reduction in his 10 subjects.

Gessler and Hansen [29] tested basal metabolism. A suggested feeling of cold produced tremors and goose pimples and a strong metabolic increase. With a general feeling of warmth hypnotically suggested, at a low temperature (12° C), the heat adjustment almost completely disappeared (increase of oxygen consumption, maximum 3 per cent), and no shivering or goose pimples were seen.

With a patient with obesity and myxedema (basal metabolism 75) I have, myself, produced, by daily hypnotic suggestion of increased blood flow in the thyroid gland, an increase of the basal metabolism to 110 and reduced body weight to normal.

Goldwyn [30] found with 18 normal persons a slight and not convincing decline in basal metabolism under ordinary hypnosis. There were slightly slower pulsation and respiration, but no changes in blood pressure, hemoglobin percentage, leukocyte and erythrocyte figures, nonprotein N, urea, sugar, or creatinine in blood.

Krafft-Ebing and others are said to have produced, through hypnosis, apyrexia (lowering of fever) in infectious diseases. Hyperthermy (high fever) up to 39.2° C is also reported to have been produced through hypnotic suggestion.

The electrical resistance of the skin of the palm was examined by Levine [31] in the waking state, during sleep, and under hypnosis. Increased resistance is evidenced in normal sleep; hypnosis gave changes weaker than in normal sleep.

Dynes [32] and others have investigated as to electroencephalography (with frontal, parietal, and occipital derivations) in the waking state, asleep, and under hypnosis. Testing five subjects, he found that electroencephalograms in hypnosis and in the waking state were identical.

REPORT ON A TEST OF CERTAIN
VEGETATIVE FUNCTIONS UNDER HYPNOSIS

The following investigation was made in collaboration with my two assistants, Dr. Sonne and Dr. DeLinde. With the permission of Dr. E. Warburg, they were conducted in the laboratory of a medical university clinic in Copenhagen. It was our intention to examine some of the vegetatively controlled functions which are closely correlated and which could be tested relatively easily during the continuous course of hypnosis by reliable methodology. The areas selected for examination were the circulatory and respiratory functions. This consisted of continuously recording electrocardiograms (precordial derivation), conditions of pulsation, and blood pressure. (These were measured intra-arterially in a. mediana cubiti through a cannula therein inserted. A record was made by an apparatus described by Dr. Tybjaerg-Hansen [33]). There was also a recording of respiration, in respect to frequency as well as type, depth (measured in liters), and ventilation (liter volume per minute). The apparatus arrangement was Krogli's spirometer, modified by Tybjaerg-Hansen and Sonne and Georg.[34]

Simultaneously with the recording of these functions, a literal recording of the suggestions given has been made, and the various suggested states have been marked on the recorded curves.

Four female subjects have been tested, all reacting with pronounced somnambulistic hypnosis. With one subject, the experiments could only be made within certain limits as she was suffering from biliary calculus for which she was in the hospital for operation. The following suggestions were given to all the subjects:

Somatic pain (toothache)

Mixed psychosomatic pain (pain in precordia or pit of the stomach)

Anxiety (an attack by a robber, detonating bomb in the room)

Comfort (staying at a summer beach)
Delight (winning a lottery prize)
Wrath (losing the prize to a rival)
Grief (death of a close relative)
Suggested bodily strain (quick running)

In between and after the individual suggestions, calm, dreamless sleep was suggested.

As an example of the procedure of the hypnosis, the verbal suggestions during one of the experiments with Subject A are quoted.

Blood pressure	Time	Subject A
195/110	14.37	(Somatic pain) You are sleeping. You cannot open your eyes. You cannot raise your limbs, cannot remove your hand from the ball (blood-pressure recorder). You are completely calm, not a bit nervous, completely relaxed, sleeping calmly—a dreamless sleep.
180/110	14.39	You are in a deep sleep. You only hear my voice. Nothing will distract you.
	14.40	Now you begin to feel a terrific pain; it is a toothache in the upper molar on the right side. It is felt like a
185/105	14.43	drill and causes great pain. You cannot move but feel great pain. The toothache grows still worse. You can hardly stand it—but you cannot wake up. Now I rub
	14.43	your cheek. Gradually, the toothache disappears. Now it is completely gone. You only hear my voice. You will
185/105	14.46	be comfortable and relieved now that the toothache is gone. Now you sleep quite calmly.
	14.47	(Anxiety) You are in deep sleep now. You cannot move. You are lying in a mysterious laboratory with peculiar machines around. On your right side stands a bomb. It will detonate in one minute, and you cannot get out. You know for certain that it will detonate in the next moment. The whole house will blow up—everything will be burned to ashes; it is an atom bomb. You are left alone; you cannot get out. Now a man is enter-
205/130	14.52	ing. He will make the pain short. He aims at you with a pistol. You cannot get away. If you open your eyes you

Blood pressure	Time	Subject A

can see him. You can open your eyes. You can see him
—there he stands with a pistol. But it now appears that it
is not a bomb. The man with the pistol only has a toy

185/120   14.54 one. He just wanted to frighten you. Now you sleep
calmly and are no longer frightened.

(Comfort) It is a lovely summer day on the Solrød
beach. You are lying prone on the beach, listening to the
gentle swish of the waves. Children are playing. Every-

185/110   14.55 thing is calm and idyllic. You feel extremely at ease. You
can open your eyes but you do not wake up. You are ex-
pecting a good supper. You are sleeping again, quite

180/110   14.57 calmly, you feel completely comfortable.

(Delight) You are at home. Your husband enters the
185/110 room. He tells you that he has played on a lottery and
has won 250,000 kronen. You can take it easy now—buy
a country home, a car. You have no concern any longer.
Now you are sleeping deeply again.

15.00 (Wrath) Now your sister comes rushing in. She tells
you that the number of the ticket is hers; your husband
and your sister are squabbling. It appears that she
has cheated you, and also cheated you of your legacy.

175/100   15.01 You are very angry. If you were able to move you
would strike her. You can open your eyes and see her—
there she stands. You are very angry and cannot under-

175/100   15.03 stand how she could do such a thing. You will have to
subdue your anger. Now you are sleeping calmly. The
whole affair was nonsense. You forget about it completely, sleep calmly, unconcerned. You are absolutely
calm, you sleep calmly.

15.05 (Grief) You have just been bereaved, your father is
170/100   15.06 dead, you have just received the message about his death.
You are deeply affected by it. It makes you very sad—
you cannot get over it. . . . Now you have recovered,
Mrs. "A."

15.07 (Anxiety) It is dark. You are surrounded by field and
forest. You walk quickly; for you hear steps behind
you. Somebody is following and gaining on you. He de-

Blood pressure	Time	Subject A

		mands money; otherwise he will kill you. You see the shine of a long knife; you cannot get away, are completely paralyzed by fear. You are begging for your life —he seems to be merciless. If you open your eyes you can see him, a big sinister person.
	15.08	Now you are completely calm again, draw a sigh of relief, and have completely forgotten that you have dreamed.
180/ ?	15.10	(Bodily strain) It is a little later than half past three. You must of necessity get home. Something significant is waiting for you. The streetcar is coming. You are far from its stopping place. You are running as hard as you can, so that you are completely breathless. You just make it and catch the streetcar. You are completely exhausted from the race—you have run a long distance, a whole kilometer—you are breathless and have a violent heartbeat. You are completely exhausted. Now you are completely calm again. Take a good rest and you are completely calm.
180/ ? 175/100	15.18	You will not remember anything of what you have been through. You do not think of it either when you wake up. You are calm and comfortable, not a bit nervous. You will not be afraid of coming here again. There is nothing to be nervous about in the laboratory. Now when I awaken you, you will feel just as calm as now, at ease after a good rest. When I count to three you will awaken. You are sleeping as comfortably as in your own bed, during a calm night. You will be awake in a moment, feeling completely well. One—two—three.

The four typical curves given herewith (Figs. 10–1 and 10–2, of the circulation; Figs. 10–3 and 10–4, of the respiration functions) will illustrate the results.

It appears that suggestions will not produce any clear effects on the electrocardiogram aside from changes of frequency. The systolic as well as the diastolic blood pressure exhibits a slight decline during hypnosis, a further decline at delight, wrath, and grief, a more pronounced increase at anxiety. The changes, however, are so small that they do not allow for safe conclusions concerning relation to the suggested states or conditions.

On the normal blood-pressure curve, slight oscillations may always

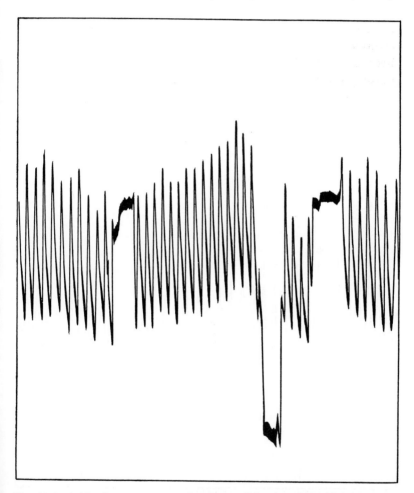

Fɪɢ. 10–1. A blood-pressure curve showing a slight rise of the blood pressure during suggested anxiety in hypnosis (Patient B). Test markings are also seen.

be observed, synchronous with respiration, and this may also be seen on the curve attached hereto (Fig. 10–2), recorded while the subject was emotionally and muscularly tranquil.

During the various emotional influences (Table 10–1), only small or no changes in the blood pressure are ascertained in our experiments, while respiration under the same influences exhibits pronounced changes. These small changes of the blood pressure may be emotionally conditioned, but the possibility also exists that they have been secondary in relation to the changes of respiration. There is a possibility that a mere voluntary change of respiration might produce corresponding changes of blood pressure. The same considera-

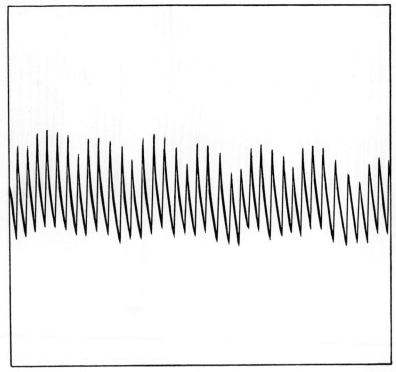

Fig. 10–2. A blood-pressure curve during emotional and muscular tranquillity under hypnosis (Patient D). The slight oscillations are due to the respiration.

tion may also apply to the rather unconvincing changes in pulse frequency.

The effects on the respiration functions will show more clearly and strongly (Table 10–2).

With suggestion of pain and anxiety the ventilation rises with all

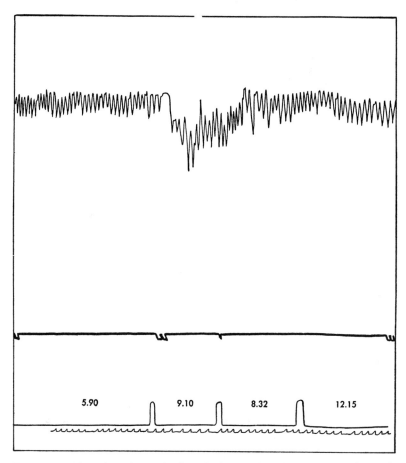

FIG. 10–3. Alterations in respiration during suggested pain under hypnosis (Patient C). The respiratory resting position is raised. This is shown on the curve as a lowering. At the bottom, markings for time, ventilation, and change of suggestion.

the subjects, as shown in Table 10–2, there being increased frequency as well as increased depth of respiration. Delight and wrath produced the same results with two of the persons tested.

With all the persons tested, the type of respiration is changed in a characteristic way at suggestion of grief. It becomes more superficial and irregular as to frequency as well as to depth. There is light breathing, with deep sighs, interrupted by expiration pauses and intermediary pauses of up to 12 seconds. With Subjects B and C the respiratory resting position is raised at the suggestion of pain, anxiety, delight, and bodily effort. At the suggestion of grief it is raised with one subject, lowered with another.

With all the subjects the suggestion of bodily effort produced increase of ventilation, less with Subject A on account of frequency

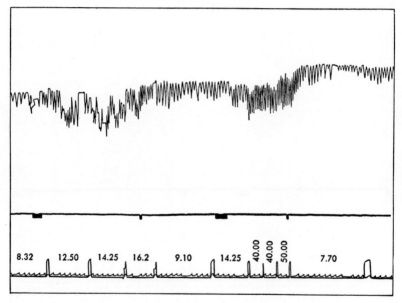

Fɪɢ. 10 4. Alterations in respiration during suggested grief (left) and bodily strain (right). The last followed by inclination toward apnea or superficial respiration (Patient C). The sorrow curve shows expiration pauses (top) and intermediary pauses. The respiratory resting position is raised during both suggestions. This is shown on the curve as a lowering. At the bottom, markings for time, ventilation, and change of suggestion.

TABLE 10-1

BLOOD-PRESSURE TABLE. SUBJECTS A, B, AND D.

	A					B					D				
	pulse	systolic max	systolic min	diastolic max	diastolic min	pulse	systolic max	systolic min	diastolic max	diastolic min	pulse	systolic max	systolic min	diastolic max	diastolic min
Before hypnosis	92	145	135	55	55	68	115	105	55	50	76	165	145	85	85
Hypnosis	92	145	140	65	65	72	110	110	50	50	80	155	135	85	85
Toothache	92	160	140	70	65	72	120	115	55	55					
Rest	88	150	145	70	70	72	115	105	55	45					
Pain in precordia	92	160	145	70	70	72	125	115	55	50	92	170	150	85	85
Rest	88	140	125	55	55	72	120	110	55	50	80	165	135	85	85
Anxiety	96	150	130	55	55	84	130	120	60	55	84	170	135	90	75
Rest	92	140	125	65	55	68	120	115	55	50	80	155	135	85	75
Comfort	88	145	135	65	55		120				84	155	130	75	75
Rest	88	145	140	70	70						76	150	130	80	80
Delight	88	140	135	60	55	72	130	110	50	50	92	175	145	95	85
Wrath	88	150	135	70	70	72	125	115	55	50	80	155	130	80	80
Rest	84	140	125	60	60	72	115	110	50	45	80	145	120	80	80
Grief	84	150	130	70	55	80	125	120	55	55					
Rest	84	135	130	70	60	72	110	105	50	50					
Running	92	140	130	70	55	76	110	100	50	50	88	170	110	100	65
Rest	92	140	140	70	70	66	120	110	55	55	76	130	100	65	50

TABLE 10-2

RESPIRATION TABLE. SUBJECTS A, B, AND C.

Suggestion	Frequency, per minute			Ventilation, liters per minute			Respiration depth, in liters			
	A	B	C	A	B	C	A	B	C	
Ordinary respiration	17		9	6,3		4,6	0,37		0,51	
Hypnosis	15	10	13	5,3	3,7	6,3	0,35	0,37	0,48	
Toothache	18	14	14	8,5	7,1	7,7	0,47	0,51	0,55	Respiratory resting position raised ½ liter by B and C
Rest	15	10	14	5,0	2,4	5,9	0,33	0,24	0,42	
Pain in precordia		17	16		7,6	9,1		0,45	0,57	Resting position raised ½ liter by B and C
Rest		11	14		3,1	7,2		0,28	0,51	
Anxiety	20	26	24	9,6	25,0	14,3	0,48	0,96	0,60	Resting position raised 1 liter by B and C
Rest	17	10	17	4,2	1,4	7,2	0,25	0,14	0,42	
Comfort	18	12	12	4,2	3,6	9,1	0,23	0,30	0,76	
Rest			18			7,2			0,40	
Delight	16	17	24	4,0	8,3	16,7	0,25	0,49	0,70	Resting position raised 1 liter by B and ¼ liter by C
Wrath	18	15	26	5,6	7,7	18,1	0,31	0,51	0,70	
Rest	17	10	15	4,0	2,8	5,3	0,23	0,28	0,35	
Grief	16	6	15	5,3	3,3	14,3	0,33	0,55	0,95	Expiratory and intermediary pauses by A, B, and C. Rest position lowered ¼ liter by B, raised 1 liter by C
Rest		12	16		3,7	9,1		0,31	0,57	
Running	28	40	39	8,4	33,3	45,0	0,30	0,83	1,15	Resting position raised ¼ liter by B and ½ liter by C
Rest	17	13	14	3,3	3,8	5,3	0,20	0,29	0,38	

increase without depth increase. With B and C the increase is very strong by reason of strongly increased frequency and depth. The resting position remained unchanged with A, while it was raised with B and C.

After such a suggestively conditioned hyperventilation, a compensatory inclination toward apnea, or superficial, slow respiration, resulted, which fact is obviously to be ascribed to the preceding strong carbon dioxide airing.

What lends our investigations a specific interest is that they have been carried out with an especially reliable technique. The material is not enough to allow definite conclusions, because of great individual variations. The experiments need confirmation. It is possible that new findings, some of them perhaps still more positive, will be the result. For instance, I have, in an earlier case, tested with a simpler technique and found a rise in blood pressure at the suggestion of anxiety of 60 mm Hg.

By means of this investigation, however, it has been evidenced that during hypnosis it is practicable through suggestion to provoke pronounced changes within a field of function which is vegetatively regulated. The changes will be more pronounced the more intimately the suggested emotional state is correlated to the relationship between the adrenals and the sympathetic nervous system.

It is probable that that which applies to the tested functional fields will also apply to other vegetatively governed functions, as appears in greater or less degree from a survey of the literature. The literature, as well as the present tests, seems to indicate also that different vegetatively governed functions show very different responsiveness to suggestive stimuli.

REFERENCES

1. Baumler: "Über die Beeinflussung der Hertztätigkeit in der Hypnose," *München. med. Wchnschr.*, **64**:1385 and 1426, 1917.
2. Löwy, M.: "Bemerkungen zur Lehre von der Hypnose und zur Pulsbeeinflussung in derselben," *Monatschr. f. Psychiat. u. Neurol.*, **44**:169, 1918.
3. Deutsch, F., and Kauf, E.: "Über die Ursachen der Kreislaufände-

rungen bei Muskelarbeit," *Ztschr. f. d. ges. Exper. Med.*, **32**:197, 1923; **34**:71, 1923.

4. Astruck, P.: "Über psychische Beeinflussung der Hertztätigkeit und Atmung in der Hypnose," *München. med. Wchnschr.*, Vol. 173, 1922.

5. Cramer, H., and Wittkower, E.: "Affektive Kreislaufveränderungen unter besonderer Berücksichtigung der Herzgrösse," *Klin. Wchnschr.*, **9**:1290, 1930.

6. Bier, W.: "Beitrag zur Beeinflussung des Kreislaufes durch psychische Vorgänge," *Ztschr. f. Klin. Med.*, **113**:762, 1930.

7. Jenness, A. F., and Wible, C. L.: "Respiration and heart action in sleep and hypnosis," *J. Gen. Psychol.*, **16**:197, 1937.

8. Stokvis, B.: "Der Einfluss der Hypnose auf den Puls," *Schweiz. med. Wchnschr.*, **19**:764, 1938.

9. Kleinsorge, H., and Klumbies, G.: "Herz und Seele (Hypnose und Elektrokardiogram," *Deutsche med. Wchnschr.*, Vols. 4 and 37, 1949.

10. Heyer, G.: "Die Magensekretion beim Menschen," *Arch. f. Verdaunngskrankeiten*, **27**:226, 1921; **29**:11, 1922.

11. Heilig, R., and Hoff, H.: "Beitrage zur hypnotischen Beeinflussung der Magenfunktion," *Med. Klin.*, **21**:162, 1925.

12. Luckhardt, A. B., and Johnston, R. L.: "Studies in gastric secretion," *Am. J. Physiol.*, **70**:174, 1924.

13. Langheinrich, O.: "Psychische Einflusse auf die Sekretionstätigkeit des Magens und des Duodenums," *München. med. Wchnschr.*, **69**:1527, 1922.

14. Wittkower, E.: "Über den Einfluss der Affekte auf den Gallefluss," *Klin. Wchnschr.*, **7**:2193, 1928.

15. Delhaugne, F., and Hansen, K.: "Die suggestive Beeinflussung der Magen und Pancreassekretion in der Hypnose," *Deutsche Archiv. f. klin. Med.*, **157**:20, 1927.

16. Heilig, R., and Hoff, H.: "Über hypnotische Beeinflussung der Nierenfunktion," *Deutsche med. Wchnschr.*, **51**:1615, 1925.

17. Marx, H.: "Untersuchungen über den Wasserhaushalt," *Klin. Wchnschr.*, **5**:92, 1926.

18. Marcus, H., and Sahlgren, E.: "Über die Einwirkung der hypnotischen Suggestion auf die Funktion des vegetativen Nervensystems," *München. med. Wchnschr.*, **72**:381, 1925.

19. Glaser, F.: "Über den klinischen Nachweis psycho-physischer Reaktionen. Die appetitsaft—leucocytosen," *Med. Klin.*, **20**:535, 1924.

20. Wittkower, E.: "Über affektiv-somatische Veränderungen. Die Affektleucozytose," *Klin. Wchnschr.*, **8**:1082, 1929.

21. Altenburger and Kroll: "Suggestive Beeinflussung der Sensibilitet," *Deutsche Ztschr. f. Nerven.*, **111**:144, 1929.

22. Marcus, H., and Sahlgren, E.: "Untersuchungen über die Einwirkung der hypnotischen Suggestion auf die Funktion des vegetativen Systems," *München. med. Wchnschr.*, **72**:381, 1925.

23. Gigon, A.: "Über den Einfluss der Psyche auf körperliche Vorgänge. Hypnose und Blutzucker," *Schweiz. med. Wchnschr.*, **56**:749, 1926.

24. Nielsen, O. J., and Geert-Jorgensen, E.: "Untersuchungen über die Einwirkung der hypnotischen Suggestion auf den Blutzucker bei Nichtdiabetikern," *Klin. Wchnschr.*, **7**:1457, 1928.

25. Glaser, F.: "Psychische Beeinflussung des Blutserumkalkspiegels," *Klin. Wchnschr.*, **3**:1492, 1924.

26. Kretschmer, M., and Krüger, R.: "Über die Beeinflussung des Serumkalkgehaltes in der Hypnose," *Klin. Wchnschr.*, **6**:695, 1927.

27. Schazillo, B. A., and Abramov, N. P.: "Über die Wirkung der Hypnose auf das Verhältnis der K und Ca Elektrolyte im Blutserum," *Ztschr. f. d. ges. Neurol. u. Psychiat.*, **112**:54, 1928.

28. Kirschenberg, E.: "Die Verändergungen der Blutviscositet während der Hypnose," Cit. from: *Zentralbl. f. d. ges. Neurol. u. Psychiat.*, **41**:326, 1925. *Folia neur. Estoniana*, **3-4**:366, 1925.

29. Gessler, H., and Hansen, K.: "Hypnotische Beeinflussung der Wärmeregulation," *Zentralbl. f. inn. Med.*, **48**:658, 1927.

30. Goldwyn, J., "The effect of hypnosis on basal metabolism," *Arch. Int. Med.*, **45**:109, 1930.

31. Levine, M.: "Electrical skin resistance during hypnosis," *Arch. Neurol. & Psychiat.*, **24**:973, 1930.

32. Dynes, J. B.: "Objective method for distinguishing sleep from the hypnotic trance," *Arch. Neurol. & Psychiat.*, **57**:84, 1947.

33. Tybjaerg-Hansen, A.: *Pressure Measurement in the Human Organism*, Disputats Copenhagen, 1949.

34. Georg and Sonne: "The relation of the oxygen tension of the inspiratory air to the chemoreceptor response during work," *Acta Physiol. Scandinav.*, **16** (fasc. 1): 52, 1948.

CHAPTER ELEVEN

The Control of the Heart Rate
by Hypnotic Suggestion

Editor's Note

So many arbitrary claims have been made as to the possibility of influencing bodily functions through hypnotic suggestion that they should be verified or disproved by scientific experiments. Dr. S. J. van Pelt has undertaken to determine whether the heartbeat is subject to such control. It is obvious that a change in heart rate can be produced through the arousing of emotions; it is equally obvious that this can be done almost as easily in the waking state as in hypnosis. Most workers in hypnosis have observed pulse changes occur as the result of simple, direct suggestions that the pulse will become slower or faster, but merely counting the pulsation is not a scientific method of experiment.

In the previous chapter Reiter has discussed past experimentation along this line, mentioning that Astruck caused both an increase and a decrease of pulse frequency by suggestion. The type of suggestions given is not stated, and this may have been merely the inducing of emotions. Bier, and also Cramer and Wittkower, produced such changes by arousing emotions with subjects in the hypnotic state. Wible and Jenness have reported that they could obtain no increase in heart rate by direct suggestion. In Dr. van Pelt's research, one electrocardiogram shows an increase of heart rate as the result of a suggested hallucination of danger, but another pictures a very definite and considerable increase from direct suggestion alone.

These variable results cause the reader to raise again the question of trance depth obtained, and the necessity of knowing more as to procedure in order to analyze the results. Perhaps an additional point may be made here that individuals will be found to vary considerably in their reactions. The editor has produced such changes rather easily in some subjects (not with controlled conditions and equipment to measure the changes) and has found other subjects who, in as deep a state, were completely unresponsive. It is likely that this is due to some fear, or, possibly, other personal reasons have prevented positive results in that particular individual. If a subject is under the impression that slowing down or increasing the rate of heartbeat might be dangerous to him, he most certainly will fail to respond to such suggestions.

This was illustrated most conclusively by one subject who was given suggestions of slowed heartbeat while a physician listened to the heart with a stethoscope. According to the doctor, the rate slowed from 80 to 50 beats per minute. However, the physician, after this stethoscopic examination, advised the subject to have a cardiogram made of his heart and seek an examination by a specialist, as it seemed that there was an organic condition present. The subjected was much disturbed and alarmed. He hastened to follow the advice and was told his heart was perfectly sound in every way. Subsequent efforts with this subject to cause alteration of heartbeat were completely negative! This was true even though the subject knew that his heart was in good condition and that no harm could result from the suggestion of change of rate.

Dr. van Pelt is one of the leading hypnotic medical practitioners in England. He has practiced in Australia, Egypt, and West Africa and has specialized in Harley Street, London, for many years. During the war, he served as a Surgeon Lieutenant Commander in the Royal Navy. He is President of the British Society of Medical Hypnotists, Editor of the *British Journal of Medical Hypnotism*. and has written several technical articles on hypnotherapy. A book *Hypnotism and the Power Within* (Skeffington and Son, Ltd., London), appeared during the summer of 1950.

The Control of the Heart Rate by Hypnotic Suggestion

BY S. J. VAN PELT, M.B., B.S.*

It has long been maintained that it was possible to influence the heart rate by means of hypnotic suggestion, and there are many references to this in the literature.

Bramwell,[1] for instance, stated that he had seen many instances where the frequency of the pulse could be altered by suggestion. He claimed that such changes could often be brought about by simply stating that they would occur. In other cases it was sometimes necessary to bring about the changes by arousing emotion in response to suggestion. He describes an experiment carried out in conjunction with Dr. Alcock, using a sphygmograph to record the pulse tracings, in which he was able to increase the normal pulse rate from 80 to 100 and slow it down to 60 by direct suggestion.

Forel[2] claimed that the pulse could be quickened or slowed on occasion, while Lloyd Tuckey[3] cited the reports of several reliable medical men to show the effects of suggestion on the action of the heart. Dr. Hack Tuke described a case where death from cardiac syncope occurred when a blindfolded man was told he was bleeding to death while warm water was allowed to trickle down his arm into a basin. Needless to say, the doctor did not carry out this experiment himself.

It is well known that certain Indian fakirs and holy men are able to so slow the circulation by autosuggestion or self-hypnosis that the pulse becomes imperceptible and they apparently die. In this condition they may be buried for some considerable time, yet recover

* Harley Street, London, W.1.

perfectly. The feat has been attested to by British physicians when performed under controlled conditions.

Braid [4] is another of the old-time hypnotists who described many cases in which he was able to influence the action of the heart under hypnosis and cured many cases of palpitation.

Coming to more modern workers, Wolberg [5] states that increased pulse rate may be produced by direct suggestion, but that evidence tends to confirm the opinion that cardiovascular symptoms occur as the result of emotion. For instance, suggestions of peace and quiet, calm and relaxation will lower the blood pressure and pulse rate as in sleep. In order to raise the pulse rate and blood pressure, it is only necessary to suggest excitement or some other strong emotion. Wolberg quotes Jenness and Wible [6] as claiming that direct verbal suggestion under hypnosis has no power to increase the heart rate without the intermediate action of emotion.

In view of this, it was decided to carry out a simple experiment to determine whether or not the heart action could be influenced by direct suggestion under hypnosis, as well as through the emotions. Accordingly, it was arranged with a consulting heart specialist that electrocardiographic tracings should be taken on a hypnotized subject.

The patient was a young man of 20 years who had suffered from attacks of asthma since early childhood. This condition had been overcome by several hypnotic treatments, and in gratitude and interest he agreed to submit to the test. However, no details were revealed to him beforehand, and it was merely stated that it was desired to make a recording of his heart while he was under hypnosis. He was an excellent subject and could easily achieve somnambulism, having indeed reached this state at the first attempt at induction. The subject was seated in an easy chair, the electrocardiograph machine was connected, and a tracing was taken during the waking state. As will be seen from Fig. 11–1, this revealed a perfectly normal heart, beating regularly at the rate of 78 beats per minute.

The induction of hypnosis was then commenced. Being a somnambulist, it could have been arranged for the subject to go into instant hypnosis. However, as it was desired to take a tracing of the heart action during the induction period, the subject was hypnotized in the manner to which he was accustomed. That is, the eyes were closed, and he was asked to concentrate on the hypnotist's hand placed on the top of his head, while suggestions of "sleep" were made.

The subject responded in exactly the same way as he had done on the first occasion when he was hypnotized, so that the experiment was conducted under conditions which approached as nearly as possible to the original induction. Examination of the electrocardiographic tracing taken during this period shows no significant changes from the normal, apart from a very slight quickening.

Hypnosis having been induced, time was allowed for the heart rate to return to normal. Then, in a quiet voice, the subject was told, "Your heart is beginning to beat faster. It is getting faster and faster. You are perfectly calm, but your heart is beating faster and faster." These suggestions were repeated a few times and, although the subject showed no distress or changes of respiration, nor, indeed, appeared to be affected in any way, the electrocardiograph revealed that the heart rate had risen rapidly from 78 to 135.

It continued to beat at this rate until suggestions were made for it to return to normal. This it did, taking a little longer to reach normal than it had to increase in rate.

After it had been normal for a short period, an experiment was made with the object of increasing the rate by means of emotion. Accordingly, it was suggested to the subject that he was sitting in a motorcar enjoying a quiet run through the pleasant countryside. It was then suggested that the driver was speeding up and, in fact, driving very fast. This did not appear to worry the patient at all. Suddenly, it was suggested that, in rounding a bend in the road, there was danger of a head-on crash with another car which was approaching rapidly from the opposite direction on the wrong side of the road. It was stated that the subject was so afraid that he could not move, but not a word was said about his heart.

Nevertheless, the electrocardiograph recorded an increase of rate,

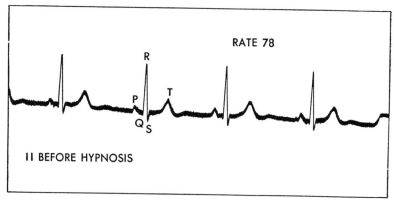

FIG. 11-1. Before hypnosis. Normal electrocardiogram (Lead II).

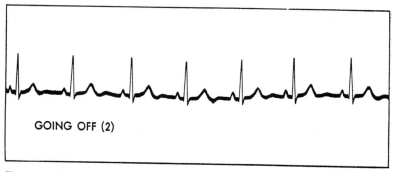

FIG. 11-2. Electrocardiogram taken as hypnosis was induced. Normal tracing (Lead II); slight increase in rate.

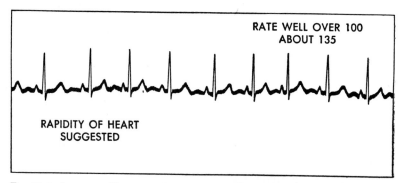

FIG. 11-3. Increase of heart rate in response to direct suggestion. Notice absence of somatic tremors indicating complete absence of fear or nervousness.

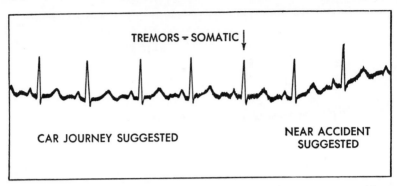

Fig. 11–4. Increase of heart rate in response to a suggestion of a car accident. Note somatic tremors which are typical of nervousness and fear.

although not to the same extent as that caused by direct suggestion. At the same time somatic tremors appeared which were typical of a nervous subject.

Circumstances made it impossible to make more exhaustive tests on this occasion, but the heart specialist who so kindly cooperated in the experiment expressed his opinion, supported by the electrocardiographic evidence, that it had definitely been proved that the heart rate could be influenced under hypnosis by direct suggestion as well as by emotion.

How are these cardiac changes brought about?

Bramwell quotes the opinion of Beaunis, who believed that the changes were brought about by suggestion acting directly upon the inhibitory centers of the heart. Moll, on the other hand, believed that they resulted from alterations in respiration and emotional ideas.

In the experiment described it may be claimed that the increase in heart rate under direct suggestion resulted from the emotion of fear. That is, it may be put forward in explanation that the patient became afraid when told his heart would beat faster. Apart from the fact that the patient showed no evidence of fear or anxiety and that he was reassured from this point of view, being told that he would feel perfectly calm and well, there remains the evidence of the electrocardiographic tracings.

For one thing, when rapidity of heartbeat was suggested directly, there were no signs of nervous tremors in the electrocardiogram. On the other hand, these signs of fear were clearly present in the tracing taken during the suggestion of a car accident. In addition, a greater rapidity of heartbeat was obtained by direct suggestion than that obtained as the result of emotion. It would therefore seem that the control of the heart rate by direct suggestion in the hypnotic state, as well as by emotion, must be accepted as a proved fact.

Direct control of the sympathetic accelerator and parasympathetic inhibitory nerve supply of the heart may seem difficult to understand at first, until it is remembered that modern experiments have revealed that the autonomic nervous system is represented in the cerebral cortex.

Hoff and Green [7] state that:

There is a mechanism by which the cortex . . . can influence . . . the cardiovascular system, and through this mechanism the cortex may bring about a finer adjustment of the activity of the heart and circulation in accordance with the exigencies of the external environment and the immediate activities of the skeletal musculature.

Accordingly, it will be seen that cardiovascular symptoms can result from direct suggestion. If the theory is accepted that it is possible for varying degrees of self-hypnosis to occur quite accidentally and without conscious knowledge of the subject,* then many cardiac disorders of apparently mysterious origin may be explained. In this state of increased suggestibility, an idea is planted in the mind and has the same effect as a hypnotic suggestion. Thus, it is not unknown for even a medical man to develop various cardiac symptoms, ranging from pain to arrhythmia, while treating a distressing case of heart disease.

Apart from the effects of direct suggestion, the experiments demonstrate conclusively the results of emotions on the cardiovascular system. The effect of emotion has long been known, and it is common knowledge, for instance, that fainting may result from the sight of blood. Any strong emotion, by disturbing the balance of the autonomic nervous system, may give rise to cardiovascular symptoms, and Katz [8] describes emotion as a possible cause of condi-

* See Chapter One.

tions such as premature systoles, paroxysmal tachycardia, and even coronary insufficiency.

Cannon [9] states that unless the emotional stress is relieved by action, then the bodily changes may upset the organism as a whole.

Fulton [10] expresses the opinion that "the heart and circulation may be worked just as hard and just as much as a detriment to the body as a whole from an armchair . . . as from a rower's seat." Certainly, in the experiment described here, the mere suggestion of a car accident was sufficient to send the heart racing, although the patient was sitting quietly in a chair and apparently at complete rest.

In view of the above experiments, which prove beyond doubt that the heart rate can be influenced under hypnosis, by both direct and indirect suggestion, it is hoped that more use may be made of this valuable method to assist more orthodox procedures in the treatment of cardiovascular disease. By removing fear and anxiety, while inducing calmness and relaxation, it could be of great value in the treatment of a serious complaint such as angina pectoris, where the emotion roused by the dread of the disease often precipitates an attack.

Finally, the experiments illustrate the point that hypnosis is akin to the waking state and is definitely not sleep. Suggestions of cardiac changes during ordinary sleep would produce no such results.

In conclusion, I should like to express my thanks to Dr. Ivor Balfour, Consulting Physician and Heart Specialist, who so kindly cooperated in the experiments and took the electrocardiograms.

REFERENCES

1. Bramwell, J. M.: *Hypnotism*, 2nd ed., Rider & Son, London, 1913.
2. Forel, A.: *Hypnotism*, trans. from 5th German ed., Allied Book Co., New York, 1927.
3. Tuckey, L. C.: *Treatment by Hypnotism and Suggestion*, 4th ed., Baillière; Tindall & Cox, London, 1921.
4. Braid, J.: *Neurypnology*, Geo. Redway, London, 1899.
5. Wolberg, L. R.: *Medical Hypnosis*, Grune & Stratton, Inc., New York, 1948.

6. Jenness, A. F., and Wible, C. L.: "Respiration and heart action in sleep and hypnosis," *J. Gen. Psychol.*, **16**:197–222, 1937.
7. Hoff, E. C., and Green, H. D.: "Cardiovascular reactions induced by electrical stimulation of the cerebral cortex," *Am. J. of Physiol.*, 1936.
8. Katz, L. N.: *Electrocardiography*, Lea and Febiger, Philadelphia, 1946.
9. Cannon, W. B.: "Some modern extensions of Beaumont's studies on Alexis St. Martin," *J. Michigan M. Soc.*, 1933.
10. Fulton, J. F.: "Cerebral regulation of autonomic function," *Proc. Interst. Postgrad. M. A. North America*, 1936 A:

CHAPTER TWELVE

Hypnosis in Obstetrics

(A PSYCHOLOGICAL PREPARATION FOR CHILDBIRTH)

Editor's Note

One of the most interesting papers incorporated in this volume is that which follows, reporting 100 cases of childbirth under hypnosis carried out in Minneapolis by Dr. Milton Abramson, an obstetrician, and Dr. William Heron, a psychologist. Heretofore, hypnotic childbirth has been used haphazardly and occasionally in this country but always with the purpose of developing as great a degree of anesthesia as possible in order to alleviate pain during parturition. In their investigation Dr. Abramson and Dr. Heron used a different approach, hypnotically developed anesthesia being merely incidental.

In a letter supplementing their paper they write:

In the conditioning of the patient it was desired to accomplish the following aims: (1) by countersuggestion to negate the erroneous ideas that the patient might have concerning childbirth; (2) to teach the subject relaxation; and (3) to teach the patient to put herself into the hypnotic state with its accompanying relaxation, that is, autohypnosis.

By these means they expected to eliminate pain from childbirth when the method was completely successful with the patient and to reduce pain in other cases where the patient failed to carry out the procedure completely. If suggestive anesthesia could be achieved, well and good; if not, they proceeded without it—such anesthesia being a secondary consideration in the experiment.

To quote further from their supplemental letter:

Failures and successes in the abstract have little meaning in cases of this sort. If we define failures as cases in which the subject felt that the training had been useless, then the percentage would be less than 1. If we define failure as those cases in which the patient failed to remain completely relaxed during labor, then the percentage would be much higher. . . . We have no estimate of the modification of the discomfort of labor except the subjective statements of the patients.

In the method employed in this test the emphasis is on proper education of the patient and on *relaxation, which automatically raises the threshold of pain*, as is well known. It is also well known to everyone experienced with hypnotism that the trance state produces a spontaneous relaxation which can be greatly increased through suggestion. In fact, this relaxation can be much greater than it is possible to produce voluntarily, sometimes approaching the cerea flexibilita witnessed at times in a catatonic stupor. Relaxation is of the utmost importance in bringing relief from pain or the discomfort of childbirth and it is only logical, then, to use hypnosis in order to produce the greatest possible degree of relaxation.

It is here that the method outlined in the following article differs radically from that which has been given so much publicity recently, which was developed by Dr. Grantly Dick Read of England and is now known as the "Read method." A number of clinics and individual obstetricians in the United States have been testing the claims of Dr. Read, and his method has been pronounced eminently satisfactory by them. Yale University School of Medicine has had more than 800 such "painless deliveries," according to *Newsweek* magazine. There are many indications from this rising interest that the method may become quite popular. Read uses patient education just as do Heron and Abramson, and he teaches relaxation through a series of exercises which *do* relax but which do not provide anywhere near the degree of relaxation which is obtainable through hypnosis.

A comment on relaxation through exercise might be made here. Various attempts have been made to work out a system of exercises which would bring relaxation. The most notable has been that introduced by Jacobson [1] and adopted by Fink. [2] It requires many hours of practice to learn it and weeks of time before the "relaxer" is successful with it. It has been termed "progressive relaxation." But in 1924 Frederick Pierce [3] promulgated a series of simple relaxation exercises which can be learned in a few moments and which produce far greater relaxation. This is accomplished by applying some psychological principles—a combined mental and physical method which is amazingly successful. It is unfortunate that it is so little known to physicians and psychologists.

In his book [4] Dr. Read freely admits the use of suggestion in his method, particularly during labor, and states that he was somewhat concerned for fear hypnosis might be involved. He therefore consulted a "prominent hypnotist" who assured him that hypnotism was not concerned. Whoever his adviser may be, he must have known little of hypnotism, for any experienced hypnotist recognizes that of course hypnotism is involved. Undoubtedly, the more susceptible patients enter an actual trance during labor. Indeed, obstetricians report that nature usually causes the patient to enter a semidazed, detached state at the beginning of the second stage of labor, which is evidently intended to relieve some of the discomfort and the pain being experienced by the tense, fearful patient. This is undoubtedly a state of hypnosis which may be light or deep at times. This condition might have been mentioned by Dr. Williams in Chapter One of this book as another instance of spontaneous trance. Dr. Read's methods and suggestions undoubtedly would tend to deepen such a naturally induced state. As confirmation, some quotations can be made from Dr. Read's book. He states (page 180): "Some of them have appeared to be lying in a trance from the beginning of their labor until the end." On page 230 he says: ". . . relaxing as the contractions come on until she was completely lifeless to all appearances"; and on page 181: "These women again sank into an amnesic, almost anesthetic state." Indeed, in the second paragraph on page 181, Read gives an excellent description of autohypnosis!

The above comments are in no way intended to indicate a belief that the Read method is not an excellent one. Undoubtedly, it is highly successful. Heron and Abramson merely carry this procedure to its logical conclusion—using hypnosis with it to the greatest degree which can be developed in the individual patient.

The main objective of Heron and Abramson is to develop a method of handling childbirth with the least possible danger to the mother and child and the least discomfort to the mother. It should be emphasized that 100 "run of the mill" patients were used, and no attempt was made to select only good hypnotic subjects. Some were probably unhypnotizable; some were fair subjects; others, of course, were somnambulists. No statistics are given as to this, though they would be of much interest.

The authors mention that they had some spectacular successes, as would be expected, though their concern was with average effects. What can be accomplished with hypnotic childbirth where a somnambulistic state can be obtained (approximately 20 per cent can reach such a state without intensive conditioning, and many more are able to if enough time is allowed) has been described by Kroger and DeLee.[5] Their series of cases consisted of 11 women, all excellent hypnotic subjects, conditioned in five or six sessions, with analgesia and amnesia produced.

Of course the disadvantages in the use of hypnosis in childbirth should also be given consideration, and the Read method, Heron and Abramson's, and the method of producing hypnotic anesthesia as described by Kroger and DeLee, which stresses suggestive anesthesia should be weighed against each other. The first involves no additional technical training; the others require a knowledge of hypnotism. A valid objection to all three is that they require time to condition the prospective mother. This is discussed by Heron and Abramson and need not be considered here. Another argument by physicians is that they dare not become known as hypnotists or their practices will suffer from public disapproval. It is doubtful if this is true at present to any great extent, because the public is becoming better informed as to hypnotism. Indeed, neurotic and other patients are beginning to ask their physicians about hypnotic treatment. The editor has recently conditioned three patients for hypnotic childbirth, each of whom requested this kind of delivery from her physician. A patient will readily accept the idea of hypnotic treatment provided that he has confidence in the physician.

Another obstacle which obstetricians have mentioned is official disapproval of hypnotic childbirth by hospitals. It would, comparably, be as ridiculous for a hospital to dictate to staff physicians as to what drugs could be used. If there are alternate facilities, an obstetrician should refuse his patronage to any hospital so backward and so prescribed in its management.

It may be said further that few obstetricians are competent hypnotists, but it is by no means difficult to become proficient.

The many advantages of the Heron-Abramson method far outweigh any disadvantages. It must be considered preferable to the Read procedure. With those patients who can reach a deep stage of hypnosis, this method will approach that described by Kroger-DeLee. Since the usual ways of handling pain in childbirth are so definitely unsatisfactory, as physicians freely admit, it is possible that the advantages of this method may secure its adoption to some extent, even in the face of general reluctance of the medical profession to accept hypnosis.

Something should be said here as to the use of hypnosis during childbirth in other countries. It has been reported as used to some extent before World War II in Germany and in Austria and to a much greater extent in Russia. It has become almost standard procedure in the hospitals of some of the large Russian cities.

In further consideration of hypnotic obstetrics, some other factors might well be studied. Nicholson [6] found that muscular fatigue could be inhibited to a large extent by hypnotic suggestion. Williams [7] confirmed this, though finding the degree of inhibition less than Nicholson reported. Since childbirth involves "labor," as Heron and Abramson point out, and labor brings fatigue, hypnotic suggestion might be of distinct benefit in relieving a large amount of fatigue during parturition.

Although never scientifically proved, many authorities believe that the rate of healing of a wound or injury can be materially accelerated by hypnotic suggestion. It should be possible to determine this, and it could be applied to healing after delivery if the results of tests were positive.

Among the workers in hypnosis in the nineteenth century were many physicians such as Braid, Liebeault, Bernheim, Esdaile, Elliotson, Wetterstrand, Von Eeden, Moll, and others. All experimented with hypnotic anesthesia in obstetrics, and some have reported being able to control the length of the duration of labor and, by suggestion, to set the time of day at which labor would start. While this may seem farfetched to an obstetrician, these physicians were competent observers, and this may perhaps be possible in some cases. It would have been interesting to know the results if Heron and Abramson had investigated the possibility in their tests. Certainly, if the hour for the start of labor and the length of duration can sometimes be controlled, obstetricians will be strongly influenced to adopt hypnotic childbirth!

Another interesting point made by many of the old-time medical hypnotists was that hypnotic suggestion could produce a definite stimulation of the mammary glands and a copious supply of milk. If true, perhaps this could be determined through comprehensive tests such as Heron and Abramson have conducted.

REFERENCES

1. Jacobson, E.: *Progressive Relaxation*, University of Chicago Press, Chicago, 1929.
2. Fink, D. H.: *Release from Nervous Tension*, Simon and Schuster, Inc., New York, 1943.
3. Pierce, F.: *Mobilizing the Mid-brain*, E. P. Dutton & Co. Inc., New York, 1924.
4. Read, G. D.: *Childbirth without Pain*, Harper & Brothers, New York, 1944.
5. Kroger, W. S., and DeLee, S. T.: "The use of the hypnoidal state as an amnesic, analgesic, and anesthetic agent in obstetrics," *Am. J. Obst. & Gynec.*, **45** (5):655, 1943.
6. Nicholson, N. C.: "Notes on muscular work during hypnosis," *Bull. Johns Hopkins Hosp.*, **31**:89, 1920.
7. Williams, G. W.: "The effect of hypnosis on muscular fatigue," *J. Abnorm. & Social Psychol.*, **24**:318, 1929.

Hypnosis in Obstetrics*

(A PSYCHOLOGICAL PREPARATION FOR CHILDBIRTH)

By WILLIAM T. HERON, Ph.D.

PROFESSOR OF PSYCHOLOGY, UNIVERSITY OF MINNESOTA,
MINNEAPOLIS, MINNESOTA

AND MILTON ABRAMSON, M.D., Ph.D.

CLINICAL INSTRUCTOR, DEPARTMENT OF OBSTETRICS
AND GYNECOLOGY, UNIVERSITY OF MINNESOTA, MINNEAPOLIS,
MINNESOTA; ASSOCIATE, DEPARTMENT OF OBSTETRICS AND
GYNECOLOGY, MINNEAPOLIS GENERAL HOSPITAL

For untold ages women have looked upon the birth of a child as an ordeal of pain and suffering, as a result of which they approach it with fear and apprehension. In some women this attitude prevents them from having children; in others the experience of having their first born convinces them that they will have no more offspring. The challenge of this situation lies in the fact that a normal spontaneous childbirth is a natural physiological process and why, then, should there be pain connected with it? It does not seem to be the plan of nature for physiological processes to be painful, since we know there is no pain connected with swallowing, blinking the eyes, digestion, evacuation of the bowels, etc., unless there are pathological conditions present. There is no pathology connected with normal childbirth, and yet many women have great pain. What, then, is the source of this pain?

* The authors have also reported their findings, more technically, in a paper, "An objective evaluation of hypnosis in obstetrics," *Am. J. Obst. & Gynec.*, No. 59, 1069, May, 1950.

The best answer to this question is that we are dealing with a psychological problem. All of us have heard a great deal, from childhood on, about the birth pains and the dangers of childbirth and, acting under these suggestions and this type of conditioning, the patient goes into labor with fear and apprehension, expecting pain, with the result that the contractions of the uterus, giving her unaccustomed sensations, immediately produce in her muscular tensions inhibiting the normal process of birth. The physiological process of birth then ceases to follow its normal course, and severe discomfort results.

It is interesting to speculate concerning the origin of the fear connected with childbirth. Perhaps it is because the development and birth of a child to the mind of primitive man was a mysterious event. Not understanding the relationship of sexual intercourse to pregnancy, the onset of pregnancy and the subsequent birth of the baby seemed to him to be without any demonstrable cause, to be spontaneous and thus mysterious. Man is almost invariably afraid of that which is mysterious—that which he does not understand. Also, under primitive conditions, a large percentage of women died as the consequence of childbirth because of the lack of asepsis. Thus, the birth of a baby produced fear in the primitive man, and with fear came tension and with tension, pain. Remove the fear, reduce the tension, and the pain of childbirth will disappear in the normal case.

There have been handed down through all the ages of civilized man traditions and tales concerning the terrible ordeal of childbirth. Thus, the curse of Eve becomes a psychological hazard and not a physiological one. For example, the golfer speaks of his mental hazards as contrasted to the sand traps and water hazards of the course itself. Similarly, the difficulties of childbirth are largely the result of mental hazards, and our problem is to reduce and eliminate these hazards. The physician frequently pays little attention to this problem. He is content with relieving the patient's mental condition by the use of drugs of various kinds for the relief of pain, thus treating the symptoms rather than eliminating the causes of the symptoms. An approach of this type, although deprecated in the theory of medicine, is in practice often used, particularly in those cases where the causes are of a psychological nature.

The alleviation of the discomforts of childbirth by drug sedation would not be undesirable except for the fact that there is no known drug used for this purpose at the present time without some element of danger in its use, either to the mother or to the baby or to both. If the drug is given in small enough quantities, the dangers are very minimal, but then, frequently, little progress is made in the alleviation of the discomfort.

It would seem, therefore, that in obstetrics as well as in other fields of medicine, it is the duty of the physician to make every effort to eliminate the cause of the fear and pain of childbirth. Meanwhile, until we are able to accomplish this adequately, we must use sedative drugs in minimal dosages.

If, as we believe, the causes of the pain in childbirth are largely psychological, it then follows that the most likely method of removing these causes is by psychological methods. By indirect suggestions since childhood, women have learned to fear childbirth as a process resulting in tension and severe pain. The most obvious way to handle this situation is to convince the woman through suggestion and training that her former concept of childbirth is not necessarily correct. The best time for this suggestion is before the mother has had her first baby, because if she has had pain at delivery, that experience reinforces her beliefs and makes it more difficult to change them. The obstetrician usually has a very short time, probably at the most 9 months, to change a belief which has been in the course of development for perhaps 18 or more years, and lifetime habits are not easily changed, whether they are habits of thought or habits of action.

Fortunately, we have at our command a very effective method of changing attitudes, provided the change is for the welfare of the individual and the patient is willing to cooperate. We can countersuggest with suggestion and at the same time teach the individual a mode of behavior which will make childbirth much quicker and easier for her. We must realize at once, however, that there is no method of eliminating the *work* associated with childbirth except by Cesarean section, which no woman would want except in special circumstances. To bear a child is hard work and is actually called "labor," involving very strong muscular contractions which in themselves are not painful. Lift a heavy weight with your hand and arm. You can feel the muscles contract. Do it repeatedly and you will begin to perspire; breathing will become deeper and quicker. You are doing work, but there is no pain. That is the way childbirth should be. It involves work to cause the baby to pass through the birth canal, even though nature has provided for increased elasticity of the birth canal at this time so that it may stretch to many times its usual size.

Therefore, it isn't the work which we can hope to eliminate nor is it the discomfort associated with hard work, for most of us will agree that hard work is not the most comfortable activity in the world. Rather it is the pain and mental anguish of childbirth which are completely unnecessary and which can be eliminated in the normal, healthy, and intelligent woman who is willing to keep an open mind and who realizes the enormous importance of psychological factors as they affect her mental state.

Since we must work quickly to re-educate the woman and since we must use powerful means to overcome a lifetime of incorrect thinking, it follows that one would naturally think of using hypnosis for this purpose. Used properly and with the cooperation of the individual, this is one of the most powerful and beneficial psychological tools known to man. It can, in some cases, accomplish results which have the appearance of miracles. It is such results which have been too much stressed in the past, while little or no attention has been given to what hypnosis can do for the average individual.

Therefore, in the discussion of our use of hypnosis in childbirth, we will not stress the spectacular results which are obtained in some women but rather indicate what benefits the average woman may obtain. Before doing this, however, it may be well to indicate briefly our philosophy in attacking the problems of childbirth through hypnosis. The various methods of inducing the hypnotic trance and the phenomena which can be produced in the hypnotic state are described and discussed in the literature generally, some of them in other portions of this book. A consideration of the phenomena may lead some people to the view that the hypnotic state is unnatural and abnormal. We believe that such a view is completely mistaken, as Dr. G. W. Williams has shown in Chapter One. We believe that what is called the "hypnotic trance" occurs spontaneously and naturally, to some degree, in every normal individual. We have all become so interested in something at times that all else save that to which we are attending is for the moment shut out. To all intents and purposes we are blind, deaf, and without feeling except for that which has completely usurped our attention. At such times movements may occur quite automatically and unknown to the person making the movement. Dr. Anita Mühl discusses this in her chapter on automatic writing.

The hypnotic state is something like this condition of fixed attention except that some control can be exercised by another person, namely the hypnotist. By the use of words he can apparently automatically control the behavior and thought of the individual, within limits.

We believe that most normal individuals can learn how to place themselves in the hypnotic state and that, in the proper hands, such learning can be exceptionally useful to the individual for various purposes, some of which are mentioned elsewhere in this book. We look upon the hypnotist, first, as a teacher whose duty it is to help and to instruct the patient to gain that degree of abstraction known as hypnosis and, secondly, then to give suggestions to the patient which will eventually enable the subject to control herself. In the words of the layman, we believe that through training under hypnosis the person can learn to control his body by his mind. In these days of increasing knowledge of psychosomatic medicine, there seems to be no escape from the position that there is definite unconscious mental control of the body, although this concept may be stated in different terms which are more acceptable to many scientists.

Our approach to the use of hypnosis may be summarized by saying that we look upon hypnosis as an aid to an educative process.

Through this education we have not only to counteract the incorrect ideas of the patient which have been learned in the past but also to teach her how to relax. In our culture of hustle and bustle, many people lose an ability which they had as babies; namely, to let tension flow out of their muscles so that they become completely limp. Look at the baby while it is lying in its crib when drowsy or asleep. Lift its arm or leg and note how it falls, when it is released, into almost any position which chance dictates. The baby is in a state of perfect relaxation, its whole body like that of a rag doll.

Now lie down yourself and try to get your body so relaxed. You will find this a difficult thing to do. You will feel a tension here or there. You do not lie quietly unless you make a distinct effort not to move, in which case you defeat your own purpose, as far as release of tension is concerned, for in making the effort to lie quietly you must of necessity use energy which manifests itself in muscular tension. Experimentation has shown that, even when asleep, people do not lie quietly for long. Now, while lying quietly, think of some occasion when you were very frightened and then note how the tension increases in your muscles; if there were a blood-pressure measuring device on your arm, you would find that your blood pressure increases. All of this will happen if you are just thinking about some state of fear, but if you were actually afraid, the results would be much more evident.

So it is with the woman when she comes to labor. She finds it difficult to relax, and this difficulty is increased by the anxiety and fear which are aroused in her by virtue of her past training. For fast, easy childbirth the muscles of the birth canal must relax and the opening must become much larger than it usually is. Therefore, to learn to relax the body is of paramount importance for comfortable childbirth, and, through suggestion and instruction under hypnosis, most normal people can learn to relax well. Using this technique, therefore, we have tried to teach patients how to relax and to put this ability under their own control so that they will not be dependent upon someone else for help in doing this. We are confident that, to the extent the patient learns to do this, she will decrease the unnecessary discomfort of labor, and both she and her baby will benefit. Furthermore, if the patient carries this training in relaxation over into everyday life she will gain great benefits from it, for we probably still have little realization of how many of our various difficulties can be traced ultimately to the constant tension which so many people in our society exhibit.

In the above paragraph we have digressed somewhat from the main purpose of this chapter; namely, to give the results of our experience in using hypnosis as a preparation for childbirth. We have tried to emphasize, however, that our conception of hypnosis is that it is a natural and useful method of training for the average individual. We have trained a large number of obstetrical patients, the only qualification in the selection of these patients being their willingness to take the training. There was no selection of good subjects for hypnosis. We made no promises to these patients, simply telling them that we were interested in determining the effectiveness of hypnosis in alleviating the discomforts of childbirth. They were told further that, if they desired drug sedation during labor, they would receive it just as though they had not had the prenatal training. We did not use hypnosis as a method of dominating the patient, nor did we represent it as a panacea of all ills. Rather, as indicated above, we tried to get the patient to look upon it as an educational process. Partly as the result of this approach, which we believe to be the correct one, we have had no negative public reaction to our program, and most of the women who were approached, both private and clinic patients, were glad to participate in the training. Statistically, this amounted to about 90 per cent. This figure may be of interest to physicians who may consider using hypnosis in this way.

Also along these lines of looking upon this as an educational process, we have tried to keep to a minimum the various traditional tests which are used to determine the depth of hypnosis. We have been mindful of the fact that many of these tests seem rather silly. For example, even the most commonly used one of inability to open the eyelids under the influence of suggestion sometimes evokes such comments as, "Well, I couldn't open my eyes, but that is ridiculous." Many persons then feel this as a deflation of their ego.

They look upon the control of their eyelids as their own private right, and they resent an invasion of its sanctity. We tell the patient that we have to use a few of these tests in order to see how well they are progressing, that they should look upon these tests in the same light as other tests which are given in the physician's office, and that we will use no more than are necessary for our purpose. Insofar as possible we also try to give the patient a rationale for his behavior and thus try to prevent the formation of an attitude that there is something mysterious going on. We believe that if hypnosis is to come into general professional use with normal persons, as in obstetrics or dentistry, the attitude of the hypnotist must be markedly different than that of the stage performer who deliberately seeks to build an atmosphere of mystery around this phenomenon. The physician, using hypnosis in his professional capacity, must respect the individuality of his patient, or else public resistance to hypnosis will again be aroused and the public will lose the benefits which are to be derived from this technique.

With these considerations in mind, patients came individually to the hospital where they were taken to a small room and a brief explanation was given to them somewhat along the lines indicated above. They were seated in a comfortable chair, preferably one which could be tilted back to the position which was the most comfortable for the individual. One or another of the ordinary methods of inducing hypnosis was then used. When the subject was apparently reacting, a few of the simpler tests were used, and efforts were then made to increase the depth of the trance, with repeated suggestions of relaxation and statements of how one feels when one becomes completely relaxed. After the subject seemed quite well relaxed and was in some degree of the hypnotic state, we would frequently leave her lying in the chair for a number of minutes. Sometimes this would induce a greater depth of the trance, but in any case it was good training for what the subject should do in labor. We would also give suggestions concerning behavior during labor and descriptions of the sensations of labor, with suggestions that the patient should not mistakenly identify the sensations coming from a strong muscular contraction as pain sensations. The whole effort was to induce in the subject at the time of labor a calm, relaxed, and detached attitude. Especially with the primipara (a woman who is having her first baby) this could only be done by forewarning her of the kind of experience she would have, so that when it came it would not seem strange and frightening to her.

No serious attempt was made to induce anesthesia in our patients as far as labor was concerned, although a number of them could have anesthesia induced in the back of the hand. There is a serious technical difficulty involved in the induction of anesthesia in the parts of the body used in childbirth: the average woman does not have the necessary language equipment by means of which these parts may be designated to her or by means of which she may represent these parts to herself. Therefore, it is difficult to formulate suggestions with reference to the anesthesia of these organs. This difficulty does not exist in those parts of the body involved in dentistry, and in many patients an anesthesia of the mouth, gums, and teeth can be quite easily induced. Furthermore, if the patient is properly prepared psychologically for labor and the attitude mentioned above is maintained, it is questionable whether there is need for anesthesia, labor proceeding without discomfort except that associated with hard work.

The use of hypnosis in preparation for and during childbirth is not an innovation. Although it has been used sporadically by many physicians, we believe that in our study we have taken a different attitude toward it than have others. If one may judge by the published reports of most of these cases, it appears that the obstetrician was looking for the spectacular and reported only those cases in which such results were obtained.

Personal communications from a number of physicians have been variable in their reaction to the use of hypnosis in obstetrics, ranging from enthusiastic approval of the technique to a noncommittal acceptance of it as another possible method of analgesia.

The older literature is replete with descriptions of the use of hypnosis in a large variety of ailments both in general medicine and in obstetrics and surgery, but to date there has been no objective attempt to evaluate it in its true perspective and from an unbiased point of view.

This we believe to be a serious error from the standpoint of establishing hypnosis as a useful technique for general use in this field. It is conceivable that the obstetrician has gone about as far as he can in the development of physiological devices and techniques of use in parturition. Certainly, great advances have been made. Possibly no chemical sedative can be devised which is entirely free from danger to the mother and baby, and certainly the introduction of any such chemical into the body is not a natural process. We can only praise the medical researcher for his concentration on the development of physiological methods and drugs to alleviate suffering at childbirth, but when his efforts in those directions begin to show diminishing returns, then it is time to approach the problem in a different manner. When we find a way, therefore, which does give spectacular results in some cases, let us not fail to explore the value of the method in the remainder. Perhaps we can develop the method to the point where we can appreciably increase these remarkable results. Of one thing we can be certain, and that is that, according to available knowledge, there is positively no element of danger to either the mother or the baby in the use of hypnosis.

In the evaluation of the effects of this kind of treatment, we must rely upon the subjective estimates of the patients or upon some objective indications, or upon both. Most of those physicians who have used hypnosis for childbirth in the past have relied upon subjective estimates of the patients or their own subjective estimates of the effectiveness of the treatment. It is highly desirable to have the patient feel that she has received help from the treatment, but the subjective estimates of the hypnotist concerning the effects of his efforts may have little or no value. We must never forget that suggestibility is a characteristic of all normal persons and that, therefore, when a person is looking for favorable results he is very likely subjectively to find them, since he may be suggesting such results to himself. Therefore, we can place most confidence in objective results.

In order to get meaningful objective results we must have two groups of patients. The one group we have trained as indicated above will be called the *trained group*. The other group will be untrained and picked at random from the hospital files and will be called the *untrained group*. We must then determine how comparable these two groups are in characteristics which have something to do with labor other than the training.

In Table 12–1 we give a comparison of our two groups in some of these characteristics.

TABLE 12–1

Comparison of Trained and Untrained Groups

	No. of Subjects	Mean Age	No. of Primiparae	Mean No. of Pregnancies	Mean No. of Living Children	Mean Weight of Baby
Trained	100	24.2	62	1.62	.55	7.1 lb
Untrained	88	24.9	42	2.15	1.03	7.3 lb

As Table 12–1 shows, these two groups are quite similar in respect to age and the weight of the baby, two factors which are related to duration and ease of labor, but in our trained group we have more women with their first baby than in the untrained group. This, though accidental, makes the interpretation of our results very conservative since the length of labor, as we will show later, is known to be longer for the first baby than for subsequent ones.

In the present experiment, the chief objective indication we have of the effectiveness of this training is in regard to the length of labor. Labor is divided into three stages:

1. The period during which the cervix or opening of the womb is dilating so that the baby may pass through. This is the stage which is so long for most women and in which they become so tired.
2. The passage of the baby through the birth canal to the outside world.
3. The passage of the afterbirth.

In Table 12–2 is shown the effectiveness of our training on the length of the first stage of labor. It is appreciably decreased.

TABLE 12–2

Comparison of Trained and Untrained Groups with Reference to Labor

	First Stage	Second Stage	Third Stage	Mean Amount of Demerol Given during Labor
Trained	8.32 hr *	35.8 min	8.8 min	103.5 mg
Untrained	10.31 hr	34.8 min	7.4 min	123.6 mg

* The record of one experimental is omitted from these calculations. She was a primipara who had a first-stage labor of 72 hours with a breech delivery. During all that period, however, she took only 100 mg of Demerol. No comparable case is included in the control group.

An inspection of Table 12–2 indicates that the mean length of the first stage is 1.99 hours less for the trained group.

Whenever a scientist looks at set figures in which a difference apparently exists because of some condition which he has introduced, he always has in the back of his mind the suggestion that the difference might have occurred anyway by chance. There is a statistical method of determining the likelihood of the difference occurring by chance. In this case, this likelihood is only about 3 chances out of 100 that this difference would occur without the training.

The reader will also note that the trained women required less Demerol (a sedative which is often used for the relief of discomfort during childbirth), on the average, than did the untrained women. This is a condition much to be desired since, as we noted above, none of these drugs is without danger to the mother and baby.

It is generally recognized that the labor of the primipara is longer than the labor of the multipara (a woman who has already had one or more children). This was true in the case of the patients with whose records we are dealing in this experiment. In Table 12–3 we see how much this difference is.

TABLE 12–3

Comparison of First-stage Labor in Primiparae and Multiparae

	Number of Primiparae	Number of Multiparae	First Stage, Mean in Hours Primiparae	Multiparae	Difference
Trained	62	38	9.65	6.17	3.48 *
Untrained	42	36	12.88	7.96	4.92 †

Probability of occurrence by chance: * 1 in 1000 † 8 in 10,000.

The reason for mentioning these facts in this report is that, as has already been said, we had 14 per cent more primiparae in our trained group than in our untrained group. Therefore, if there had been no training, we should have expected the former group to have an appreciably longer first stage than the latter; consequently, the training probably had a greater effect than is indicated by the difference of 1.99 hours.

This probability becomes more likely when we consider the effects of the training on the primiparae as compared with the multiparae. This difference is shown in Table 12–4.

TABLE 12–4

Comparison of the Reaction to the Training of the Primiparae to the Multiparae in Terms of the Mean Length of the First Stage of Labor

	Mean Hours, First Stage	Mean Difference in Hours
Primiparae		
Trained	9.65	3.23 *
Untrained	12.88	
Multiparae		
Trained	6.17	1.79 †
Untrained	7.96	

Probability of occurrence by chance: * 3 in 100. † 4 in 100.

As we would expect, the training shows greater benefits to the girl who is having her first baby. This is partly because her first stage of labor is longer than for the multiparae, and, therefore, there is more possibility of reduction. No doubt, also, the woman who has had a bad time with her first baby is harder to train, since her personal experience tends to support her belief that childbirth is an ordeal.

In addition to the objective data which are presented above, we could add the testimony of our patients with reference to the help which they felt they had received from the training, ranging from extreme enthusiasm to the belief that the training did little or no good. This latter type of report is in the extremely small minority. No one expressed a belief that the training was detrimental.

The reader may naturally wonder why the training was not universally successful. The reasons for this are several and varied:

First, in this as in almost everything else, some people learn quicker and better than others. At the present time there is no known method of overcoming these individual differences.

Second, some people are still a bit afraid of hypnosis and therefore unconsciously draw back from it, although not to the extent of refusing to take the training. This difficulty will disappear as the public learns to appreciate the true nature of hypnosis and the benefits to be obtained from it.

A third difficulty is that the obstetrical nursing staff is not adequately trained to handle patients under hypnosis. A patient in the hypnotic state must be handled differently from one under the influence of a sedative. She should be spoken to quietly and gently, should not be questioned unless absolutely necessary, should be told of any manipulation by the nurse or physician before the manipulation is done, and, while it is in progress, should be given suggestions frequently of relaxation and hypnotic sleep, and undue noises should be eliminated, especially cries from the delivery room and complaints of other patients. These are not difficult measures to take, but when one is accustomed to working with patients under drug sedation, it becomes easy to disregard these small irritations; irritations, nevertheless, which help to make it difficult for the patient to remain relaxed since consciousness is never lost in the hypnotic state.

However, even if these and other difficulties could be overcome, it is still questionable whether the use of this method will become general. The greatest limiting factor is the time needed for training the patient, since most obstetricians feel that they cannot spend so much time with each patient. The solution to this difficulty could be to have some one person, who makes hypnosis his business, give such hypnotic training under the direction of the physician. We feel that an even better solution is to try to develop a technique by which the training can be given to groups of 8 or 10 patients by the physician himself. We believe, or at least hope, that such a technique can be developed, and we expect to continue to work upon it.

SUMMARY

Despite the various difficulties, we have been able to reduce the length of the first stage of labor by about 20 per cent and with the aid of less drug. This is an average figure and does not stress the spectacular results which are obtainable in some patients.

To exchange 1 or 2 hours spent in pleasant, comfortable prenatal training for some of the hours spent in the first stage of labor is a bargain which most women would be glad to make, especially when it results in less danger to themselves and to their babies.

Furthermore, we believe that this result can be improved in the future as knowledge of better training methods is gained. We believe that, eventually, childbirth can be accomplished in the normal case with no discomfort other than that attendant upon hard work.

CHAPTER THIRTEEN

Hypnodontics

Editor's Note

The most surprising development in the history of hypnosis is the recent adoption on a somewhat wide scale of the use of hypnosis in dentistry. For over a hundred years there have been occasional tooth extractions performed with hypnotic anesthesia, in most cases as a demonstration of an interesting and unusual phenomenon. However, most dentists have felt that hypnosis had no place in actual dental practice. In isolated instances a dentist might become interested and, at times, resort to hypnosis, but fears of damaged reputation among patients have been sufficient to make such use very rare.

Within the past few months the various dental journals have published more articles on hypnosis in dentistry than in their entire previous history, indicating the degree of interest now being shown by the profession. This interest is still confined to certain localities but is rapidly spreading to others. It has arisen very largely from the fervent and enthusiastic efforts of Dr. Thomas A. Burgess, a psychologist of Moorhead, Minnesota, who has lectured on and demonstrated the use of hypnosis in dentistry since 1927. It has been further supplemented by Dr. Aaron A. Moss, a "hypnodontist" of Bernardsville, New Jersey, and in Southern California over 100 dentists have studied hypnosis in classes given by psychologists.

Dr. Burgess might be said to have become a self-appointed missionary as to *hypnodontia*, a splendidly descriptive word coined by Burgess and Moss during a conversation. He is head of the psychology department of Concordia College in Moorhead, his spare time being devoted to lecturing about and teaching techniques of hypnodontics. Additionally, he is in private practice as a clinical psychologist. Burgess has appeared before dozens of medical and dental groups in many different parts of the country, and also in Canada, often conducting classes and teaching his methods to dentists who become interested after hearing a lecture or reading some of the technical articles on the subject.

In the Northwest Central states, use of hypnosis in dentistry has become a regular procedure with many dentists and is resorted to on occasion by many more. At first, some dentists who learned hypnodontics were reluctant to call it to the attention of patients, fearful of losing them if the dentist became known as a hypnotist. Those who ventured to recommend hypnosis were somewhat surprised to find most patients receptive to the idea if it would bring freedom from pain. They also discovered that patients, pleased with the results, were voluble in recommending the method to friends. In many towns and cities it is now commonplace for a patient to visit the hypnodontist asking for hypnotic escape from pain. Instead of losing patients, the hypnodontist finds word-of-mouth advertising is bringing him new ones. When this is reported, other dentists lose their reluctance to employ hypnosis and take up this new technique in dentistry.

As hypnodontia is a field for extensive practical utilization of hypnosis, the next two chapters are devoted to discussions of the subject. The paper by Burgess is from the leading teacher of hypnodontics; that by Moss is contributed by a dental surgeon who has used hypnosis extensively in his practice for over ten years. It will be noted that they approach the subject from a somewhat different viewpoint. Dr. Moss feels that the most important consideration in hypnodontics is producing the hypnotic trance which results in such a degree of relaxation that there is an automatic rise in the pain threshold. Whether or not complete analgesia can then be obtained through suggestion is immaterial, though highly advantageous. If not, the threshold of pain has been changed to permit further analgesia by use of only a small amount of Novocain or other drug.

The approach of Dr. Burgess differs in that he believes it is possible to obtain analgesia with a very large percentage of patients, and hence hypnotic anesthesia is of primary importance. Results, as reported by dentists who have studied his methods, seem to bear out his contentions. Experienced workers in hypnosis find his statistics as to the production of successful analgesia most surprising. However, he is undoubtedly correct in his analysis of the reasons. He believes that this high percentage is due to the motivations of the patients who subject themselves to hypnotic anesthesia, and to the fact that they are above average in intelligence.

Freud has called attention to the fact that one of the two strongest of all human drives is the avoidance of pain, the other being the pursuit of pleasure. The dental patient is aware that much dental work involves pain—very considerable pain. His dental experience has probably been most unpleasant, and he has found drug anesthesia not too satisfactory, as a rule, either at the time or in its aftereffects. His desire to avoid pain provides the strongest motivation to accept both hypnosis and the analgesia which, he is informed, can be produced under hypnosis. He is not only ordinarily suggestible; his need for escape from pain makes him eager to accept any suggestion which will enable him to avoid it. Therefore, he is far more likely to enter a trance than is the average person under other circumstances, and also to produce analgesia when it is suggested. His great need brings successful results. It is this fact that leads Dr. Burgess to emphasize the use of suggestive anesthesia in hypnodontics. At the same time, he recognizes that success cannot be universal with all patients. Both Dr. Moss and Dr. Burgess agree that best results for the dentist and for the patient are only possible if the dentist is adequately trained in techniques.

Hypnodontics

By AARON A. MOSS, D.D.S.*

To coin a convenient technical term, *hypnodontics* may be said to be that branch of dental science which deals with the use and application of hypnosis or any other form of controlled suggestion in the practice of dentistry.

The dental profession is showing a definite trend at the present time toward an interest in learning and applying this new science of hypnodontics. This is being manifested extensively, not only by individual members of the profession but by various dental societies and groups. The leaders in the field of hypnodontics are receiving numerous requests for lectures and information, and there are many inquiries as to the availability of postgraduate courses by dental schools. The interest has reached such proportions in some sections that three regular organizations have been formed. The American Society for the Advancement of Hypnodontics was established in New York in 1948 with about 12 members, as of January 1, 1950, having a paid-up roster of 75. With headquarters in the Middle West, the American Society of Psychosomatic Dentistry has an even larger roll and is growing rapidly, its members being certified and accredited in the use of psychosomatic sleep, as they have termed hypnosis. In Los Angeles the Hypnotic Study Club meets regularly, with a membership mostly of dentists but including a few physicians and psychologists. With over 60 members, it, too, is rapidly expanding.

A comprehensive presentation of both the theoretical and the practical approach to the subject of hypnodontics has been made by the author of this article in a full-length textbook, *Hypnodontics,*

* 20 Morristown Rd., Bernardsville, N. J.

or Hypnosis in Dentistry, published by Dental Items of Interest Publishing Co. In this book the uses, advantages, and indications, as well as the disadvantages, contraindications, and limitations are discussed in detail. The many techniques of induction are presented, together with tests for susceptibility to hypnosis. Until now there has been very little material on the subject available for the dentist which has been written by a member of the profession. The dentist has been obliged to obtain all information either from a psychologist or, unfortunately, from a lay hypnotist, such instructors being without dental training. With the present rapid increase in interest among the dental profession, a number of dentists are now qualified as hypnodontists and will be able to teach its application.

The present paper is, essentially, a summary or digest of some portions of the above-mentioned textbook. It is intended to familiarize the reader with some of the uses and applications of hypnodontics. It is also intended to consider some of the problems confronted and to give a word of caution to the dentist who is now using hypnosis or who plans to take up this new branch of dentistry.

A thorough familiarity and knowledge, together with practical experience in the technique of inducing hypnosis, is fundamental for the application of hypnodontics. The following presents the minimum information which the hypnodontist should possess, in addition to basic training in induction technique.

The application of hypnosis in dentistry is usually identified as a matter of anesthesia for painless tooth extraction. This misconception holds true not only in the minds of the lay public but also in the minds of those psychologists and others who work in the field of hypnosis. The reason, perhaps, is that as far back as 1837 the literature describes the extraction of teeth by Oudet, a French dentist, while in 1890, Henry Carter and W. Arthur Turner, two dentists of Leeds, gave sensational clinical demonstrations before various British medical gatherings. The literature on hypnosis is full of descriptions of such demonstrations of the use of hypnoanesthesia in medical and dental surgery. This may explain why this concept of the limited application of hypnodontics exists.

If there were no other application than for anesthesia, hypnodontics would be nothing more than a spectacular phenomenon, but one quite impractical for general dental application. This is because only a small percentage of people are susceptible to complete or profound hypnoanesthesia. Actually, there are other wide uses to which hypnosis can be applied in dentistry aside from anesthesia. Space limitations prevent more than the presentation of high lights on these applications.

The uses of hypnodontics fall into two categories:

1. Hypnodontal therapeutics
    a. Patient relaxation
    b. Elimination of the patient's fears and anxiety as to treatment, etc.
    c. Removal of objections to orthodontic or prosthetic appliances which are necessary for treatment, after such treatment had previously been accepted by the patient
    d. Maintenance of patient's comfort during long, arduous dental work or operation
    e. Accustoming the patient to orthodontic or prosthetic appliances
2. Operative
    a. Anesthesia or analgesia
    b. Amnesia for unpleasant work
    c. Substitution for and in conjunction with premedication in general anesthesia
    d. Preventing of gagging and nausea
    e. Control of saliva flow
    f. Control of bleeding
    g. Postoperative anesthesia

It should be mentioned that the science of hypnodontics does not necessarily do away with the present use of drugs. It should be stressed that hypnosis is used as an adjunct to the present dental armamentarium. With this thought in mind, there is no danger of overselling the use of hypnosis to the dental profession.

Before going further into the discussion of the above applications, the writer would like to sound a strong warning to dentists interested in using hypnosis in their profession. *Hypnodontics should not be abused by the dental profession.* The dentist using hypnosis has the means at his disposal of probing into the unconscious of an individual. With only a little experience he can produce the peculiar phenomena characteristic of hypnosis such as age regression, hallucinations, illusions, catalepsy, etc. These phenomena lie in the fields of either psychotherapy or experimental psychology. The type of training and background of a dentist does not qualify him for this work. These are highly specialized fields of medicine or of psychology, requiring special training and experience which the dentist lacks.

This does not mean that the dentist should be hesitant in using hypnosis in dentistry. On the contrary, like a lancet, hypnosis is a very valuable instrument in the hands of a dentist, but the fact that a dentist may have the legal and moral right to use a lancet does not give him the right to open an abdominal cavity and remove an appendix. The dentist, as well as the physician, can and should and does borrow from all fields of medicine and science to apply whatever knowledge he can to alleviate pain, suffering, and discomfort, and for improving the general welfare of mankind. Not only is he entitled to do this, but he has an obligation to his patients to do it. It is with this ethical and moral approach that the dentist should avail himself of hypnosis and apply it in his dental practice. The lancet and hypnotic technique, like anesthesia and drugs, are instruments and armamentarium that belong to the dentist as well as to the physician.

There is in the field of hypnosis, just as in the field of anesthesia, a school of thought which aims at denying such rights to dentists. Those who feel this way fall into two groups:

1. Those who feel that hypnosis is associated with witchcraft or mysticism
2. Those who feel that hypnosis is an instrument of such a nature as to be dangerous in the hands of anyone but a physician or psychotherapist or psychologist

Of course the position of the first group is utterly ridiculous, and the public is gradually becoming better informed as to hypnosis. But the second group includes physicians and psychologists who are influenced by instances of abuse or misuse of hypnotism. The only insurance against this in dentistry is for the dentists to set up their own code of ethics and limitations for the use of hypnosis.

Preparatory to the use of hypnodontics, the dentist, in his training, should be given enough understanding of psychology or psychiatry to let him realize that he is not dealing with a simple thing if he steps out of his field in using hypnosis. For instance, before attempting to cure the smoking habit he should appreciate that smoking is a peculiar manifestation, at times, of a very complex and complicated personality structure. He should know that there is in smoking a certain necessary release and outlet of nervous and psychic energy. He, the dentist, must know that smoking, like thumb-sucking, constipation, headache, inferiority, etc., is often the resultant of many hidden, powerful, unconscious forces. The removal of any nervous or neurotic symptom or habits may throw the entire psychic mechanism into turmoil and confusion and unbalance. The untrained person may be satisfied with the removal of a symptom, but the trained eyes and understanding of a psychiatrist or psychologist will see a powerful threat to the entire personality structure. Such interference as the superficial symptom removal may have a psychological traumatic effect and is nothing less than a "bull in a china shop."

The American Society for the Advancement of Hypnodontics has passed a strong resolution banning the use of hypnosis by dentists for any form of psychotherapy other than such as may relate to dental problems. The society members are fully aware of what such abuses imply and, since hypnodontics is a young infant, the society guards its charge with zeal and jealousy. The American Society of Psychosomatic Dentistry is also on record in the same way.

Psychodental therapy, however, is strictly within the province of dentistry. Elimination of fear and anxiety for dental work, such as drilling, surgery, etc., has always been a problem for dentists. Where necessary, the dentist has always resorted to drugs such as sedatives and in premedication. Hypnosis is extremely useful here as a substitute.

One of the chief uses of hypnosis is in obtaining relaxation, which is so desirable for dental work. Obviously, for this hypnosis need not be deep, a light or medium trance being sufficient. About 90 per cent of the people are beneficially susceptible to a light state of hypnosis, and it will be remembered that relaxation is a symptom of the first or hypnoidal stage of hypnosis. The patient is fully conscious but, in this relaxed state, has a somewhat euphoric feeling. Also, with the relaxation achieved in a light hypnosis, the pain threshold is generally raised spontaneously.

Elimination of fear and apprehension is somewhat more difficult, owing to the deep roots in the unconscious of such fear and anxiety. It is hard to convince a person that he will not have pain, when all his life's experience tells him otherwise. It must be pointed out here that the oral cavity is a very important erotogenic zone. All parts of the oral cavity have great psychic importance, the oral mucosa, the tongue, the lips, the teeth, etc. Exposing these areas to the manipulation of another individual has highly disturbing significance to many individuals. It is from these roots that fear and anxiety spring. Many patients will remark that they know that the impending extraction will not hurt and that there is nothing to it, yet they cannot understand why they are quaking so violently. The dentist should know something of the reasons. For instance, extraction of teeth may be associated unconsciously with punishment, sadism, or even castration. The patient knows nothing consciously of this, yet the hypnodontist should be aware of it.

It is not possible to remove or even reduce all fear in all patients because of these facts, but it is possible to remove all fear in some people, and some fear in most people. More than one sitting may be required to accomplish this. Before dental work is started, perhaps two or three sittings should be devoted to the removal of fear. Highly nervous, neurotic people, particularly, will require extra time and effort, but it pays dividends in the end. As to the time element, once fear and anxiety have been eliminated, or if anesthesia has been produced, in all subsequent sittings this can be accomplished almost instantaneously. In other words, once induction has been successfully accomplished, hypnosis can be produced almost instantly at subsequent sittings; and therapeutic good can be accomplished by means of posthypnotic suggestions.

The writer has encountered several cases where patients were placed in the hypnotic trance and suddenly would begin to cry miserably or to tremble. This need cause the dentist no alarm. Usually, it will be found that the patient has been wrought up and under tension for a long time. His nerves have been taut owing to financial, domestic, or other pressures. Such an outburst of tears is the manifestation of "release" of tension. They are "letting go." It is best not to work on the patient at that sitting but to permit and encourage the patient to "let go" even further. These patients find a release of nervous tension under hypnosis. Although it may be somewhat alarming to the dentist, it is not only harmless but actually beneficial to the patient. Such a spontaneous outburst of tears should not be identified with the outburst of crying a patient may experience under the probing pressure of analytic psychotherapy. In the latter case a condition of emotional conflict is brought about deliberately by the psychotherapist. He is equipped to handle such a situation.

If a patient undergoes this spontaneous release of nervous tension with crying, he should be encouraged to complete his crying spell and to let go even more while under hypnosis. Before he is awakened, always explain how much better he will feel as a result of having released such tension. He should be told that he will feel a complete relief when he has awakened; that he will feel better than he has felt for a long time, as, in fact, he will. The author has had cases of patients crying in trance during which it was possible for work to be done. Upon awakening, as a result of posthypnotic suggestion, amnesia for the crying experience was developed. The patients always felt relaxed and better upon awakening.

Another example of dental hypnotherapy is the conditioning of a patient to wear a prosthetic or orthodontic appliance. This is accomplished by giving him in the trance positive, firm, posthypnotic suggestions that there will be no difficulty in becoming accustomed to the appliance. There are times when it may be necessary to question the patient while in a trance to get at the root of a problem in this connection. Although this is permissible, a dentist should realize that certain difficulties may have ramifications which take the patient into the field of psychotherapy. This should, therefore, be handled only by a qualified psychotherapist.

Only some 20 to 25 per cent of people are capable of achieving complete anesthesia, and in some cases several sessions may be necessary. This would be very time consuming. In the majority of cases where the operation will be painful, the writer does not depend entirely on hypnoanesthesia. Where the reduction of pain is not sufficient to permit operation, as in drilling a tooth or where surgery is to be performed, hypnosis is supplemented with other established means of anesthesia. Unless hypnoanesthesia can be established easily and quickly, its use in dental surgery without drugs is limited to demonstrations for other dentists or at a clinic for the profession or for experimental purposes.

The deeper the degree of hypnosis, naturally the more complete will be the anesthesia which can be produced. It is for this reason that anesthesia is limited in application. On the other hand, there are many instances in which anesthesia is possible even in the lighter hypnotic stages. If the anesthesia is not complete there may be pain reflexes present, but with suggestion of amnesia before taking the patient out of the trance, it is possible to drive away all recollection of pain.

Where complete anesthesia is present, in operative work it must be remembered that the same rules hold true as for the usual drug anesthesia. The dentist must not overheat the tooth. This may result in pulp injury. Therefore, he must work slowly while the assistant sprays water on the tooth, at the same time aspirating so that the patient need not arouse himself to spit while in trance. Some patients have a tendency to wake when they are not in a deep trance, even though they may have hypnoanesthesia. Hence the dentist demands little cooperative activity from the patient, treating him as though he were under a general anesthetic. Of course with a deep somnambulistic state this would be unnecessary, but, as was mentioned earlier, most patients are unable to reach a deep state.

It is important for the hypnodontist always to terminate the anesthesia before awakening the patient from the trance; or a time may be set by suggestion for termination of the anesthesia in the posthypnotic period. This may be from 15 minutes to 2 hours or more after the patient leaves the office. The dentist tries to complete the entire dental operation before taking the patient out of hypnosis. For instance, if a tooth has been prepared for filling purposes, with hypnoanesthesia, it is desirable to insert the filling while the patient is still hypnotized because sterilizing and filling the tooth after the trance may then bring pain. This might awaken the patient's memory for pain while in trance, such a memory not being otherwise re-called. It is also best not to question the patient about pain after he is awakened but to assume that anesthesia or amnesia was present. In addition to operative dentistry and surgery, hypnoanesthesia may be used for purposes of periodontal scaling and curettage.

It must be emphasized that hypnoanesthesia can be a substitute for the present drug anesthetics in only a small percentage of individuals. While it may be used alone for decreasing the quantity of pain, it is more often employed along with Novocain or general anesthetics such as nitrous oxide, which are then given in lesser amounts.

In an article appearing in the *Journal of Anesthesiology*, Dr. Bernard B. Raginsky [2] mentions that fear of anesthesia may be due to fear of loss of consciousness, or of mutilation, or of loss of life, or of the unknown. He states that it results in changes of blood pressure, heart rate, capillary permeability, urinary output, coronary flow, rate and depth of respiration, and the carbon dioxide content of the blood. Raginsky writes:

He [the anethesiologist] must learn the structure of normal personality, and see how and to what degree the patient to be anesthetized deviates from that normal. With this knowledge [hypnosis], he can quiet the patient more effectively, use much less of the anesthetic agent and have a smoother anesthesia. . . .

He believes the anesthetist should be more of a physician who makes the patient less fearful, as well as a technician.

Goldman [3] made the same point when he said that anesthesia does not depend upon gas-oxygen balance alone. He suggests that the tone of voice of the operator be calm, slow, and suggestive of sleep. He points out that the tone is more important than the content, and that, at about the fifth to twelfth breath, the voice of the anesthetist should take on the character of a drone, conducive to relaxation and comfortable sleep. Any textbook on anesthesia makes this point. The experienced and skilled anesthetist instinctively applies himself in this way.

Cherry and Pollin,[4] in an article describing the technique and method of employing music in conjunction with nitrous oxide anesthesia, say:

In this method designed to reduce reflexed irritability without resorting to depressing pre-medication, the nitrous oxide oxygen mixtures were maintained with a minimum of 24 per cent oxygen. Nausea, retching, excitement, jactitation, soft tissue obstruction, aspiration and swallowing have been conspicuously absent.

The authors describe an elaborate setup of earphones attached to the patient's ears, connected to a phonograph, with a microphone allowing the anesthetist to speak directly to the patient. Selected music which is soothing and suggestive of sleep is used, such as "Clair de Lune," "Moonlight Sonata," "Evening Star," etc. Actually, this is a form of hypnosis, having all the advantages of the disguised technique explained later.

Raginsky also suggests that the technique of quieting and reassuring the patient prior to general anesthesia can easily be learned, becomes second nature and easy to use. Thereafter, the anesthesiologist will need no more than 5 minutes for the process, with the results, in most cases, well worth the effort.

An important application of hypnosis is in eliminating the gag reflex which is so frequently a nuisance to the dentist. It is not necessary to place the patient in a trance for this purpose because the elimination of gagging can be accomplished exceptionally well by waking hypnotic suggestion. The writer and other dentists to whom he has taught this technique have had most gratifying results in this area.

Controlling the flow of saliva is not a matter of surprise since the autonomic nervous system is subject to some control by the subconscious mind through hypnosis. It is possible, in the experimental laboratory, to bring about through hypnotic suggestion vasoconstriction or vasodilation of peripheral blood vessels and to produce blushing or even blanching of a hand or the face. It is therefore not surprising that the flow of saliva can be affected in the same way. The advantages for the dentist are obvious. Fortunately, a patient need not be in a very deep stage to obtain this control. The salivary flow can be influenced not only during the trance but for a reasonable time thereafter by means of posthypnotic suggestion.

Laboratory experiments with scientific controls which prove that bleeding can be hypnotically controlled are lacking, but such claims are common in the literature. The author has been able to corroborate these statements through practical experience. It is obvious that such control must be true if vasoconstriction and dilatory functions are affected by hypnotic suggestion. Numerous bloodless extractions of teeth have been reported. Dr. Samuel Samet of Newark, New Jersey, demonstrated to a group of about 75 dentists at a meeting of the American Society for the Advancement of Hypnodontics in October, 1949, with the extraction of two upper bicuspids and one lower bicuspid all on the right side. No drug or chemical anesthetic was used. The teeth were firm, and radiographs revealed a normal amount of bone present. Dr. Samet lifted away the periosteum and extracted the three teeth without the slightest indication of pain and without bleeding, while the patient remained in a deep trance. Posthypnotically, there was no sign of bleeding or recollection of pain. Suggestion produced the anesthesia and inhibited the flow of blood.

It has also been stated that healing can be made more rapid as a result of posthypnotic suggestion. Although this is difficult to prove, and controlled experiments are lacking, it would seem possible. Many of the early hypnotists, such as Braid and Bernheim, believed this to be true

Due to the existing prejudices in the minds of the public, the method of approach in suggesting use of hypnosis to the patient is of paramount importance. If not properly presented, the patient may refuse to undergo induction. Sometimes prejudices are so deeply rooted that, even with the proper approach, consent to hypnosis cannot be obtained. There are two ways of handling this matter, one being a circumvention of the problem:

1. The direct technique
2. The disguised technique

With the direct technique the patient is told either by the dentist himself or by his assistant of the many advantages of hypnodontics. It is very helpful if he is permitted to observe another patient being operated on while in a hypnotic state. The role of the dental assistant is of great importance, and in many instances she can, by a careful approach, induce the patient to request hypnosis from the dentist without the dentist having even suggested it.

In the disguised approach nothing is told the patient which would make him aware that he is about to be put in a hypnotic state. He is simply told that he is to relax; that he should make himself comfortable and let his arms and legs become loose and heavy. It is explained that in a relaxed state the threshold of pain is markedly raised, and also that fear and apprehension can be lessened if he remains completely relaxed physically and mentally. Through this means, step by step, he is gradually brought into a trance state. The patient is then unaware that he has been hypnotized. While such a method is usually successful, it must be understood that a patient might realize what is transpiring and become resentful, with a consequent bad relationship ensuing. The writer has had this happen, with the patient refusing to return for further treatment. There is also a medicolegal aspect to the use of the disguised induction of hypnosis and a question of liability. In writing malpractice insurance, one company insists that permission always be obtained from the patient for the use of hypnosis, preferably in writing. The reason stated by the company is that hypnosis in dentistry is, as yet, not an accepted and standardized procedure.

Since the writer practices dentistry in a small town, most of his patients are aware that hypnodontics is an established method in his work, and therefore the disguised technique is unnecessary. Many patients now actually request the use of hypnosis because of the writer's reputation as a hypnodontist.

The hypnodontist may give the patient posthypnotic suggestions which will serve as a protection from the experimental amateur or vaudeville hypnotist. The wording of these suggestions could be somewhat as follows: "In future no one will be able to hypnotize you except a dentist, a physician, or some other qualified person such as a psychologist; unless you expressly desire to be hypnotized, no one can hypnotize you." It is important not to close out all future susceptibility. The patient's desires should be learned, as he might at some future time wish to be a subject for therapeutic purposes.

Before dismissing any patient who has been in a hypnotic trance it is imperative to observe two things:

1. To remove any hypnotic suggestion that might continue to operate in the posthypnotic period
2. To make certain the patient is wide awake

Any suggestions which might have been given, perhaps as tests, such as paralysis of a limb, should be removed. If, for any reason, countersuggestion is not made, there is a possibility that such a paralysis may continue to operate in the posthypnotic period. It is important to set a time limit to any analgesia or anesthesia in the posthypnotic period. If a hallucination has been produced in the trance, it is important to remove it before awakening the patient. These are always important considerations whether or not the operator is a hypnodontist, psychologist, psychiatrist, or amateur hypnotist.

The hypnodontist, as well as the psychotherapist, is legally and morally responsible for a patient's condition and welfare at the time he leaves the office, after he has been in a trance. This is just as true for hypnosis as it is for general anesthesia. If a patient, because of a partially depressed state owing to incomplete awakening or recovery from trance, should meet with an auto accident, it might involve the practitioner in legal complications as to responsibility, as is true after the administration of general anesthetic drugs. For this reason some hypnodontists make it a practice to hand each patient a cloth dampened with water with which to wipe his face after he has been awakened. This precaution is necessary only when a patient has been in a very deep trance. It is wise, however, to observe every patient for a short time and converse with him before dismissing him. This will serve to ascertain the complete recovery from the trance.

Of course hypnodontics is no panacea. It is not a substitute for existing techniques nor for the drugs now employed in the practice of dentistry. It must be stressed that it has certain limitations which are, primarily:

1. Limitation of susceptibility to deep trance
2. Uncertainty of results
3. Existing prejudices

Not every patient lends himself to the various benefits and advantages which may be derived from hypnodontics. Complete anesthesia can be developed at the first sitting with only about 10 to 15 per cent of patients. However, with several sittings, a patient can be conditioned to a point where the percentage is doubled. Partial analgesia is obtainable in about 50 to 75 per cent of patients. On the other hand, the use of drugs eliminates all uncertainty and is 100 per cent successful.

Another marked disadvantage in using hypnosis is the time consumed in conditioning a patient. Many busy dentists will find it impractical and undesirable to spend so much time in view of the uncertainty involved. Many practitioners also feel that the necessary training and experience required for a high percentage of success is an obstacle. Insofar as time is concerned, it must be pointed out that reinduction of hypnosis is a matter of only a few seconds or a few minutes when proper posthypnotic suggestions to this effect are given, after the trance has been induced the first time. Also, a psychologist trained in hypnosis or a hypnodontic specialist may be called upon to condition a patient, either at his own office or that of the dentist, with a transferring of rapport. There are more skilled psychologists capable of such work today than at any time in the past, owing to the growing use and interest in hypnosis in fields other than dentistry.

Against the above disadvantages there exist a number of advantages which have been discussed throughout the text. Hypnosis is extremely useful and successful in relaxation of nervous and excitable patients, eliminating fear and tension, making long, arduous sittings more tolerable. The hypnodontic patient approaches his dental appointments with pleasant anticipation instead of dread and anxiety. There is a definite enhancement in the prestige of the hypnodontist, because of his added service, skill, and ability. It is the usual experience of hypnodontists that new patients seek appointments and request hypnosis, when word-of-mouth information is spread by patients who have experienced hypnotic treatment.

Hypnosis can, on some occasions, be used alone for minor dental surgery and frequently for drilling cavities. More often, it is used in conjunction with local or general anesthesia, being very valuable for this purpose. It very definitely reduces the amount of anesthetic agent required for successful anesthesia. Where drug anesthesia is contraindicated, as in a bad heart condition, hypnosis should always be attempted.

Because of the added time and service, the hypnodontist is, of course, entitled to an additional fee. Many charge a fee ranging from $10 to $100, depending on their clientele, experience, time necessary, and demand of patients. When a dentist has become established as a hypnodontist and has gained a reputation for this work, patients will refer other patients who request this service, and patients will also be referred by other dentists and physicians. The hypnodontist definitely creates a demand for his services, although some dentists have hesitated to adopt hypnosis for fear that some of their patients might be offended.

The question of who will make a good hypnodontist can be answered briefly by saying that any dentist who applies himself and receives proper clinical training and instruction can easily develop the skill required. No special abilities are needed other than a good personality and the techniques which come with experience.

No supernatural or special powers are involved. Naturally, the temperament of the individual dentist will vary. The amount of time required for acquiring skill is hence variable, though the total number of hours is not great. Of course some work, study, and experience are indispensable.

The question of where proper and adequate postgraduate training can be obtained is at present difficult to answer. Several dental colleges are contemplating offering such courses. In several localities well-qualified psychologists are offering special courses for dentists, teaching them in small groups at reasonable cost. The reader may obtain the latest information by applying to The American Society for the Advancement of Hypnodontics, Dr. H. W. Marcus, Secretary, 200 Central Park West, New York City, New York; or The American Society of Psychosomatic Dentistry, Dr. Thomas O. Burgess, Moorhead, Minnesota; or The Hypnotic Study Club, Dr. James Hixson, 6253 Hollywood Boulevard, Hollywood, California.

The dental colleges planning to offer such courses in their graduate curriculum should include as part of the proper training:

1. General principles of psychology
2. Principles of psychosomatics in medicine and dentistry
3. Theory of hypnosis
4. Practical clinical training in induction of hypnosis and hypnodontics

Any graduate dentist receiving such training would be well qualified to practice hypnodontics. Of course, practice can be begun with less training, until such courses are available. In many instances dental colleges will be obliged to utilize the teaching services of a psychiatrist or a psychologist. At present there are too few dentists willing to teach or qualified to administer postgraduate training in hypnodontics. However, with so much recent interest, an adequate number of dental teachers will soon be available.

REFERENCES

Moss, A. A.: *Hypnodontics, or hypnosis in dentistry*, Dental Items of Interest Publishing Co., Brooklyn, N. Y., 1952.

2. Raginsky, B. B.: "Mental suggestion as an aid in anesthesia," *J. Anesthesiology*, p. 467, September, 1948.
3. Goldman, J. D.: "Better and safer gas oxygen anesthesia for exodontists," *Dental Items Interest*, **67**:359, 1945.
4. Cherry, H., and Pollin, I. M.: "Music as a supplement in dental nitrous oxide–oxygen anesthesia," *Dental Digest*, **54** (10):455, October, 1948.

CHAPTER FOURTEEN

Hypnosis in Dentistry

Hypnosis in Dentistry

By THOMAS O. BURGESS, Ph.D.

DEPARTMENT OF PSYCHOLOGY, CONCORDIA COLLEGE,
MOORHEAD, MINNESOTA

INTRODUCTION

One hundred and seven dentists here in the northwest and twenty-three in nearby Canada have been trained in the use of hypnosis in dental operations. Most of them are using the technique. More are being trained. . . .

We conservatively estimate that several thousand dental operations have been done.

The above pithy statement by Hyde [1] appears as an editorial in the January, 1950, issue of *North-West Dentistry*. It gives a fair summary of the status of *hypnodontia* (hypnosis as applied to dentistry) in the Middle Western states for the 2-year period 1948–1949. Since then, a great many more dentists have received such training.

The application of hypnosis to dentistry is not new. In 1837 Jean Etienne Oudet, a dentist, told the French Academy of Medicine of the extraction of teeth during what he called "magnetic sleep." Eight years later a series of rather quaint but interesting reports emanated from England. A typical one is presented as follows:

From *The Critic* of May 31, 1845,[2] addressed to Dr. John Elliotson.

On Tuesday, Feb. 4th, before a numerous company assembled to witness the operation, I extracted a large molar tooth without the knowledge of the patient whilst in the state of mesmeric sleep. The patient is a girl . . . previously mesmerized only a few times. . . .

Signed by William Curtis, Surgeon.

Curtis mentioned that the public of the time was skeptical as regards mesmerism but he believed it could be a most valuable force for the relief of human suffering. He described the operation as borne with no sign of suffering and with complete postoperative amnesia present.

During the intervening hundred years, men of science have not advanced very far in their general acceptance of hypnotism as an aid to medicine in general and dentistry in particular. Most medical men have shied away from hypnosis as a tricky and rather sinister phenomenon. But not all of them have felt this way; modern doctors have explored the use of hypnosis in many medical specialties. In the field of dentistry, a new impetus to a revival of interest in hypnodontia was given through the reporting on Nov. 16, 1948, of a carefully controlled piece of research on the part of seven hypnodontists trained by the writer. Securing the cooperation of 250 patients drawn from their daily practices, it was found possible to place over 95 per cent in the trance state. Of the number, only 11 failed to enter it at the first induction; 3 of the 11 entered the trance in subsequent sessions and responded normally; 3 others were later placed in a deep trance but were unable to produce anesthesia. The remaining 5 were complete failures.

To determine if hypnoanesthesia could function in all dental situations without the use of supplementary chemical anesthesia, every possible type of dental operation was performed, including preparation of deep cavities and filling of teeth, extractions, removal of impacted teeth, removal of a vital pulp and the endodontic treatment of a necrotic pulp, and maxillary surgery. Bleeding and salivation were controlled, gagging was prevented, the patient was accustomed to prosthetic or orthodontic appliances, and there was no pain or discomfort either during or after the dental operations.

The ages of the patients treated ranged from 5½ to 71 years. It was discovered that elderly patients with well-established personality structures were not so responsive as younger subjects. The best response came from the teen-agers.

Some of the patients treated had previously feared dental work and refused to enter the dental chair. After being placed in the trance and told the work could now be done without discomfort, such a child willingly and alone walked into the dental office and climbed unaided into the chair. The child subjects had their dental work done without any anxiety or fear and usually awakened with a smile or a look of wonderment.

The Middle Western dentists trained by the writer formed the American Society of Psychosomatic Dentistry. Its purpose is to promote the study of hypnodontic techniques and to encourage research in the field. Hypnodontists from all parts of the United States, Canada, and a few from England are being admitted to membership upon demonstration of their qualifications. It is estimated that the organization will have a membership of more than 300 by the end of 1952.

As of early in 1952, reports indicate that there are more than 900 dentists in the United States and 30 in Canada using hypnosis to some extent. Reported cases of the use of hypnoanesthesia since March, 1948, number over 8,000. With many dentists in the Middle Western area the use of hypnodontics is gradually becoming routine practice. In a recent 10-week period a unit of 10 dental trainees conditioned 183 patients drawn from their respective clienteles and performed a total of 248 dental operations on these patients. The surgery included 45 extractions, 4 impactions, 3 three-quarter crown preparations, 45 distal occlusions, 109 mesial occlusal distals, 6 gingivectomies, and 1 root-canal therapy. Hypnoanesthesia, as indicated previously, lends itself to any type of dental situation. Furthermore, because of the routine use of posthypnotic analgesia, the patient experiences no postoperative discomfort such as is common following the use of drug anesthesia.

From the present growing and extensive use of hypnodontia, it appears that it is here to stay. It is gradually being placed on a firm foundation. The biggest present problem is that of adequate training of prospective hypnodontists by teachers of recognized standing. Dental schools will soon see their obligation relative to this. Training should be offered in these schools, where more adequate control of the personnel and the training situation may be maintained, or teachers may be certified to carry on the training of practicing dentists through extension service.

VALUE OF HYPNOSIS IN THE FIELD OF DENTISTRY

The objections to the use of hypnosis as an anesthetic in general surgery do not necessarily hold true for dentistry. Medical surgeons must treat all types of personalities with varying degrees of intelligence. In the medical situation an objection is that it is only possible for good subjects to reach the necessary depth of trance for anesthesia, many never going beyond the light stage. In dentistry the patient pattern is almost the reverse. The dentist deals with a very select group of individuals. They are not only usually more cultured, higher in intelligence, well-organized personalities who have a high sense of value of their personal worth, general health, and personal appearance, but also they seek out the dentist. As a consequence, they cooperate well. The patient of low I.Q., low mental stability, and low socioeconomic status is generally not interested in his general health or personal appearance. True, if he experiences severe discomfort caused by a decayed tooth he will seek out a dentist, primarily as a means of relieving pain. This factor acts as an automatic screening process so that the clientele of the dentists is largely made up of people more susceptible to the induction of hypnosis.

Such a clientele frequents the dental office at periodic intervals. The patients become accustomed to "taking orders" from the dentist. This conditioning is a prime contributing agent in the high percentage of induction successes which the hypnodontist is able to secure. Over a long period of time the dentist has unknowingly been preparing his patients to become successful hypnotic subjects. Thus, hypnoanesthesia is not difficult to induce.

The medical surgeon's patients are seldom repeaters; not so with the dentist's. A little time spent in teaching a young patient to be a good hypnotic subject conditions him for life. He may then have the benefits of hypnoanesthesia scores of times with only a few moments needed for its induction.

Each dentist has a clientele of perhaps up to a thousand regular patients. If he built up a practice of hypnotically conditioned pa-

tients, the induction-time element would be negligible. One hypnodontist in the Middle West expects to bring his clientele to at least
90 per cent conditioned patients. Many of them now enter the trance
quickly and achieve mouth anesthesia far faster than by any known
chemical anesthesia.

Some hypnodontists train their patients in autohypnosis so that
the person may place himself in the trance, bring on anesthesia, control salivation and bleeding, and, on signal, awaken himself. Such a
patient can also induce posthypnotic anesthesia and rapid healing
of tissue. This may seem fantastic, but it is routine practice with
several certified hypnodontists. A patient trained in this way may
be treated by a dentist unfamiliar with hypnosis, with all the benefits of hypnosis. With autohypnosis the only direction given the
dentists is "please let me know when you have completed the work,"
and when the patient has been told it is finished, he will awaken himself fully refreshed.

The skilled hypnodontist can talk to the hypnotic patient and be
answered just as in the waking state. The hypnotized patient is instructed to move his body and limbs at will so as to be as comfortable
as possible. He remains fully at ease and relaxed (something all good
dentists strive to achieve in their patients). As a distraction, while
the dentist proceeds with his work, the hypnotized patient can be
directed to hallucinate and enjoy through hallucination his favorite
music, a trip through a land of beautiful scenery, or perhaps again
enjoy a recently seen motion picture.

In one such instance a hypnodontist directed his 24-year-old
female patient to hallucinate and enjoy the music of her choice. She
was told to indicate to the doctor the tempo of the music to which
she was listening by means of tapping the index finger of her right
hand. Hallucinations of music readily set in, and she informed the
dentist that she was listening to dance music. This continued for 20
minutes, then stopped for no apparent reason. When questioned as
to why she had stopped the finger motion, the dentist experienced a
real chuckle when she replied, "Oh, we're sitting this one out."

While dentists are legally entitled to use hypnoanesthesia, some
hesitate to do so, usually because they do not know how to induce

the trance or are afraid of failure if they attempt it. The initial hurdle, like the solo flight in learning to fly a plane, is a difficult one, especially since the dentist usually transmits his uncertainty to the patients, if the dentist has a fear of not succeeding. This factor alone may cause failure.

REACTION OF PATIENTS TO ANESTHESIA

Gross [3] has stated that practically everyone fears pain more than the facts warrant. Most prospective dental patients regard the prospect of pain with actual terror and will do anything to escape it.

When a man comes to the dentist for professional attention he is given another label. He is called a "patient." Literally, that term means one who endures and suffers. He is expected to endure and suffer. In turn, he accepts his fate as something inescapable. In the past the dentist did little or nothing to change this; now he has access to the techniques of hypnodontia.

The dentist untrained in hypnodontia must accept the fact that his services are not looked upon with pleasure. They may be appreciated and considered necessary and important, but they are not liked. Fears, anxieties, phobias, and the like enter into the patient's attitude toward his dental experience. For 90 per cent of dental patients these attitudes can be greatly alleviated, if not removed entirely, by the application of hypnodontics.

Fear of the dentist is a postnatal acquisition that has come into being by living in a society that is decidedly expressive of its fears. The young child is a good patient provided he has not been preconditioned by an atmosphere of expressed familial fear. Many parents carelessly pass along their prejudices, fears, and intolerances. Unfortunate is the dentist who must set the dental world aright for the child. The best medium yet discovered is hypnodontia.

It has been said that fear is a premonition of pain. When a child has been conditioned against dental experience in advance of any unpleasant sensory experience, the dentist has a problem on his hands even before attempting treatment. A single episode of conditioning the child to fear by the parents or others may prepare the way to a lifetime dental phobia. If such a fear has been set up, regardless of the age of the patient, it is still not too late to relieve this fear of the dentist in whole or in part through hypnodontia.

Sometimes when a patient is in a deep trance state, he will moan and groan while either instrumentation or drilling is taking place. Yet the hypnodontist knows that the mouth is hypnoanesthetized because he has tested carefully. When questioned as to whether he is experiencing any discomfort, the patient will reply in the negative. Still as the dentist proceeds with his work, the groaning and/or moaning will continue. This should not disturb the hypnodontist. It can be ignored, or posthypnotic suggestion may be made that henceforth the patient will no longer react in this way.

The writer witnessed an amusing incident of this nature in the office of a trainee hypnodontist in South Dakota. The patient, a middle-aged man of high intelligence, had been moaning and groaning during a cavity preparation. Even the initial opening of the mouth elicited a moan. Finally, when all the work, including filling, was completed and the patient was still in the trance, he was informed that the tooth had been filled. A few moments later when a belated invited observer arrived, the patient was asked merely to open his mouth for inspection. The moans and groans were again produced, despite the fact that not a single portion of the mouth cavity was touched.

Occasionally, the hypnodontist will be faced with a patient in need of surgery or an extraction who, despite the fact that he has talked to another patient who has described the comforts of having dental work done with the use of hypnoanesthesia, still cannot be convinced that it is possible for him to have a similar experience. For this type, preanesthetic medication is indicated. Premedication refers to the preparation of the patient, before hypnosis, with sedatives, hypnotics, or sleep-inducing agents. The basic objectives of preanesthetic sedation are:

1. Control of preoperative pain, if any is present
2. Control or lessening of fear and apprehension
3. To decrease the amount of anesthetic agent required for good anesthesia with or without drug anesthesia in addition to hypnosis

4. Fortification against effects of the anesthetic drug in case any is used

The last is not so important since untoward symptoms from nitrous oxide seldom occur for reasons other than lack of oxygen.

Following premedication, the hypnodontist next proceeds to bring the deepest possible trance state. Premedication greatly facilitates this. The relaxed condition resulting from a fairly deep stage greatly lessens the amount of drug anesthetic needed for the impending operation.

A patient's reaction to anesthesia and surgical intervention is the sum total of all the stimuli that reach the brain. Oral and dental surgeons are inclined to minimize the effect of the emotional and psychic phenomena on a patient about to undergo an operation. To the surgeon it is a commonplace experience, and he is not on the receiving end. To the patient it is an adventure of terrifying magnitude.

Dental surgeons have reported in the literature that, contrary to the usual teaching, local anesthetics are contraindicated more frequently than general anesthetics. However, in more prolonged operations the possible harmful sequelae of the general anesthetics seem to outweigh the local. Under ether, authorities agree, septic pneumonia may develop, and with most gases anoxia and asphyxia may result. Another disturbing factor is the discomfort caused with a local anesthetic by visual awareness of the needle, the injection, and the fact that the patient knows exactly what is going on. This may develop a severe psychic effect. There is also the inevitable discomfort postoperatively following local anesthesia.

The disadvantages of nitrous oxide–oxygen over local anesthesia are: (1) more skill required of the operator; (2) responsibility greater on the part of the operator; (3) not all patients are suited to it; and (4) sometimes nausea and depression follow. No drug anesthetic can be safely administered to a patient with heart dysfunction or any circulatory irregularities. Nitrous oxide is contraindicated in many conditions, including mitral stenosis, heart condition, hyperthyroidism or hypothyroidism, asthma, nasal obstruction, tuberculosis, status lymphaticus, anemia, circulatory conditions, aortic regurgitation, infections or tumors of the neck and air passages, exophthalmic goiter, diabetes, malaria, influenza, diphtheria. There are still other situations, such as pregnancy, where nitrous oxide is contraindicated, and it is not for young adolescents and children under 4, or for patients who are excessively fat.

Local anesthesia is contraindicated with extremely nervous patients, those whose mouths are in a highly septic condition, where a needle must be inserted in acutely inflamed tissue, with patients having influenza, acute fever, puerperal fever, boils or carbuncles, or suffering from general debility.

From these long lists it is evident that drug anesthetics cannot be used with many patients. With a skilled operator, hypnodontia has no such limitation for any type of patient.

In addition to benefiting the patient, the dentist is also benefited in three direct ways. He has fewer cancellations owing to fear of pain; he has more operative hours through the elimination of "breathing spells" for the patient, and he will develop a larger clientele because the dentist who "doesn't hurt" is sure to become a topic of frequent conversation.

Hypnosis can be utilized to alleviate fear and anxiety as to future surgery, to produce anesthesia at the time of surgery, and to continue the anesthesia postoperatively. In addition to the usual forms of dental surgery, hypnoanesthesia is a great asset for other oral operations such as removal of cysts from the jaw or tongue, neoplasms of the tongue, tumors of the mouth, and the like.

It is generally believed by many experimenters that in the majority of cases four or five induction sessions will be required before a surgical operation with hypnoanesthesia is possible. However, it has been the finding of experienced hypnodontists that for average dental work but one or two sessions are needed.

TECHNIQUES EMPLOYED IN CONDITIONING THE PATIENT

The hypnodontist desiring to increase his percentage of successes in conditioning patients—on first as well as later inductions—will find the following hints helpful.

Before the patient is ushered into the operating room, it should be in order. All equipment needed or anticipated should be on hand and in orderly arrangement. The armamentarium should be checked, and all instruments except fixtures should be covered with sterile towels so as to be out of sight of the patient.

The hypnodontist should assume a bearing and a tone of assurance and confidence. Fears, imaginary or real, should be dispelled and the patient given to understand that he will experience no discomfort. In case premedication is to be used, he should be informed of the sensations which may be felt.

Prior to being seated, the patient is asked to empty his bladder. Tight clothing, particularly about the neck and waist, is loosened or removed, though appliances such as hernia belts need not be removed. The chair should be comfortable. The patient is placed in a position so that he is inclined slightly backward, and the headrest is adjusted to give him the utmost comfort.

In order to attain a high percentage of successful inductions with dental patients, the following points should be noted:

1. Each new induction should be started with the point of view drawn from LeCron and Bordeaux [4] that ". . . every normal person should be hypnotizable under proper conditions by a skilled operator."

2. Hypnosis should be undertaken only with cooperative and normal persons, those who express a desire to have their dental work performed under hypnoanesthesia. It is a well-known fact that most cooperative persons can be hypnotized almost immediately.

3. Whenever possible, the prospective subject-patient should be allowed to observe a previously conditioned patient being placed in the trance and undergoing dental work. Noting the calmness and relaxed state of the hypnotized patient in the chair during actual surgery gives the prospective subject-patient extreme confidence in the operator and a desire to use the procedure.

4. Prestige should be used from the start. The patient must be led to believe wholeheartedly in the ability of the operator to hypnotize him. The operator must exude confidence and let the patient know there is not the slightest doubt of success—that he will most certainly be hypnotized.

5. The special techniques to be observed during the first induction of hypnosis are as follows:

a. If it can be avoided, the patient should not be told that hypnosis is to be employed. He should be informed that he is to be relaxed; that he will feel drowsy and comfortable; that this is a relaxing technique sometimes called "psychosomatic (mind-body) sleep." The writer highly endorses this term. It will help place the patient at ease and give him a preliminary mind-set.

b. Prior to induction the patient should not be overexcited or led to an overactive cooperation. This has a negative effect.

c. The beginning hypnodontist may use a small unit light as a matter of expediency. Most patients respond to it quickly, saving time and energy for the operator.

d. Suggestions should be phrased carefully and correctly. They should be clear, precise, and logical. It is highly important to avoid negative suggestions, particularly with a new subject-patient. Also, through constant repetition, the mind of the subject must be narrowed to one thought—that is the voice and directions of the operator.

e. The induction method should be one of calm, quiet relaxation; the manner and voice of the operator soft and persuasive, yet definite.

f. For many patients a light stage of hypnosis will be adequate for the production of the anesthesia needed for the average dental operation. Unless tests show the patient to be in a deep stage, only minor dental work should be attempted during a first induction.

A high percentage of successful inductions of anesthesia in the mouth cavity requires some understanding of the possible dynamics of the phenomenon of hypnoanesthesia. Hypnosis involves the assumption of a trance state on the basis of a unique and particular type of relationship to the hypnodontist. Because the patient is provided with certain incentives to go into a trance, he submits himself to specific suggestions, in the course of which there is a temporary dissociation and deadening of higher cortical centers. It is imperative that the operator capitalize on this transference.

The hypnodontist has much in his favor at the very outset. The patient desires his dental work done without discomfort. The dentist gives tentative promise that this will take place provided the patient cooperates with him while in the trance. He enters the trance expecting to cooperate. So it is important at the very outset to affirm that he will comply—will relax when asked to do so, breathe deeply when so ordered, and so on through a series of positive suggestions to the point when a test is made for anesthesia. By cooperating and accepting the suggestions, there is no discomfort from the dental situation.

To produce hypnoanesthesia in about 30 to 35 per cent of dental patients (note "dental patients" and not the general public) who quite readily enter the deep trance stage is really no problem. The mere suggestion that certain areas are anesthetized, are senseless and frozen, together with gentle and brief massage of such areas, is sufficient to produce anesthesia. The problem of the untrained dentist is how to produce oral-cavity anesthesia in the remaining number, of whom about 5 per cent will be failures.

Space does not permit discussion of all possible techniques of inducing anesthesia. One which will be successful in perhaps over 40 per cent of the nondeep trance cases is offered.

The deepest possible trance should be secured which may require two or more sessions. If the trance permits glove anesthesia, this phenomenon is explained. This is the beginning of acceptance of anesthesia in the mouth tissue. The procedure to be followed is adequately presented by Wolberg.[5] For best results it is preferable to use the word "discomfort" instead of "pain." The word "pain" has a decided negative effect because of preconditioning.

When a test of the presence of anesthesia is made, an affirmation by a nod or other signal should be secured that "no discomfort" is felt. There should be a distinct pause following the suggestion for anesthesia to allow time for it to become effective. Then a test is made, gently at first, then more firmly. Carelessness in handling this phase of the total procedure may result in delay in securing anesthesia, or in complete failure. The cause of possible failure probably lies in the patient's inability to accept the possibility of "no discomfort." At the crucial moment he loses confidence.

In some instances it is not possible for the dentist to anesthetize the mouth cavity of a patient who has never had Novocain or other similar anesthetic. The patient simply does not know what it is like to have a sensation of numbness, so his subconscious mind is unable to reproduce it. In such cases an effective procedure is to first inject a little Novocain so the patient can have the experience of numbness in the jaw. Immediate suggestions to the effect that the entire jaw or any portion of it is anesthetized will become effective.

When the patient is only in a light stage and might react to the insertion of the needle, proceed first to use a topical anesthesia to deaden the area of insertion of the needle, then make the Novocain injection.

This technique, in fact, will serve as a routine procedure for 50 per cent or more of the patients unable to reach a medium to deep stage of hypnosis upon first or second induction. The time of the dentist is valuable. This technique will hasten the acceptance of anesthesia in the mouth cavity. It has been developed by careful experimentation and by testing hundreds of patients. It need be used but once on each patient in order to implant the idea of numbness in the oral cavity.

The operator also must have confidence in the success of any test. The patient easily detects the least uncertainty on the part of the operator, such as tremor of the voice, trembling hand or uncertain touch, or hesitancy in making positive statements.

Once the patient has accepted and affirmed the anesthesia, the next problem is to sustain it, which calls for added skill. As soon as anesthesia is accepted in the hand, it should be transferred to the mouth. This may be accomplished somewhat as follows: The patient is told, "We will now transfer this numbness and insensitivity from the hand to your jaw here." *The operator then touches the quadrant of the mouth where anesthesia is desired.* "As I count to three, a complete transfer of the anesthesia from your hand to your jaw will take place. As soon as you observe that your jaw is numb and insensitive, let me know by raising the index finger of your left hand." At this point the operator speaks very slowly. "Ready now, *one*, it is starting to enter the jaw; *two*, the transfer is almost complete; *three*, your jaw is numb, frozen, and woody, just as with Novocain. You can feel the tingling sensation." In case the patient does not raise the designated finger, indicating a numb sensation, a further statement should be made, "Go ahead and raise your finger to let me know it is there. That's right. It is getting 'number' every moment. It is so numb that all feeling is gone." The positiveness of this remark usually acts as an added suggestion and causes the patient to give the signal.

Normally, the posterior portions of the mouth do not become numb under Novocain. In keeping with this fact, the suggestion of numbness should be confined to other sections of the oral cavity.

Light instrumentation or drilling of a tooth may now be carried out in the anesthetized area. In the absence of caries, an explorer may be used on a portion of the gum. If there is to be an extraction, minor work should first be concluded, confirming to the patient that he has produced anesthesia. Following this, anesthesia is produced by further suggestion in the quadrant containing the defective tooth. A tooth should never be removed until the dentist is certain that anesthesia is present in the area of the tooth to be extracted. If an extraction is the only operation to be performed, all the above precautions should be observed, and in addition a small amount of Novocain (a third portion) should be injected to enhance the suggestion and ensure complete absence of discomfort as the tooth is extracted.

The period of training required to induce anesthesia hypnotically varies with the individual. In one test case a female patient, aged 20, with no previous hypnotic experience, was timed, beginning with the moment she was seated in the dental chair. Induction was made, anesthesia induced, an upper third molar removed without the use of Novocain, bleeding was controlled, and a blood clot formed. When the patient was awakened, a total time of 5 minutes had elapsed. While this is an exception, it can easily be duplicated under proper conditions. However, any reasonable length of time spent is justified by the fact that once achieved, hypnoanesthesia can be obtained almost immediately for years thereafter.

For the average patient, a reminder should be given every few moments that, "The harder I press the more numbness there will be." Patients seem to like this phraseology. It gives assurance of no discomfort resulting from instrumentation or drilling because the very act of pressing any dental instrument or the rotating of a burr on the sensitive tooth will act to cause more numbness and insensitivity.

As a distraction during dental work with hypnoanesthesia, hallucinations such as listening to music may be induced, as has previously been described.

CLASSIFICATION OF TRANCE STAGES AND
EXPLANATION OF HYPNODONTIA GRAPH

As stated by LeCron and Bordeaux,[4] "There is no doubt that every human being is more or less susceptible to suggestion, and most people could be hypnotized—perhaps all—if better methods were available." Let us add that the dentist deals primarily with normal people who should be hypnotizable if the operator is skilled.

Authorities differ as to the division of the trance into various stages. Some give a three-stage classification, while LeCron and Bordeaux have set up a 50-point scoring system. Over 25 years ago the writer set up an arbitrary set of 9 stages for his own personal use in professional practice and experimentation. Hundreds of observations have caused him to cling to this, for it roughly serves its purpose.

Through observing hundreds of instances with scores of different types of subjects, it has been possible to trace the probable curve of a composite subject as he enters hypnosis and proceeds into lower and lower stages. The reader is reminded that no two subjects necessarily reach the same depth upon first induction. Some will go into only a light state, while others enter the deeper ones without the slightest hesitation, all within a few seconds.

It is generally agreed by experimenters that the subject remains

HYPNODONTIA: HYPNOANESTHESIA AS APPLIED TO DENTISTRY

(DESIGNED BY THOMAS O. BURGESS)

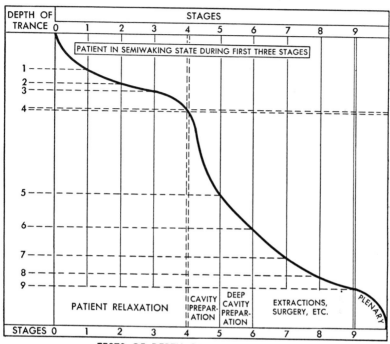

TESTS OF DEPTH OF TRANCE STAGE

Hypnoidal **Light Trance**	1. Flutter of eyelids. Heaviness of limbs. Suggestions of local warmth are effective.
	2. Suggested catalepsy of limbs possible. Catalepsy of eyelids.
	3. Consciousness remains almost complete. Automatic movements possible.
Medium Trance	4. Recognition of trance. Hears only voice of operator. Glove anesthesia. Tactile illusions.
	5. Complete catalepsy of limbs of body. Hyperacuity to atmospheric conditions.
Light Somnambulistic Trance	6. Fixed stare when eyes are open. Ability to open eyes without affecting trance. Possible to effect amnesia on waking by suggestion.
Deep Somnambulistic Trance	7. Complete amnesia on waking. Complete anesthesia. Posthypnotic anesthesia. Eye coordination lost. Rigidity and lag in muscular movements and reactions.
	8. Age regression. Positive auditory and visual hallucinations. All phenomena of posthypnotic suggestion possible.
Plenary Trance	9. Stuporous condition in which all voluntary (that is, spontaneous) activity is inhibited.

FIG. 14–1.

in a semiwaking state during the initial stages (1 to 3 on the accompanying graph, Fig. 14–1), and that this state terminates as soon as he reaches a depth wherein he usually hears only the voice of the operator. Another test for the termination of this state is successful production of a glove anesthesia.

The accompanying chart gives a fair concept of the probable path followed by the patient as he proceeds through the various trance stages, and it serves as a guide in use of hypnosis in dental practice.

The table which forms a part of the graph will be found useful in estimating the trance depth and anticipating the phenomena that can be expected at different stages. In dentistry it is useful to know what type of dental situation will successfully lend itself at the depth of hypnosis a patient is able to attain. It is useless to attempt surgery if the subject is able to reach only a light or medium trance. Similarly, posthypnotic anesthesia cannot be produced unless hypnosis is sufficiently deep. Attempts to produce phenomena beyond those to be expected at any given hypnotic stage may destroy the confidence of the patient in hypnodontics.

The first stage of the prehypnoidal state is marked by heavy sensations in the limbs. The first stage of the hypnoidal state brings drowsiness. Indications of the next stage are fluttering of the eyelids and closing of the eyes and the possibility of producing psychobiological therapy (reassurance, relaxation, persuasion). Physical indications near the bottom of the hypnoidal stage are increased heaviness of limbs and complete physical relaxation, accompanied by mental relaxation and partial lethargy of the mind. When called upon to move a hand or arm, the subject, when questioned later, often complains at the effort required to move and says he would have preferred to be let alone.

The hypnoidal stage is one between waking and either sleep or hypnosis. It is distinct from the lighter stages of hypnosis. Like sleep, it has different levels of depth. Whereas the sleep curve rises steadily, the hypnoid consciousness fluctuates, at one moment sinking into a sea of dreaminess, then rising toward the waking threshold. Emotional excitement subsides, voluntary activity changes to passivity, and suggestions meet with little resistance. This subwaking state is mainly one of rest and physical and mental relaxation.

It is while the excitable patient is in this state and hesitates to "let go" into a deeper state that the hypnodontist begins his therapy. This stage offers an excellent starting point for the removal of mild obsessions and phobias relative to the impending dental situation. Often, the immediate success with deeper trance states is won or lost at this time. The hypnoidal stage is not less important for therapeutic purposes than the full hypnotic states, especially in view of the popular objections to hypnotism to be overcome by the operator, and the difficulty of inducing hypnosis in some patients. The hypnoidal stage is one of increased suggestibility, so that the operator is able to break down inhibitions to entering the trance. At times he must be content with only this stage at first. He must realize that inhibitions may be deep-rooted and long standing, so that several sessions may be required to remove them.

In early sessions the patient should always be given the suggestion that at the next session he will go as deep as he is then and a little deeper. Sometimes it is wise to have the next session immediately. After making this suggestion of increased depth, the patient is awakened, the situation is discussed, and any questions are answered, with assurance that he can now go deeper. He may be asked to stand, to walk about and stretch, then return to the original chair. Then he can be informed, "We are now ready for the next session." At times this second session results in a very deep trance in which the dentist may proceed with deep cavity preparations.

Questioning will sometimes disclose the reason why a deep state is not reached. A dental patient, a girl of 16, was referred to the writer as a refractory case for conditioning. She said she was willing to enter the trance and, in fact, wished the dental work to be done with hypnoanesthesia. There was a general discussion of hypnotism, and induction was attempted, but only the hypnoidal stage was attained. Several sessions failed to change the situation. Finally, she was informed that she must have something on her mind and that she should disclose it if it was not of a personal nature. She then said, "What I want to know is, will my dentist be able to place me in the trance when you are not here?" She was assured that he could. She promptly entered a very deep state and became a somnambulistic subject. Her mild anxiety was easily brushed aside in this way. If anxiety is on the unconscious level, the operator will have more success by making the inquiry while the patient is in the hypnoidal or light stages.

It must be emphasized that the accompanying table, like any other scale, must not be accepted literally despite the utility claimed for it by scores of dentists who use it. Until the patient has reached the fourth stage, there can be no expectation of obtaining anesthesia of the mouth. There is a rather distinct plateau following the hypnoidal stage, as shown in the hypnodontia curve, during which the patient is experiencing "patient relaxation." From the viewpoint of the hypnoanalyst this downward curve would take a somewhat different shape. The hypnodontia curve is designed to serve the purpose of the dentist who is using hypnosis primarily for anesthesia. He must know, relatively, in what stage his patient is at any given moment. This is determined by tests and observations of behavior. Some of these tests are listed below the graph. A more elaborate set of tests will be found by referring to LeCron and Bordeaux.

Serving as a guide, the hypnodontia graph indicates that only minor cavity preparation and filling should be attempted while the patient is in the fourth stage. Deep cavity preparations may be carried out in the fifth stage. Extractions, impactions, or surgery on the palate, jaw, tongue, and elsewhere in the oral cavity should only be attempted if tests show the patient is in the sixth or a deeper stage. Occasionally, a patient will drop into the plenary stage. While this is rare, the writer has observed this three times in a period of 3 weeks. It is very difficult to perform dental work while the patient is in such a deep state, and it is better to restore a lighter stage and then proceed.

If the dentist is very careful to make an injection without discomfort to the patient, mild drug anesthesia may be used successfully while the patient is in one of the "patient relaxation" stages. The drug anesthesia may then be accepted as hypnoanesthesia. During the next session no drug will be needed, provided that the patient goes into a deeper trance, as is usually true following a successful operation using drug anesthesia. However, the hypnodontist must stay within the bounds of the dental situations suggested on the graph.

IMPORTANT PROCEDURES TO REMEMBER

In addition to using some guide such as the graph showing the stages of hypnosis, the operator should carry out the following procedures when hypnotizing a previously *untrained* subject:

1. There should be a brief discussion period prior to induction with the patient told:
   a. What is to be done by the operator.
   b. What *he* is to expect.
   c. What the *operator* expects of him.
   d. He should be given a signal for awakening.
2. The hypnodontist must adapt himself to the patient's needs, must win his confidence, and must correct his preconceptions. It should be pointed out that once he has been trained to go into a trance he can always afterward enjoy dentistry without discomfort, provided he seeks the services of a dentist trained in hypnodontia.
3. The patient must be made comfortable in an easy chair, preferably in a semidarkened room. The limbs and neck should be in a comfortable position, the collar loosened if necessary, so as to facilitate easy breathing.
4. Then hypnosis should be induced by any one of the several methods.
5. Posthypnotic suggestions should be given relative to the next and future sessions. This is a very important timesaver.
6. Before the patient is awakened, the various points on the following list should be checked.

CHECK LIST—TERMINATING THE TRANCE

1. The subject-patient should be informed that he is about to be awakened—"In a few moments I'm going to awaken you."
2. He should be given a suggestion that, in future, he will easily

and quickly enter the trance when the operator's hand is placed over his eyes (or some similar signal).

3. It should be suggested that no one can place him in the trance except some other qualified dentist, physician, or psychologist.

4. If any hallucination has been suggested, such as hearing music or visioning a motion picture, it should be removed.

5. If suggestions have been given as to salivation, they should be removed.

6. If anesthesia has been induced, normal sensitivity should be restored except in such designated areas as are desirable.

7. Posthypnotic analgesia can be suggested if necessary.

8. In case dental surgery was of a severe nature, total amnesia for this particular trance state should be suggested. This should be repeated several times. The patient should be reminded that no purpose is served by remembering the happenings in the trance except that it was a very pleasant experience.

9. It should be suggested that he will experience no headache, dizziness, heavy feeling, or other similar sensations on awakening.

10. He should be told that he will awaken feeling relaxed and refreshed and *will awaken with a smile.*

11. The patient should be awakened slowly. It is well to have him awaken himself by slowly reciting the alphabet until he reaches a designated letter. This has a good psychological effect.

12. It should be made *sure* that the patient is awake before being dismissed. Having him wash his face with a damp towel will assure this.

13. He should be dismissed with a smile and reminded of the pleasantness of his experience.

ADDITIONAL HYPNODONTIC HINTS

Once a patient has been conditioned to produce suggestive anesthesia, a posthypnotic suggestion can be made so that, at some given signal, he will immediately enter the trance state and spontaneously be totally insensible to any discomfort from instrumentation or extractions and will remain undisturbed by noises. When anesthesia has been produced, it can be localized in any area or in all of the mouth.

There are many instances where hypnosis should be used in conjunction with chemical anesthetics, but hypnosis should have preference because there is an absence of nausea and nervousness as is frequent with drugs, and there is complete freedom from dangerous reactions. Hypnosis may be used merely to free the patient's mind of fear and apprehension through suggestion. This will make it easier to use a chemical anesthesia if necessary.

While in the trance the facial muscles are relaxed so that it is easier for the dentist to work on the mouth. Better cooperation, such as keeping the tongue out of the way, is obtained from the patient. The trance permits the patient to keep his mouth open without fatigue, and gags, mouth props, and retentive devices need not be utilized. The period in the dental chair is one of rest and relaxation, so the patient leaves the office feeling refreshed and rested.

It should be standard practice to remind the patient during every instrumentation that it is a pleasant experience which he is enjoying and that he will have no memory of the time in the dental chair except as having been pleasant.

Prior to drilling the suggestion may be given, "The harder I press, the more numb it gets." For extractions it may be worded, "The harder I press or pull, the more numbness you will feel."

When possible to obtain it and when needed, full use of posthypnotic suggestion to maintain postoperative anesthesia should be made, this being an advantage not to be had with drugs.

During cold months of the year the patient should be kept warm and comfortable while in the trance. A light shawl or other wrap placed over the lap and legs may be employed.

Refractory cases or unresponsive subjects can be made more receptive by light oral dosage of Sodium Amytal administered about half an hour before trance induction.

The time for training the subject in hypnosis and for anesthesia is justified by virtue of the fact that, once achieved, it can be obtained immediately for an indefinite number of years. The writer has tested this with two subjects, one for 20 and another for 21 years.

Excess salivation can be controlled in the trance by saying, just before instrumentation is begun, "Your mouth will not water any more. These glands here and here (gently touching the areas) will stop flowing. Now swallow everything in your mouth. Make it dry. As I count to three, the glands will stop flowing. Ready—one, two, three. They have stopped. Now again swallow any moisture in your mouth. And now keep a dry tongue until I have finished with your dental work."

In a deep trance it is quite possible to control bleeding of tissue by suggestion. Evidently, this results from a contraction of the blood vessels which cuts off the circulation. Control may be effected through suggestions worded about as follows: "When I count to three, the blood will stop circulating in this area (with a finger the area is massaged). One—two—three. It has stopped." If an extraction is performed, when the tooth has been removed, a 2-by-2 gauze is held against the gum, circulation is ordered to start again to fill the socket, and then the suggestion is given for circulation to cease again.

In suggesting awakening from the trance a recommended standard procedure is to have the patient awaken himself by saying a designated number of letters of the alphabet as "A—B—C, I am awake." Often this is done by counting, instead. However in using Sodium Pentothal, the usual technique to learn the patient's progress is to have him count until there is confusion, or unconsciousness. In one case a girl subject was awakened from the trance but was completely mute thereafter. Questioned, she replied by writing that she felt lightheaded and experienced a feeling of tonic contraction in and around the throat. Her speech was partially restored through relaxation and suggestions, and next day she was completely normal—even amused at the experience.

In an effort to discover the reason for the temporary mutism, she was rehypnotized. She then stated that Sodium Pentothal had been administered to her a few months previously for minor surgery and she had been required to count as she was going under. Raimy [6] who reported the case, indicated that the counting technique served as a stimulus for two conflicting responses both involving a change in consciousness. In the one situation (Sodium Pentothal anesthesia) use of the counting technique was connected with loss of consciousness; in the other, counting was designed to cause her to awaken from the trance.

As hypnodontia is a relatively new technique, minor mishaps with hypnosis, such as this, should be guarded against. It is therefore good practice to keep carefully prepared records of each patient. Those hypnodontists who belong to the American Society of Psychosomatic Dentistry use the accompanying form, keeping a copy for their own records and forwarding one to the secretary of the society. Over 8,000 of these are now on file and will be of aid in the society's continuing program of research.

CASE RECORD: DENTAL TREATMENT
WITH HYPNOANESTHESIA

Name of patient_____Case number_____
Address_____
Age_____
Phone_____
Have you ever walked or talked in your sleep?_____
Have you ever experienced: ether_____; nitrous oxide_____; Sodium Pentothal_____; Novocain_____; a fainting spell_____; or other similar experience?_____
What sensations did you have just as you lost consciousness?

Preliminary Testing and Induction   Date_____
   1. Technique used_____
   2. Time (in minutes) required for induction_____
                                      Number of minutes in trance_____
   3. Deepest stage obtained (Burgess classification *)_____
   4. Remarks: (temperature of room, humidity, outdoor weather condition, patient's condition, temperament, attitude, etc.):

   5. Sensations experienced during the trance, as reported by the patient:

* See Fig. 14–1.

Report of Dental Surgery (or Treatment)

1. Time required for induction:

   _____sec.

2. Nature of dental work_____

   _____

3. Reactions of patient while in the trance state during treatment:

Surgery number_____

Date_____

Time of day_____

Conditions:_____

Burgess "stage"_____

Posthypnotic anesthesia induced for _____ hr
(State number of hours.)

4. Report of patient as to the effectiveness of anesthesia, etc.:

5. General remarks by dentist:

Reported by_____D.D.S.

HYPNOANESTHESIA CASE REPORTS

As typical of the thousands of case reports now being accumulated for research in hypnodontic techniques and study of the progress in the use of hypnosis in dentistry, some are given here. These reports were drawn from the records of dentists practicing in the Middle Western portion of the United States and were published in the July, 1949, issue of *North-West Dentistry*.[7]

Young woman, 18 years of age. Gas anesthesia was suggested for this patient, a highly nervous person, but she asked for hypnosis. She was very co-operative, and the first induction took less than ten minutes. The nature of the operation was two cavity preparations for a DO and MO filling. No chemical anesthesia was used in this case.

This patient expressed great gratitude, being so well pleased that she recommended it to her sister and a friend. She was completely relaxed during the operation, and that made it much easier for the operator.

This patient and many others on whom I have used hypnosis are well pleased. I therefore feel that hypnosis has a very important place in dentistry.

V. J. EASTMAN, D.D.S.

Man, age 33. Thirty minutes were required for the first induction. I did no work until the third induction. The patient had anesthesia for cavity preparations. He liked the experience very much and is no longer afraid of having dental work done. Working was easy because the patient was perfectly quiet.

Woman, age 30. Fifteen minutes were required for the first induction. Four cavities were excavated and filled at the first sitting. At the second.

sitting, induction required only five minutes. Four cavities were excavated and filled. At the third sitting, induction required five minutes. Two cavities were excavated and filled. At no sitting was any chemical anesthetic used. This patient no longer dreads dental work. The work was very easily accomplished because the patient was very quiet and co-operative.

H. A. ANDERSON, D.D.S.

M.C., a boy, age six, was placed in the hypnotic state in one and one-half minutes from the time the first instructions were given. Prophylaxis and first application of sodium fluoride were completed during this induction. The patient awakened bright and smiling, and requested that we play the "sleeping game" again. Two succeeding appointments, one week apart, completed the course of fluoride treatment with the same favorable results and comments.

The successful completion of a dental operation for a juvenile patient who ordinarily gave the operator much concern and difficulty by his curiosity, apprehension, wiggling, forcing cotton wicks from position and incessant talking was a source of satisfaction. In the hypnotic state quietness, relaxation and complete cooperation were in evidence at all times.

C. B., a young man, age 24, had been placed in the hypnotic state twice previously while submitting to operative dentistry. During this third induction the patient was tested for greater depth than previously, and it was decided to attempt the extraction of a carious upper third molar without benefit of supplementary chemical anesthesia. The operation was done accordingly. The patient was awakened in the customary manner, and the first comment was to ask if the tooth had been removed. Upon being assured it had, his remarks were to the effect that this was a perfect procedure as far as he was concerned. The patient was fully relaxed throughout the entire procedure. He had no recollection of any pain or unpleasantness whatsoever. There was no postoperative pain because of countering such reaction with posthypnotic suggestion. Recovery was uneventful.

Summary: Extractions can be painlessly done without supplementing with chemical anesthetics provided a deep hypnotic state is induced in the patient.

WINSTON L. LEE, D.D.S.

To illustrate a dental situation of another type, the writer received a 27-year-old patient, a practicing dentist, suffering from bruxism (the grinding together of the teeth during sleep). The grinding was a nightly affair and so noisy as to annoy other occupants of the bedroom. In addition, it was a constant problem of repair of the cusps of the molar teeth.

At the fourth session, a deep somnambulistic trance was produced. Appropriately worded posthypnotic suggestions were given as to his difficulty. There was total amnesia following his awakening. Fifteen minutes later the subject was placed again in a deep trance and was asked to repeat the suggestions and instructions given him relative to his problem during the first trance. The purpose of this procedure was to have the patient play an active part in reinforcing the suggestions on the subconscious mind. He was again awakened with amnesia and assured that he would not longer grind his teeth. Passage of time has shown the method successful, although the condition was one of long standing. The case is reported as an example of an experimental approach to the solution of a specific problem (bruxism) which had not been cured through conventional approaches.

THE USE OF HYPNOANESTHESIA IN OBSTETRICS

While hypnoanesthesia in childbirth would seem to be a different field from hypnodontia, both aim at eliminating pain, and, in fact, the hypnodontist may contribute something to the obstetrician who wishes to use hypnosis.

It is a known fact that, because of many factors, the caries rate among pregnant women usually increases. Therefore, the expectant mother should visit the dentist for restoration and care of her teeth. Then the dentist trained in hypnoanesthesia may serve the obstetrician both in conditioning the patient in hypnosis and in producing anesthesia. Arrangements can be made with the obstetrician to be present when anesthesia is induced and work is performed. While the patient is experiencing hypnoanesthesia in the oral cavity, she is placed *en rapport* with the obstetrician, and, by suggestion, the anesthesia is transferred to the pelvic area. The effectiveness of the anesthesia in the dental work makes it easier to obtain it in the pelvic region during actual delivery, and the presence of the obstetrician in the dental office will facilitate this.

DeLee and Greenhill [8] state:

Hypnosis has been used in obstetrics for a long time and should be employed more often. . . . Even if complete hypnosis is not desired, physicians should remember that repeated suggestions, . . . can accomplish a great deal in labor, particularly for the relief of fear as well as the pains of labor.

The writer has trained seven obstetricians in the techniques of hypnosis as related to obstetrics. Securing the cooperation of a group of hypnodontists, a series of experiments was conducted using the above method of inducing anesthesia in the pelvic area. In a control group the obstetrician conditioned the patients in hypnosis and in obtaining anesthesia in the ordinary way. It was found that, in general, using the method where the physician and hypnodontist cooperated, the patient experienced less discomfort during delivery than with the other method.

Up to this writing, these seven obstetricians have delivered more than 100 babies with hypnoanesthesia, with varying results. While a full report is not ready to be made, some interesting observations may be revealed. When one group of patients was taught the Read method and this was supplemented during delivery by hypnoanesthesia, and a second group was conditioned and delivered with hypnosis alone, less discomfort was experienced by the latter group. A probable reason for this may lie in the reference to "pain" with the Read method. This acts as a suggestion to the patient that pain will be felt. With the second group no reference was made to the Read method. It was routine during training to use such statements as "You will experience pleasant sensations," "You will enjoy the experience," and suggestions that labor contractions would be a pleasant experience produced this result.

These statements must not be construed to mean that the Read method is not effective. These findings only indicate that hypnosis used in conjunction with the Read method is not so effective as when used alone for delivery.

A FINAL STATEMENT

The employment of hypnodontic techniques calls for certain personality qualifications and specialized skill in the dentist. For greatest success he must be relatively free from personality problems. Training and experience, particularly supervised experience, is essential. Books and articles on the subject are helpful, but practical experience and training are required. It is best if these are obtained at some training center.

Although there is still some prejudice against hypnosis, adequate education of the public will permit hypnodontia to assume its proper place in dentistry. It has definite advantages which should bring it into more and more use. With the recent progress toward its acceptance, the writer believes a new era in dental service is about to be launched.

REFERENCES

1. Hyde, W.: "Psychosomatic sleep" (editorial), *North-West Dentistry*, **29**:55, January, 1950.
2. *The Critic*, May 31, 1845 (a letter from William Curtis).
3. Gross, M. L.: "How much does it hurt?" *Sat. Eve. Post*, **222** (23):29, Dec. 3, 1949.
4. LeCron, L. M., and Bordeaux, J.: *Hypnotism Today*, Grune & Stratton, Inc., New York, 1947.
5. Wolberg, L. R.: *Medical Hypnosis*, Vol. I., Grune & Stratton, Inc., New York, 1948.
6. Raimy, V. C.: "A note on hypnotic technique," *J. Clin. Psychol.*, **5**:423, 1949.
7. Hyde, W.: "Case reports," *North-West Dentistry*, **28**:154, July, 1949.
8. DeLee, J. B., and Greenhill, J. P.: *Obstetrics*, W. B. Saunders Company, Philadelphia, 1947.

FURTHER REFERENCES NOT CITED DIRECTLY

Ament, P.: "Relaxation of excitable patients," *Dental Digest*, **54**:402, 1948.
Burgess, T. O.: "Hypnodontia—Hypnosis as Applied to Dentistry," *Brit. J. M. Hypnotism*, **3**(1):49, (2):48, 1951, (3):62, 1952.
Lundholm, H.: "An experimental study of functional anesthesias as induced by suggestion in hypnosis," *J. Abnorm. & Social Psychol.*, **23**:337, 1928.
Moss, A. A.: *Hypnodontics*, Dental Items of Interest Publishing Company, Brooklyn, 1952.

Pattie, F. A.: "The genuineness of hypnotically produced anaesthesia of the skin," *Am. J. Psychol.*, **49:**435, 1937.

Rosen, Harold: "The Hypnotic and Hypnotherapeutic Control of Severe Pain," *Am. J. Psychiat.*, **107:**917, 1951.

Shaw, L. J.: "Hypnotism in dental work," *Brit. J. M. Hypnotism*, **I** (1): 38, 1949.

Stein, M. R.: "Anaesthesia by mental dissociation," *Dental Items Interest*, **42:**941, 1930.

Stolzenberg, Jacob: *Psychosomatics and Suggestion Therapy in Dentistry*, Philosophical Library, New York, 1950.

CHAPTER FIFTEEN

Extrasensory Perception and Hypnosis

Editor's Note

The question of whether or not there is such an ability as extra-sensory perception (ESP) is one in which scientists in general have shown little interest. They have consistently closed their minds to the possibility of such phenomena, most of them refusing even to investigate. This includes most psychologists. The findings of Dr. J. B. Rhine and other researchers are only slowly being accepted. Reports which indicate the possibilities of ESP are generally dismissed by these incredulous scientists as based on faulty mathematical calculations, or else as the result of the utilizing of minimal cues by the subjects of ESP experiments. There is a sound basis for some of this criticism. The ability of the subconscious mind to interpret minimal cues is sometimes astounding, but it cannot work over long distances and through stone walls. Such contentions do not necessarily apply to the more carefully conducted ESP experiments. As a matter of fact, Rhine's mathematical figures and statistics have been thoroughly checked by a number of eminent mathematicians and certified as correct in public statements (for example, by The American Institute for Mathematical Statistics).

It is only natural that Dr. Rhine, who courageously began his famous research on the subject of ESP a number of years ago, should be the target of ridicule and attack by other psychologists. Until he began his experiments at Duke University, most investigation of parapsychology was uncontrolled and uncritical, although the societies for psychical research have tried to be extremely critical in investigating psychical phenomena. Science has never accepted the unorthodox until forced to do so.

About a dozen years ago a poll of psychologists belonging to the American Psychological Association was taken on the opinions of members as to the validity of Rhine's work on ESP. Only some 5 per cent of those who replied indicated acceptance of Rhine's findings. It is probable that the percentage would be much larger today.

Many members of a comparable group of scientists, the psychiatrists, are at present showing considerable interest in ESP. A single issue of the *Psychiatric Quarterly* [23 (2), April, 1949] contains articles by Jan Ehrenwald on "Ques. for 'Psychics' and 'Psychical Phenomena' in Psychiatric Studies of Personality," and by Eric Berne on "The Nature of Intuition." There is also a lengthy editorial dealing with psychiatric interest in the controversial subject of parapsychology. It is suggested here that this is an appropriate field for psychiatric exploration. It calls attention to the unwarranted scorn accorded parapsychology, hypothesizing that it is largely based on fear. It quotes a questionnaire sent out in 1948 by Dr. R. G. MacRobert of New York to 2,510 psychiatrists to which 723 answers were obtained. Of these, 495 stated that they believed a useful purpose would be served if psychiatrists and neurologists were to sponsor research to see if ESP has a place in psychodynamics, and 453 felt that identification with psychical research would not discredit their professional standing. In addition, 163 reported having personally witnessed occurrences of ESP. These figures are rather surprising from any scientific group.

Rhine's work has had considerable publicity, both scientific and popular. Not so well known is the fact that various other groups of scientists are working along the same lines in other countries, notably in some of the English universities and also in the Scandinavian countries, where interest is high. These investigations serve largely to confirm Rhine's.

In writing an introduction to Rhine's article, which follows, the editor feels that his own personal position as to ESP should be stated. His experience with ESP is nil. He has made no study of parapsychology and hence is not in a position to express any opinion one way or another. It should be said that he has no definite convictions as to ESP but possesses a normal curiosity. This introductory material is on a purely objective basis, but he believes parapsychology is worthy of intensive investigation.

Hypnosis has long been associated with magic and the esoteric, and most scientists feel that ESP is largely a magical or related matter. Many scientific workers in hypnosis are strongly of the opinion that hypnosis is still too closely associated with magic in the minds of the public for it to be discussed in connection with ESP. The editor feels that it is a mistake for scientists of any persuasion to be of such closed mind. If there is such a capacity as ESP, it should be subject to proof, and only carefully controlled research will provide proof. If ESP can be shown to have no validity, disproof would also be of the utmost value. At present there seems to be a preponderance of evidence which seems valid and cannot lightly be dismissed.

To comment on Dr. Rhine's article, some suggestions might be offered as to further investigation of hypnosis and ESP in combination. Anyone who has read the old books written by the early mesmerists cannot but be impressed with the ESP phenomena reported by them in connection with mesmerism. Many of these writers, and Pierre Janet of a later period, cannot be considered gullible simpletons. Too many of them were of the highest scientific standing in their time. DeLeuze's book is an excellent example of this literature.

In 1892 T. R. Hudson published *The Law of Psychic Phenomena*, which is a thoroughly sane, objective treatise. Long before Freud, Hudson described perceptively the activities of the subconscious mind in a most modern way, arriving at conclusions later reached by Freud. Hudson recognized the role of minimal cues and subconscious activity in psychic manifestations, dismissing all but a small percentage of psychic phenomena as fakery or misinterpretation. He accepted a small portion as inexplicable in the light of the knowledge of his time. Hudson offered an excellent discussion of ESP phenomena in mesmerism, and made a most pertinent suggestion for research along this line. He contended—as does Rhine—that ESP faculties must be in the realm of the subconscious. Not in accord with Rhine, he considered that hypnosis is a state in which the subject's responses are also largely in that realm. Hudson believed that ESP abilities would be easiest demonstrated and developed by having the ESP subject placed in a state of deep hypnosis. Also, the hypnotist should himself then be hypnotized (the hypnotist to be the transmitter in any telepathic experiment). With both in the trance, and the subject in rapport with the hypnotist, Hudson theorized that the greatest possible results would be obtained because there would be subconscious activity on the part of both.

This conjecture is interesting, especially in respect to the reports by Erickson and Kubie [1] and others as to the ability of one hypnotized subject to interpret the dreams and automatic writing of another hypnotized person. Also, it is known that one hypnotized subject can instantly determine whether or not another person is in a hypnotic trance.

As a pertinent digression, an interesting field of research in hypnotherapy would be to utilize a good hypnotic subject (preferably another psychotherapist) to attend analytic sessions during hypnoanalysis and to have him listen and assist in interpreting the material produced by the analysand. In line with the above statements, some surprising results might be anticipated.

In Dr. Rhine's work with hypnotized subjects and ESP, the question arises as to the depth of trance obtained. In Erickson's chapter, the importance of deep stages in any hypnotic experiment is stressed, and it is stated that in deep stages it is the subconscious mind of the subject that is dealt with, to a large degree. Rhine, instead, describes hypnosis as a centering of conscious attention. This is true to some extent, but in deep somnambulistic states there is undoubtedly much subconscious mentation and activity, as Erickson has mentioned in his chapter.

Modern hypnotists seldom take a long enough time for the induction of deep hypnosis. The old-time mesmerists often found that their subjects entered the trance within a short time, but their descriptions of trance induction by mesmeric methods frequently mention protracted efforts lasting from 2 to 5 hours. One wonders if the reason for their obtaining ESP phenomena, if they did obtain them, does not lie in the fact that the subject was very deeply hypnotized. Perhaps such ESP abilities develop only in deep states, with the greater accompanying dissociation, though of course ESP abilities may appear without hypnosis.

The average person probably has little perceptible ESP faculty, or does not recognize and know how to activate it. On the other hand, according to the investigators, a few individuals seem to have unusual ability along ESP lines. It has often been observed that about 1 person out of 5 is a good hypnotic subject, though more can be conditioned to somnambulism. Every worker in hypnosis occasionally discovers an exceptional subject in whom deep hypnosis, with all the attendant phenomena, can be quickly induced. These remarkable subjects are rare. No statistics are available, but a guess may be hazarded that such a subject is found in perhaps 1 person out of 200. There is a possibility that it is this type of hypnotic subject who would also show the greatest ESP abilities, a matter for investigators in parapsychology to determine.

Every dabbler in hypnosis is likely to attempt to produce "traveling clairvoyance" in a subject. Invariably, a good subject will respond and "project" his mind to the suggested scene. Many subjects will claim that they "saw" the scene and the events which they describe to the hypnotist. Whether or not such clairvoyance is possible is, of course, a moot point, but the production of hallucinations is not. The obliging subjects may conform by producing a hallucination. Scientific check of the validity of the scenes reported is something else again.

Whether or not one accepts the findings of Rhine and other ESP workers, his historical data as to ESP and hypnosis are most interesting, and it is to be hoped that there will be further research along the lines projected by Dr. Rhine.

REFERENCE

1. Erickson, M. H., and Kubie, L. S.: "The translation of the cryptic automatic writing of one hypnotic subject by another in a trance-like dissociated state," *Psychoanalyt. Quart.*, **9** (1):51, 1940

Extrasensory Perception and Hypnosis

BY J. B. RHINE, PH.D.

PARASYCHOLOGY LABORATORY, DUKE UNIVERSITY,
DURHAM, NORTH CAROLINA

The combination of two unknowns rarely, if ever, makes a known. Bringing together hypnosis and extrasensory perception, or ESP (perception without the use of the recognized senses—as by telepathy and clairvoyance), will not explain either one. Probably no one ever thought that it would. Certainly, our present effort is not made with that anticipation. Rather, our objective is to see what we find in the way of illuminating relationships leading to a better understanding of either of these little-understood phenomena of human personality.

Whatever other connection we may find between hypnosis and ESP, we may certainly speak of their historic relationship. From the very beginning of hypnotism, dating back to its mesmeric stage, we find phenomena of extrasensory perception closely associated with it—so closely, in fact, that for a long time they were taken to be incidental products of hypnosis.

Mesmer, himself, encountered phenomena of what would now be considered ESP, and referred to instances of it.* He wrote: "Sometimes through his inner sensibilities the somnambulist can distinctly see the past and future."

Among Mesmer's followers, though never with Mesmer himself, the ESP phenomena threatened in some instances to become the major aspect of the mesmeric manifestation. This was so with the discoveries of the two Puységur brothers, especially the younger, Count Maxime, whose subject, Victor Race, demonstrated what ap-

---

* Goldsmith, M.: *Franz Anton Mesmer*, Doubleday, Doran Company, New York, 1934, p. 165.

peared to be clairvoyant awareness of the illnesses and physical condition of his fellow patients. This led to the use of hypnotic ESP for diagnosis, a practice that became widespread and lasted to some extent for at least a century.

Some idea of the degree to which the ESP aspects of hypnotic phenomena captured the interest of the day may be obtained from the report made by the Second Commission on animal magnetism of the French Academy of Science, in 1831. From this it will be seen that the extrasensory powers of the somnambulist make up a prominent part of the recorded evidence. The commission was much concerned with demonstration of the ability on the part of blindfolded somnambulists to identify cards or read from an open book put in their hands. While we may have our reservations about the adequacy of the conditions obtaining during these demonstrations, there can be no mistake about the degree of interest among medical and other scientific men of the time in the clairvoyant aspect of the performance of mesmerized subjects.

Even though a new commission only a half dozen years later squelched the interest in mesmerism in general, it did not kill it completely, and not only in France but in Germany and England and later on in America there were occasional reports of the transcendent mental powers of the somnambulist. Combining the mesmeric trance and its superior powers with the theories of Swedenborg and some mysterious happenings in America, occurring about the middle of the nineteenth century, the spiritualist movement developed and grew so extensively that, for a time at least, spiritualism became one of the major religious groups of the Western world. Its actual claims, however, were not scientifically substantiated and remain as much a matter for faith as those of any other religious group.

In the latter half of the nineteenth century science began to take hold of the more verifiable claims of the hypnotists (as the mesmerists became known with the introduction of the artificial-sleep theory of the phenomenon) and introduced a more experimental approach. A French physician, Dr. E. Azam, was one of the first of these experimenters. He found that a hysteria patient in whom

he had induced hypnosis gave evidence of appearing to taste substances which Azam had casually put in his own mouth, and he carried out a series of tests with substances which he would taste without
giving sensory evidence of having done so to the patient. In each
case, the patient responded that she tasted the appropriate substance,
to the extent of convincing Dr. Azam that there was some unex-
plained transmission of a sensory experience.

The experiments of Edmund Gurney and Frank Podmore of
Cambridge University in the transfer of pain sensation from hypnotist to hypnotized subject were carried out with a considerable
amount of precaution to prevent the transmission of cues by sensory
means. The hypnotist, standing behind his blindfolded subject, was
pinched at some point on his body, and the subject was told he
would feel the pain in the appropriate location. A high order of
success was reported by Gurney and Podmore, as well as by other
observers in similar tests, among them Pierre Janet, the eminent
French psychiatrist. Still another development was represented by
the reports of Dr. A. A. Liebeault, who is best known for introducing the suggestion theory of hypnosis. Liebeault encountered subjects who were able to perceive visual images being experienced by
the hypnotist. In a series of tests with one of these patients, he
satisfied himself that words and sentences which he wrote and visualized could be reliably apprehended by the patient.

The introduction of a mathematical analysis of the data from these
tests of ESP in the hypnotic state began with the eminent French
physiologist, Professor Charles Richet. His patient, the famous
Léonie, was reported to be able, in the somnambulent state, to identify playing cards enclosed in envelopes. Richet applied the mathematics of probability to the results, finding them significantly different from the degree of success expected from chance alone.

On the English side of the Channel, Professor and Mrs. Henry
Sidgwick, at Cambridge, carried out ESP tests between hypnotist
and subject, using numbers as the stimuli, and they, too, obtained
results significantly above mean chance expectation. They did so
even with the hypnotist and the subject located in different rooms,
although the results were less striking with the separation.

As everyone knows, the history of hypnosis itself is studded with dramatic occurrences; the history of ESP is no less so, although its drama is somewhat less tangible and is much less familiar. We should expect, then, a rather phenomenal story whenever the two types of manifestation were combined, although it is difficult, indeed, to be able to appraise just exactly what took place. This is especially true with historical material in which the report did not anticipate all the questions which students might subsequently raise. It may be worth while, nevertheless, to mention a few lines of the more dramatic combination of these two interesting manifestations of the normal human personality—ESP and hypnosis.

Surely one of the most striking types of human behavior ever reported is what is called "traveling clairvoyance." It had early been noted that the entranced subject seemed not to be restricted in his perceptual powers by time and space. Numerous instances were reported of the perception of things at a distance. One classic example, although it concerned a trivial incident, comes from Mesmer, himself, in which a somnambulist "saw" a pet dog which had been lost being carried on the street at a certain corner in Paris and gave such instructions as enabled a gendarme to locate and retrieve the lost animal for its owner. The incident is cited by Goldsmith.

Someone conceived the idea of "sending" the subject mentally traveling to a distant scene and reporting what he observed. Janet wrote of having "sent" Léonie (from Le Havre) to report what Richet was doing in his laboratory in Paris, Léonie then became excited and said that the laboratory was in flames. It had actually burned to the ground that day.

Sir William Barrett reports similar traveling clairvoyance tests which yielded surprisingly accurate information unknown either to the subject or to himself. Barrett followed up with more controllable tests, using playing cards concealed in a book and located some hundreds of yards from the subject. He obtained such conclusive results that he was emboldened to present his findings to the British Association for the Advancement of Science in 1876. It is not surprising that his courageous gesture was not well received.

The most astonishing reports in the literature as to traveling clairvoyance are those presented by Dr. Alfred Backman of Sweden. He sent his peasant-girl subject traveling to many quarters strange to both herself and the hypnotist, with what were reported as phenomenally accurate results. The claim was made that in some instances she made her "presence" felt by the persons whom she visited. But, while it is a great shame to the science of the day that more was not done to follow up these remarkable claims, it is not possible to draw final conclusions regarding them because of the difficulty of appraising certain problems of control. They stand simply as provocative challenges to the explorer of the future.

Another combination of hypnotism and ESP almost as dramatic as traveling clairvoyance is the hypnotization of a subject at a distance, first attempted by the French physicians Gibert and Janet. Demonstrations of this effect of what might be described as an exercise of telepathic suggestion upon a hypnotic subject were made by other French physicians during the last quarter of the nineteenth century, but the experiments of Janet will serve to illustrate. They are all concerned with the subject Léonie, who was discovered by Gibert and brought to Janet's attention, later to be turned over to Richet for further experimental study. It was discovered that Léonie appeared to be so responsive to those who had been hypnotizing her that she was in some way seemingly bound to them even when they left her bodily presence. For example, a day or so after having been hypnotized by Dr. Paul Janet, Pierre's brother, she screamed at the instant when Paul burned his arm accidentally in a room near by where he was at work on an experiment. Léonie rubbed her elbow at the point where Janet had received his burn.

It was decided to try to put Léonie into the somnambulistic state and cause her to "go to sleep" from a distance of a kilometer away from her. They chose random points of time on the clock, simply asking the housekeeper to record the times when she went to sleep. Both Gibert and Janet were quite successful in bringing about the hypnotic trance at approximately the hour and minute agreed upon, the selected times ranging from 11:00 A.M. to 11:35 P.M. No one present in the house knew of the experimental plan. Janet reports in his autobiography that there were "sixteen times out of twenty when somnambulism exactly coincided with a mental suggestion made at a distance of one kilometer." Richet was not so successful but had some success, obtaining 9 positive results out of 35 trials, 6 more being doubtful. (These experiments furnished the suggestion for the plot of the famous Du Maurier story of *Trilby*.)

Again, one could wish for more evidence and for certain precautionary measures that are always easier to think of afterward than at the time a pioneer experiment is being conducted. One wonders, above all, why Janet could have abandoned so completely puzzling and challenging a phenomenon of this type, but it took more boldness for a young professional man of ambition in those days to depart on so unorthodox a line as hypnotization at a distance. Janet would doubtless have said that, after all, his job was healing the sick.

When we come to the more advanced and better-controlled period of ESP experiments and ask what we have to offer by way of combination ESP and hypnosis from this later era, we have nothing so dramatic to report, although it is entirely safe to say that what we do have to report can be taken with a great deal more confidence.

In the initial experimental work of the Parapsychology Laboratory at Duke, we tested subjects in both the hypnotic state and the normal condition to discover whether they could show evidence of ESP ability. Slight deviations above the expected chance average were obtained in both conditions. There was not sufficient advantage resulting from hypnotic suggestion to warrant the greater expenditure of time and effort which that method called for, and it was abandoned. Moreover, some of the subjects who scored highest in the early Duke period were not hypnotizable by methods in use today. These and other findings seemed to indicate clearly enough that there was at least no *necessary* connection between hypnotizability and ESP. That idea had, it is true, been given up long ago by workers in the field of parapsychology, and for half a century or more most of the tests of telepathy and clairvoyance had been carried out with subjects in the waking state. But most of the earlier conclusions, with regard to both ESP and hypnosis, were in need of later re-examination.

The general feeling we had at the Duke Laboratory was that we did not know what to tell the hypnotized subject to do to increase his ESP scoring rate. The generalized hypnotic suggestions of increased confidence that he could see through the opaque screen which hid the card or that he could penetrate to the mind of the telepathic sender and perceive his thought were not, in themselves, sufficiently helpful to the subject. Assuming that there was some basis for the earlier reports of exceptional success in ESP in the hypnotic state, we could only suspect that we did not yet know what specific directions to give the hypnotized subject to make him an effective ESP subject as well.

Some years later, after the Duke work with ESP and hypnosis, John Grela,[1] a senior psychology student at St. Lawrence University, undertook to secure a difference in performance on the Duke ESP procedures by giving the subject different hypnotic suggestions at different test sessions. At one session there was no hypnosis, at another there was hypnosis with neutral suggestion, at a third there was strong positive suggestion of ESP ability and of interest in scoring high on the card test. Finally, the subject was given a fourth session in which negative suggestion with regard to ESP was administered. He was told that ESP was impossible and that he had no such ability. The total of all four sessions gave significantly high score averages, and the session which gave the highest was that in which positive suggestion was given. The lowest was that in which the negative suggestion was made, with the other two conditions falling between.

It is interesting, however, that the correlation studies on the data showed that the subject tended to follow his own scoring level to a significant extent; that is, the subjects differed among themselves more than the group as a whole differed from one condition to the other. It looks as if hypnotic suggestion, as used by Grela, made a dent, but not a deep one, on what goes on in the ESP process. This result is, however, encouraging, and more work on similar lines is going on at the present time.

We can be fairly clear about the limiting factor in the case: it is our lack of knowledge of what specific conditions favor and hinder ESP. Without this information we cannot expect to be able to induce those conditions by hypnotic suggestion. It is not a fair test of hypnosis to tell a subject in blanket fashion that he will score high, that he will be able to see the concealed object, or anything else of the kind.

Also, we are dealing in these more recent experiments with relatively unselected people. Most of the older records involving a combination of hypnosis and ESP, came from physicians dealing with what were then called hysteria patients, a very special group indeed. It may well be that among our college student populations, which were dealt with in our more recent experiments, we have very few people, if any, showing any of the characteristics of personality which furnish the crop of interesting cases in the older literature. There are likely many other factors of difference, too. One of them is the statistical one; that is to say, the cases that came to the attention of physicians and were placed in the records were really only a few out of thousands, while today we are reporting on everyone tried in a given experiment. Our findings would naturally look thin by comparison.

Perhaps the main thing that should be said is that finally the ESP side of the hypnosis–ESP combination has reached the point of having clear-cut methods developed so that we can find out just what is actually going on. The stricter control over observation has taken a good deal of the dramatic out of many a case and claim, not merely in parapsychology. But this reflection on the older reporting of ESP under hypnotic and mesmeric conditions probably does not warrant rejection of all of these colorful cases. Their suggestive value is high and should not be underrated. There is undoubtedly much more to be found out, both about hypnosis and about ESP, than is yet known. What is more, each may yet have a big role to play in the future research on the other. As we find out more about what to do to a subject to induce more favorable performance, we ought to be able to use hypnosis to implant those conditions and to fix the mental state needed. If we are able to learn more, these two capacities can be made to work together in a reliable way of application. If so, we hardly dare dream of the consequences that could follow.

Another thing is clear, or at least reasonably so. ESP, on its part, is still a definitely unconscious process. The subject is not aware of the way ESP works in him, even though he may be using it with remarkable success. Its operation does not register in consciousness.

Hypnosis, on the other hand, is not so much a phenomenon of unconscious nature as of limited consciousness. Hypnosis is a state of highly restricted consciousness to the point where attention is focused in a highly controlled fashion on a small area designated by the hypnotist. If he says, "You will hear only my voice," attention (in the responsive subject) is restricted to that. If he says, "You will feel nothing," attention shifts away from feelings of all kinds. Within the focus of this highly concentrated and limited attention, however, there is full consciousness. The hypnotist may direct the focus of attention and consequent consciousness to anything within the subject's range but not to ESP functioning, not to the way in which the ESP impression is received or the time when it is received, or the awareness as to whether or not a given response is correct.

Hypnosis, then, can be seen to be not the kind of thing we need at this stage in the ESP research, that is, unless someone working with hypnosis can find out how to penetrate to the true area of unconsciousness involved in ESP—not just to the zone of forgotten things, but to things which were never conscious. That would revolutionize ESP research.

Has the ESP research anything on its part to contribute to the study of hypnosis? Our understanding of the basic nature of hypnosis is limited by our ignorance of the character of the thought-brain relation. Naturally, we can go only a limited way on a purely descriptive level, and a host of mysteries remain among hypnotic phenomena as long as the connection between suggestion and the nervous system remains unknown. Now it is the special merit of the ESP research that its findings go right to the heart of the body-mind problems that have baffled psychology throughout its entire history.* Hypnosis, which has never fitted into a mechanistic psychology, and which demands a more complex foundation in personality than brain physics alone can offer, may be expected to enter a new phase of its progress as the full import of the ESP findings is realized.

(Note: After writing this chapter I became better acquainted with the work of John Björkhem, S.T.D., Ph.D., M.D., of Sweden and his really vast experience with hypnosis. Working both with mental patients and with normal subjects, Dr. Björkhem has done literally thousands of experiments over the last 20 years, but because of language barriers this work is but little known outside of Sweden. He has, in a number of exceptional cases out of thousands of subjects tested, found good confirmation of some of the earlier reports of "travelling clairvoyance" like those of Janet, Backman, and Barrett. Some of this material is still awaiting publication, but a part of it appears in his technical book on hypnosis *De hypnotiska hallucinationerna*, published in 1942, and some of it in a popular book *Det ockulta problemet* (1939 and 1951). Effort will now be made to have this work presented in English. It would appear to supply an important missing link between the older explanations and the current types of experiment.)

REFERENCE

1. Grela, J.: Report published in *Journal of Parapsychology*, Duke University Press, September, 1945.

* A discussion of this aspect of the ESP research may be followed in my book, *The Reach of the Mind*, William Sloane Associates, New York, 1947.

CHAPTER SIXTEEN

Antisocial Uses of Hypnosis

Editor's Note

"Is hypnosis dangerous?" is a question frequently asked by the uninformed person whenever the subject of hypnotism is discussed. It can be safely said, and all authorities will agree, that hypnosis, in itself, is completely harmless. No bad effects, either mental or physical, from the mere fact of being hypnotized have ever been incurred by anyone. Yet, with those who know little or nothing about it, fear of hypnosis is almost universal, owing, unfortunately, to popular misinformation and misconceptions.

There is another way in which hypnosis might be dangerous to the subject—or others. Perhaps he can be hypnotized by an unscrupulous person and led to commit some antisocial or criminal act. The question of whether or not this is possible has been threshed over ever since the days of Mesmer and has never been answered satisfactorily to all authorities. It has been discussed in many of the older books, with most of the writers claiming that no one under hypnosis could be made to do anything which he would not do when in the waking state. Modern researchers have tried to formulate experiments to prove the matter one way or another, and great controversy has arisen over the results.

In the following chapter, Dr. Paul C. Young undertakes a discussion of this matter and of the conflicting evidence from past experiments. The various tests and results, both pro and con, are described and analyzed. Young's article, with a well-conceived, well-executed experiment to back up his contentions, would seem to cover the situation most adequately. Critics will find it difficult to refute his arguments that hypnosis *can* be used to produce antisocial behavior. The tests made by Young with eight subjects were arranged to substantiate, if possible, Rowland's previous experiment, but under conditions which would not be subjected to the same criticisms made of Rowland's work. It is worthy of note that, until recently, Young has been on the other side of the fence, and his views have been completely changed as a result of his consideration of the problem after publication of articles by Watkins, Schneck, and others.

Dr. Young is a veteran in hypnotic experimentation, and he has contributed a great deal to our knowledge. As was mentioned in the introduction, he was the first experimenter in hypnosis to use the controlled experiment and is a pioneer in modern scientific research in the field. For some time he has been engaged in psychological practice for the Veterans Administration in Dallas and Houston, Texas, but recently has returned to academic work as acting head of the Department of Psychology at Louisiana State University.

As has been stated previously, hypnosis is now in a period of renaissance. In looking back over the history of mesmerism and hypnotism, it is noticed that interest has been cyclic in the past, with a peak of interest reached approximately every thirty years. Such a peak is being approached at present, one perhaps destined to be the highest yet attained and which may be maintained. Formerly, a rise of interest has been followed by a decline brought on by various factors. These have included scientific discrediting, as by the French commission which investigated Mesmer and quite unwarrantedly negated his work; attacks by the medical profession, such as followed the work in England of Braid, Elliotson, and Esdaile; and because of ridiculous and disgraceful stage performances and demonstrations. Not the least of the reasons for seeking to discredit hypnotism has been that the public and scientists alike have feared it.

In one way, it is most unfortunate that, with this rising and healthy interest, there should appear popular and scientific articles which tend to arouse further fear—articles by the very men who sincerely believe that hypnosis has something of great value to offer. Pointing out that it can be dangerous in unscrupulous hands is bound to develop and increase such fears. Most workers in hypnosis feel that hypnosis is of great potential value to mankind, a science which has, so far, been almost completely ignored. Popular fears of its dangers will certainly restrict its use in the future, as they have in the past and do at present.

On the other hand, if hypnosis can be dangerous to the hypnotized subject, then the public is entitled to know the facts. There can be no question of this. However, the facts must be weighed and carefully analyzed before conclusions are reached, perhaps too hastily and in error if there is not full scrutiny of the situation.

One fact seems certain from weighing the results of experiments and from our knowledge of what can be accomplished with modern techniques. A person in a deep hypnotic state *can* be caused to commit antisocial acts. It is obvious that many people have criminal trends and many others are actual criminals. With such people, it should be no great task to cause them to commit an antisocial act under hypnosis. This will be granted by any hypnotic authority. It is the honest, conscientious, law-abiding subject who must be considered. He, too, can undoubtedly be deluded into committing such acts.

Yet, let us look into other facts. Experiments such as Young's, and all those which he describes, require somnambulistic subjects. For effective research, extremely good subjects are necessary. Young relates his method of selection of his subjects from large groups. Undoubtedly, every authority will agree that *only* good subjects under hypnosis can be led to exhibit antisocial behavior. Such subjects are not at all common. It is likely that not more than 1 person out of 50 or even 100 is a sufficiently good one to be in any danger whatsoever of being victimized by a hypnotic Fagin.

When one reads an article on hypnotic experiments, the discussions of phenomena and the results of tests may lead the reader to believe that hypnosis is, indeed, a magic wand. A wave of the wand and a command from the omnipotent hypnotist and the subject promptly does almost anything conceivable that is suggested to him. The hypnotist may seem to be an unbottled jinni. Actually, it is not so easy to obtain the reported results, even with excellent somnambulistic subjects. Hallucinations—and other phenomena—do not always result at the mere order of the hypnotist. Yet, with proper techniques, they can be obtained.

In considering these technical papers, it is surprising how researchers often give every evidence of viewing the hypnotized subject as nothing but an automaton—a guinea pig who is unable to speak and is unconscious. Few seem to think of asking a subject's views as to the results of a test or why he has exhibited certain behavior. Conjectures and rationalizations, perhaps quite erroneous, are made by the experimenter when a simple, direct question asked the subject might produce the real answer to a problem of motive or behavior. The subject is not an automaton when he is in a deep hypnotic state, nor is he unconscious. He thinks and is rational, though he may be hallucinated and deluded. In considering antisocial actions provoked under hypnosis, it is quite likely, if the hypnotist's purpose is criminal, that the subject would analyze and detect his nefarious purpose and would refuse to accept suggestions, despite the subject-hypnotist relationship. Furthermore, even with the most devious and best of techniques, the hypnotist will not find it easy to overcome the censorship of the subject's superego.

Dr. Young tells of the possible use of hallucinations, delusions, illusions, induced complexes, transidentification, etc., as techniques available for inducing antisocial behavior. Of course he is quite correct in his contentions that they could be employed and should at times be successful. Young quotes Erickson as admitting that a subject can be deluded when hypnotized into performing some objectionable act, but that the deception would not be dependent upon the hypnosis. This an extremely important point. Deceit may be easier, at times, under hypnosis, but certainly most of us can be deceived more or less readily, and hypnosis is not a requisite. The newspaper columns and court actions show that deceit is common and "suckers" are plentiful. The unhypnotized person can be led to commit objectionable and criminal acts by deceit and delusion with no necessity for hypnosis.

Another important fact is that any hypnotist who sets out seriously to cause a subject to commit a crime—and the hypnotist would not be interested in a mere antisocial act which would offer no benefit—must, of necessity, be highly skilled if he is to achieve such a purpose. No large number of hypnotists have such skill or knowledge. Undoubtedly, many are adept and would be potentially able to victimize a subject, but few would be amateur or lay hypnotists. Most of them are reputable psychiatrists and psychologists. Certainly it is possible that a psychiatrist or psychologist might be criminally inclined, and the point that a hypnotist might be unscrupulous and criminal cannot be entirely dismissed. But the fact is that it is not at all likely for any prospective hypnotic subject to ever encounter a villainous hypnotist possessed of the requisite skill.

Granted that antisocial and criminal actions could be brought about under hypnosis and that there are hypnotists both unscrupulous and adept, what is the possibility of the hypnotist "getting away" with such a projected scheme? We can imagine many crimes that might be attempted, from murder on down the scale. In the commission of any crime there is a strong likelihood of detection—our penal institutions are well populated with convicted criminals. What would happen if the victimized subject who had committed a crime were haled into court? Theoretically, amnesia would have been suggested, and the hypnotist therefore would feel safe. (If he were competent he would know he was not safe.) Would an amnesia stand up if the subject could save himself by recollection? We cannot be dogmatic, but almost certainly the motivation would be so strong that the subconscious mind of the subject would rescue him by dissolution of the amnesia, and he would recall having been hypnotized and remember the suggestions given him. He would then be able to explain his victimization, and the hypnotist would be exposed.

As a matter of fact, this actually happened, according to Wetterstrand's [1] translator who cites a case occurring in Kansas in the 1890's. The crime was a murder committed by a hypnotized person at the instigation of a hypnotist, somewhat along the lines considered possible by Young and others. Under pressure of the trial, the subject's suggested amnesia was broken, he was freed, and the nefarious hypnotist was hanged! But one wonders if the alleged hypnotist could not have been an innocent victim instead of a malefactor.

The mere fact that a criminal act might be carried out by a hypnotized subject is no guarantee to the hypnotist that he would escape responsibility and punishment. Any hypnotist intelligent enough to work out the intricate techniques necessary successfully to accomplish his purpose is more likely to pass up a procedure so doubtful of results and so full of danger for himself and to resort to his own efforts in carrying out his projected crime, knowing there would be less chance of apprehension.

Any prosecutor who could bring hypnotism into a criminal case, or any defense attorney who could plead hypnosis as a defense, would leap at the opportunity, with the resultant publicity and prejudice of jury and judge. The newspapers sometimes, though rarely, report such attempts. The results are usually disappointing to those who have brought up hypnosis. Any real danger of the type under discussion would be reflected in the law courts.

Interesting as is the problem, and it is important because of the mistaken conceptions of the public, it must be regarded as most impractical as to real danger. Hypothetically, there may be said to be danger. Practically, the possibilities may be regarded as nil. We can say that it *can* be done, but one is inclined to ask, "So what?" There is about as much danger for one to become involved in such hypnotically inspired antisocial actions as there is to being struck by a flying saucer.

Even if the danger were real and definite and likely to be encountered, there is a simple prevention of any danger—a most effective safeguard. Complete safety lies in the prospective hypnotic subject making sure that a third person, whom he knows and trusts, is present at all times when hypnosis is induced. With this precaution, any unscrupulous Svengali is rendered quite impotent.

REFERENCE

1. Wetterstrand, O.: *Hypnotism and Its Application to Practical Medicine*, G. P. Putnam's Sons, New York, 1897.

Antisocial Uses of Hypnosis

By PAUL C. YOUNG, Ph.D.

PSYCHOLOGY DEPARTMENT, LOUISIANA STATE UNIVERSITY,
BATON ROUGE, LOUISIANA

ASSUMPTIONS

In any serious discussion of the question of the antisocial uses of hypnosis, definition becomes paramount. Some writers speak of antisocial uses, immoral or criminal acts; others of harmful or dangerous acts. To prevent confusion it must be understood that harm, crime, antisocial acts, dangers, etc., are to be taken in their common-sense meanings. The harm may be done to oneself or to others, just as the danger may involve oneself or others. The emphasis, of course, must be on the results of the act, that is, the end product, not on the attitude of the subject. An act is harmful or antisocial or dangerous if damage is done or danger is run, whether or not the actor performs the act knowingly and willfully. Thus, certainly, the acts of the mentally ill, the alcoholic, the drug addict, or the hypnotized subject are to be considered dangerous, harmful, or antisocial if these acts put in jeopardy the health, life, property, or morals of the actors or others.

The point being labored here, and it is crucial, is that an act, to be antisocial, need not be willfully so or even consciously so. It is enough if it is antisocial only, but really, in its actual or potential *effects* upon the actor or others. In fact, the criterion of danger or immorality must be the judgment of observers who themselves are not hypnotized, rather than the subjective appraisal of the situation by the hypnotized subject. By all means, the state of the subject's mind while he is accepting or rejecting antisocial suggestions should be investigated; but the point at issue is whether *antisocial* actions can be induced in hypnosis if an unscrupulous operator should go all out to induce them. Furthermore, it seems logical to assume that, if a hypnotist were to seek to induce antisocial acts, he would not do it like a gentleman,

A further assumption is that experimental situations can be so arranged as to answer this question without requiring a corpus delicti. Estabrooks'[1] conviction (in spite of his maintaining that antisocial acts are possible) that the problem cannot be finally solved because real danger involves possible (or necessary) loss of life or limb, is ill-founded. Erickson[2] and others rightly see that antisocial actions form a graded series, from mere annoyances, impertinencies, and petty thefts on up to criminal actions, and that any clear-cut antisocial acts, if they are out of keeping with the subject's customary code of behavior, would be definitive. Moreover, real danger may be in the small as well as in the large. Even though the amount of danger involved in a psychological experiment cannot be so nicely weighed as in physical experiments, unbiased observers can judge what does and does not constitute an antisocial act. Moreover, it is the experimenter's business to evolve criteria by which his results can be evaluated. This matter will come up later in criticizing Erickson's methodology. Contrary to the opinion of Erickson, and others, the experimental conditions in the laboratory are not necessarily inferior or "vitiating" but are often superior to the conditions existing in a hospital or clinic. Moreover, in Watkins'[3] successful experiments the setting was an Army installation rather than a psychological laboratory and was, apparently, fully as "informal" as Erickson's. Judging by Erickson's reports, the knowledge that they were being experimented upon rankled in the minds of his subjects in the hospital setup more than has been the case with subjects experimented upon by others in laboratories. Besides, we must emphasize again, it is by what the subjects will actually do, as evaluated by observers themselves unhypnotized, that the question must be settled. Where the actions take place is immaterial except as it allows for full play of the hypnotic techniques and for the commission of the antisocial actions. There might be a positive handicap in antisocial suggestions being given in a hospital by an experimenter whose use of hypnosis for therapy is well known—as Erickson's was.

It must be admitted that for the most part the question at issue is more theoretical than practical. By and large, hypnosis is in the hands of psychologists in universities, colleges, and clinics, and of psychiatrists and other physicians in clinics and hospitals. Still, it is more than an academic question. Watkins [4] reports that, according to a recent Associated Press dispatch, a hypnotist was sentenced to prison upon conviction of a breach of the "felony morals act" on a young woman. Moreover, commercial entertainers often use hypnosis in a manner which might lead imitators to attempt to exploit it. Whatever one's decision is in regard to dangers, the scientific and therapeutic use of hypnosis need not be affected. Even if hypnosis is innocuous, it is no less powerful therapeutically, as has been shown often. If it is potentially dangerous, it is so on the basis that the more powerful the instrument, the greater the possible damage in unworthy hands.

Lastly, it should be assumed that only somnambulistic subjects, who show uniformly all the classical phenomena of hypnosis, including posthypnotic amnesia for trance activities, will be used in this type of experimentation.

THE PRESENT STATE OF THE PROBLEM

The situation regarding antisocial uses of hypnosis is not so simple as Weitzenhoffer [5] has described it in his efforts to reconcile the contradictory results reported by experimenters. His analysis is to the effect that those, like Erickson and Wolberg [6] who report failure to bring about antisocial acts in hypnosis, have failed because they put the matter baldly to the subjects, as if to say: "Take your roommate's money"; whereas those who report success, like Wells,[7] Brenman,[8] Rowland,[9] and Watkins, have made the situation acceptable to the subject by saying in effect: "The money is yours, take it." For simplification here we shall let Erickson represent one group, Wells the other group. Weitzenhoffer describes the situation as follows:

In either groups of experiments, the results indicate the behavior of the subject was in every instance appropriate to the situation *as defined by the hypnotist* . . . the behavior of the hypnotized individual seems to be entirely a function of the stimulus-pattern as perceived by him under hypnosis. If the situation appears socially, or in other ways, acceptable to the subject, he probably can be induced to commit "anti-social" acts. If he perceives the situation as contrary to his own ethical system, it is very unlikely that he can be made to carry out "criminal acts."

Weitzenhoffer's penetrating analysis, however, is incomplete on two counts. In the first place, Wells's group has reported antisocial acts even though the situation had been defined as antisocial, the subject having been told in effect, "This is bad, but do it," as, for example, Watkins in extracting military secrets and Rowland in making subjects hurl acid which had been described to them as corrosive. In the second place, Weitzenhoffer does not attempt to deal with the questions of (1) the validity, the "reality" of the antisocial actions reported, and (2) of the efficiency, the experimental adequacy for the purpose, of the methods that fail. His analysis of the methods that fail is essentially correct: by these methods the subject "perceives the situation as contrary to his own ethical system."

Weitzenhoffer does not come face to face with the question whether (in spite of the criticism that these results are artefacts of the experimental situation) the antisocial actions reported are really what they purport to be. His reconciliation satisfies neither side because it throws doubt on the work of Wells and others who report subjects doing dangerous actions *after* the danger has been pointed out to them; and (contra Erickson and others) it seems to accept as bona fide, antisocial actions brought about through a falsification of the experimental situation.

Erickson explains Wells's results as being mere artefacts of the laboratory, with its experimental atmosphere and its subject-hypnotist relationship, including the attitude, "This looks dangerous, but it is not, because you—the experimenter—are a reputable person." * On the same account many psychologists have questioned the reality of antisocial actions induced in hypnosis. Typically, Pattie says

* The present writer's phrasing.

about Brenman's results, in which subjects took money, "∴ . . . yet these experiments were performed in the atmosphere of a laboratory and the subjects were well aware that the situation was experimental." Indeed, the orthodox position has been that the dangers elicited are more apparent than real. Weitzenhoffer seems to share this opinion, or at least to be in doubt, inasmuch as he has put *antisocial* and *criminal* within quotation marks, as if they were pseudo-antisocial actions.

The methods that fail do not attempt to define the situation as socially acceptable to the subject, or—and this is the nub of the criticism brought by Wells and others—the methods that fail do not use the full repertoire of hypnosis in the way that a skilled and unscrupulous operator certainly would, by inducing hallucinations, illusions, delusions, using the hypnotist's prestige, etc. Put baldly, the controversy is as follows: on Wells's side there is a denial of the adequacy of Erickson's methods for inducing antisocial actions in hypnosis; on Erickson's side, a denial of the reality of the dangers induced by Wells's method.

The problem, then, is twofold: do the methods used by Erickson, in seeking to induce antisocial actions, exhaust the possibilities for inducing them; and are the actions elicited by Wells really dangerous?

The second question seems more important, because it is much more to the point to find out *whether* Wells succeeded than to understand *why* Erickson failed. Yet, if we see clearly why Erickson failed, we may have some basis for judging whether it was possible for Wells to succeed. This is possible if, for example, it should appear that Erickson failed to use methods which have been successful in inducing behavior as startlingly different from the subject's normal reactions as antisocial behavior is from his usual behavior. Also, if methods rejected by Erickson have in them aspects which make the induction of antisocial actions seem logically possible and probable, and if, finally, the heart of Erickson's criticism of the successful methods (the subject-hypnotist relationship) should logically appear to be closely related to induction of behavior entirely out of keeping with the subject's usual behavior, such as is seen in antisocial acts, then this may lay a basis for judging not only whether it was possible for Wells and others to succeed, but also why Erickson's much-quoted and highly regarded criticisms of the successful experiments should have little or no theoretical weight. These results can then be judged by strictly objective standards as to whether, in fact, antisocial behavior has been induced.

We shall be better able to judge the matter if we study carefully, first, the methods that have admittedly failed to produce positive results even in the hands of very good experimenters such as Erickson and others; second, the results theoretically to be expected in view of the well-established phenomena of hypnosis; and, finally, the conditions under which the reportedly successful results have been produced. In this way we may be able to resolve not only the question whether antisocial actions are theoretically possible, but also whether they have actually rather than artefactually taken place.

METHODS THAT FAILED TO INDUCE ANTISOCIAL ACTIONS IN HYPNOSIS

A criminal, intent upon the antisocial use of hypnosis, as Wells points out, would employ every trick of hypnosis, that is, vivid hallucinations, realistic illusions, and delusions in keeping with the personality needs of the subject and the ulterior purposes of the hypnotist. In addition (something Wells did not mention), he would use the apparent innocuousness of the situation, including the hypnotist-subject relationship of dominance on the one side and trust and compliance on the other. Thus, if one were seriously attempting to induce antisocial behavior (and if the problem is real, such an assumption must be made), he would seek to falsify the whole external and subjective situation for the subject, stepwise, of course, giving the subject only such suggestions as he could assimilate and giving him time to consolidate them, in a way which Erickson [10] points out in his description of building up a complex. Into such a misperceived and misconceived world, the hypnotist with criminal design would insinuate his orders. As will be shown in the next section, the recent work on the reality of hypnotic hallucinations, age regressions, circumvention of ego, transidentification of the ego, etc., points to the possibility of the hypnotist's building up within the subject such an altered conception of reality (including the subject's own identity as well as the identity of the hypnotist) as might induce the subject to act in accordance with the altered concept of himself and the world. It is possible that such action might be directed into antisocial channels.

As will be shown later, this theoretical possibility should be considered presumptive of success for antisocial suggestions until such time as these powerful hypnotic measures shall have been energetically used and, in the judgment of objective observers, found incapable of bringing about antisocial behavior.

This is just what Erickson did not do in seeking to induce such action. In both experimental and therapeutic work in other connections, he has reported the successful use of varied and energetic methods in implanting complexes,[11] in bringing about age regression,[12] and in inducing transidentification.[13] He used hypnosis in this thorough and ingenious way to demonstrate the psychopathology of everyday life, to attenuate and thus eradicate a complex. But when he attempted to induce antisocial behavior, he resorted to only the most meager of hypnotic techniques, that is, bare suggestion of wrongdoing, under the impression, apparently, that in a more complicated "experimental" situation it becomes impossible to tell to what aspects of the situation the subject is responding.

Erickson not only did not build up a case by the use of hallucinations, etc., to obviate conflicts in the subjects, but he held before them the objectionable aspect of the act suggested, thus guaranteeing a moral conflict in the subject. He explains his method and gives his reason for this restricted technique in the following words:

> In all instances every effort was made to induce either an actual performance or an approximation of the suggested act, so that, whatever the degree of the experimenter's responsibility and guilt or the extent of possible protective measures, there would still be the unescapable fact of the subject's own participation in an undesirable performance directed either against himself or against others.

Erickson's criticism of the methods of experimenters who have reported success shows his willful rejection of any of the powerful means available to confuse the subject through disorienting him as to time, place, and person (his own person included); through implantation of complexes of overwhelming fear, guilt, hate, or cupidity; and through trading on the strong subject-hypnotist relationship to bring about obedience, etc. He points up his rejection of the classical hypnotic phenomena for this purpose in the following language:

That these experimental findings [that is, Rowland's] are valid as to their apparent significance is to be questioned, for the reason of the serious oversight, except for slight hints summarized in the tentative explanation offered for the results, of the definite and highly important subject-hypnotist relationship of trust and confidence which could account fully for the findings. . . . Schilder and Kauders have made an excellent survey of the literature and offer, in relation to various aspects of the entire problem of the misuse of hypnosis, a wealth of general opinions based upon their own experience and that of others. They declare, "The hypnotized person is always aware of the general situation, . . . conscious of the fact that an experiment is being made . . . he must be well aware that the hypnotist is not inducing him to commit an actual murder, if the hypnotizer is a man of respected social position."

To top off Erickson's conviction about this matter, I quote: "Yet, at a mere experimental level, where the purposes of the act are defeated by the nature of the setting, full obedience may be obtained."

I shall not labor here the fact that Schilder and Kauders,[14] as well as Erickson, assume that the experimenter will be a man of "respected social position" and that the subject is always *au courant* with the situation, both assumptions being quite unfounded, the first as shown by any logical definition of the question, "Can antisocial actions be induced?"; the second by such work as Erickson and others,[15] Wolberg,[16] Lindner,[17] and others, following Luria,[18] report in profusion. The latter type of contradiction will be dealt with in the next section.

Erickson did not use a varied, ingenious, and energetic methodology in seeking to induce antisocial actions, as is palpable. He did not use illusions, hallucinations, delusions, etc., the real stock in trade of hypnotic influence. Quite the contrary. Not only did he not induce such classical phenomena; not only did he not trade upon the trust and submission inherent in the subject-hypnotist relationship; he willfully abstained from these measures. He did so because he demanded that the subject face up to the actual situation, that is, to "the unescapable fact of the subject's own participation in an undesirable performance directed either against himself or against others." In other words, Erickson's definition of an antisocial act in hypnosis is an act which the subject has been made to see as antisocial. It cannot be a bad act which the subject has been misled into believing is a good or at least a necessary act. For Erickson, it must be a bad act which the subject sees as a bad act. As he phrases it:

Furthermore, it is doubtful if any definite answer to the general question can be obtained *except by an experimental situation in which the suggested anti-social act really can become an accomplished fact, obviously and unmistakably so, and without the protection afforded by a falsified situation which can serve only to vitiate or negate the experimental procedure for both subject and investigator.* (Erickson's italics).

Fearing to complicate the situation by confusing the subject as to what was right and wrong—a squeamishness which no antisocial user of hypnosis would bother about—he developed the mistaken thesis that such an act can be diagnosed as right or wrong only if the actor is conscious of his own immorality.

In seeking unequivocal results, he simplified the experimental situation so that if the subject took the suggestions, the antisocial behavior would be plain. But in so doing, he robbed his method, in his hands at least, of the power to induce the actions he so nakedly suggested. Later, it will become obvious that antisocial actions were induced, but they did not take the direction suggested. Instead of complicating the situation and bringing about "obedience"— which Erickson admits is possible—and then judging the reality of the behavior by means of objectifying the observational conditions, he clings to the thesis that only by a direct attack, without falsification, can the question be settled.

Erickson says his subjects resented his commands:

Rarely did the subjects show equal resentment [against the experimenter] in both the waking and the hypnotic states and still more rarely was the waking displeasure greater than the trance emotion. Also, it is of interest to note that certain of the subjects actively inflicted punishment and humiliation upon the experimenter in retaliation for his objectionable commands, the possibility of which has been noted by Schilder and Kauders.

Faced with a conflict between the hypnotic tendency to carry out suggestions and the natural repugnance to do the unpleasant (and sometimes the immoral or the dangerous), the subjects turned in resentment "almost invariably" upon the perpetrator of the conflict and heaped upon him the antisocial actions the hypnotist had meant for others. And well might subjects resent being commanded to do disagreeable things, without being motivated by either reward or punishment, much less by the implantation of an overwhelming complex built up around an act in keeping with their past and pictured as essential for their future welfare.

Erickson makes much of this resentment:

Despite their well-established trust and confidence in the experimenter, almost invariably the experimentation . . . caused them to develop intense resentments and antagonisms to him . . . apparently, in attempting to induce felonious behavior by hypnosis, the danger lies not in the possibility of success, but in the risk to the hypnotist himself.

One is reminded of an incident Estabrooks reports:

He attended a stage exhibition and arrived late. He was horrified to see a respectable acquaintance stripped to his underwear with a broom handle for a flute gamboling around the stage under the delusion that he was a Greek faun. Highly gratified also to see the faun knock the hypnotist flat the moment the trance was removed.

Through the hypnotist's failure to incorporate the act into a satisfactory setting for the ego and to induce complete posthypnotic amnesia, the subject felt resentment at having been forced into a slightly antisocial act.

For lack of any hallucinatory or delusionally induced motivation, Erickson's bald suggestions served only to arouse such mental conflict and aggression as resolved itself in the heaping of punishment and humiliation upon the hypnotist—actions which are antisocial in fact, whether or not the subject so regarded them. It is not that

Erickson's antisocial suggestions were lost; they simply backfired.* The subjects inflicted the identical antisocial acts upon the suggester. Far from being without antisocial effects, Erickson's report is replete with them; but he failed to use a method that would direct them toward third persons. The hypnotist got them all.

Since Erickson's thesis is that unequivocal judgment in this matter can arise only if an antisocial act be defined as one in which the subject sees the issue and chooses to do the wrong, and since he has firmly held to a methodology in keeping with it, his results can logically prove no more than that thesis. Therefore the only justifiable conclusion Erickson can draw from his 35 "accounts" is that, in his clinical setting, his subjects, who were under no illusion as to the meaning of the commands given them, would not carry out unvarnished suggestions to commit "objectionable" actions against the intended victims but did, in many cases, carry out identical actions against the ingenuous hypnotist. His experiments were successful in inducing antisocial action, but, for lack of proper motivation, those actions were directed upon the suggester rather than upon the suggested victims. His actual conclusions, as published, however, jump from this narrow thesis, with its necessarily restricted methodology and its retaliatory antisocial results, to the following conclusions embracing hypnosis in general:

> Hence, the conclusion warranted by these experimental findings is that hypnosis cannot be misused to induce hypnotized persons to commit actual wrongful acts either against themselves or others, and that the only serious risk encountered in such attempts is incurred by the hypnotist in the form of condemnation, rejection, and exposure.

Thus, we see hypnosis in general equated with hypnosis as delimited in Erickson's report, that is, hypnosis devoid of illusions, hallucinations, delusions, falsification of situations, implantation of motives, etc. In fact, Erickson says flatly:

* It should be noted, however, that in accounts 2 and 11 the subjects in hypnosis actually carried out the suggestions, burning a finger and divulging intimate information, before turning against the hypnotist in irritability and in violent anger, respectively. (See Ref. No. 2.)

In that type of setting one might deceive a subject into performing some objectionable act, but the deception would not be dependent upon the hypnosis. Rather it would depend upon entirely different factors and the hypnosis as shown repeatedly above, could easily constitute an actual obstacle to a deception based upon other factors.

Here, Erickson differentiates the hypnosis of hallucinations, etc., from the hypnosis of unvarnished suggestions, and treats the latter as the only true hypnosis. Really, of course, hypnosis includes whatever can be induced by the well-known techniques. The person experimenting in the field of antisocial uses of hypnosis must not emasculate his methodology for fear he cannot evaluate his results. Rather, he must ingeniously plan to objectify these results so that they can be evaluated.

It is clear, then, that Erickson's methods fall far short of the methods which should be tried in this field of research, and that, if he had succeeded in inducing antisocial behavior directed against third persons, he would have elicited only one very restricted type of antisocial actions, namely the type in which the subject realizes that the act is wrong and still does it. Other experimenters, it is true, claim full success even under the conditions Erickson imposed upon himself. But to argue, as does Erickson, that such a limited method is the definitive method of experimentation in this field, and his results therefore are more trustworthy than those obtained by using a more varied and ingenious approach, is quite unwarranted. Other experimenters have used a much more varied, and hypnotically more powerful, attack and report successes.

The present point is not that such fuller and motivationally more powerful methods would necessarily result in producing antisocial acts, but rather that any method that purposely stops short of some such use of the full armamentarium of hypnosis should not be considered an adequate method in the premises. The uncritical acceptance of Erickson's results, as well as of his strictures of method, can be explained on the following bases: (1) the sheer quantity of proof, that is, 35 different "accounts" of persons being asked to do things ranging from the picayunish to the near-libelous; (2) the easy confidence with which, as a physician, he declares that his method-ology, used for the most part in "informal situations," was scien-tifically unimpeachable; (3) and most important of all, his results confirm the beliefs, or at least the desires, of most of his readers.

In reality, however, Erickson's failure to induce antisocial actions against third persons, using a meager methodology, gives him no license to impugn the results of others who used a motivationally much stronger method. In science one does not criticize another's results without having duplicated his methods or without having shown the logical or practical inapplicability of his method. Erickson has done neither.

The fact that Erickson, using an incomplete technique, failed does not mean that others, using the full arsenal of hypnosis, would neces-sarily succeed. But the phenomena of present-day hypnosis certainly lead to that assumption. Let us review some of the recent findings.

HYPNOTIC PHENOMENA PRESUMPTIVE OF THE POSSIBILITY
OF ANTISOCIAL USES

To show that we might logically expect the well-authenticated phenomena of hypnosis to make possible induction of antisocial actions, it is only necessary to outline some of the recent reports. First, the sheer power of hypnotic techniques should be emphasized. Pattie [19] has written:

The results of the work of experimental psychologists on hypnosis have been to a considerable extent negative in character—they have shown what hypnosis is not, that it will not do certain things claimed for it. . . . Despite these negative factors the effects of hypnosis are acknowledged to be remarkable even by the most tough-minded scientist; by its aid illu-sions and hallucinations can be produced, anesthesias for major surgical operations can be induced, old memories not available in the normal state can be recovered and peculiar alterations of personality can be brought about. . . . It is now established that susceptibility carries with it no stigma of neuroticism. To say this, however, is not to deny that there are certain striking similarities between the phenomena of hypnosis and the amnesias, paralyses and anesthesias of hysteria.

The hypnotic phenomena which are similar to those of certain

neuroses and even certain psychoses—though on a temporary basis—
may be listed as follows:

1. "Powerful and primitive unconscious forces . . . [which] come
to light in the hypnotic trance." (Fisher) [20] (Italics are mine.)

2. The subject's belief in the magical power of the hypnotist, that
is, that "alterations take place in the external world at his [hypno-
tist's] mere wish. For the hypnotized, at least, he is the great magi-
cian, who alone is capable, by his wish and will, to produce creative
changes in the universe, to eliminate objects from the universe or
supply them to it." (Schilder and Kauders) [14]

3. Removing repressions. "Hypnoanalysis is equivalent to a
surgical removal of barriers and hazards; it pierces the psychic sub-
strate and raises the repressed to the level of awareness." (Lindner) [17]

*4. A minimization of outside reality and an alteration of body sen-
sation and of body image*, changes in self-awareness, in modes of
thought, and in motor expression. (Brenman, Gill, and Hacker) [21]

5. A "limitation of the spontaneous mental life of the subject and
the consequent limitation of attention to the stimuli provided by the
experimenter." (Leuba) [22]

6. Hallucinations, so real according to Erickson [23] that hypnotically hallucinated color blindness had the correct (hallucinated)
afterimages. Estabrooks reports using such a hallucination to moti-
vate a subject to perform an antisocial act.[24]

7. Hallucinations of unbearable pain. "I am convinced that he
would not have suffered more if there had been an actual hot iron
pressed against his forearm all the time." (Wells) [25]

8. Satisfaction of infantile needs. Love, passive compliance, and
the wish to participate in omnipotence. (White) [26] Presumably, a
skillful but unscrupulous hypnotist might play upon these unsatisfied
needs.

9. "Hypnosis offers an opportunity to control and direct thinking,
to select or exclude memories and ideas, and thus give the patient
the opportunity to deal individually and adequately with any selected item of experience." (Erickson) [27]

10. Rapport, "a condition in which the subject responds to the
hypnotist and is seemingly incapable of hearing, seeing, sensing, or

responding to anything else unless so instructed by the hypnotist. It is in effect a concentration of the subject's attention upon and awareness only of the hypnotist and those things which the hypnotist wishes included in the situation, and it has the effect of dissociating the subject from other things." (Erickson) [28]

11. Artificially induced complexes, apparently possessing all the effects of actual deep-lying conflicts in persons "without expressed neurotic problems." "He complained of . . . dizziness, . . . took two or three steps then fell backward remarking that he felt so faint that he could hardly walk. His face was blanched and when his pulse was taken it was found to be rapid and thready . . . cold perspiration . . . began to shiver . . . generalized muscular tremors . . . agitated, and complained of such great physical distress that I found it necessary to rehypnotize him and remove the conflict." (Wolberg) According to McDowell, in a case of his, an artificially induced conflict promptly proved much more efficient than months of psychotherapy.

12. Complete compliance. Lindner claims, "With hypnoanalysis it is as if surgical removal of such barriers and hazards (resistances and natural reluctances) has been accomplished. . . . Training in hypnosis [should be continued until] posthypnotic suggestions are carried through in a fashion that leaves no doubt of the mastery of the situation by the hypnotist." Wolberg states, "Analyses of fantasies in deep trance states in both normal subjects and neurotic patients frequently shows the hypnotist to be an omnipotent individual vested with protective and punitive powers, whose commands cannot be resisted."

13. Reorganization of psychic life, as Erickson states, through "the recovery of memories, development of amnesias, identifications and anesthesias, the causing of dreams, emotional conflicts, hallucinations, disorientations and so forth"; or, as White [30] puts it: "For hypnotism is one of the few experimental techniques applicable to human beings whereby it is possible to produce major changes in the organization of behavior. Without discomfort or danger to the subject, provided certain precautions are taken, it is possible to effect an extensive alteration in those patterns of experience which constitute the self and in those controls of behavior which we know as volition." Wolberg says (after referring to the loss of the reality sense and installation of a regressive type of thinking), "It is possible that hypnosis removes barriers between the cortical and sub-cortical areas analogous to the situation that exists in the infant prior to myelizination of higher neurones."

14. Age regressions, according to Wolberg, Erickson, Lindner, Watkins, and others, are real. (See Chapters Seven and Eight.)

15. "Circumvention of the Ego resistances," via the hypnotic trance, according to Brenman and Knight,[33] is the common factor in divergent applications of hypnosis. Wolberg speaks of loss of demarcation between the ego and the outside world.

16. The compulsory nature of hypnotic phenomena. Are the hypnotic phenomena real? Arnold's [34] answer is, "They are real in the sense that any functional defect is real. . . . The process of focusing has become so efficient, so selecting, that nothing else exists and therefore no other possibility of action is available to the subject." Wolberg speaks of inducing "an irrepressible impulse" of "infantile dependency by leaning on the godlike figure of the hypnotist"—and summarizes his own and others' work in this respect as follows: "In subjects capable of deep hypnotic states, it is possible to produce obsessive ideas, compulsions, phobias, ideas of reference, persecutory trends, grandiose ideas, depressive and nihilistic delusions, ideas of unreality, hypochondriacal ideas and delusions of influence."

17. Assumption of another's identity, described by Erickson in his experiments on transidentification as follows: "The subject seemed actually to experience the same emotional response that Dr. D. would have had at such a time. Finally, because he appeared to be entirely resistive to simple suggestion, it was necessary to induce hypnosis by indirect methods. This rather astonishing result offers a technique for the experimental investigation of the phenomena of identification, and of the unconscious incorporation of parental emotions by children."

18. Summary. The various techniques and processes of hypnosis mentioned above can be so woven into a progressive, mutually supporting pattern that the subject is gradually led to take suggestions which, if given earlier in the experiment, or given brashly, would have been rejected. Thus, as if composing a melody, the hypnotist plays upon the subject until, as described by Erickson's report, a complex is so elaborated into the subject's real experiences that it becomes an integral part of him.

Conclusion. If the phenomena of hypnosis actually are as described above—and the listing, though only a tithe of what could have been brought forward, does not overemphasize the ego-changing aspects inherent in hypnosis—it is theoretically possible to use them to induce antisocial actions.

Hypnosis, as outlined here, differs as daylight from dark from the poverty-stricken suggestions to which, according to Erickson's thesis, antisocial experimentation is limited. If, however, we study Erickson's techniques in dealing with all other hypnotic problems, we find him using a methodology varied and rich, and consequently effective. If, in the case of antisocial experimentation, we should wish to imitate Erickson's well-formulated methods (formulated in other connections), it would be something like this:

1. By elaborating the suggestions by means of preparatory and terminal suggestions.
2. By allowing the subjects time subjectively to elaborate these suggestions.
3. By appealing to motives latent in the normal state but easily aroused in hypnosis—motives of love, compliance, and desire for omnipotence.
4. By regressing the subject to an age when he was (as most have been) susceptible to immoral urges.
5. By bringing on transidentifications with persons who are rich, or who live freely, or who are venturesome, or even with historical persons who lived according to customs different from our own.
6. By wording the suggestions so that the hypnotist-subject relationship itself serves the antisocial purpose.
7. By refraining from any hint that what is being done or is to be done has anything antisocial about it; rather, by eliminating

all moral conflict by appealing to the highest and strongest motives but so distorting the subject's perception of external reality, including personal relationships by hallucinations, that acting on such motives is in line with the hypnotist's nefarious purposes.

8. By implanting complexes which are in line with personal vanity, pride, honor, self-defense, revenge, cupidity, lust, drive for power, or desire for submission, etc.

We would make use of all the above ancillary techniques, so that there is no point where the subject can stop and say to himself "This is wrong: I must not do this"—thus using some or many of these techniques and weaving them into patterns to fit the individual case. By these means the antisocial suggestion could be placed in a milieu in which it would seem not only right and proper but necessary or inevitable.

The antisocial suggestion could be put in such a context and couched in such terms that the line of demarcation between fact and fancy, truth and falsehood, would disappear, and, as has been demonstrated in other connections, the resistances of the ego would be circumvented. It is illogical to think that this technique would be successful in elaborating all sorts of complexes, but would fail if skillfully used in inducing disguised antisocial behavior. There is no such clear-cut division between what is social and what is antisocial, as those who hold the negative on this question seem to assume. Change one's perception of the situation, one's belief about himself or others, and, presto, what without falsification of reality would be an antisocial act becomes for the hallucinated or deluded subject a social act. All of us harbor inclinations which are inhibited or repressed by just those ego or superego concepts which the well-authenticated work of Erickson, Wolberg, and others, as referred to, has shown can be circumvented by falsification of the situation in hypnosis. It is scientific naïveté to think that these powerful hypnotic techniques, used for all they are worth, can perform wonders up to, but not beyond, the point where antisocial actions would be induced.

Watkins has expressed views similar to those of the present writer, saying:

The psychoanalytic point of view holds that in the unconscious part of personality known as the Id there exist in everyone primitive instinctual drives of a hostile and erotic nature. These are controlled in the normal person by the development of the Super-Ego. The Super-Ego, governed by the duty principle, forces the Ego to adjust and reconcile the pleasure-seeking Id drives to the realities of ethical and social demands. In deep pyschoanalysis immoral and criminal impulses are commonly found in every person analyzed. There are sound biological and anthropological reasons for hypothesizing their universality. Hence, it would not be illogical to assume that if under hypnosis Super-Ego controls might be temporarily blocked, anesthetized, or even softened, these more primitive impulses might be made operative and initiate actual anti-social behavior.

There is ready to hand an example which shows how this technique could without doubt have been used to induce antisocial actions. It is part of an extensive set of experiments reported by Erickson on the psychopathology of everyday life. A digest of this experiment on "the assumption of another's identity under hypnotic direction" follows:

During hypnosis the subject was informed that after awakening he would be Dr. D. and that Dr. D. would be Mr. Blank, and that in the role of Dr. D. he would talk to the pseudo Mr. Blank. Additional suggestions . . . were given to complete the trans-identification. After the subject was awakened a conversation was begun. The pseudo Mr. Blank questioned him about his work in the seminar, as though he were Dr. D.; the subject responded by giving an excellent talk about his experiences in the seminar and his reactions to the group, talking the phraseology of Dr. D. and expressing the personal attitudes of Dr. D. . . . he adopted Dr. D.'s mannerisms in smoking and . . . introduced ideas with certain phrases characteristic of Dr. D. When the pseudo Mr. Blank challenged his identity, the subject contradicted "Mr. Blank" politely and seemed profoundly amazed at "Mr. Blank's" remarks. . . . "Mr. Blank" then questioned the subject about his "wife," to which the subject responded in a way that would have been natural for the real Dr. D. When asked about children he assumed an expression of mild embarrassment and replied, "Not yet, but you never can tell." . . . Finally, when an attempt was made to rehypnotize him in order to restore his own identity, the subject displayed the emotional attitude of resistance towards the induction of hypnosis which would have been entirely characteristic of the real Dr. D. . . . Because he appeared to be entirely resistive to simple suggestion, it was necessary to induce hypnosis by indirect methods.

That the subject in Erickson's experiment was not only willing but anxious to play the role in life that Dr. D. played to the point of taking over Dr. D.'s prerogatives and privileges is the clear implication of this report—or else it was mere play acting. Writing a check in the name of Dr. D. for value received or responding to Dr. D.'s wife as Dr. D. would have done—both equally antisocial acts in the circumstances—would have been perfectly in keeping with the described behavior of this subject, who, wishing to play to the hilt the role of Dr. D., was so resistant to any suggestion to terminate his transidentification (or, as Erickson says, was responding even in this respect as Dr. D. would have responded) that Erickson had to reinduce hypnosis by indirect methods. If transidentification of the sort described is a reality (even though arrived at by a falsification of the situation), the possibilities of its use for antisocial purposes are so varied and so obvious that it is not necessary to elaborate them. In fact, almost any meaningful action performed by a person in such a state would be, *ipso facto*, antisocial behavior. But Erickson's thesis would require that the moment such a subject (acting under the delusional system of a false identity) committed some antisocial act, assuming that that could happen, the experiment would thereby become vitiated and negated, however valid such a falsified situation is for other experimentation. It is regrettable that Erickson's thesis has prevented his using as full a repertoire in experimentation on antisocial uses as he has used in this case cited above.

SUBJECT-HYPNOTIST RELATIONSHIP

This aspect of hypnosis, the one which Erickson and others consider too complicated and too confusing to make use of in researches on antisocial behavior, and the use of which, therefore, they declare actually invalidates the experiments, is so important that it should be dealt with separately, even though it belongs with the hypnotic phenomena listed previously and is referred to in items 10, 12, and 16, above. This relationship, depending, as many think, upon the infantile need for love, for compliance, for masochistic subservience, and for participation in omnipotence, is by most psychologists considered one of the most powerful motivational forces in hypnosis. Wells and others refrain from "suggesting," from using indirection. They produce "a completely helpless obedience" and simply tell the subject what to do. As mentioned earlier, Erickson maintains that this very obedience invalidates the whole experiment.

The type of "trust and confidence in the experimenter," "full obedience . . . at an experimental level, where the purposes of the act are defeated by the nature of the setting" (as described by Erickson) is, per se, potentially dangerous. If the subject *considers* it an experimental setting, whereas (if an unscrupulous hypnotist is performing) it is *not* an experimental setting; if, furthermore, "trust and confidence" are given uncritically because of the setting (and nobody doubts they are so given), whereas the question we are considering assumes that confidence *may* be displaced, then, *ipso facto*, it becomes possible to induce antisocial actions by use (or rather abuse) of this subject-hypnotist relationship.

If, in an experimental situation the subject trusts an experimenter to protect him, even though the experimenter tells him he is not going to protect him—that the snake is a real snake and a dangerous one, that the acid is real acid and will corrode (Rowland); when, moreover, the subject's senses of sight, sound, and even smell give him evidence that the situation is as dangerous as the experimenter says it is—if, after that, the subject acts on the assumption that the situation is different from what it appears to be, he is acting unrealistically and, in the situation described, potentially dangerously. It makes it no less potentially dangerous if he believes, in line with hallucinations suggested by the hypnotist but against the evidences of his own senses, that it is not dangerous, or complies because the experimenter wants him to. It is much more dangerous if, as Erickson contends, the actual sensations, for example of sight, can be controlled so that the situation is not only believed to be different but *is* different from what it would be without the hypnotically induced hallucinations. In any of these cases potential danger becomes real danger by substituting a criminal for a reputable scientist.

There is nothing in the setting, in the subject's confidence, or in the subject's obedience to distinguish between scientist and criminal. That the situation is an "experiment," that the subject-hypnotist relationship is all-pervasive and confusing as to responsibility, that, in addition, hallucinations and illusions may be used to define the situation as the hypnotist wants it defined (in Erickson's words, "falsifies" it) does not lessen the potential danger. In fact, the dangers are increased thereby. It seems palpable that a subject who trusts another person in spite of the evidence of his own senses (Rowland, Watkins) is in a situation where safety, or danger, lies in what the experimenter will request rather than in what the subject has ability even to perceive, much less to resist. In such conditions the greater the trust, the greater the danger.

A word must be said about a supposed obstacle to the reality of the dangers in the subject-hypnotist relationship, namely that the subject has a hypersensitive, not to say telepathic, ability to perceive not only the hypnotist's intention, but also and more specifically, the details of the experiment (for example, invisible glass) which unhypnotized persons cannot perceive. This ability is assumed to exist even though no suggestions for arousing it are given by the hypnotist. Thus LeCron and Bordeaux [35] and an anonymous expert in Estabrooks' account endow Rowland's subjects with visual hyperacuity, the former two thus explaining the subject's imperturbability contrasted with the perturbation of unhypnotized persons who looked upon the rattlesnake behind the invisible glass. Erickson also mentioned this supposed ability of the subject as one reason for rejecting all "falsification" of the situation in this field of experimentation. In answer, it must be said first of all that such hyperacuity of visual or auditory perception is very doubtful, even when suggestions for heightening have been given, much less when no such suggestion has been given. In the second place, according to Rowland's description, they behaved as if they could not see the glass. In the third place, a sufficient explanation for the subject's apparent calmness is ready to hand in their full and complete trust in the hypnotist's omnipotence, not only to keep things from going wrong but to take all responsibility if they should go wrong. It is totally unwarranted, then, to explain the subjects' behavior on the basis of unproved perceptual powers; whereas it can be fully explained on the basis of well-authenticated aspects of the subjects' trust and confidence in the experimenter. Besides, the conditions of the experiment, as well as the results, must be adjudged by objective observers, themselves unhypnotized. If such observers see the situation as so dangerous that they would not dare enter into it, then it must be defined as dangerous; and the subjects' willingness to enter into it must be put down not to their seeing the external situation more clearly than the observers, but to their having more trust and confidence in the hypnotist than the observers have, or than the subjects themselves would have in the normal state. This is shown, for example, in Rowland's subject when apprised of her hypnotic behavior.

From a hurried review of the literature it appears that there are no theoretical obstacles to the possibility of antisocial uses of hypnosis. On the contrary, the cumulative effect of the reported results is so great as to convince one that antisocial actions are not more deviant from the normal behavior—and no more difficult to induce— than are many of the actions which have been carried out by subjects motivated by artificial complexes, age regression, transidentification, etc. In fact, if a skillful hypnotist should use such techniques as those just mentioned and should go all out to induce antisocial results, theoretically it is very likely he would succeed. Additional strong presumptive proof lies in the subject-hypnotist relationship of dominance submission which makes possible not only the falsification of the subject's internal and external world but also, apparently, compliance with the hypnotist's suggestions even when assured he is facing danger.

This presumptive proof is not weakened, but rather strengthened, by such negative results as have been reported, for example, by Erickson. Wells has pointed out that negative results do not prove anything really; certainly not unless everybody gets negative results. But that is not the basis for the present writer's discounting the reputedly negative results that have been dealt with in this paper. Rather, the criticism is on the basis of theoretical insufficiency of the experimental design and the consequent poverty of the methods

chosen to test the hypothesis. Erickson's results, though he interpreted them otherwise, were successful in inducing antisocial behavior. He does not appreciate the possibility that if unmotivated
suggestions to commit antisocial acts, far from being without effect,
result in the suggested actions being inflicted upon the hypnotist,
then strongly motivated suggestions in wrongdoing, using the full
repertoire of hypnotic methods rather than unvarnished suggestions,
might just as logically result in punishments being inflicted upon
the suggested victims.

Since there is no experimental bar to an open-minded appraisal,
but, on the contrary, a strong presumption that a varied and vigor-
ous technique would result in antisocial actions, we are ready to
turn to the experiments that are reported as successful. It may be
mentioned, though, that several textbooks—Winn's,[36] Estabrooks',
Watkins', LeCron and Bordeaux's (the last-named with no great
conviction)—agree that under certain conditions antisocial actions
can be brought about. In the next section we shall deal only with
such experiments as have been described in some detail. There are
not many of them. We shall keep in mind the simple question: "Were
the actions induced in hypnosis such as an objective observer would
consider dangerous or otherwise antisocial?" We are not interested
in knowing whether the subjects *thought* they were acting anti-
socially, or whether the situation was one of pure suggestion in an
unfalsified situation, the subject responding, therefore, in his own
identity, being *au courant* with the actual situation; or whether the
subject's own identity was changed, the external situation falsified
for him, and the real motivation (of the hypnotist) quite different
from that suggested to the subject. What the subject *thinks* he is
doing is immaterial; what he actually does is all that matters. And
what he does, whether it is an innocuous action or a noxious action,
can only be judged by people who ostensibly, at least, are in their
right minds and know danger when they see it.

EXPERIMENTS REPORTING ANTISOCIAL USES OF HYPNOSIS

The extensive *experiments of Wells and of Brenman* are scientifically rigorous. They are so well known it is not necessary to

quote from them. The subjects were motivated to commit actions which they would not otherwise have done, being amnesic for their actions and resentful of accusations that they had done such things. The criticism that they knew they were subjects in an experiment and that they trusted the experimenters is not relevant. All hypnotic work (especially the work of Erickson and others) is experimental; and since they trusted the experimenter to the point of doing what they never would have done (all but one, who, it transpired, was a thief all along), they trusted not wisely but too much. The question of who was responsible for the subject's behavior is interesting, but not relevant as to whether or not it was antisocial.

Estabrooks' experiment, already referred to above, is utterly lacking in the experimental aura adversely criticized by Erickson and others, but it nevertheless eventuated in patently antisocial behavior, as may be seen from the following description:

During the last war I experimentally put one subject in a murderous frame of mind toward his best friend. "Alfred is really a Nazi spy," I told him. "When you wake up, he will enter the room and offer you a smoke from a cigarette case. Look closely and you'll notice a Swastika engraved on the inside of the lid." The subject "saw" the Swastika, which was not there, and had to be forcefully restrained from attacking his bosom pal. We were obliged to re-hypnotize him to "unswastika" his mind.

Rowland's technique was that of so using invisible glass that subjects could plainly manifest their willingness to carry out suggestions to handle a rattlesnake and to throw sulphuric acid on the experimenter, without a corpus delicti. We need do little more than quote from Rowland to show that the results were quite different from those that could be elicited from unhypnotized observers. Rowland says:

By way of control, forty-two persons, of every age and degree of sophistication, were asked to come to the laboratory and pick up the snake. . . . With one exception all the persons were not only badly frightened at the appearance of the snake, but would not come close to the box; only a few were finally persuaded to pick up a yard stick and try to touch the snake. They all seemed bewildered when they touched the glass which they could not see. The exception referred to was as follows: A young woman was told to reach for the snake and she did so at once, of course striking the glass. When asked why she complied so readily, she said that of course it was an artificial snake and she was not afraid of it. Assured that the snake was real, she made a closer examination of it. She then became frightened, and even though she knew she was protected, would not go near the box.

Erickson's and LeCron and Bordeaux's criticisms of this experiment have been dealt with above. It is gratuitous to assume, as the latter do, that the hypnotic subjects, without any suggestion of hyperacuity, or with one, could see what 41 other persons in full waking consciousness failed to see. It is more likely that they behaved as did the forty-second person; they trusted the experimenter more fully than was in keeping with the objective situation. It is to be noted that this experiment had two aspects: in one the situation was falsified (the snake was described to the subject as a "coiled rubber rope"); in the other it was not falsified. ("There is a rattlesnake in that box.") The results, however, were the same. The experimental laboratory aspect of the situation was as patent to the 42 unhypnotized as it was to the 5 hypnotized subjects. The main difference was that the experimental subjects had accepted certain suggestions and, apparently, were in a certain relationship to the experimenter. It is farfetched to explain their behavior in terms of hyperacuity or telepathic communication. It is scientifically more economical to explain it as blind confidence, as did one of the subjects, who awake, a week later, tried to formulate her reasons for her hypnotic behavior.

Watkins induced antisocial action under conditions informal enough for anybody who fears that the experimental laboratory atmosphere may vitiate the results obtained in this type of research, as do Erickson and others. In six different case studies Watkins induced antisocial actions, some with and some without falsification of the situation by the use of hallucinations and delusions; some, therefore, with moral conflict present and some without it. Regardless of the motivation present and whether the situation was or was not falsified, the actual behavior in all cases was strictly antisocial and was so judged by the unhypnotized observers. Only one of the six experiments will be quoted, one in which the situation was falsified and the subject had his conscience salved. So, in accordance with Erickson's thesis, the value of the whole experiment would on that account be considered vitiated and negated. But on the very face of the report the results were bona fide and antisocial aplenty. The verbatim record of this case is as follows:

The subject this time was a private with a very good record . . . about 20 years of age. He was respected by the other men as sincere and earnest. Several members of the medical staff of the Neuropsychiatric Division of a station hospital were present. The subject was placed in a trance.

E: In a minute you will slowly open your eyes. In front of you, you will see a dirty Jap soldier. He has a bayonet, and is going to kill you unless you kill him first. You will have to strangle him with your bare hands. (A lieutenant colonel, the head psychiatrist . . . was placed directly in front of the subject and about ten feet away.)

(The subject opened his eyes. He then slanted them and began to creep cautiously forward. Suddenly, in a flying tackle he dove at the lieutenant colonel, knocking him against the wall, and with both of his hands [he was a powerful, husky lad] began strangling the man. It will be recalled that for an enlisted man to "attack" a commissioned officer is a serious offense in the Army. It took the instantaneous assistance of three others to break the soldier's grip, pull him off the officer, and hold him until the experimenter could quiet him back into a sleep condition. The lieutenant colonel reported that the man's grip was strong and dangerous, and that he might have been killed or injured if assistance had not been available to drag the soldier back.)

It will be noted here that the man did not violate his own conscience. He was attacking what to him was a Jap soldier and not an officer of the Army. He was acting under an induced hallucination. Yet, had he been permitted to continue his act, he would have committed murder from the social viewpoint and would have been punished if the prosecution had "proven" to the resulting court martial that "people cannot be made to commit crimes under hypnotic trance." [3]

Another aspect of dangers in hypnosis concerns the question of inducing hypnosis against the subject's best efforts to remain unhypnotized. Here, again, without the complications of a laboratory technique or much, if any, of the "protection" inherent in the subject-hypnotist relationship, the subjects could not resist hypnosis. The situation is described by Watkins as follows:

Case Study F. The subject was a corporal who had been hypnotized once before but he had not been connected to any posthypnotic "yellow pencil" suggestion. The purpose of this study was to see if a person could be made to enter a trance against his will. The subject was shown a ten-dollar bill which was placed on a table before him. He was seated and told to look at the bill.

E: Now, George, this ten-dollar bill in front of you is yours under one condition. I want you to look at it carefully. You can have it if you will *just not let me make you go to sleep.* Keep from entering a trance. Remember, you are to try your hardest not to enter a trance. . . . But it won't do you a damned bit of good because I am going to count up to twenty-five and by the time I get there you will be sound asleep. 1, 2, 3, . . . 25.

(The subject was in deep trance. His eyes closed at the count of twenty while staring directly at the ten-dollar bill in front of him. Of course this individual was very highly hypnotizable, but the experimenter has observed several others who were equally so.)

Schneck [37] reports a most informal experiment by way of inadvertently arousing a conflict between a posthypnotic suggestion and a soldier's assignment to military duty. The posthypnotic suggestion was carried out: the soldier deserted his duty. The antisocial nature of the outcome is without doubt—regardless of the other possible complications in the experiment—the subject-hypnotist relationship, the falsification of the situation, or any of the other possible vitiating factors described by Erickson and referred to above.

The writer's experimentation will be merely sketched here. This research used eight consistently somnambulistic subjects, the residue of extensive trials: first in large classes where the likely subjects were picked out, secondly in smaller groups where these selectees were tested further for depth of hypnosis, and finally in individual sessions with those subjects who had proved somnambulistic through the previous series of experiments. The experimental conditions were similar to those of Rowland, except that in Series A, with four subjects, the invisible glass was used, and in Series B, with four subjects also, there was no glass between the individual subjects and the ostensibly dangerous objects, namely, four snakes and a glass dish filled with nitric acid. Furthermore, half the subjects in Series A were told the stimulus objects were very dangerous, half were told they were perfectly harmless, and the same for Series B. Thus, the invisible glass was used in the experiments with half the subjects, and danger was emphasized in experiments with half the subjects. All eight subjects had been individually conditioned, however, during the first part of the crucial experimental session, to reach through the aperture to the inside of the box, where later the experimental objects were to appear. This was accomplished by requesting them to hand the experimenter in a certain order three different innocuous objects lying there (knife, pencil, paper clip). Somewhat as in Rowland's research, faculty members who were tested by being introduced into the experimental room prior to the experimentation with the hypnotic subjects were completely baffled by the invisible glass and greatly perturbed at the sight of the snakes. None saw the glass, and, after touching it, could not later judge whether or not it was in place guarding the aperture.

The water snakes used (*Natrix rhombifera*) were not dangerous, but they are so similar to the water moccasins (*Agkistrodon piscivorus*), which the hypnotist suggested they were in half the experiments, that one must be something of a herpetologist to differentiate them. After the experiments were over, only one subject answered affirmatively the question whether he knew the difference between the harmless natrix and the poisonous moccasin.

For Series B (no glass between subjects and the stimulus objects) the nitric acid having been demonstrated as in all other cases (with the sight of a penny disintegrating in it, and the subjects being made to smell it), a like-sized dish of methylene-blue water, continuously kept "boiling" by miniscule droplets of barium peroxide, was substituted for it by an assistant hidden from the subjects' view by the body of the hypnotist, who for the ostensible purpose of "deepening" the subjects' hypnosis had stepped between the subjects and the aperture. This innocuous water was then ordered to be thrown on the assistant through the aperture.

Seven of the eight subjects carried out the instructions, both as regards attempting to handle the snakes and to throw the "nitric acid" on an assistant. In Series B, with the invisible glass out of the way, three of the four subjects actually threw the substance (in one case pure nitric acid) on the assistants and caught the snakes and put them in a large can. One subject, a male music student, in tremulous conflict over the instructions, was so inept in the long-continued alternate approach and withdrawal of his hand near the snake's head that he was bitten by the snake and fainted dead away, only to be brought back to hypnotic consciousness and pushed by the experimenter until he, too, captured the snake of which he was mortally afraid. First aid was handy for him in hypnosis, for he never waked up; it was, also, for the assistant upon whom another subject threw real nitric acid, a most regrettable mistake in technique, but due to the fact that in this case, as happened more than once, the experimenter and his (a second) assistant could not tell which was methylene blue and which was nitric acid. The other times the experimenters themselves suffered only hand burns.*

The results show that seven of the eight subjects would enter into a situation which unhypnotized observers shrank from, the subjects carrying out suggestions to handle snakes and throw nitric acid under conditions from which they themselves recoiled in the waking state. Three of the eight actually reached into the box to carry out instructions for which they had been conditioned by three different reaching operations through the same aperture immediately prior to the critical experiments; as, also, had the four subjects in Series A, whose attempts to carry out the instructions to handle the snakes and hurl nitric acid were frustrated by invisible glass, so invisible indeed, that the experimenter had to keep his eye on the written schedule of the experiments to tell him whether or not the glass was to be used in that individual experiment. In this research, as in Rowland's, the

---

* Note: Thanks are due Harcourt Stebbins, D.D.S., for his temerity in taking chances as the victim. On account of the promptness of remedial measures, no scars were left on his face; although his heavy uniform (that of an ROTC student) deteriorated in large areas where the acid struck.

Robert Harold Schulingkamf is to be thanked for his continuous service as the second person who assisted in this arduous research.

subjects may have been deluded or they may have been masochistically trustful or subservient. In either case they entered into a situation from which unhypnotized subjects—and they themselves when unhypnotized—recoiled. As it turned out, it was, actually, a dangerous situation.

CONCLUSIONS

In keeping with the recent findings of experimenters that at least certain types of hypnotic hallucinations are real; that by means of illusions, delusions, age regression, transidentification, and other powerful devices available in hypnosis, the personality can be temporarily so altered as to circumvent the ego demands and implant complexes which are as bona fide as those of a neurosis or a psychosis; that the subject-hypnotist relationship itself satisfies certain infantile needs for love, subjection, and feelings of partaking in omnipotence, resulting in an obsessive type of compliance or helpless obedience, there is a strong presumption that a skillful hypnotist could induce antisocial behavior in hypnosis. This presumption is strengthened by an analysis of Erickson's classical experiments in which he reported his subjects refusing to perform antisocial actions against the suggested victims but turning against the hypnotist almost invariably to heap on him the resentments aroused by the suggestion of unpleasant actions in the most naked and unpalatable fashion, without using any of the techniques mentioned above. The results of Erickson's meager techniques, springing from his mistaken thesis that an antisocial act in hypnosis is one which the subject must see as antisocial, can by no means be taken as representative of results to be expected from using the full armamentarium of hypnosis, as used by Erickson and others in all types of experimentation save only in that of inducing antisocial actions. Since the criterion of antisocial actions must be the judgment of unhypnotized observers, there is no theoretical obstacle to an objective appraisal of the work of those who report success in inducing antisocial hypnotic behavior. The work of Wells, Brenman, Rowland, and the writer, all done in experimental situations under good conditions, resulted in the subjects performing such actions as they shrank from or denied when apprised, in the normal state, of what they had done; actions, moreover, which un-hypnotized persons refused to contemplate. These actions were aroused whether the situation was defined as harmful or harmless. In like fashion, in a more informal setting, without the intervention of any complicated subject-hypnotist relationship, Schneck, Esta-brooks, and Watkins demonstrated the effectiveness of antisocial suggestions, the latter two eliciting actions which were so patently real that unhypnotized observers were hard put to it to protect the lives of the suggested victims.

Although the question dealt with here has more theoretical than practical importance, inasmuch as hypnosis is for the most part in the hands of reputable persons, still its potential antisocial use by other types of persons should not be lightly regarded. If in skilled and worthy hands hypnosis is as powerful and salutary an instrument as its recent application, for example, in hypnoanalysis indubitably indicates, then in *skilled but unworthy* hands it might become an instrument of danger. From the present rather extensive review of both the theoretical and experimental findings—with particular con-sideration of the results of those who think hypnosis powerful only for good—it seems clear to the writer that this logical conclusion is the only possible one, and that hypnosis, therefore, must be thought of as a two-edged tool to be wielded with caution only by those who possess both an understanding of the motivations it releases and also the desire to use these dynamisms for scientific and therapeutic purposes.

REFERENCES

1. Estabrooks, G. H.: *Hypnotism*, E. P. Dutton & Co., Inc., New York, 1943.
2. Erickson, M. H.: "An experimental investigation of the possible anti-social use of hypnosis," *Psychiatry*, **2**:391, 1939.
3. Watkins, J. G.: "Anti-social compulsions induced under hypnotic trance," *J. Abnorm. & Social Psychol.*, **42**:256, 1947.
4. Watkins, J. G.: *Hypnotherapy of War Neuroses*, The Ronald Press Company, New York, 1949.
5. Weitzenhoffer, A. M.: "The production of anti-social acts under hypnosis," *J. Abnorm. & Social Psychol.*, **44**:420, 1949.

6. Wolberg, L. R.: *Medical Hypnosis*, Vol. I, Grune & Stratton, Inc., New York, 1948.

7. Wells, W. R.: "Experiments in the hypnotic production of crime," *J. Psychol.*, **11**:63, 1941.

8. Brenman, M.: "Experiments in the hypnotic production of anti-social and self-injurious behavior," *Psychiatry*, **5**:49, 1942.

9. Rowland, L. W.: "Will hypnotized persons try to harm themselves or others?" *J. Abnorm. & Social Psychol.*, **34**:114, 1939.

10. Erickson, M. H.: "The method employed to formulate a complex story for the induction of an experimental neurosis in a hypnotic subject," *J. Gen. Psychol.*, **31**:67, 1944.

11. Erickson, M. H.: "A study of an experimental neurosis hypnotically induced in a case of ejaculatio praecox," *Brit. J. M. Psychol.*, **15**:34, 1935.

12. Erickson, M. H.: "Hypnotic investigation of psychosomatic phenomena: III. A controlled experimental use of hypnotic regression in the therapy of an acquired food tolerance," *Psychosom. Med.*, **5**:67, 1943.

13. Erickson, M. H.: "Experimental demonstrations of the psychopathology of everyday life," *Psychoanalyt. Quart.*, **8**:338, 1939.

14. Schilder, P., and Kauders, O.: *Hypnosis*, Nervous & Mental Disease Publishing Company, New York, 1927.

15. Huston, P. E.; Shakow, D.; and Erickson, M. H.: "A study of hypnotically induced complexes by means of the Luria technique," *J. Gen. Psychol.*, **11**:65, 1934.

16. Wolberg, L. R.: "Hypnotic experiments in psychosomatic medicine," *Psychosom. Med.*, **9**:337, 1947.

17. Lindner, R. M.: *Rebel without a Cause*, Grune & Stratton, Inc., New York, 1944.

18. Luria, A. R.: *The Nature of Human Conflicts*, Liveright Publishing Corp., New York, 1932.

19. Pattie, F. A.: "Some American contributions to the science of hypnosis," *Am. Scholar*, **12**:444, 1943.

20. Fisher, C.: "Hypnosis in treatment of neuroses due to war and other causes," *War Med.*, **4**:565, 1943.

21. Brenman, M.; Gill, M. M.; and Hacker, F. J.: "Alterations in the state of the ego in hypnosis," *Bull. Menninger Clin.*, **11**:60, 1947.

22. Leuba, C.: "Hypnosis as a method of controlling variables in psychological experiments," *Am. J. Psychol.*, **59**:686, 1946.

23. Erickson, M. H. "The induction of color blindness by hypnotic suggestion," *J. Gen. Psychol.*, **20**:61, 1939.

24. Estabrooks, G. H.: "Hypnosis: its tremendous potential as a war weapon," *Argosy*, **330**:26, February, 1950.

25. Wells, W. R.: "The hypnotic treatment of the major symptoms of hysteria: a case study," *J. Psychol.*, **17**:269, 1944.

26. White, R. W.: "An analysis of motivation in hypnosis," *J. Gen. Psychol.*, **24**:145, 1941.

27. Erickson, M. H.: "Hypnotic techniques for the therapy of acute psychiatric disturbances in war," *Am. J. Psychiat.*, **101**:668, 1945.

28. Erickson, M. H.: "Hypnosis in medicine," *M. Clin. North America*, **28**:639, 1944.

29. McDowell, M.: "An abrupt cessation of major neurotic symptoms following an hypnotically induced artificial conflict," *Bull. Menninger Clin.*, **12**:168, 1948.

30. White, R. W.: "A preface to the theory of hypnotism," *J. Abnorm. & Social Psychol.*, **36**:477, 1941.

31. Bergman, M. S.; Graham, H.; and Leavitt, H. C.: "Rorschach exploration of consecutive hypnotic age level regressions," *Psychosom. Med.*, **9** (1):20, January–February, 1947.

32. Wolberg, L. R.: *Hypnoanalysis*, Grune & Stratton, Inc., New York, 1945.

33. Brenman, M., and Knight, R. P.: "Hypnotherapy for mental illness in the aged: case report of hysterical psychosis in a 71 year old woman," *Bull. Menninger Clin.*, **7**:188, 1943.

34. Arnold, M. B.: "On the mechanism of suggestion and hypnosis," *J. Abnorm. & Social Psychol.*, **41**:107, 1946.

35. LeCron, L. M., and Bordeaux, J.: *Hypnotism Today*, Grune & Stratton, Inc., New York, 1947.

36. Winn, R. B.: *Scientific Hypnotism*, Christopher Publishing Company, Boston, 1939.

37. Schneck, J. M.: "A military offense induced by hypnosis," *J. Nerv. & Ment. Dis.*, **106**:186, 1947.

CHAPTER SEVENTEEN

Hypnosis and Dissociative States

Editor's Note

No condition in abnormal psychology is more fascinating to the psychologist than the strange cases of multiple personality which occasionally come to light and have been described from time to time in the literature. From earliest recorded history until relatively modern times, they have been ascribed to demonic possession, and it is significant that, in the past, the personalities which have been manifested have themselves accepted this role of being demons. At least this is true of those which have been described in history. Invariably, those possessing consciousnesses were considered to be evil. Stevenson's classic story of Dr. Jekyll and Mr. Hyde is based on this type of manifestation, good and evil thus being fictionally personified.

The modern psychological explanation of multiple personality is to attribute the phenomenon to dissociation. Semantically, the word *dissociation* is most unsatisfactory. It has so many connotations that one psychologist trying to discuss dissociation with another psychologist must make elaborate explanations in order to convey his proper meaning. The matter is so confused even to a psychologist that to the layman it is chaotic. Dissociation is usually defined as a split or disunion of mind where a group of ideas and complexes separates to form one or more coconsciousnesses in varying extent. This conception covers many entirely unrelated conditions ranging from the state of hypnosis (according to one theory) to schizophrenia, including such varied conditions as hysteria, mediumistic trances, multiple personalities, and such simple subconscious activities as crystal gazing, automatic writing, and dreaming. Deep hypnosis has definite dissociative attributes, but certainly hypnosis induced in an intelligent, normal person has no relationship to the catatonic stupor of schizophrenia, although there may be a similarity in some of the phenomena of each. Yet the word "dissociation" is applied to both of these conditions. Our technical terminology in this instance is sadly lacking and confusing.

While true dual or multiple personality can hardly be regarded as a common phenomenon, it undoubtedly is evidenced much more frequently than has been realized. There are many hundreds of people who profess to be mediums, with the control personality or personalities appearing in a way that is very similar to the true type of such cases. Of course many of the mediums are out-and-out fakes who do no more than pretend to enter a trance. However, many others do hypnotize themselves, with the so-called "control" then taking over.

As to the incidence of multiple personality of the true type, Dr. Milton Erickson once wrote an article on the subject which appeared in the *Psychoanalytic Quarterly*, a journal which certainly is not widely read outside of psychological circles. He was surprised to receive several letters from persons with multiple personalities or who suspected their presence. As Dr. Odencrants mentions, psychotherapists who recognize the possibility of their occurrence are not infrequently able to detect them.

The spiritualists claim that most of these personalities are the disembodied spirits of people who have lived at some former time, who are able in some way to enter, at times, a living body. Although still held in some cultures, in our present civilized society the idea of these entities being "demons" has almost disappeared. And the personalities themselves no longer accept this conception, usually describing themselves as the spirit of some deceased person.

Some of the reported cases are most puzzling to explain and afford the adherents of spiritualism good ammunition. The case of Patience Worth is one such which confounded scientific inquiry in the early part of this century, and there have been others. This writer knows of a somewhat similar one, a woman who is well adjusted and normal in every way. Over an extended period, through automatic writing she has produced the apparent autobiography of another person who lived in Revolutionary times who claims to be carrying on the writing. Details of her life and of where she lived have been written, some of which could be verified, and it has been impossible to ascertain where the living woman could possible have obtained much of the automatically written information which she theoretically draws from her subconsciousness. In the chapter on Automatic Writing will be found an illustration which pictures this woman's script, automatically performed.

It is such ascertainable facts which make some of these cases so puzzling and difficult to explain, although the scientific theory assigns all such matters to subconscious mental activity and hypersensitivity to minimal cues. This undoubtedly does adequately explain most of these matters. Perhaps, if we knew more, all could be rationalized in this way, especially if the "psi" factor of parapsychology ever receives scientific acceptance of its actuality.

Most multiple-personality conditions can be explained by the dissociation theory. Yet here again, there are some which seem to be exceptions to the rule, and the personality is such a complete entity that the matter is hard to fathom.

In the treatment of multiple personality, analysis may locate the reasons behind the dissociation which frequently results from some trauma, as was true in Prince's case of Miss Beauchamp. Blending of the personalities, or rewelding them into the original status, ends the condition, often permanently. To obtain such a result it is usually necessary to secure the cooperation and agreement of the secondary consciousnesses, for such a blending is often impossible to achieve through mere insight.

Using hypnosis and hypnotic suggestion, reintegration is much easier to effect. In fact, without it there may be refusal of cooperation and therapeutic failure. The suggestibility of the secondary personality is usually such that, with persuasion and suggestion, agreement can be reached and the reintegration accomplished. Hypnosis is also invaluable in securing the appearance of the secondary consciousnesses. Often, it is found that placing the primary personality in a state of hypnosis automatically produces the secondary, or one of them if there are more. At other times this is not true, and the hypnotized primary consciousness does not lose possession of the body. Then the secondary personality, when it is evidenced, can also be hypnotized. Here we encounter much confusion again in terms of dissociation. The primary personality is dissociated through hypnosis; then the dissociated secondary personality is further dissociated in another way by hypnotization! It might be added that most individuals with multiple personalities are good hypnotic subjects and also write easily automatically.

Dr. Odencrants has encountered a number of cases of multiple personality during his practice of psychotherapy in Stockholm, Sweden. He specializes in hypnoanalysis and has become one of the leading European authorities on hypnosis.

Hypnosis and Dissociative States

By GERARD ODENCRANTS, M.D.*

Attacks of unconsciousness or changes of consciousness can be extremely divergent in type and in degree. The underlying factors range from uncomplicated and grossly organic causes to others that are extremely obscure and difficult of diagnosis. Among the latter there is a type usually classified as hysterical. These cases are markedly divergent in character, varying from a simple and opportunistic kind, bordering on simulation, to such types as seem to have no ascertainable causative agent even on analysis of the situation or when psychoanalysis has been employed.

It is striking that the family history of some of these cases reveals suicidal tendencies in the patient or in the family. Sometimes there are also periods of mental obsession, a craving for alcohol or narcotics, and other symptoms which seem alien to the usual character of the patient.

During the period of apparent loss of consciousness, which may occur regularly, or unexpectedly and irregularly, a distinct and separate personality may appear which is not the patient's usual self. Sometimes more than one secondary personality is evidenced at different times. After such a "spell" there is total amnesia on awakening, the primary personality having no knowledge of what has occurred during the period of unconsciousness.

Those who have had the occasion of studying trance mediums will find a great similarity to these patients, especially in mediums in the developmental stage. It is obvious that these fits of unconsciousness are uncontrolled phenomena of a medial type found in predisposed individuals. Hereditary traits of mediumship are often found

* Bragevägen 9–11, Stockholm, Sweden

in the case history, and the mediumistic trance is one form of such dissociations, one or more "controls" appearing and taking over. In spiritualistic circles these personalities are accepted as entities or beings which take possession of the medium, coming from the spirit world.

In multiple-personality cases where the individual does not purport to be a medium and is not an adherent of spiritualism, the personality or personalities do not profess to be spirits and regard themselves as living beings, but they are unable to account for their existence or explain where they have come from. Sometimes they claim to have been present since the birth of the individual in whose body they are incarcerated.

"Possession" has been a phenomenon recognized throughout the history of every race and every civilization. Many churches and religions have rituals prescribed for the casting out of the possessing "demons," for as such they were always regarded until modern times. In many cultures even today "demonic possession" is considered factual. In such cases, however, no distinction was made between those persons suffering from various forms of psychosis, where behavior became irrational, and those having multiple personalities but definitely to be regarded as sane. Historical accounts mainly describe insane persons. However, the incidence of multiple personality is far greater than is usually realized, even by psychiatrists and psychologists. Hidden personalities avoid allowing their existence to become known lest the individual be thought odd or crazy. Those who have become interested in the phenomenon and sought to uncover these split-off personalities find them by no means uncommon.

Though they make frequent appearances, friends, members of the family, even a spouse, may notice nothing, accepting the changes witnessed as moods of the individual. The principal or primary personality usually knows nothing of the other personalities unless informed of them by someone else. Lapses of consciousness and amnesic periods which are experienced may cause confusion and concern. Because of this, treatment may be sought, and if the therapist is cognizant of such matters the other self or selves may be led to appear. Very frequently, they are overlooked by the therapist. They may be summoned, or may reveal themselves voluntarily through automatic writing, crystal gazing, trance states, or through hypnotic suggestion. Dr. Anita Mühl,[1] leading authority on automatic writing, once had a patient who displayed at one time or another 23 different personalities. Five were exhibited by "Miss Beauchamp," the classical case studied by Dr. Morton Prince.[2]

As Prince learned, in the treatment of these cases hypnosis is of the utmost value and may be the only means of obtaining therapeutic results which will end the condition. It is of but little value merely to relieve the symptoms by means of suppressive suggestion. Instead, a causal therapy is demanded in order to prevent the symptoms from recurring. Psychoanalysis may be helpful. For further information on this, the reader is referred to the works of Dr. Titus Bull.[3]

During treatment it is of importance to consider every word uttered by the secondary entities of the patient and to try to link them up with what may be learned later. Usually, there is a very one-track mentality in the personalities contacted. They expect to be taken seriously, and it is imperative for the psychotherapist to maintain an interested, sympathetic attitude, or contact may be lost. He must humor such a consciousness, be deferential and polite, for slights, irony, or impatience will be resented. Sometimes, the personality may be quite childlike and immature, like Miss Beauchamp's "Sally." At other times they are found to be amazingly well developed mentally, intelligent and superior, seemingly complete entities.

Strangely, Rorschach and other personality tests may show the secondary character to have entirely different traits from the primary personality. Their interests may be extremely variant, and tastes, likes, and dislikes may be opposed to those of the primary self. There may be no evident change in appearance or behavior when another personality takes over control; in other cases the whole expression changes, voice tone is different, awkwardness may become grace, and the new personality has little resemblance to the primary one.

It is frequently difficult to obtain contact with the being behind the front of consciousness. Under hypnosis it may be possible, by suggestion, to cause the second personality to come, or to select which one is to appear if more than one is present. It is of value if such a personality reveals its name, and invariably it has selected a name for itself. On questioning, it is remarkable how the patient will react if the correct name is revealed, then becoming willing to communicate. Very dramatic situations can arise. If the situation becomes too disquieting, a touch on the forehead of the patient seems to have the effect of an electrical discharge, and the usual consciousness returns. Patients of this type reveal a sensitivity that is very different from that of the average individual.

During treatment, analysis may show the causes for the dissociation, such, perhaps, as a trauma. Aside from the usual analytical procedures, argument and persuasion may be most effective in reintegrating the personalities, uniting them into one normal mentality. The personality is frequently open to reason and may be led to promise to disappear or to blend itself with the primary personality. The spiritualists who are most experienced in these matters make use of arguments and prayers.

Commonly, the personality which appears declares itself to be an individual who has lived at some former time, believing itself still living in that time. The defective orientation in time is most striking. In other cases the personality may declare that he is dead and has returned into the body of the patient. He (she) may tell of events of his (her) former life. It may be possible to convince these personalities that they are dead and should leave the body, or if they already consider themselves as dead, they may be persuaded to leave through rational argument. Elimination of the secondary consciousnesses should not be forced. It is noticeable that the patient, after the dissociation has been ended, often feels weak and fatigued, but, on the other hand, more harmonious.

Those who have not seen such cases at close hand can hardly appreciate them. They are not products of suggestion but are spontaneous. Often very puzzling and difficult to treat successfully, unless through the use of hypnosis, they are a most interesting aspect of abnormal psychology. In the literature on this subject, Janet [4] and Oesterreich [5] will be found of value.

REFERENCES

1. Mühl, A. M.: *Automatic Writing*, T. Steinkopff, Dresden, 1930.
2. Prince, M.: *The Dissociation of a Personality*, Longmans, Green & Co., Inc., New York, 1925.
3. Bull, T.: *Nature, Man and Destiny*, 1933; and *The Imperative Conquest*, 1936, Jas. H. Hyslop Foundation, New York.
4. Janet, P.: *Un Cas de Possession et d'Exorcisme Moderne* (Neuroses et idées fixes), Vol. I, Alcan, Paris, 1919.
5. Oesterreich, T. R.: *Possession*, Routledge and Kegan Paul, Ltd., London, 1930.

CHAPTER EIGHTEEN

Automatic Writing and Hypnosis

Editor's Note

Few psychotherapists have taken advantage of the opportunities which are offered by automatic writing and drawing for probing the subconscious. There are several reasons for this approach having been so slighted. The more orthodox analysts do not favor such a direct approach; others have believed it difficult to develop the facility for automatic writing; and still others have found it too difficult to interpret the symbolism and the cryptic material usually produced, which may be much more involved than in dreams. Furthermore, many psychotherapists know little about automatic material and do not know the best ways of producing it. Those who have worked with hypnoanalysis, and some others, have found automatic writing one of the best means of exposing conflicts, bringing out repressed material, and recalling other forgotten memories. It is true that it may be difficult to unravel, for the devices used by the subconscious to protect the ego from intolerable knowledge are indeed devious.

During the first few sessions where automatic writing is attempted, little information may be gained, though sometimes the writing is lucid and fluent from the start. When facility and the cooperation of the subconscious have been won, suggestion and urging may produce smooth writing with only a small amount of concealment and little need for "translation." This is sometimes easier to obtain if the subject is able to remain in a somnambulistic state while writing, with subsequent amnesia developed for the material which has been released, which will protect the patient from too great anxiety.

Before clear, lucid writing is obtained, or if it cannot be obtained, the symbolism may be very involved and the concealment may be most cryptic. Condensations, phonetic spelling, atrocious punning, neologisms, rebuses, upside down and mirror writing, and other such devices are common. As an example, the word "before" may be written B4. Dr. Mühl had one patient who wrote one line in the ordinary way, then followed each such line with mirror writing from right to left across the page, the lines alternating. A bilingual client of the editor would write a few words in English, then switch to Spanish, alternating between the two languages. Erickson [1] and Erickson and Kubie [2, 3] have written most interestingly of the use of automatic writing and drawing in psychotherapy, giving excellent examples of how cryptic it may be, and of how it was translated. Two different instances of dual personality were uncovered through spontaneous automatic writing. Dr. Mühl has encountered a number of similar cases which were betrayed through the writing.

Wolberg [4] tells of having the automatic writer, while in hypnosis, translate his own automatic writing, giving the full meaning of his communications underneath his automatic productions. Wolberg says: "Because the automatic writing is so fragmented, it is best to permit the patient to do the translating himself in order to supply missing material that he has eliminated or condensed."

It is also possible to obtain a good translation of such writing from another subject while he is hypnotized. In a deep trance such a subject will often understand perfectly the mechanisms of the automatic writer and can explain their meaning. Incidentally, such a subject can also translate dreams with the same facility. Not all somnambulists seem to be able to do this; some are amazing in their insight. The language of one subconscious mind is understood by the other subconsciousness.

Dr. Mühl emphasizes that only a light hypnosis is needed in order to develop subconscious writing activity, or it may be produced without the aid of hypnosis at all. Indeed, she prefers a light state or no hypnosis. But most hypnotic authorities feel that the deeper the hypnosis, the greater the dissociation, and the easier it is to influence the subconscious. Posthypnotic suggestion given during a light state to the effect that the subject will be able to write is often effective, but there should be more probability of success if the trance is deep enough so that the subject can open his eyes without waking and, while remaining in the trance, carry out the writing activity.

The question arises as to whether any substantial percentage of people can produce automatic writing, this being of prime importance if considering its use in therapy. No great amount of time is usually required, and Dr. Mühl, from her extensive experience, believes that at least 80 per cent of us can become "automaters," though some will take much longer than others to develop the facility.

Dr. Mühl is undoubtedly our leading authority as to the phenomenon of automatic activity. Her book, *Automatic Writing,*[5] published in 1930, serves as an excellent text on the subject. Since it appeared, she has continued her investigations and has learned much which, it is to be hoped, she will soon publish in book form. With this technique she has been able to reach subconscious depths which as yet are little understood. She has formulated a most interesting concept of the subconscious, and her work may be of more value than any such investigation since Freud propounded his theories. It will require an entire volume to coordinate and express the ideas she has developed, and it can only be said briefly here that she believes that man's unconscious can be said, for illustrative purposes, to be divided into seven different sections or "layers," each with different characteristics and functions. Her work seems to confirm the theories of Jung as to the "collective unconscious." Not only has she propounded new theories, but she has worked out a definite method of dealing with the unconscious in order to lead it to integration and the resolving of conflicts, that is, to overcome neuroses.

One of our leading women psychiatrists, Dr. Mühl is now retired from active practice and at her home in La Jolla, California, is devoting much of her time to research in handwriting from the standpoint of character analysis and diagnosis in emotional disturbances and delinquent behavior. She has had much institutional and lecturing experience in psychiatry, as well as a long private practice, both in this country and abroad. She is the author of more than 50 articles on medical and psychiatric subjects, as well as two books.

REFERENCES

1. Erickson, M. H.: "The experimental demonstration of unconscious mentation by automatic writing," *Psychoanalyt. Quart.*, **6**:513, 1937.
2. Erickson, M. H., and Kubie, L. S.: "The use of automatic drawing in the interpretation and relief of a state of acute obsessional depression," *Psychoanalyt. Quart.*, **7**:443, 1938.
3. Erickson, M. H., and Kubie, L. S.: "The permanent relief of an obsessional phobia by means of communications with an unsuspected dual personality," *Psychoanalyt. Quart.*, **8**:471, 1939.
4. Wolberg, L. R.: *Medical Hypnosis*, Grune & Stratton, Inc., New York, 1948.
5. Mühl, A. M.: *Automatic Writing*, T. Steinkopff, Dresden, 1930.

Automatic Writing and Hypnosis

By ANITA M. MÜHL, M.D.*

The methods of reaching the unconscious and of ascertaining its functions are numerous. The ones most frequently heard of are hypnosis, free association of ideas, word association, and the tracing of dreams to their source through analytical procedure. Automatic writing, when developed and used correctly, is another extremely useful method.

The term "automatic writing," as I use it, refers merely to script produced involuntarily and has nothing to do with so-called occult messages. Automatic writing may be produced while the subject is reading out loud or is talking to someone or is otherwise distracted, and it may occur while the subject is in a state of mental quietude and not in any way distracted. It may appear spontaneously or it may be induced through suggestion as a posthypnotic phenomenon.

The most common example of automatic writing is the scribbling people do when they are telephoning. Sometimes they write numbers while they are talking, others write words or funny little phrases, while others again draw pictures, designs, scrolls, and arabesques. I have seen many people look with comical dismay at their telephonically induced automatisms and say: "Now what on earth ever made me do a thing like that? I was not even thinking about anything like that as far as I know."

Automatic writing, in its simplest form, may be defined as script which is produced involuntarily by the writer and, in some instances, without his awareness of the process. When people who know nothing of the mechanism of automatic writing first have any ex-

* 571 Sea Lane, La Jolla, Calif.

perience with it, they are apt to be very surprised by some of the things that they write. A very common form of the writing is in the "spiritistic messages." Because they are so at variance with the average conscious expression, these "messages" are thought to come from the unknown and are usually ascribed to the supernormal, whereas they generally come from the less constructive parts of the unconscious.

If undirected, the writing may deal with stupid and usually unconstructive ideas, or it may produce nonsense or poetry. Undirected automatic writing rarely deals with recall of actual early events. If directed by a trained and responsible person, the records of automatic writing can describe, accurately, events of very early childhood which have been forgotten consciously by the subject.

Frequently, unpleasant ideas and expressions have appeared in automatic writing which have seemed at great variance to the normal personality of the individual. The person who dabbles with automatic writing merely as an evening's entertainment is very possibly going to be annoyed because he may write profanities and obscenities so at variance with his conscious thinking and cultural background that he is disturbed for some time afterward.

In past ages automatic writing was considered a supernatural phenomenon. In early Christian times and in the Middle Ages, too, people who did automatic writing were apt to be considered sorcerers and were frequently thought to be possessed by a devil.

Perhaps one of the most famous references to automatic writing occurs in the Bible where the handwriting on the wall of the palace in Babylon is mentioned. Automatic writing and demoniacal possession are both mentioned in the days of Babylon, but no explanation is offered from the standpoint of the unconscious.

In Dublin in Trinity College Library, in a glass case, is a volume containing some writing purporting to come from the devil. The card of description reads:

The Devil's Autograph. Spirit writing in the 11th Century. The first book with printed Syriac characters—A certain physician having invoked the devil to answer a question about concealed treasure, the pen at once

was taken up into the air by an invisible hand. The author of this book (Theseus Ambrosius) says he received the writing from one who was present.
Papiae (Io. Mar. Simoneta) 1539.

The writing finished with a signature said to be his satanic majesty's! This was more than two thousand years after the Babylon episodes, and they were still letting themselves accept the same prescribed explanations.

At this point, I must say that in the more than 300 cases of automatic writing I have investigated, I have never seen any writing in which the pen or pencil moved without the agency of a human hand.

In a previous book of research work published under the title *Automatic Writing*, the various forms of expression found in automatic writing and the uses to which it could be put constructively were discussed.

It was found to be useful (1) in unearthing hidden conflicts, (2) in obtaining access to the early thought forms of childhood, (3) in discovering latent talents, and (4) in helping the subject organize the personality more efficiently.

It was further found that automatic writing (1) may indicate destructive or constructive mental activity, according to the manner in which it is directed; (2) may be an expression of dissociation as seen in hysteria, dual or multiple personality or schizophrenia, or it may be an expression of constructive association as seen in "inspirational writing," or again, it may indicate a reversal of personality; and (3) may express ideas which are varied and unexpected and frequently antagonistic to the ordinary conscious thought ideas of the writer.

All people who have well-defined dissociative potentialities of any kind can develop automatic writing with facility, while those who do not can learn to write automatically, though the time required to establish the habit takes longer. If relaxation combined with light waking hypnosis is used, it is easy to get the individual to write whether he is a natural "automater" or not.

The advantage of having the person write automatically is that there is complete awareness of what is happening, that is, the patient knows he is reading, knows he is writing (though as a rule he does not know what he is writing), and knows he can stop at any time he wishes. There is none of the feeling which occurs sometimes in hypnosis alone, that ideas are being imposed from without. He knows that what he is writing is coming from himself, no matter how much he consciously disapproves of what he is writing.

As to the method of procedure: it is always advisable to have the arm clear the table by at least an inch so that any impulse, no matter how slight, may move the hand. In order to get this clearance the arm may rest in a sling attached to the horizontal arm of an iron retort stand clamped to a table. The patient must sit high enough so there is no sense of physical strain at the shoulder joint. The sling consists of a strong 2-in. bandage and is made just long enough so that when the full weight of the forearm is suspended it clears the table by about 1 in. A large handkerchief folded to a size about 3 by 6 in. is placed in the bottom of the sling, and the forearm rests on this pad.

With the arm in place in the sling, the subject is given a distracting book to read (the type of book, of course, depending on the taste and interest of the reader) and instructed to read aloud. As soon as he is very much engrossed, a pencil is slipped into his hand (the usual writing hand is always tried first) and placed in position on the paper. After the pencil is placed at right angles to the paper with the pencil point touching the paper, one waits to see what happens. If marked automatic activity exists, there will be a movement at once, and connected statements may be recorded, but this does not occur too frequently. As a rule, for several attempts nothing happens—not even a slight move of the pencil. Then perhaps a further attempt will cause an uncertain movement of the pencil, producing wavering lines and long sweeping ones; spirals and circles; little sharp-pointed lines; scrolls and arabesques—an almost limitless jumble of lines and symbols of various kinds, gradually increasing in rhythmic ease and freedom of expression.

As a rule one period of this type of movement is used to get the motor activity well established; then one may begin by asking simple questions which can be answered yes or no. If the automater continues to make scrolls and waves, then the experimenter should raise the hand of the subject by the wrist each time the question is asked until an answer is obtained. Once the system of answering a whispered question or of following a whispered suggestion is established, the most difficult part of the work is over as far as getting the subject to write automatically is concerned. The experimenter should sit to the right and a little back of the subject in order to change the pages when necessary and to be in a position to whisper questions in such a way that the writer is not distracted from his reading.

If it is wished that the subject should not see what he is writing, a simple screen made of light-weight cardboard or strong muslin with a slit for the arm to pass through is satisfactory. This is of value only when the subject gets so interested in the movement of his arm that he interrupts his reading in order to see what he has written and thus blocks the free flow of ideas. This, of course, interferes with the ease and continuity of the automatic performance. Once the path from the unconscious has been cleared, the sling may be dispensed with and the subject be allowed to write with the hand in the natural writing position.

If the method of distraction does not work, then the combination of relaxation with the suggestion, made during a waking hypnotic state directing the subject to write automatically with ease, generally produces the necessary results. The waking hypnotic state is of extreme value, as the subject feels in complete control and feels assured that he knows all that is happening to him.

Much stress should be placed upon the suggestion that the experiments be staged always at the same time of the day, daily until the habit is established successfully. The reason for this is that, if the same time is used daily and expectancy of possible activity is set up, a motor habit becomes established which is of real importance. In every case it is better to use the same time in order to develop a rhythmic interval of automatic *writing activity* and of automatic *writing inactivity*.

It is often difficult to decipher the first records. Unless one knows about it, many valuable early statements may be lost because of the tendency to form one letter on top of the other instead of writing straight ahead. If it is observed that the subject is doing this, a slight pressure with one finger on the wrist is often sufficient to guide the writing hand in the proper direction until the correct habit is formed. Early writing attempts do not separate words, as a rule; neither do they cross t's or dot i's. The experimenter must learn to be exceedingly alert and read the writing as it appears, letter for letter; in this way one develops facility in deciphering even piled-up words. Incidentally, it is very good training in learning to read even the worst voluntary writing on record!

One other suggestion should be given here, and that is with regard to the formation of closed letters. These are very often left open, while *i, y, u,* and *t* may frequently be looped so that the tangle which appears to be a meaningless group of letters may often be perfectly good words and sentences. One example of this was an apparently senseless repetition of letters spelling "eeel." This was thought to be "eel" but the hand wrote "*no*—eeel." Later, several other words followed which gave the clue, and the word was found to be *eat*: the *a* had been left open and looped, and the *t* was looped and not crossed.

Some of the greatest difficulties are to be found with the following letters: *a* which appears as *ee* or *u*; *d* which looks like *el* or *cl*; *g* which turns into *v*; *m* which often seems *eee*; *n* and *u* which are often confused; and *o* which is mistaken for *v*, and vice versa, with great ease. For the person interested in automatic writing as a research problem, not one of these details is too trivial for· consideration.

Illustrated here is an example of automatic writing (Fig. 18–1) in which some of these points will be noted.

Translated, this reads:

Would you like to hear about the ways of the new england housewives there were not as in the south servants as such servants were unknown but many had help which lived as part of the family the old wives ruled and the family was a unit an impregnable unit and as such functioned in the community many women bemoaned their fate when children multiplied at the rate of one a year but large families made a stronger unit

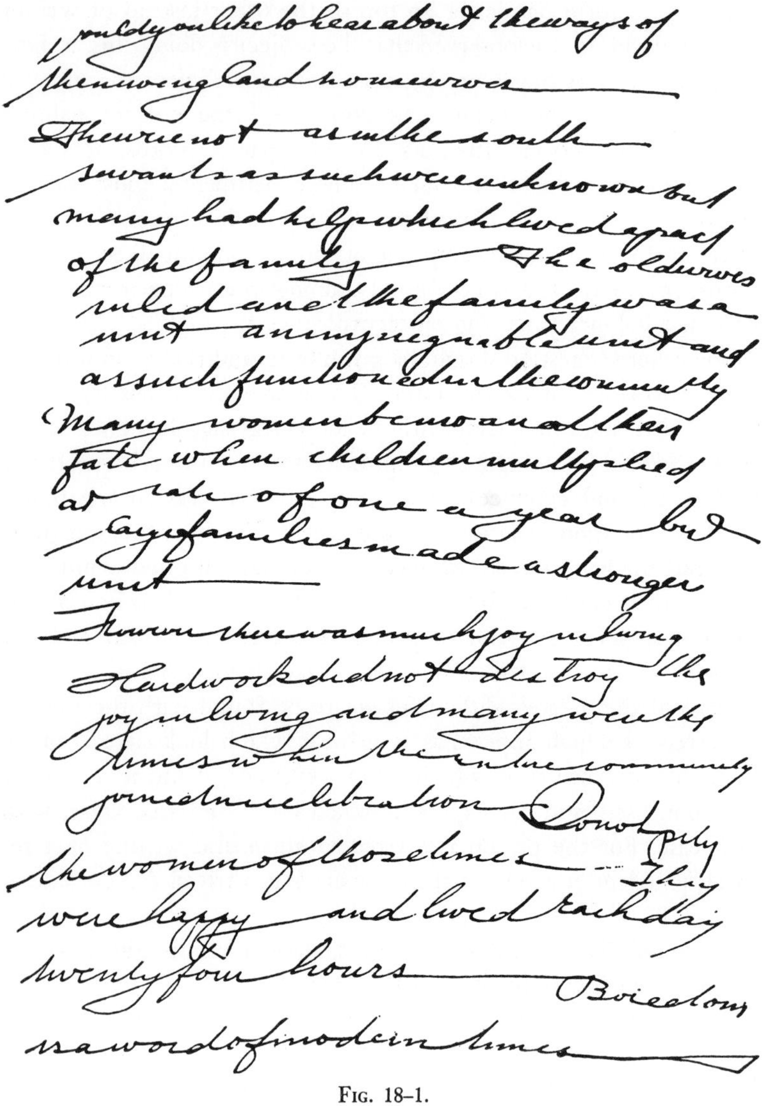

Fig. 18–1.

however there was much joy in living hard work did not destroy the joy in living and many were the times when the entire community joined in celebration do not pity the women of those times they were happy and lived each day twenty four hours boredom is a word of modern times.

The unconscious is apt to be prankish at times and will use various amusing devices to make it difficult for the experimenter to decipher the records. Several such records were about to be discarded when it became obvious that the writings contained really important material. One patient, a vivacious, stubborn, quick-tempered, sensitive, and markedly sadistic individual, produced an interesting variation in writing. She had indicated previously urethral and oral-anal erotic tendencies which had not been well sublimated. While reading aloud one day, she covered page after page with relevant conflict material written in a normal automatic script. Suddenly she began writing upside down. After she had written several pages this way, she was asked to stop both reading and writing and was then requested to write voluntarily upside down, from dictation, the sentences she had written automatically that way. She was utterly unable to do this, though she tried really hard. The pages written automatically upside down dealt with deeply hidden guilt feelings.

Another case in which a syllable written over and over was a valuable clue was that of a young unmarried woman who was well educated and who had high ideals. She had been physically ill for 5 years and showed a marked toxic reaction at the menstrual period, consisting of premenstrual irritability, nausea, flatulence, abdominal distention with rise of temperature the first day (generally 102° to 104°F), followed by increased coughing and expectoration and, as a rule, terminating with slight pulmonary hemorrhage. It seemed obvious that the reaction was psychogenic and not toxic, as others had determined. Through an odd repetition in the automatic writing, the problem was solved.

It was difficult to get this young woman to write automatically with any ease, but she produced page after page of *er, er, er, er*. When asked to write all of the words she could think of with *er* in them, she produced a large assortment beginning with *er*, ending in *er*, and having *er* anywhere between the beginning and the end. The word fun*er*al was repeated. Association of ideas with the other words with *er* established a series of occurrences and fantasies the relationship between which the patient had not noticed. Menstruation, unconsciously, had been associated with colds, tuberculosis, pregnancy fantasies (nausea, distension which the patient used as a disguise for fantasies of abortion), and other subjects distressing to her. The pregnancy and abortion ideas were fantasies only but carried an enormous weight of guilt.

There was also a great unconscious struggle going on over the fact that if she got well and married the man to whom she was engaged, she would become pregnant and this would undoubtedly mean death for her. Her religion precluded the idea of birth control. (Funeral was one of the recurrent words.) At every menstrual period this whole unconscious conflict was restaged, with the resultant physical manifestations. Following the exteriorizing of these ideas, the next menstrual period progressed with none of the toxic symptoms to complicate it.

Another patient, after having written every day for several weeks in a very sedate and conventional automatic manner, suddenly wrote several pages very rapidly of what appeared to be nothing but gibberish. She then resumed her normal writing for two pages, after which she again wrote her peculiar-looking words. Finally, one word provided a clue, and it was then evident that she had spelled all of the words backward. This was done during one writing period only and never was attempted again. The following is an example: "Won I ma a elzzup ot eht eye lli yas os. I ma a elzzup. Rof eht hturt fo eht rettam si, na eretsua nam emac ot eht esuoh dna eh dias os"—"I dias tuhs pu, tuhs pu Tuhs Pu, uoy era daed, daed. Uoy era a llams dlihc. I llahs eveiler uoy won." "Og yawa—no siht noisacco siht si ym yad."

There was being staged a war between two conflicting factions of the personality, as the impolite *tuhs pu* indicated. However, the claims of the rival factions were settled amicably, and the two quite tolerantly eventually occupied the same conscious abode. The patient, who had a very keen sense of humor, was highly amused over her "unknown selves" and when writing of herself always spoke of both parts "so that neither can be offended at me," as she said.

These records were made while the patient was reading aloud with a screen set up so that she could not see the writing hand. The patient was asked to write the same words backward voluntarily and she accomplished it, but very slowly and with numerous mistakes. One short sentence spelled backward automatically without a single mistake and no hesitation in 8 seconds, with voluntary effort required 128 seconds and contained six mistakes.

Much of the automatic writing, after it is well developed, relates coherently whole episodes of early childhood, often accompanied by profuse illustrations and even diagrams. Clear-cut impressions from the first year have been obtained which have been confirmed by members of the family who thought the patient could not possibly have any knowledge of the situation written about.

One patient, 50 years of age, who had come because of a state of almost constant fatigue, mentioned one symptom which embarrassed her very much and which, she said, had caused her considerable humiliation all her life. No matter where she was or how entertaining her environment might be, she always got very sleepy after her midday meal and felt the necessity for going to sleep. She said she had never been able to break herself of this habit. She was a good automatic writer so she was asked to explain this symptom. She wrote: "It is a little girl in a red hammock and an old lady in black and she has a bottle with a picture like this on it [picture of skull and crossbones] and she has a spoon and she gives the little girl a big spoonful to make her go to sleep."

Asked if she had any conscious memory of this, she said she thought it must be pure fantasy as she remembered no red hammock or old lady in black. However, the next time she came, she brought a picture she had painted. (She said she had never been able to draw or paint consciously.) The picture indicated trees, a red hammock slung between the trees, and a figure in black standing at one end of the hammock. Asked to explain this picture automatically, she wrote: "This is the reason she wants to go to sleep after her noon meal." Asked to elaborate further she wrote: "I mean that the nurse used to take her to the back lawn overlooking the river where the *red hammock* was. She would put her in the hammock, pull out a big bottle and a spoon (the bottle looked reddish too and had the funny picture on it) and she would give her a big spoonful of the sweetish-tasting stuff. She got very sleepy after she had the stuff and the lady in black went walking off with a friend." Asked how often this occurred, she wrote "every day."

Contemporary members of the family who were questioned about this said they thought it was pure imagination, as they had no knowledge of black-robed dispensers of pink fluid out of a poison bottle. Finally an aunt, 70 years old, in another part of the country was reached, and her response to the picture and the written record was very interesting. She wrote that she could not understand how X—— could have any memory of this occurrence, as it had happened in her first year and she knew there was an agreement between the parents and herself never to mention the circumstances to anyone.

It developed from the aunt's account that the nurse (who always wore a *black* uniform) had been giving the baby a large dose of paregoric every day after midday so that she would go to sleep and stay asleep and thus make it possible for the nurse to go off with her friend. In this way a conditioned response was set up for the child for the situation: midday—food—rest—sleep. This situation had been in existence apparently for months before it was discovered, so that a distinct habit had been formed. The nurse was discharged, and the subject from that time on was not discussed. The aunt was definite on this point, for she lived with the family at that time. If it had not been for this verification, the automatic drawing and report would have been ascribed to fantasy instead of being established as a rather remarkable instance of actual recall.

In automatic writing we may say that we have two great divisions of exteriorization: (1) fantasy and (2) actual recall.

Under actual recall we have two subdivisions worth remembering. (*a*) Actual memories of incidents, situations, and ideas which have been repressed through unfavorable reactions such as fear, shame, guilt, or humiliation. (*b*) Actual memories which have faded simply because they had no intense feeling of any kind associated with them or were crowded out because of other more vivid and intense impressions.

Under fantasy we have many subdivisions among which, to mention a few, are (*a*) so-called "spirit messages," (*b*) deeply rooted universal destructive instincts, (*c*) fairy stories, (*d*) philosophic expression, (*e*) religious expression, (*f*) symbolic poems, (*g*) symbolic drawings, (*h*) fantasy based on elaborated actual experience, and (*i*) the highest esthetic type of creative expression in painting, music, writing, and all forms of art.

The material which is obtained under recall or fantasy may be *either destructive or constructive*. This is especially true of fantasy. Where it results in asocial behavior or develops an unstable personality, it must be considered destructive, and we must speak of it as dissociation. But, on the other hand, if it leads to a satisfactory adjustment and a stabilized emotional condition, then we can use the term "association."

Fairy stories which come from the unconscious are generally delightful and gay. The philosophic discussions are often amazingly profound, considering the educational and cultural background of the writer. However, the most constructive use of automatic writing is in locating hidden abilities. Many people who have no realization that they are capable of writing begin to produce good essays, fiction, and drama. Many who do not know that they have artistic ability find that they can paint and eventually paint well. Others discover practical abilities such as designing, writing for the pulps, and journalism.

The use of automatic writing in conjunction with hypnoanalysis is invaluable in getting at unconscious processes quickly. The combination of automatic writing and hypnosis is particularly useful in anxiety and panic states where the patients have a strong degree of suggestibility. This combined method is unusually successful in simple amnesias and in dual and multiple personalities where the two methods combine very well to produce analysis and integration.

After the various personalities have "written themselves out," it is possible through hypnosis to direct the patient *consciously to remember* every part of the submerged material. This is often extremely painful to the patient, therefore in directing the patient to remember, the direction should be given *to remember and accept the memory without too great emotional stress*. This relieves a great deal of unnecessary strain and tension. The next hypnotic suggestion is for the patient *consciously and subconsciously to reject* useless, destructive elements of the personality and *consciously and subconsciously to accept* the useful, creative elements. The next hypnotic suggestion is for the patient continuously to integrate on a constructive level. The patient learns to make use of a technique which, if followed consistently, will keep the constructive integration functioning satisfactorily.

In conclusion, it may be well to emphasize that either automatic writing alone or hypnosis alone can produce excellent results from both a therapeutic and a research approach, but that the two combined give a splendid method of depth analysis and constructive integration.

CHAPTER NINETEEN

Projective Hypnoanalysis

Editor's Note

Therapeutic measures for the treatment of mental disorders are generally recognized as entirely unsatisfactory. This applies both to the results and to the time and expense involved. None of the various "schools" of thought or methods of psychotherapy are as successful as their proponents would like to claim. As a matter of fact, psychotherapists who secure the best results seldom are followers of any particular school and, from their experience and knowledge, work out individual methods of their own, eclectical and empirical. These are seldom publicized, for many workers in this field may not be interested in writing or, when busy in practice, do not care to take the time to pass on their methods to others.

The student of psychotherapy is usually at an age when he tends to believe the written word and to accept somewhat blindly the instruction given him in school or training. In most institutions which teach psychotherapy, the orthodox Freudian methods are indoctrinated, usually by instructors who have placed Freud on a pedestal and are unwilling to accept anything which he did not advance or of which he did not approve. It is this factor which has prevented most analysts from even investigating hypnoanalysis. The student is apt, in later practice, to continue to follow the pattern taught him. This is unfortunate, because new and improved techniques are badly needed. The conservative and the middle-of-the-road types then tend to follow rigidly what they have learned, and medical and psychotherapeutic training are definitely along conservative lines; strangely enough, in the latter case, since it is a relatively young branch of medical practice which should not yet have become so fixed and dogmatic, particularly when it fails to produce very good results. As a rule, those who introduce new methods are decidedly not conservative. Radical thinkers are more likely to experiment and to formulate and try new methods, when they have attained their education and are engaged in practice or teaching. It is from them that new and better procedures will come.

In the following paper Dr. Watkins has advanced some new techniques, or it would be more proper to say that he has taken various known techniques, elaborated them, and combined and coordinated them into a methodology which offers distinct advantages, particularly as to brevity, as he explains in his article. In reality, this article is a brief condensation of material which he is now preparing and elaborating into book form. It serves as an outline for a projected publication to be titled *Projective Hypnoanalysis*. This will be a companion volume and will supplement his *Hypnotherapy of War Neuroses* (The Ronald Press Company, New York, 1949).

Dr. Watkins has had much experience, both academic and practical, in clinical psychology and psychotherapy, teaching in various colleges prior to entering military service in 1943. He was Chief Clinical Psychologist at Welch Convalescent Hospital when he left the service in 1946. He now occupies the same position in the Mental Hygiene Clinic of the Veterans Administration in Chicago, Illinois. He has become one of our leading authorities in the field of hypnosis.

Projective Hypnoanalysis

By JOHN G. WATKINS, Ph.D.

CHIEF CLINICAL PSYCHOLOGIST, MENTAL HYGIENE CLINIC,
VETERANS ADMINISTRATION REGIONAL OFFICE, CHICAGO, ILLINOIS.*

NEED FOR BRIEF THERAPY

The greatest challenge today in the treatment of neurotic disorders is the development of therapeutic procedures which will bring some measure of relief in a shorter period of time. Since psychiatric illness has become so widespread, and the recent war has focused attention on our treatment inadequacies, we find ourselves faced with the fact that there are far more patients seeking psychotherapy than can possibly be treated by the available psychotherapists. Attempts to alleviate this situation naturally take two directions: first, the training of more psychotherapists both among physicians and among competent adjunctive workers within the psychological and social-work professions; second, the experimentation with, and development of, more active treatment measures whereby the maximum therapeutic gain can be secured for a given amount of the therapist's time.

EXPERIMENTATION WITH BRIEF THERAPY

With due credit to the classical procedures of analysis developed by Freud,[1] there are many who believe that therapeutic technique can be improved, with the aim of initiating significant personality changes without the expenditure of several hundreds of hours per patient. This experimental attitude seems to be growing within the

---

* Reviewed in the Veterans Administration and published with the approval of the Chief Medical Director. The statements and conclusions published by the author are the result of his own study and do not necessarily reflect the opinion or policy of the Veterans Administration.

ranks of the psychoanalysts as well as among those who hold some-what different psychological frames of reference.

The recent work of Alexander and French [2] appears to support the claims of significant results within comparatively short treatment periods such as earlier keynoted the writings of Stekel.[3, 4, 5] Still others among the analytical ranks have exerted great effort in ex-perimenting with brief treatment, notably Ferenczi,[6] Frohman,[7] and, more recently, Deutsch [8] with his "sector therapy."

During the war the method of treatment in military hospitals em-phasized the "team" approach and employed considerable flexibility aimed at the maximum integration of therapeutic skills of the psy-chiatrist, clinical psychologist, and psychiatric social worker (Men-ninger [9]). However, most of this treatment was not "depth" therapy but a stressing of the ego-supportive and environmental factors.

METHODS OF STUDYING UNCONSCIOUS MOTIVATION

At the present time there appear to be three basic approaches to the understanding of unconscious conflicts—psychoanalysis, hyp-nosis, and projective techniques. They have largely been used in isolation from each other, although some analysts have experimented with hypnosis (Kubie [10]), and there is now in psychoanalytical circles a wider acceptance of the values of the Rorschach test.

It will not be possible here to consider the first two at length. Psychoanalysis, of course, does its "digging" into unconscious men-tation through free association, dream analysis, and the analysis of transference reactions.

The induction of hypnosis and the various hypnotic phenomena that can be initiated have been quite adequately described in such standard references as Bramwell,[11] Brenman and Gill,[12] LeCron and Bordeaux,[13] and Wolberg,[14] as well as in other chapters of this book, so no attempt will be made to review them here.

The third kind of procedure for "plumbing" the unconscious depths of the human mind, namely projective techniques, is a young and lusty child which had its chief origin in the ink-blot test devel-oped by Herman Rorschach.[15] These methods are at the present the center of much research and controversy, especially by clinical psychologists, and are deserving of some further definition before we proceed.

THE PROJECTIVE HYPOTHESIS

Projection, as a psychological mechanism, implies that the individual projects himself into objects in the outside world, attributing to them ideas, emotions, and feelings which are the constructs of his own mind. This is the essential mechanism in paranoid disorders. It has been found that a subject tends to structure a relatively unstructured stimulus situation in terms of his own personality needs.

Projective Techniques

Rorschach showed his patients cards containing ink blots and asked them, "What might this be?" The different reactions to this query were found to reflect both personality structure and dynamic content. The techniques of analyzing subject responses have been described in detail by Klopfer and Kelley [16] and Beck.[17, 18]

At Harvard University, Murray [19] developed still another projective technique in the Thematic Apperception Test, usually referred to as the TAT. In this test, loosely structured pictures are presented to the subject, and he is encouraged to make up a story about what he sees in the illustrations. These stories are found to contain many of the strivings, both conscious and unconscious, of the subject, as well as to reflect many of his underlying attitudes and values.

The more recent Make-A-Picture-Story (MAPS) Test (Schneidman [20]) is a somewhat equivalent procedure. Readers wishing a recent survey of these projective techniques are referred to Bell.[21]

Projective techniques are not really new. They only represent a further extension of principles that are a recognized part of psychoanalysis. For example, dreams are actually projective techniques in which the patient projects out into fantasies the symbolized, elaborated, and disguised representations of his unconscious conflicts utilizing relatively unstructured content material drawn from everyday experiences.

In transference reactions the analyst is the "ink blot." He usually is seated somewhat out of sight of the patient and becomes a vague and relatively unstructured person. The analyst keeps himself "unstructured" by avoiding social contact with the patient. In this way he does not permit the patient to react to him as a "real" person. The patient then tends to transfer (hence projects) onto the analyst feelings and emotions related to earlier figures in his life.

THE "TEAM" APPROACH

We now come to the main thesis of this paper. If modern wars require an integration of land, naval, and air weapons for greatest efficiency; if general psychotherapy is most expedited through a combination of the services of the psychiatrist, the clinical psychologist, and the psychiatric social worker, why do we not employ a more comprehensive and flexible *integration* of our various "depth" techniques for the resolution of unconscious conflicts? If insight into unconscious motivation is our therapeutic aim, why should we not experiment with *all* known approaches to the unconscious utilized simultaneously and in an integrated manner? This does not alter the basic strategy of treatment; it only offers more tactical opportunities. It is not even necessary for the therapist to change his concepts of treatment or his therapeutic "school." It means only that the therapist uses a wider number of tactical tools in developing his psychotherapeutic strategy,

In this paper no basically new developments will be heralded. The treatment examples described here are presented only because they represent an integration of procedures which have already been separately developed by professional workers of different disciplines and too largely kept discrete from each other.

PROJECTIVE HYPNOANALYSIS

This title is applied to a manner of treatment which attempts to utilize combined tactics drawn from the areas of psychoanalysis, hypnosis, and projective techniques. It employs free association, dream analysis, and transference reactions as these are *projected* onto relatively unstructured stimulus situations within the hypnotic state. It is here proposed that, in doing this, we reach more rapidly and more deeply into the maze of unconscious, conflictual material. In addition, tactical devices will be described which are aimed at meeting the two most critical and controversial points in the procedure: first, protecting the patient's ego from developing more anxiety than it can safely handle; and second, assuring that the insights received represent a real "working through" of resistances and not a bypassing of them—a criticism which has been leveled at hypnotic procedures (Freud, A.[23]).

Prerequisites for the Use of Projective Hypnoanalysis

It is not essential that there be a deep trance, although this is desirable. Many fantasies may be projected in a light hypnoidal state. Accordingly, the procedure is not limited to those patients in whom deep trance can be initiated.

However, it is most essential that the patient have a vivid and active fantasy life to furnish adequate content for analysis. Frequency of dreams, elaborated production of TAT story material, and the existence of a number of movement responses on the Rorschach test are perhaps the best indicators of this. It should be remembered that often patients are severely constricted in fantasy production early in treatment. Later, in the safety of a well-developed therapeutic relationship, they will begin producing such images. Lack of fantasy does not necessarily contraindicate use of the method but will certainly restrict the results to be gained from it. Supportive and ego-building procedures would be generally indicated first in this case. Projective hypnoanalysis may then be employed later in the treatment.

Initiating Fantasies

In psychoanalysis the spontaneous dreams which are produced and reported by the patient are considered, and may be interpreted, by the analyst. In projective hypnoanalysis we do not wait for their natural production but actively intervene to suggest fantasy production on any particular topic or problem desired. For example, if the patient is wrestling with a conflict involving his relation to his mother, he is informed under trance that he can dream about this, either at once or during the next period of natural sleep. If this relationship is considered highly charged with conflictual affect, he is protected by being told that he may use highly disguised symbols or that he need not remember the dream when he is awakened from the hypnotic trance. Everything possible is done to protect his ego from being overwhelmed by anxiety at premature confrontation with its unacceptable impulses.

We may permit him to choose his own symbols, or we may give him a set of symbols to work with. One patient was told while under trance that bricks would be father, flowers would be mother, an animal would be himself, etc. The next day he spontaneously brought in a dream about a small animal faced with the necessity of jumping off the Empire State Building (which, he said, was composed of bricks). Through devices of this type the therapist can understand the dreams in advance without having to rely on associations to the dream elements.

The patient may be shown TAT pictures and asked to make up stories about them under trance or under regressed trance. Various endings to these stories may be suggested to him for "testing" under trance.

Another fruitful starting point for the initiation of dream fantasies is to have him associate and elaborate upon movement and original responses in the Rorschach test. These are considered by clinicians to stem from deeper personality sources than mere form responses.

Elaborating Fantasies

Once fantasies have been secured, either through spontaneous or hypnotic dreams, or through projective techniques,* they may be reworked under hypnosis by testing each element, suggesting specific outcomes, securing associations, and initiating new projections at resistance points.

For example, a patient brings in a dream about a house on fire There are no decipherable associations to it. Under hypnosis the "house" is reconstructed, and it is suggested that he can enter the

---

* The author conceives of any type of fantasy production as analogous to dreams, hence TAT or MAPS material. Except for the element of more conscious control and hence more censorship, the subject is usually trying in all of these procedures to solve internal conflicts symbolically, just as in dreams.

door. He reports seeing an empty hall (resistance), whereupon he is told to wander down the hall until he finds a door to which he is "drawn." (The therapist remains flexible and adjusts his suggestions to the demands of the moment and the potentialities for therapeutic advantage as he infers them at the time.) The patient follows the suggestion and "locates" the door. He hesitates in front of it and is then told that he is very, very strong and can go in. (Direct suggestion is used to increase ego strength temporarily so as to enable him to look into the "hidden room.") He goes into the room and says that he doesn't see anything (more resistance). He is next told that if he will look around the floor he will find an object. He looks and, after some prodding, locates a handkerchief with the initial "M" on it. When it is suggested to him that "M" is his mother's initial, he shows considerably more resistance but finally accepts the suggestion, although with anxiety. Now that he is able to tolerate a mother symbol in the room, he is told that he will notice a rocking chair. He sees this. It is now suggested that the owner of the handkerchief will gradually appear in the chair. He then sees his mother. He is next told that something will happen. At this particular point the patient actually saw himself drawn toward his mother, who spread her legs apart, and he was gradually drawn into a dark oblivion between her legs.

The foregoing example from a treatment case illustrates how strongly repressed material such as the Oedipus fantasies, which would ordinarily have required months of analysis before they could be spontaneously produced, can be elicited in projective hypnoanalysis. We started with the manifest dream material merely of a house on fire and gradually developed the latent incestuous fantasies which lay behind. Notice that the final fantasy material produced is not suggested by the therapist but is developed by the patient through constant projection into the unstructured stimulus situations selected by the therapist from the material at hand and presented to the patient.

Many different hypnoanalytical techniques may be called upon at any time in the fantasy production, hence regression, dissociated handwriting—actual or hallucinated—crystal gazing, motion-picture-screen or stage-play projection, scrambled words, "ticker tape" running between the fingers, etc.* The material which is readily present in the fantasy is used as new, unstructured stimulus material. For example, our patient dreams of a mountain. His attention is called to the "fact" that there is a burned-off place in the forest on its slope and that this place is in the shape of a letter. He "observes" this, and after some resistance he reports the letter. A black pen writing on a sheet of paper is next hallucinated for him, and he is told that the pen will write a scrambled word whose initial letter is that of the letter on the mountain. After some unscrambling and deciphering we may find a word which stands for mother, father, or some other close, intimate (and emotionally ambivalent) figure for which the mountain is a symbol.

Or again, houses may have numbers over the door which will become letters when inverted. This may tell us for what or whom the house stands. Unknown figures may be wearing coats. If we ask the patient to report the color, we may be able later to associate them to some important person in his life—or perhaps to some impulse which is characterized by the color.

In projective hypnoanalysis there is a constant and flexible weaving back and forth between projections, associations, and new projections. All of the regular defenses used by the unconscious to disguise unacceptable impulses and translate them into acceptable manifest dreams, symptoms, or behavior are used in reverse by the therapist. By consciously and purposively furnishing the necessary displacements, projections, symbols, and all the other customary defense mechanisms to the patient's ego, the therapist induces (or forces) the unconscious to do its expressing in a code which has already been deciphered and therefore is controlled and immediately translated by the therapist at will. Instead of having to follow the patient's unconscious, we lead it.

A typical example of this might be as follows: We suggest to the hypnotized patient that he can see a fantasied animal carrying out

---

* Description of many of these hypnoanalytical procedures may be found in Brenman and Gill, LeCron and Bordeaux, Wolberg, Watkins, and Erickson.[24, 25, 26]

some bestial crime. (We know wild animals are often used in dreams to symbolize "wild" impulses, so we provide one in advance and hope that the unconscious will identify it so and use it in elaborating the motivation needs.) After the patient has "seen" and described the sadistic act, he is told to watch as the animal escapes and finally falls off a cliff into a pool of water and disappears. We might now make suggestions tending to dissociate him as to time and place—leaving the "wild animal" still in the "water" but attempting to mislead the unconscious into feeling that the subject is being dropped. Next, he is told to visualize a lake. When he reports he can see it, the suggestion is given that something is floating on the surface of the water. He reports seeing a stick. We give him permission to examine the stick closely. He tells us that it has carvings on it. To this he associates that he used to carve sticks and carry them in his pocket when he was about 12 years old. When asked to associate to the age 12, he recalls that at that time his father used to beat him a great deal.

Thus, we have elicited through projection, association, and dissociation of ideas that it is he who hides sadistic impulses. We get some idea of the nature of these fantasies and arrive at the inference that the object of the original bestial crime (impulse) was probably father.

A technique of initiating and developing fantasies similar to this, but without the use of hypnotic trance, has been practiced by the analytical psychologists [27] who follow the theories of Jung.

Testing Symbolization

Dream and other fantasy symbols may be tested by *progressive substitution*. For example, we take the strange man in a dream and we ask the patient to put on a "mask" of his brother's face, friend's face, the therapist's face, or father's face and see which one will "stick." We suggest to the frigid female patient that she is in a room with a man in brown and a man in gray standing, respectively, on each side of her. To which is she drawn? It had been previously elicited in an earlier interview that her husband prefers brown suits and her father gray suits. We test prognosis in the treatment by asking her to repeat the choice as it will be 1 month in the future, 1 year from now, etc. On numerous occasions patients have quite accurately predicted the future course of their treatment. One patient predicted in November the subsiding and disappearance of her depressive symptoms in the following March—an event that occurred according to her schedule.

The unconscious, given enough protection through disguised fantasy projections under hypnosis, will often make known its true purposes and strengths.

The Principle of Separation

If we are to avoid censorship of ideas, we may develop them in separation from one another when their contiguity would be anxiety provoking. Hence, we may talk about the attributes of wives and sexual partners in the early part of an interview. Perhaps the patient characterizes them as "affectionate and understanding." Fifteen minutes later, again under hypnosis, he may characterize mothers as "affectionate and understanding." We do not put the ideas together until his ego is strong enough to accept the responsibility for incestuous desires.

Protection of the Ego

The problem of ego strength and when the patient may be confronted with his fantasy productions is a real one. True, the Rorschach test and other psychodiagnostic tests may give us an estimate in advance as to whether he has a strong ego or is deteriorating into a psychotic disorder, but frequently informal tests must be made during therapy. This may be done by "asking" his unconscious ego whether it is strong enough to remember the fantasy and its meaning upon awakening. The unconscious is a good judge of the ego's strength. I have never known a patient who gave "permission" under trance for the therapist to suggest that he would remember traumatic material upon awakening, who was unable to handle and integrate the material when he was brought out of trance. If necessary, we may reconstruct the traumatic fantasy with several progressively disguised elaborations and suggest that the patient will remember each "stairstep" in turn back to the original fantasy as he becomes strong enough to do so. In this way the therapy is kept near to but just below the anxiety tolerance level. This moves the treatment as fast as is possible, preventing a panic or psychosis, and still keeping it from dragging with interminable resistance.

Recognition Therapy

Another directive feature is the use of recognition rather than recall. When someone asks us to remember who sat in front of us in the eighth grade, that is recall. When he asks us if it was John Jones, that is recognition. We recognize much that we cannot recall. Nondirective and psychoanalytical therapies wait until material is spontaneously *recalled*. As part of the treatment process described here, the therapist anticipates and suggests under hypnosis memories, feelings, and interpretations for "testing." The patient *recognizes* by selecting from several interpretations one to which he reacts-- either with acceptance or with anxiety and resistance. Desensitization and reassurance may permit acceptance and insight later. So, in projective hypnoanalysis, we utilize the recognition principle as much as the recall one. This often speeds the relearning process, which is the essence of psychotherapy. Although he did not refer to it in the same terms, Kempf [28] has employed a similar technique in the active analytical treatment of cases of schizophrenia.

In this brief paper it will be possible to present only a few sample parts of therapy sessions illustrating these treatment methods, although a more comprehensive publication discussing them is envisioned in the near future.

CASE EXAMPLES

A 21-year-old girl volunteers as a subject for hypnotic demonstration and experimentation. She is highly hypnotizable, being able to enter a deep trance within a few seconds. Before being placed in trance she is asked whether she recalls any recent dreams. She reports that she had one some time ago but that it has been largely forgotten. The only thing she can remember is that it had something to do with "Mother" and that she awakened with terrific pains in both sides of her head. Nothing of the dream content remains, but she does recall that her mother was at that time sick with a physical disorder involving pains in both sides of the head.

She is now placed in a deep hypnosis and the session continues as follows:

"You are free to go back to the time when your mother was sick and to relive your experiences at that time."

"I am alone in the house with Mother. I lie down to take a nap. When I wake up I remember vaguely that I dreamed of Mother. Both sides of my head hurt."

"What did you dream about?"

"I don't know—I can't remember."

"What comes to your mind in connection with this incident?"

"I don't seem to be able to think of anything." (Resistance.)

At this point we do not get hypermnesia. Regression also has failed. Furthermore, the patient is blocked in her associations. We now shift to projective hypnoanalysis to try to break through this resistance and determine what is behind it.

"You are walking down the main street of a town. Can you see yourself?"

"Yes."

"As you walk along the street you see a movie theater on the other side of the street. Can you see it yet?"

A brief pause ensues followed by, "Now I see it."

"You feel like going in to the show. Can you see yourself going in and sitting down?"

"Yes."

"You notice now that you have pains in both sides of your head. Can you feel them?"

The subject makes a pained face and puts her hands up to the sides of her head.

"These pains seem to have started as soon as you walked into the theater. Look up at the screen and tell me what the show is about."

"The screen is a picture of fog—just thick fog." (Resistance again.)

"You begin to feel an increased impression of strength within yourself. As this feeling of greater strength comes on you, you will notice that the fog in the picture gradually melts away. Can you see it doing that?"

"I think I can see a point of land now jutting out into a body of water."

"And what else?"

"And also I see a number of people. I wonder why they are dressed in black?"

"Why do you think they are dressed in black?"

"I don't know."

"What does black mean?"

The patient shows considerable anxiety. This anxiety becomes too great, and the protective factors in the ego bring her out of trance.

"My, I must have been asleep quite a while?"

"Well, for a little while. Do you remember what happened or what we talked about while you were asleep?"

"No, I guess I don't. It just seems to be blank."

The patient is now rehypnotized.

"You will see a number of people dressed in black. Can you see them now?"

"Oh, yes, I see them. Somebody must have died."

"Who might have died?"

"I wouldn't know."

"Look up in the air. You will see a number of spinning spots. Now they begin to look like mixed-up letters. Can you see them?"

"Yes, I see them. They don't make much sense."

"These mixed-up letters will begin to come out one at a time and you can read them off as you see them."

The subject slowly reads off, "R—O—H—T—M—E." This is obviously a scrambled form of "MOTHER." By constant associative projection she has led us from her headaches (the same as Mother's) and her forgotten dream to the idea of "the point," which consists of people in black, who obviously must be mourning a death, and out of the air we get the scrambled word "MOTHER." The headaches must be her punishment through identification with mother for her unconscious death wishes toward her mother. In this case no interpretations were made. She was given "permission" to forget the entire material and awakened from trance. She showed total amnesia for all that had been discused. This dynamic material emerged during the first hypnotic session the author had with the subject and within about 15 minutes after first meeting her. The session was nontherapeutic but was serving as a demonstration of projective hypnoanalytical techniques for a professional colleague.

The following is an example of another projective hypnoanalytical session illustrating the flexibility of the technique. Because of its length it will not be reported in the word-for-word manner as in the previous case.

The patient was a young and deeply depressed professional man. He had previously received 1 year of once-a-week psychotherapeutic interviews in another city, conducted along psychoanalytical lines. These had helped him considerably. However, about 6 months after discontinuing treatment, his depression returned deeper than ever. After reading about the possibilities of self-analysis (Horney [29]), he undertook such self-treatment for about 3 months without noticeable results. At this point he came to the therapist seeking help. The first 3 of our hours were spent in psychodiagnostic testing. Discussion of social-history material and working through TAT stories used about 8 hours more. At the beginning of this period of treatment he reported that at the end of his first year in treatment he had reached the stage of insight where he accepted the idea that he was sexually in love with his mother. At the time of terminating this treatment he was convinced that this was the basic cause of his guilt and depressed feelings. It could not be determined whether he had received a genuine insight into an Oedipus attachment or whether this understanding was only intellectual. The following is a report of the thirteenth and fourteenth sessions which this therapist held with the patient.

Thirteenth Session

He was placed in hypnosis rather rapidly, to a medium trance stage. It was suggested that he would dream of his present status and that he would also dream of the future direction of the therapy.

He reported one dream in which he was trying to get to a truck in a railroad station which contained a number of men. He was blocked by a metal screen. The truck pulled out, and he ran around through the station, seeing it in front. He then dashed through the front entrance of the building and climbed on the truck.

Next he reported seeing himself plunging a knife into the groin of a man. After he had ripped him open, he inserted his erect penis into the wound. No attempt was made in this session to analyze these dreams.

Fourteenth Session

The subject was placed in a moderate degree of trance and told that he could remember and interpret his dreams of the other day. He then stated that "these men" were childhood associates who had gotten on the truck (growing up into maturity). He had been blocked off and had missed it. By running through the station (psychotherapy) he could get on the truck. He was reminded of the present date and asked just where in the process he was. He replied that he was just beginning to get on the truck.

He then discussed the other dream and, after revivification of the fantasy, "noticed" that the man he had stabbed had "blond hair." His association to blond hair was the therapist. He then "tried" the face of the therapist on the man and found that it would "stick." The fantasied faces of several other people in his life were "tried" on the man. No other such face was found to "stick."

We then discussed transference reactions and why he might project these sadistic, homosexual desires onto the therapist (the discussion being entirely under hypnosis). He mentioned that he had become vaguely aware during his period of self-analysis of his homosexuality and sadism but didn't know either how to handle these impulses or why they arose.

He was given the hallucination of a writing desk on which was a sheet of paper and a pen writing on it. The "pen" was asked to give some information regarding the origin of this homosexual sadism. There was initial resistance. The pen would not write.

It was then suggested that the pen would write a scrambled word. Whereupon it wrote "AEBDRS." He was then told that these letters could be fed into a whirlpool. After he visualized this he was told that the whirlpool would throw out a new word. It threw out the word "BREADS."

He associated "sweetbreads (sweet breads)" to this—something nice to eat, and then thought of eating people's organs. We then discussed oral forms of sadism.

He was next told he could walk along a street and that he would come to a theater which was showing some rather gruesome movies. He could enter, sit down, the lights would go off, and the play would start.

He then reported seeing a "monster eating a man's decaying body." His own face could be made to "stick" on the monster. He was next told that the motion-picture reel would stop and would go backward and that in this way he could see the man before he was dead and determine his identity. At this point he screamed, "My God, it's my mother."

He then associated that his mother seemed to be "manlike." He was now regressed back to the first year of life and reported seeing himself as a crying, hungry baby. Mother had plenty of milk but wouldn't give it to him. He said he wanted to bite her and get it. When asked why, he responded with "If I could incorporate her then I would have her in me all the time and wouldn't go hungry."

There followed some discussion of how men were "Mother" and hence, his "homosexual" sadism toward them. They were all rejecting mothers (mother was a man). He reported that the meaning seemed quite clear for him and would account for his inability to develop any sound emotional ties with either men or women and his wish to retreat from social relationships.

He was next asked whether he would want to remember all this when he was awakened from trance, and he said that he wanted to do so. He did not have any amnesia for this material on emerging from trance.

Following trance, there was discussion and interpretation regarding his transference of mother to the analyst via the blond man in the dream who was then sadistically made into a woman and raped. This was related to his feelings toward all men—staying away from them to protect himself from the "homosexual" sadistic feelings toward them (mothers).

There is not space here to report the entire case except to say that there appeared to be a rather substantial improvement during and subsequent to the fairly brief treatment (only 18 sessions being possible before he made a change of residence).

EVALUATION OF PROJECTIVE HYPNOANALYSIS

During the past 5 years, projective hypnoanalytical techniques have been used and integrated with other therapeutic tactics in quite a large number and wide variety of cases. Failures and successes must both be numbered among these, but the "batting average" appeared to be as high as or higher than the published reports for other forms of treatment including traditional psychoanalysis. The number of sessions per patient varied from 1 to more than 100, but the average was in the range of 20 to 30. Of course, no real scientific comparison of this therapeutic approach with others can be made unless we can establish objective standards of evaluating the initial degree of psychopathology and the amount and duration of more stable adjustment subsequent to therapy.

A few cases from among those considered successfully treated by the method might be reported here. These are not considered to be atypical.

1. Syphilophobia, severe, chronic for 2 years. Apparent recovery after 41 sessions. No return of symptoms or equivalent ones during a 2-year follow-up. The patient is making a successful school and work adjustment. Six months after the termination of his treatment this patient independently and voluntarily requested that the Veterans Administration discontinue his disability pension on the grounds

that he no longer had a neurosis. He informed the therapist of this action afterward.

2. Hysterical conversion, photophobia, third recurrence. Loss of the symptom followed apparent insight during a projective hypnoanalytical session after a direct suggestion failed to affect the symptom. No return of symptom or equivalent in 1-year follow-up. Treatment time, 4 hours.

3. Neurotic depression and character disorder. The depression had lasted for 2 years. Previously, there had been a record of lifelong maladjustment and "acting out" of antisocial sexual promiscuity. Treated by projective hypnoanalysis, after 2 years of intermittent traditional analysis had not relieved the depression nor affected behavior. Apparent insight, relief of depression, normal adjustive behavior including cessation of promiscuity, falling in love, marrying, good marital adjustment, and birth of child. This 31-year-old woman was treated for a total of 22 hours. Her subsequent adjustment was followed for a period of 1½ years.

In many cases projective hypnoanalysis was used only occasionally throughout the treatment, so it would be difficult in these to evaluate its role in the recovery or lack of it. As previously mentioned, not all patients are amenable to this approach. Therefore, it is not suggested that this method of therapy can be used in all cases as a substitute for standard analysis. Rather, it may be employed in selected cases to speed up the usual psychoanalytical procedures.

PRECAUTIONS TO BE OBSERVED

It is obvious that this type of treatment usually keeps the anxiety level quite high, since it is designed to elicit and work through a great deal of repressed material in a relatively short time. For this reason proper safeguards must be taken against precipitating psychotic or suicidal reactions in individuals with weak egos. This involves first establishing a warm, permissive, "giving" relationship with the patient so as to make him accept help. He needs the strong support of an emotional loan by the therapist during projective hypnoanalysis even more than in other therapies because he must face and work through so much more material in a short period of time. This intensive relationship with the therapist keeps him from being immobilized by his anxiety or overwhelmed by concrete unconscious material before he can integrate his new self-discoveries into his self-structure.

Some comparisons as to technique might be made at this point between projective hypnoanalysis and traditional psychoanalysis.

Psychoanalysis	*Projective Hypnoanalysis*
Relaxation and restriction of attention from external stimuli—the couch.	Further relaxation and more drastic restriction of attention from external stimuli—hypnotic trance.
Strengthening of patient's ego through identification and relationship with the analyst.	Protective "mantle of hypnosis" over patient's ego plus strong supportive relationship with therapist.
"Projecting" of patient's infantile fantasies on the analyst. Skillfully timed interpretation by analyst. Period of reality testing by patient with working through of resistance. Release of affect, followed by insight because seeing (experiencing) is believing.	"Projecting" of patient's infantile fantasies on unstructured stimulus material suggestively guided by therapist. Interpretations by questions. Period of reality testing by patient with working through of resistance. Release of affect permitted first in the protection of trance only, followed by working through and integration consciously as patient's ego strength permits.

In psychoanalysis, especially when the insight has been achieved through the initial establishment of a transference neurosis, there is often difficulty in breaking the transference, since the analyst is a real, live person who continues to exist in reality.

In projective hypnoanalysis the transferences are largely to projected fantasies and not quite so much directly onto the "ink blot of the analyst." Accordingly, the danger of an undissolvable transference neurosis is somewhat lessened. This advantage, however, can be offset in some cases where the secondary gain of enjoying the pleasant hypnotic relationship is strong.

SUMMARY

There is great need today for briefer forms of therapy. Psychoanalysis, hypnosis, and projective techniques are the three best-known avenues to unconscious motivation. Because they have been developed by different disciplines and somewhat in separation from each other, they have not been integrated into a comprehensive, flexible, therapeutic approach. A set of treatment procedures is here proposed which uses all three simultaneously in an integrated combination. An extended period of experimentation and use with these procedures indicates that disorders requiring deep therapy can be successfully treated and often in a comparatively short period of time. Further study, experimentation, and development in this area are needed.

REFERENCES

1. Freud, S.: *Basic Writings*, Modern Library, Inc., New York, 1938.
2. Alexander, F., and French, T. M.: *Psychoanalytic Therapy*, The Ronald Press Company, New York, 1946.
3. Stekel, W.: *Peculiarities of Behavior*, Vols. I and II, Liveright Publishing Corp., New York, 1924.
4. Stekel, W.: *Frigidity in Women*, Vols. I and II, Liveright Publishing Corp., New York, 1926.
5. Stekel, W.: *Impotence in the Male*, Vols I and II, Liveright Publishing Corp., New York, 1927.
6. Ferenczi, S.: *Further Contributions to the Theory and Technique of Psychoanalysis*, Hogarth Press, London, 1926.
7. Frohman, B.: *Brief Psychotherapy*, Lea & Febiger, Philadelphia, 1948.
8. Deutsch, F.: *Applied Psychoanalysis*, Grune & Stratton, Inc., New York, 1949.
9. Menninger, W. L.: *Psychiatry in a Troubled World*, The Macmillan Company, New York, 1949.
10. Kubie, L. S.: "Use of induced hypnogogic reveries in the recovery of repressed amnesic data," *Bull. Menninger Clin.*, 7:5–6, 172–182, 1943.
11. Bramwell, J. M.: *Hypnotism, Its History, Practice and Theory*, J. B. Lippincott Company, Philadelphia, 1930.
12. Brenman, M., and Gill, M.: *Hypnotherapy*, International Universities Press, New York, 1947.

13. LeCron, L. M., and Bordeaux, J.: *Hypnotism Today*, Grune & Stratton, Inc., New York, 1947.

14. Wolberg, L. R.: *Medical Hypnosis*, Vols. I and II, Grune & Stratton, Inc., New York, 1948.

15. Rorschach, H.: *Psychodiagnostics*, Hans Huber, Berne, 1942.

16. Klopfer, B., and Kelley, D. M.: *The Rorschach Technique*, World Book Company, Yonkers, N. Y., 1942.

17. Beck, S. J.: *Rorschach's Test*. Vol. I; "Basic Processes," Grune & Stratton, Inc., New York, 1944.

18. Beck, S. J.: *Rorschach's Test*. Vol. II; "A Variety of Personality Pictures," Grune & Stratton, Inc., New York, 1945.

19. Murray, H. A.: "Techniques for a systematic investigation of fantasy," *J. Psychol.*, **3**:117–143, 1937.

20. Schneidman, E. S.: "Schizophrenia and the MAPS test: a study of certain normal psycho-social aspects of fantasy production in schizophrenia as revealed by performance on the Make A Picture Story (MAPS) Test," *Genet. Psychol. Monogr.*, **38**:145–223, 1948.

21. Bell, J. E.: *Projective Techniques*, Longmans, Green & Co., Inc., New York, 1946.

22. Watkins, J. G.: *Hypnotherapy of War Neuroses*, The Ronald Press Company, New York, 1949.

23. Freud, A.: *The Ego and the Mechanisms of Defense*, Hogarth Press, London, 1937.

24. Erickson, M. H.: "The experimental demonstration of unconscious mentation by automatic writing," *Psychoanalyt. Quart.*, **5**:513, 1937.

25. Erickson, M. H.: "Hypnosis in medicine," *M. Clin. North America*, May, pp. 639–652, 1945.

26. Erickson, M. H.: "Hypnotic techniques for the therapy of acute psychotic disturbances in war," *Am. J. Psychiat.*, **101**:668–672, 1945.

27. Adler, G.: *Studies in Analytical Psychology*, W. W. Norton & Company, New York, 1948.

28. Kempf, E. J.: "Bisexual factors in curable schizophrenia," *J. Abnorm. & Social Psychol.*, **44**:414–419, 1949.

29. Horney, K.: *Self-Analysis*, W. W. Norton & Company, New York, 1942.

CHAPTER TWENTY

The Hypnoanalysis of
Phobic Reactions

Editor's Note

In the following pages will be found a discussion of methodology and reactions in the hypnoanalysis of two persons with phobias—the fear of water in one patient, a cat phobia in the other. The entire analysis is not given, only extracts in each case of such part of the analysis as pertains to the phobic symptoms and their causes.

The dynamics, resultant behavior, and the mechanism of the phobias become understandable as the result of the use of hypno-analytical techniques. These serve to shorten considerably the time which probably would have been required to obtain the necessary information as to causes by more orthodox methods. With the gain of insight and knowledge of the motivations of the phobia by the patient, it is seen how the condition is therapeutically corrected. Utilization is made of some of the projective techniques.

During the past few years Dr. Schneck has become one of the leading investigators in the field of hypnosis and hypnoanalysis. He is the author of a large number of scientific articles most of which have dealt with various aspects of research in these subjects.

Dr. Schneck is a psychiatrist whose experience has included association with the Menninger Clinic, the U.S. Army Medical Corps during and after World War II, and the Veterans Administration. At present he is Clinical Associate in Psychiatry, College of Medicine, State University of New York; Psychiatric Consultant, Westchester County Department of Health (New York); and also is engaged in private practice.

Instrumental in the founding of the Society for Clinical and Experimental Hypnosis (26 West Ninth Street, New York 11, New York), Dr. Schneck is president of the organization.

The Hypnoanalysis of Phobic Reactions

By JEROME M. SCHNECK, M.D.*

Read before the Society for Clinical and
Experimental Hypnosis, November, 1949.

The depth and duration of therapy for phobic reactions depend on the number and nature of components involved. These relate to the type of phobia, the personality of the patient, the dynamic importance of the symptom as a defense in intrapsychic conflict, the implication of repressed memories, and the ease or difficulty involved in their ultimate availability for conscious awareness, and the relationship of the phobia to other symptoms and to the character structure of the patient. These and other considerations influence attainment of temporary or permanent relief, with or without insight on the part of the patient. As for effective treatment and its opportune time there would have to be taken into account the necessary insights in regard to over-all personality functioning and perhaps other specific problems before attempted resolution of the phobia. Thus, some symptoms may be evaluated and eliminated early in treatment, and others may have to await rectification of deeper characterological problems.

Methods of treating certain problems have been described by the writer in earlier papers.[1, 2, 3, 4] Elimination of an animal phobia during an early phase of therapy has been described in detail elsewhere.[5] Transference relationships are carefully evaluated in analytic therapy, and indications of how they are taken into account and the role that they play have been discussed.[6, 7]

The manner in which phobias were resolved for two patients will be described now. Both patients were in hypnoanalysis. One had a

* 26 West Ninth St., New York 11, N. Y.

water phobia involving a fear of swimming, and the other had a cat phobia. The symptoms in both cases were attacked after the patients had been in treatment awhile and after various aspects of personality functioning had been disclosed, at least in part.

Case 1. For about 1 year this patient, in her middle twenties, had a water phobia. She was a good swimmer, enjoyed the sport very much, and was puzzled by this fear. It had started a few months prior to her entering treatment. With the onset of the phobia there had been numerous dreams about water, but she could not recall the details.

Following the induction of hypnosis during a hypnoanalytic interview, it was suggested to the patient (not specifically in connection with the phobia) that various past memories would be re-evaluated and rearranged unconsciously in connection with the rectification of current problems. (This technique may be used within a particular interview for immediate investigation or as a posthypnotic suggestion in preparation for future work, as has been described elsewhere by the writer.[4]) She was then given an opportunity for spontaneous verbalization but had nothing to say. (Frequently, in similar situations, such absence of ideas constitutes a form of resistance in treatment. Its various implications can be determined on the basis of knowledge about the patient from data already made available.) The patient was then told that she would visualize a crystal ball and in it there would appear an important memory from childhood. (This technique, and many variations, may be employed readily with quite a few patients who, for its accomplishment, do not have to be in somnambulistic states. Thus, it is particularly helpful for extending hypnoanalytic therapy to include patients who cannot enter deep hypnosis. This and similar methods are also indicative of an active approach which may be employed during hypnoanalysis. In so doing, also, resistances may be either circumvented or analyzed, depending upon the nature and purposes of therapy.)

The patient revealed, "It's in the country—A-ville. Chickens. And there's a cow. And some cousins. And wide-open spaces on one side of the house and in front of it and back of it." The patient sighed considerably and grew uncomfortable. This occurred frequently with her as she approached dynamically meaningful material. "My cousin B—. B— and I are—are walking away from the house. (The patient frowned.) She's putting her arms around me— she's touching me and kissing me. We're playing games." (The use of the present tense is indicative here of the manner in which she tended to relive experiences under hypnosis. It did not always occur but would do so frequently. The intensity of her emotional involvement in hypnosis was invariably quite pronounced.) (Pause.) (*Yes?*) "And that scene ended." (*Any other scene come up?*) "Just about A-ville. About the chickens. A man used to come and kill them on Friday. The cows. The fields, and going out berrypicking." (The patient smiled.)

The memory of her cousin was clearly related to homosexual material. Her discomfort may be explained briefly. During treatment the patient became gradually aware of the fact that in many ways she had made a masculine identification. This stemmed from an inadequately resolved Oedipus situation. Her attachment to her father had been considerable, and her mother was regarded as an interference. She began to feel rejected by her father, however, and eventually developed considerable antagonism toward him. The early masculine identification represented many things, among them an effort to please him, a rejection of things feminine associated in part with her mother, and a defense in relation to competition with her mother for her father. The discomfort in relation to the country scene with her cousin stemmed from a stirring up of this conflict. Also, the material served as a prelude to the dynamics involved in the water phobia which was to be dealt with shortly thereafter. The comments which permitted the patient to smile indicated movement away from anxiety-producing material. The man killing the chickens is a camouflage for more meaningful hostility, but for the patient the disguise permitted sufficient reassurance.

(*Yes?*) "Some songs—we used to sing them in the evening. And one of those swings that four people sit on—I don't know what you call them. It was very pretty up there. There was a neighbor down the road who had twelve children—had one every year. (The patient was in conflict about having children.) We used to go swimming. (She moves into the phobia material.) There were two places. One underneath a trestle of some sort. I remember once my foot got caught in the bottom. It was a rock bottom. That's not what I started to say. (That is exactly what she *wanted* to say.) I started to say I'd catch tadpoles there and take them home and want them to grow into frogs. (And now she is drawn back to the traumatic memory.) My foot did get caught. I got very frightened. (Patient smiled. The emotional implications of the experience for her current problems are still adequately repressed.) (Pause.) When we traveled home from A-ville, probably at the end of the summer, I used to sit in front of the truck—it was a small car. My father used to attach a string to his hand and my hand. (This reflected her marked attachment to him at that time, but she did not say this. She proceeded to reveal how on an occasion, when it was dark, a man offered her an apple, whereupon she was frightened, thought it was poisoned, and did not eat it. She believed it resembled a fairy tale. Whether fairy tale, fantasy, screen memory, or actual memory, it reveals her ambivalence toward her father and follows immediately a memory indicative of marked attachment.)"

The patient was asked further about the string, and she explained that she would pull it if she wanted something and her father would stop the car. Then, still in hypnosis, the patient started to strain. "Saturday night at the wedding (which she attended) I put my arms around my father and kissed him and he said, 'What goes on here?' and I said I kissed him because I loved him. He said, 'I'm sorry, I don't feel the same way about you.'" The patient teased him and said she would tell her doctor (the writer). He then said he felt the way he had just indicated. The patient felt like crying but restrained herself because other people were there. (*The string wasn't there any more.*) She started to cry. "I don't believe it!" Her father's comment was apparently typical of him in his relationship with his daughter. An irregularly changing seductive (substantiated by other data) and rejecting approach could only induce conflict, confusion, and ambivalence, which it did.

The remainder of the hypnoanalytic hour was devoted to material in connection with the cousin mentioned above.

During the next interview the patient felt anxious but claimed she did not know the reason. However, she was fearful of having to discuss her father. She had begun to experience conscious feelings of antagonism toward him. She was asked about the water episode referred to during the previous hypnosis, and she revealed the feeling of loss of control. She had gulped water, felt she was drowning, and someone pulled her out. Although she had hitherto scrupulously avoided deeper discussions about her father, she had, at the start of treatment, discussed her mother a good deal. She was now asked about her mother, and she revealed feelings about her mother's attempts to control her. Then when the patient would feel she was losing control in her relationship with her mother, she would become anxious and resentful. The loss of control obtained in water situations now, and she feared the water would become the controlling agent. (Thus, this aspect of the phobia was introduced, but the emotional impact of the dynamics of the phobia had to wait until her father was reintroduced.)

Following this, the patient's fear persisted. She ventured into the ocean but only in low water, and she swam parallel to the shore line. It was an accomplishment even to go into the water. In treatment, she realized how little thought she had been giving to her father, although now she recognized being troubled about their relationship.

Under hypnosis again, the patient was encouraged to work further on her problems and was told that she would visualize a crystal ball in which an important scene would appear—a product of the unconscious work being performed. She became uncomfortable. "They keep changing!" (Pause.) "They keep changing all the time. One is the day my grandfather bought me skates; I went fishing in a boat with an uncle of mine; then my father getting me a doll; and I'm sitting, talking with T—; (T— was her lover who had been unconsciously identified with her father); and something that happened in the water yesterday—my father taking me in the water and going out further than I, and he kept beckoning me to go out further."

(*Anything else?*) (Patient smiles.) The latter again was a frequent occurrence with her when she was able temporarily to escape anxiety-producing material. "No, no scenes now."

The patient was told she would see a scene which would have much meaning for her. She would describe it even if the meaning at first was not clear to her. (This technique may frequently be used to obtain material the implications of which the patient might be unable to tolerate at the time. Gradual tolerance may be achieved later, but in the meantime the therapist may obtain important clues.) Again, the patient became uncomfortable. "It's with T—." (Pause, patient squirms.) "Last summer on the beach with T— together. We had an argument. He went into the water without me. I went into the water in another direction. I didn't want to come back. I kept swimming and swimming and didn't want to come back. All of a sudden I kept getting sorry for my mother and father. It would make them very unhappy. I turned around and started back. I wanted to drown." (*Anything else?*) (Patient nods.) "I want to get up." (*Why?*) "I'm uncomfortable. I'm very restless." (*Do you know why?*) "Because I can't think." (*What do you mean?*) "I just don't think I am thinking about other things I should think about." (This remark is of interest. On the one hand it seems to denote her resistance to dealing with the dynamically meaningful material which is arising; on the other hand it is pertinent in that the "other things" are the precipitating circumstances of the phobia and its implications.) (*What was the meaning of the last scene?*) "It seemed to me—at the time it just seemed to me that nothing was important." (*Yes?*) "I guess my mother and father were, or maybe I just didn't want to die." (*Any relation to your fear of water?*) "I went into the water after that." (*Were you afraid after that?*) "I don't think so." (*You sure?*) "I don't think so." (The last comment would appear capable of possessing a double meaning.)

The patient was told she would see a scene which would represent the first occasion on which her water phobia appeared. (Patient squirms.) "I don't know. The only thing that comes into my mind are those dreams I had." (*Yes?*) "There was someone drowning or someone needing help in very rough water. It seems I was the only one there to swim." The patient revealed afterward that, although in the dream she was the only one who could swim out to help this person, she did not.

She was told she would dream again the most meaningful of the series of dreams she had had centering around her fear of water. (This approach was utilized in an effort to avoid the circuitous path of attempting recall of many dreams related to a specific problem. If the technique proved effective, much time and effort would be saved while the most pertinent data would be obtained.) (Pause.) (*Tell me about it.*) (Patient sighs repeatedly.) (*Tell me about it.*) "Well, there's a—a very steep hill but it's not a hill because it's much larger." She said it was like the side of a mountain. "It's quite barren on one side and thick shrubbery . . . (covered part of it). It's hot and dry and very steep and I'm going down in an old car. There's a lake at the bottom of the hill. It's not really a lake because it's got different locks in it like a canal." There were three locks. Shrubbery was there. People were diving from the hill into the water. The patient rowed across and away. (*Anything else?*) "The scene switches. It switched to the Hudson River." (*Yes?*) "No, not the Hudson River. It's something that happened last year also. I was swimming in the Delaware River and I got caught under the bridge and the current was pulling me downstream. I was trying very hard to get to the other side of the river or at least to one of the foundations of the bridge." She planned on swimming diagonally in the direction of the current. She reached her goal but was badly frightened. "That was something like the dream I had—the one where someone was drowning in rough water. It was also underneath a trestle." The Delaware River incident was an actual event preceding the dream just mentioned.

The crucial point was now reached. She was told she would visualize a crystal ball. In it she would see the face of the person drowning during the dream in which she, the only person who could swim, did not go to assist. "It's my father!" she exclaimed, as she experienced an attack of anxiety with marked hyperventilation. Direct suggestions for relaxation were then administered, and she burst into tears. In view of the intense anxiety associated with this material, she was asked whether she desired posthypnotic recall. "Yes!" she stated emphatically, and she did remember on awakening. The water phobia disappeared completely.

The phobia served as a defense against her unconscious death wishes toward her father. These were represented in at least one crucial dream involving water and swimming. The dreams apparently occurred when her unconscious conflict about her relationship with her father reached a climax. The dreams about water followed an actual experience in which the patient's life was in danger. The nature of the experience found some representation in the water dreams. This actual experience also bore an emotional tie with a traumatic episode involving water, earlier during the patient's childhood. Conflict with and about her lover who was identified with her father also was connected through an actual event with a water situation. In addition to the death wishes toward her father and the ordinary association of death with swimming in water based on actual traumatic experiences, there was her conflict about suicide which also bore a relationship to a swimming scene. Finally, her relationship with her mother enters the problem through an association between conflict over personal control and the powerlessness experienced by the patient in relation to the force of a large body of water. To avoid swimming would serve the purpose of avoiding at least all of the above associations. She could channelize her anxieties into this area and erect a phobic defense.

Case 2. This patient, also in her middle twenties, had a phobia involving cats for as long as she could remember. The phobia was resolved during her hypnoanalysis. Again, the symptom was explored after some dynamics in regard to interpersonal relationships had been uncovered earlier in treatment. It will be observed that emotional reactions in relation to the investigation of the phobia were, in appearance, less marked and intense than with the previous patient. Here there was exhibited more of a tendency to evaluate thoughts and feelings as they appeared. The impression is less dramatic. It is illustrative of differences in hypnoanalytic work as engaged in by various patients. A complete evaluation of the latter is neither practicable nor intended in this report.

The patient was free-associating within the hypnotic state. She had been telling about her mixed feelings toward her husband, especially her antagonism. She had been wondering whether the marriage would be terminated. Her husband, incidentally, had been identified in various ways by her with her mother. The identification was based on certain passive, feminine characteristics. Then, (pause), "You know, I was just thinking about cats." (The meaningfulness of the sequence of associations will become apparent.) "I don't know what it is about them that bothers me. . . . I once saw a picture called *The Cat People*. . . . It frightened me. . . . I don't think I ever liked cats. . . . I'm sure it's tied up with a female figure. I was trying to think of something to make sense. I had a sudden picture of an Indian woman leaning against the wall, half bent over in grief . . . sort of praying, with an attitude of prayer and great grief. I don't know what connection the two have, if any." There was an unplanned interruption, and the patient then left this subject. As the hypnotic interview came to a close she was given posthypnotic suggestions for further work on her problems.

By the time one week had passed, the patient no longer avoided cats—something she had always done. Also, the choked-up feeling experienced when seeing them disappeared immediately following the last hypnosis. She felt that cats symbolized her mother owing to certain aggressive connotations. She had heard that cats "turn on" people despite close associations. She was once told of a cat that had badly hurt its mistress so that the latter had to be hospitalized. A dish of milk had simply been moved.

The choked feeling was also related to high collars. After revealing this, the patient mentioned that recently her daughter showed her some tropical fish. A mother fish was kept apart from the off-spring because, she was told, they would be eaten. The aggressive implications in this recalled to the patient an early childhood experience. She became angry with her mother about something, whereupon she started to choke on some gum she was chewing. She felt at the time that this was deserved punishment. She also felt now that all of these associations were related to the cat phobia. The cat's tail impressed her, but she could not account for it. Neither could she account for the Indian woman during the last hypnosis.

Another hypnotic state was induced. The Indian woman was the starting point for her associations. "In connection with the Indian woman. I still don't understand the figure, but . . ." (and the patient recalled a West Indian woman she had known. The woman had three children. Her husband appeared white. He looked Danish. His children with her looked almost white. His children with a former wife were dark with one exception.) "In connection with Z— (the West Indian), I recognize my feelings today as being jealousy of her children whom she loved very much. . . . I guess I was jealous of the love she had for her children because it was something I couldn't get from my own mother. (She described the woman singing hymns.) This whole feeling of family life. . . . (She described how she envied it.) The things that stand out in my mind are the hymns. In connection with her husband, I wanted him very much to like me. . . . I realize today what a pest I was. . . . I wanted to be thought well of by him. . . . Something else happened this week. I was sitting in the orchestra (with which she played) watching G— (the conductor) and was thinking I'd enjoy having him as a lover. . . . It was a very deliberate feeling. . . . The thought came to my mind I'd never want him as a husband. . . ." (*Why do you mention this after telling me about the West Indian woman?*) The patient replied that this was related to feelings about her husband. K—, a man she had once been interested in, and G— were both different in type from men she had imagined she would be attracted to sexually. The several men mentioned, incidentally, were being identified in certain ways with her father. (*Why was the Indian woman grief-stricken?*) "This I didn't figure out yet unless it's because I was trying to take my father away from my mother." The patient felt that this applied also to her feelings about the husband of the West Indian mentioned above. (*Are you identifying Z— with your mother?*) "Yes."

(*Then you have Z—, Indian woman, your mother,*) the patient interjected, "And cats with long, long tails that also remind me of penises. Yet cats are represented in my mind by a female figure. . . ." (*Is your mother masculine?*) "Well, she's domineering, and I associate that with normally accepted masculine traits. She's domineering. She succeeds in dominating my father. I just bit my lip this minute when you asked me if she's masculine. I've been doing it this week. I associate it with self-punishment. . . ."(*Does your mother wear the pants?*) "Does that explain the cat's tail? Uh-huh (Patient appears to be in thought.) Makes sense." (*And sensuality?*) The patient had indicated that there appeared to be something sensual about cats. "There it got me—why would I have a sensual feeling toward my mother? You mean in a general way?" (*Yes.*) "I have a feeling the tail of the cat is directly related to my femininity." (*Or masculinity?*) "Oh! Wait a minute, it does make sense! If I wanted to be like my mother so my father would love me I would try to be masculine, because I never could understand why my father permitted himself to be taken in by my mother. . . ." She revealed she tended to identify herself with her mother only insofar as the masculine component was concerned. Her over-all masculine identification was utilized in part as appeal to her father who had apparently liked and accepted this. There were no boys in the family. The patient was the younger of two sisters. "It makes terrific sense to me." The cat phobia did not reappear.

This phobia reflected the patient's ambivalence toward her mother. The concept of the phallic mother, the cat with the tail, apparently developed during her very early years. Ideas about an unpredictable, untrustworthy, aggressive animal were paralleled in her image of a hostile female figure. She identified herself in part with the phallic aspects of her own mother as she assumed more and more the masculine identification which apparently appealed to her father. The cat phobia embodied her fear of her mother's hostility. At the same time it reflected a projection of her own hostility as well as her fear of this, too.

SUMMARY AND CONCLUSIONS

Extracts from the hypnoanalysis of two patients have been presented with the purpose of supplying data on the techniques used for removing a water phobia, in one instance, and a cat phobia in another. Methods and reactions are readily illustrated. In view of the fact that these data are removed from the context of total treatment, it must be realized that the dynamics involved had their antecedents revealed, at least in part, during earlier phases of therapy. They continued to reappear constantly, too, during later phases. In order to permit proper evaluation and facilitate understanding of the data, explanatory comments have been introduced throughout the accounts. The dynamics presented, in addition to others which did not apply directly, were of considerable significance in relation to other symptoms and to basic characterological problems worked through during hypnoanalysis. An evaluation of transference relationships was an integral part of therapy with both of these patients, although no specific reference to them was indicated in these extracted data. A wide variety of hypnoanalytic techniques have yet to be published, and many areas for additional investigation are being explored currently.

REFERENCES

The following articles are by the author of this chapter.
1. "Psychogenic cardiovascular reaction interpreted and successfully treated with hypnosis," *Psychoanalyt. Rev.*, **35**:1, January, 1948.
2. "The role of a dream in treatment with hypnosis," *Psychoanalyt. Rev.*, **34**:485–491, October, 1947.
3. "Lückenschädel in a patient with amnesia amenable to hypnotherapy," *J. Nerv. & Ment. Dis.*, **104**:249–262, September, 1946.
4. "The hypnotic treatment of a patient with amnesia," *Psychoanalyt. Rev.*, **35**:171–177, April, 1948.
5. "Hypnotherapy of a patient with an animal phobia," *J. Nerv. & Ment. Dis.* (in press).
6. "Some aspects of homosexuality in relation to hypnosis," *Psychoanalyt. Rev.* (in press).
7. "Hypnoanalysis, hypnotherapy, and Card 12M of the Thematic Apperception Test," *J. Gen. Psychol.* (in press).

Index of Names

Index of Subjects